MAGDALENA COLINE

THE LAWRENCE STONE LECTURES

Sponsored by

*The Shelby Cullom Davis Center for Historical Studies
and Princeton University Press*

A list of titles in this series appears at the back of the book

Magdalena Coline

A LIFE BEYOND SLAVERY
IN MEDITERRANEAN EUROPE

DANIEL LORD SMAIL

PRINCETON UNIVERSITY PRESS
PRINCETON & OXFORD

Copyright © 2025 by Daniel Lord Smail

Princeton University Press is committed to the protection of copyright and the intellectual property our authors entrust to us. Copyright promotes the progress and integrity of knowledge created by humans. By engaging with an authorized copy of this work, you are supporting creators and the global exchange of ideas. As this work is protected by copyright, any reproduction or distribution of it in any form for any purpose requires permission; permission requests should be sent to permissions@press.princeton.edu. Ingestion of any IP for any AI purposes is strictly prohibited.

Published by Princeton University Press
41 William Street, Princeton, New Jersey 08540
99 Banbury Road, Oxford OX2 6JX

press.princeton.edu

GPSR Authorized Representative: Easy Access System Europe - Mustamäe tee 50, 10621 Tallinn, Estonia, gpsr.requests@easproject.com

All Rights Reserved

ISBN 9780691253800
ISBN (e-book) 9780691253831

British Library Cataloging-in-Publication Data is available

Editorial: Priya Nelson and Emma Wagh
Production Editorial: Sara Lerner
Jacket Design: Haley Jin Mee Chung
Production: Erin Suydam
Publicity: William Pagdatoon
Copyeditor: Karen Verde

Jacket Credit: Art Collection 2 / Alamy Stock Photo

This book has been composed in Arno

Printed in the United States of America

10 9 8 7 6 5 4 3 2 1

CONTENTS

List of Illustrations and Tables   ix
Conventions   xi
Dramatis Personae   xiii

Prologue: The Spoils of War	1
1 Practices of Slavery	**15**
The Topography of Servitude	19
Slavery and Gender	22
A Marginal Phenomenon?	25
Slavery as a Social Fact	28
2 Slavery in Marseille, 1248–1491	**29**
Slavery Comes to Marseille	29
The Anomalous Register of 1248	31
The Tatar Phase	34
Vectors	37
The Slave Owners	40
Lives Beyond	42
Catherina of Tartary	44
3 Peire the Privateer	**49**
An Obscure Lineage	50
Peire the Privateer	53
Peire's Partners	54
The Women of the Family Huguet	56

vi CONTENTS

4 The Expedition to Naples   60
The Revolt of Provence   61
The Dogs of War   64
The Expedition to Naples   67
The End of Angevin Patronage   70

5 Magdalena Comes to Marseille   73
Off the Roads of Naples   73
Amazigh Origins?   77
In the House of Peire and Bertomieua   82

6 The Wheel of Fortune   91
A Litigious Man   92
Falling Out with Antoni de Lueys   95
The Abyss of Debt   97
Sitting on a Man   100

7 Magdalena Gets Married   103
Why Now?   106
Dowry Makes Free   108
Manumission and Marriage   113
Forgetting   118

8 Magdalena the Moneylender   123
Money and Credit   125
The Neighborhood Pawnbroker   129
Women Lend Money   131
Magdalena Learns How   134

9 Alaeta and Her Friend   139
Magdalena's Network   140
Alaeta the Highlander   144
Setting Up House   149

CONTENTS vii

10 A Roll of the Dice 153
Magdalena Speaks 155
Peire's Bind 157
The Neighbors Vote 159
Justice Bends Toward Magdalena 164
A Servile Bitch 167

11 A Pyrrhic Victory 170
Legal Peril 171
Peire Is Undone, Again 176
The King Rules 177
Coda: Bertran Gombert 182

12 Afterlives 185
The Corridors of Time 187
There Was Slavery on French Soil 189
Magdalena Moves On 192
A Shattered Man 193

Acknowledgments 199
Notes 203
Bibliography 225
Index 239

LIST OF ILLUSTRATIONS AND TABLES

Illustrations

1. The maritime neighborhoods of Marseille, ca. 1400	3
2. The Western Mediterranean basin	17
3. The rate of slave sales in Marseille, 1270–1499	30
4. The Bay of Naples, ca. 1400	68
5. The neighborhood of the Lansaria	84
6. The changing identity of Peire Huguet	92
7. "For Theodora, formerly a slave"	119
8. The business world of Alaeta Columbe	148
9. Rubric for a house purchase made by Alaeta Columbe and Gassenda Blanque	150
10. The cover of the second Magdalena register	186

Tables

1. Names given to enslaved women in Marseille, 1248–1491	114
2. Women named "Magdalena" in Marseille, 1382–1465	116

CONVENTIONS

Names and Translations

Where known, personal names have been translated into their equivalents in the local vernacular, an eastern dialect of Occitan also known as "Provençal." Thus, the Latin name *Petrus Hugueti* has been translated into "Peire Huguet." Since *Magdalena* was not a name normally given to newborn girls in Provence and therefore lacked a vernacular equivalent, I have left the name in the original form. A number of personal names, such as the woman's name typically spelled *Garcendis* in Latin, have a variety of spellings in both Latin and eastern Occitan. I have normalized these names to a typical spelling. All translations from passages in Latin, French, and eastern Occitan are my own unless noted.

Dates

In late medieval Provence, the new year began on March 25th. All dates in the text and the citations have been updated to match the modern Gregorian chronology. Thus, a date identified as January 26th, 1407, when Peire Huguet launched his second appeal, appears as January 26th, 1408.

Currencies

Two moneys of account operated simultaneously in the city of Marseille around 1400. Sums given in the imperial system of pounds, shillings, and pence are represented by the abbreviations l., s., and d. There were 20 shillings per pound and 12 pennies per shilling. The other system was florins and gros, with 12 gros per florin. A florin was worth 32 s., a sum equivalent to several hundred US dollars in today's currency. When considering prices, a rule of thumb is to multiple a value in florins by 500 in order to arrive at an approximate modern equivalent in dollars. Around 1400, the average price of an enslaved person was 50 florins, roughly equivalent to $25,000.

DRAMATIS PERSONAE

The Neighborhood of the Lansaria

Magdalena Coline and Her Circle

MAGDALENA COLINE, a formerly enslaved woman. Born ca. 1372 (?) in North Africa. Before 1387, she was seized by slavers and came into the possession of the admiral of Sicily, in all likelihood an aristocrat named Manfredi Chiaramonte. At some point she was almost certainly baptized and given the Christian name "Magdalena," a name commonly assigned to enslaved women. The source of her surname is unknown, though there is a faint possibility that it is Amazigh or Arabic in origin. Early in the year 1388, she was brought to Marseille as the slave of the shipwright and privateer, Peire Huguet. In August of 1399, Magdalena married Johan Petre. In the dowry contract that records this marriage, she is described as a *pedicequa*, or housemaid. After the marriage, she and her husband continued to reside with Peire, although Johan died two years later. Later, she married Hugonin de lo Chorges. Through Hugonin, she initiated the lawsuit against Peire Huguet in August of 1406.

JOHAN PETRE, a shipwright and immigrant from the town of Sluis in Flanders. He was probably employed in Peire Huguet's shipyard. Johan married Magdalena in 1399 but died shortly after, in 1401.

HUGONIN DE LO CHORGES, a shoemaker and immigrant from the village of Chorges in Savoy. He married Magdalena in late 1401 or soon after and took a young apprentice in 1406. Although he formally initiated the first lawsuit in 1406, he rarely appeared in court, leaving the litigating to his wife.

ALAETA COLUMBE, alias *la Gavota*, or "the Highlander." Alaeta was an immigrant from the highlands of Var who had settled in Marseille early in the 1390s and became a moneylender. She specialized in lending goats. She and her intimate friend, Gassenda Olivarie, may have mentored Magdalena in the art of moneylending. Alaeta provided crucial testimony for Magdalena in the first trial.

xiii

GASSENDA OLIVARIE, another moneylender and used-clothing seller who occasionally appears in contracts with her friend Alaeta Columbe. Gassenda also testified for Magdalena.

Peire Huguet and His Circle

PEIRE HUGUET, a shipwright and privateer, son of Gassenda and Peire Huguet senior. He was probably born around 1350 and may have been in his late thirties when he acquired Magdalena in 1387. In 1391, he fell out with a fellow privateer, Antoni de Lueys, one of several events that triggered Peire's slide into debt. He married at least twice, to Bertomieua and then Guillelmona.

GASSENDA HUGUETE, Peire's mother. She appears to have given Magdalena several very fine garments, although Peire claimed that Magdalena had stolen them.

BERTOMIEUA HUGUETE, Peire's first wife. She probably died in 1399, and if so, this event may have trigged Magdalena's wedding in that same year. She left Magdalena a legacy of 10 pounds, which subsequently became a bone of contention because Peire, as his late wife's executor, refused to honor the legacy.

GUILLELMONA HUGUETE, Peire's second wife. Guillelmona figures in witness testimony and is independently attested in a notarial act from 1403. She reportedly borrowed money from Magdalena around this time.

LAZARET HUGUET, also known as Lazar, son of Peire and Bertomieua. Lazaret married his stepcousin Hugoneta, the daughter of his uncle's wife, Alaseta Huguete, in 1393. He appears to have had a falling out with his father over Hugoneta's dowry, although father and son patched things up by 1412.

JOHAN HUGUET, Peire's younger brother. He joined Peire on the expedition to Naples, where Magdalena was seized as a spoil of war, and fraudulently hid some of the war booty. He married Alaseta, the widow of Peire Bertran.

ALASETA HUGUETE, née Coline, Johan's wife. Alaseta was born in Ceyreste, a village east of Marseille, and may have immigrated to Marseille as a housemaid. There, she met and married Peire Bertran and gave birth to two children, Hugoneta and Peyret. Following her first husband's death, Alaseta married Johan Huguet in 1391 or 1392. Alaseta and Johan never had any children together. They lived until at least 1429.

HUGONETA HUGUETE, née Bertrana, also known as "Hugona" later in life. She married her stepcousin Lazar in 1403. Hugoneta sued her father-in-law, Peire, for the return of her dowry. The dispute dragged on until 1410, when officials of the bankruptcy court, acting on her behalf, plundered Peire's estate to recoup her dowry.

The Expedition to Naples

ANTONI DE LUEYS, a ship captain and privateer. Formerly Peire's partner, Antoni had a dramatic falling out with him in the wake of the naval expedition of 1387. In 1391, Antoni sued Peire for hiding spoils of war that should have been shared equally.

NICOLAU DE SALA, a prominent barber-surgeon. He participated in the expedition to Naples and provided crucial testimony about Magdalena's enslaved condition, which was then repudiated when Alaeta Columbe and Gassenda Olivarie testified that he was in a state of hatred with Magdalena, having become irate when she rejected his sexual advances. Nicolau was one of the surgeons who inspected the corpse of the merchant, Antoni Gracian, murdered by Jacme Limosin.

ISNART DE SANT GILLES, a draper and businessman. In addition to being one of Peire Huguet's neighbors, Isnart was also an important investor in Peire's privateering business. His shop probably supplied fabric for the trousseau of Hugoneta Huguete at the time of her wedding in 1393 to Peire's son, Lazar.

JACME LIMOSIN, a shipwright. Like Peire Huguet, Jacme was a shipwright turned privateer, and lived a few doors down from Peire on the Lansaria. He murdered his neighbor Antoni Gracian in 1391. Brother of Guilhem.

GUILHEM LIMOSIN, a shipwright and brother of Jacme. He owned shares in the galley captained by Antoni de Lueys and was present when the Angevin flotilla seized the galley of Corrado Doria, on which Magdalena Coline was taking passage. Guilhem provided testimony about these events in Peire's lawsuits.

NICCOLÒ SANFRAMONDI, the count of Cerreto. A Neapolitan nobleman who had a falling out with Charles of Durazzo and, for a time, threw his support behind the Valois Angevins.

JACME MARTIN, a nobleman and admiral of the Angevin flotilla that set out for Naples in December 1387.

BERTOMIEU AYMERIC, one of the four Massiliote captains of the Angevin flotilla.

BERTOMIEU SIMONDEL, a businessman. He was one of Peire's major investors and creditors.

ANTONI GRACIAN, a merchant, businessman, and close neighbor of Peire Huguet on the Lansaria. He was murdered by Jacme Limosin in April of 1391.

The Law

ANTONI ARNAUT, Magdalena's first procurator and lawyer.

BERTRAN GOMBERT, Magdalena's second procurator and lawyer. He may have provided pro bono services.

JOHAN DE YSIA, Peire's procurator and lawyer.

JOHAN RAYNAUT and ANTONI DE RAUDE, judges of the two lesser courts of first instance in Marseille in 1406 and 1407. They presided over the early phases of the dispute.

ELZIAR AUTRICI (also spelled Audrici), lieutenant judge of the Palace court in 1407. The disputes originally filed in the two lesser courts were subsequently transferred to the Palace court in May of 1407.

GUILHEM ARNAUT, judge of the court of first appeals. Following an appeal lodged by Peire, Guilhem ruled in Magdalena's favor in November of 1407 but later testified for Peire against Magdalena, reporting an insult that Magdalena had hurled at Peire. As judge, he also issued a second ruling against Magdalena in July of 1408, following Peire's successful petition to King Louis II.

HUGO VINCENS, judge of the Palace court in 1408. He issued a ruling in Magdalena's favor in June of 1408, prompting Peire Huguet's second appeal.

The Contenders for Naples

The Valois Angevins and Their Ally

QUEEN MARIE OF BLOIS (d. 1404), wife of Louis I, Duke of Anjou (d. 1384) and mother of Louis II. During her regency, the Valois Angevins temporarily recaptured Naples but lost the city again in 1399.

KING LOUIS II (d. 1417), son of Louis I and Marie, count of Provence and titular king of Naples. He initially responded favorably to a petition lodged by Peire Huguet, but then reversed himself following Magdalena's petition.

CLEMENT VII (d. 1394), the Avignonese pope. He provided major financial support for the Angevin cause, using them to pursue his adversary, Pope Urban VI.

The House of Durazzo and Their Allies

MARGARET OF DURAZZO (d. 1412), wife and widow of Charles III of Naples (d. 1386), queen-regent of Naples during the minority of her son, Ladislas of Naples.

LADISLAS OF NAPLES (d. 1414), heir to the Neapolitan throne through his father, Charles III, a younger cousin of Johanna I of Naples (d. 1382).

URBAN VI (d. 1389), the Roman pope. At one time he supported Charles of Durazzo, though their relationship fell apart in 1385.

MANFREDI CHIARAMONTE (d. 1391), admiral of Sicily, father-in-law to Ladislas of Naples, and one of the great noblemen of the Aragonese realm. It is likely that he was Magdalena Coline's first enslaver.

CORRADO DORIA, a Genoese ship captain and member of a distinguished Genoese family. Magdalena was aboard a small galley captained by Corrado Doria when it was captured in December 1387 by the Angevin flotilla.

MAGDALENA COLINE

PROLOGUE

The Spoils of War

ALONG A STRETCH OF Mediterranean coastline east of the Rhone river, nestled inside a great basin formed by majestic ramparts of white limestone, a cove pierces the shore between two low hills. Long ago, on a day that legend places in the year 600 BCE, a group of ships rounded the southern headland and made their way into the harbor. The ships carried settlers from the Greek town of Phocaea searching for a likely spot to form a new colony. Drawn to the beauty and safety of the Lacydon, the name they gave to the little calanque, the Phocaeans settled on the northern shore and erected a new city. To honor their gods and their customs, these strangers in the lands of the Gauls erected proud temples, a theater, and other monuments on the slopes and summit of the northern hill. They cut stone and used it to build docks in a corner of the harbor. Today, the temples and theater are long gone, and the site known as the Old Port is much changed. The rocky beaches and salt flats that once ringed the cove have been replaced by concrete and tarmac, and the surrounding basin is filled in by the fabric of a modern city. But the site remains as stunningly beautiful as it was 2,600 years earlier, at the founding of Massilia.

Marseille, as we call it now, is the oldest city in modern France and one of the oldest cities in the western Mediterranean basin, rivaling Rome in its antiquity. The city's fortunes have waxed and waned through the ages, though it has always been a destination for people on the move. After 1800, it became home for new waves of immigrants, first from Italy, then from France's colonies in North Africa. In the last few decades, the arrival of the Euro-Mediterranean project, coupled with the engineering of a rapid train line connecting Paris to Marseille, has dramatically altered the fabric of the mid-twentieth century city, bringing even more waves of visitors and settlers. From the cruise ship terminals in the north through the heart of the Old Port and stretching south to the manufactured beaches of the Prado, Marseille is a city for young people and travelers. Flocks of tourists navigate the quays of the Old Port and embark on boats to tour the islands dotting the choppy seas around the Château d'If. They visit the ancient monastery of Saint-Victor and climb aboard trolleys to make the ascent to the basilica of Notre-Dame-de-la-Garde, where they marvel at the stunning views. A few take a moment out of the sun to visit the ancient Greek docks. In the adjoining museum, they contemplate the skeletons of the sailing vessels that sank into the muck long ago and have been painstakingly restored and put on display. The remnants of these vessels bear witness to Marseille's long history as a land of moving landscapes, a city of settlers, a city of displaced persons.

———

On the north shore of the Old Port today stands a row of buildings erected by the architect Fernand Pouillon in the years after the Second World War. The buildings were commissioned to fill the gaping wound left when the Nazi occupiers demolished parts of the old city in 1943 to punish the locals for their acts of resistance.[1] Cafés and restaurants occupy the ground floors, with tables for outdoor seating stretching out under canopies that shelter clients from the heat of the Mediterranean sun. One summer, I came to visit an establishment situated in one of these buildings. I wanted to commune with a woman, a most unwilling immigrant, who had lived here, long ago.

Six centuries ago, when Marseille was still Massilia, the space presently occupied by the restaurant "Chez Madie Les Galinettes" was on a street known as Lansaria, at the eastern edge of a zone favored by shipwrights (figure 1). The heart of the shipwrights' quarter, the "Canton of the Masters of the Adze," was situated a few blocks to the west. The profession took its name from the adze, an ancient iron tool like an axe whose cutting blade has been rotated 90 degrees. This orientation allows the skillful craftsman to shape timber by striking off thin shavings of wood in successive blows. The trade was an active one, and the workshops and houses of the shipwrights spilled out of their eponymous quarter eastward, along the Lansaria, above the shelving strand that descended to the quay. Further to the west, in a zone extending to the headland where the Fort Saint-Jean now looms, lay the quarter of the mariners and fishermen, nestled beneath the parish church of Saint-Laurent on its rocky prominence. The need to manufacture and repair the fishing smacks known as *lahuts* and other boats, coupled with ease of access to the water's edge, explains the proximity of the shipwrights to their seagoing neighbors. Members of other maritime trades, including caulkers, coopers, and oarmakers, clustered in the same neighborhood.

When this story opens, a house located at the eastern end of the Lansaria, where it spilled out into the Plaza of the Shipyards, belonged to a hard-charging shipwright named Peire Huguet. One day, early in the year 1388, Peire and his younger brother, Johan, were in the hall of Peire's house, laying out

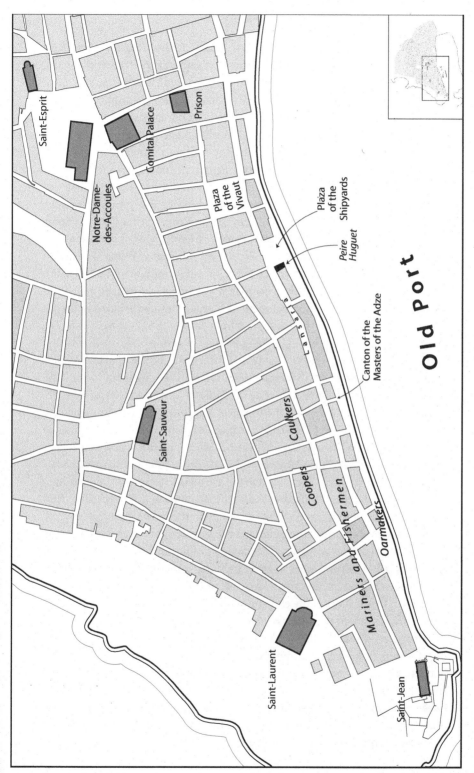

FIGURE 1. The maritime neighborhoods of Marseille, ca. 1400. *Credit:* Marc Bouiron / Scott Walker / Dan Smail.

treasure on the dining room table. Though Peire had begun life as a shipwright, his restless ambition had drawn him into other walks of life. During the 1380s, when in his early thirties, Peire acquired the wherewithal to purchase a share in *La Stella*, a vessel known as a "subtle" or narrow galley. The subtle galley was an agile warship favored for naval campaigns and raiding expeditions against enemies of all sorts, both Christian and Muslim. In acquiring *La Stella*, Peire became more than a simple shipwright. He became a ship's captain and a privateer, hiring out his services to his sovereigns, the Valois Angevins.[2]

At the time, the house of the Valois Angevins was led by the equally hard-charging Queen Marie of Blois. A few months earlier, in September of 1387, Peire Huguet had visited Marie's court in Aix-en-Provence, requesting confirmation of rights granted to him several years earlier by Marie's deceased husband, Louis I of Anjou, scion of the French royal house of Valois. The queen was glad to accede, for the crown had need of loyal servants experienced in the art of galley warfare. Since July, a campaign was underway to capture Naples from the rival house of Durazzo and place Marie's young son, Louis II, on the throne. In December, six galleys set out from Marseille to complete the conquest, and *La Stella*, captained by Peire Huguet, was one of the galleys taking part in the expedition. After a victorious skirmish off the coast of Naples against naval forces loyal to Margaret of Durazzo, queen-regent of Naples, the flotilla triumphantly entered the Bay of Naples and landed troops, who defeated the guard ensconced in the tower of Mergellina. A few days later, the victors paraded through the streets of Naples, displaying the standards of Louis II and Pope Clement VII of Avignon. Much plunder was seized.

A few weeks later, Peire Huguet and his brother Johan returned to Marseille, flush with treasure. But their share of the plunder consisted of more than the golden coins, the jewels, and the precious items of gold and silver that glittered on the dining room table. Elsewhere in the house, perhaps working in the kitchen or laundry, or quietly serving water and wine, was a young Amazigh woman. Her name was Magdalena Coline. The plunder seized from an enemy galley several weeks earlier included a man and a woman whom witnesses, in later years, described as slaves, and when the plunder was distributed among the leaders of the expedition, Magdalena was divvied out to Peire as part of his share of the spoils of war.

No one present at the time could have anticipated the events that unfolded over the next two decades, although the resentment that Magdalena evidently felt about her enslavement to Peire may have afforded her some inkling of the trajectory of things to come. Perihelion in their fiery circuit was reached between 1406 and 1408, when Magdalena Coline, now a freedwoman, faced off dozens of times against Peire in court. At the outset of the first of a series of trials, not quite twenty years after her arrival in the city, Magdalena had become a respectable moneylender and a married woman in her mid-thirties, fluent in the eastern dialect of Occitan, culturally attuned to the customs of the people, knowledgeable in the subtle ways of the law, and comfortably settled in networks of women's solidarity. She had come a long way. The ostensible purpose of the suit that she and her husband filed in August of 1406 was to recover a loan of 6 gold florins, the equivalent of several thousand dollars in today's currency, supposedly owed by her former enslaver. But there is no need to assume that any lawsuit is really about what it purports to be about. In this case, much more was at stake.

Outraged by Magdalena's audacity, Peire countersued, claiming that she had never been manumitted and accusing her of the grievous fault of ingratitude. In the teeth of a series of adverse legal rulings that smacked him down again and again, Peire stubbornly persisted in his claims and appeals. Along the way, he took every opportunity to demean and degrade Magdalena, calling her a slave woman, an ingrate, a thief, and a servile bitch. In August of 1408, he was on the point of victory when an adverse decision by the king pulled the rug out from under him and brought him down with an ignominious thud. Five years later, Peire was a broken man, drowning in a sea of debt, his dreams of glory shattered by the workings of fate and his own vainglorious pride.

———

In the annals of slavery in late medieval Mediterranean Europe, the spectacle of an enslaved North African woman clawing her way to freedom against the wishes of an obdurate master is unusual if not unprecedented. Elsewhere, there is ample evidence of the practices that enslaved people deployed to escape bondage. Various medieval laws and ordinances point to the ubiquity of flight.[3] Genoese and Venetian legislation reveals an even more extreme solution to the unbearable condition of enslavement, for legislators were consumed by a fear that disgruntled slaves with access to pharmacies might acquire the wherewithal to poison their masters.[4] Slavery also offered opportunities for escape within its own workings: through manumissions of various types, in cases where masters were amenable; through freedom suits and petitions, in cases where they were not.

If there is anything particular to be learned by following Magdalena's passage from slavery to freedom, it lies in what the story contributes to our understanding of the phenomenology of slavery. By this, I mean an approach, pioneered by scholars such as Ariela Gross and Rebecca Scott, that considers the degree to which slavery was a condition defined not so much by a set of laws as by a series of performances.[5] In societies that have slaves, the positive law goes to some lengths to articulate the distinction between servitude and freedom and to explain the rules and procedures that govern the passage from the one to the other. In this sense, it is easy to say what slavery means in the abstract. What is sometimes more difficult is to point to any given person and declare, with conviction, that that person is a slave, for the supposedly clear definitions of slavery, in practice, were threaded with ambiguity.[6]

A formal reading of the law of slavery in late medieval Mediterranean Europe might suggest that slavery and freedom were distinct conditions, where manumission allowed the enslaved to pass abruptly through the membrane separating the two. But this is not how slave status was actually determined in this world, at least in places like Marseille, located as it was in the borderlands of slavery where the practice was unfamiliar and the habitus undeveloped. Imagine instead a spectrum running continuously from enslaved to free, where the observed performances of master and slave alike, constantly evaluated by members of the community, served to locate any given person somewhere along the spectrum. In a metaphor deployed by Natividad Planas, the spectrum takes the form of the basin formed within the locks of a canal.[7] An enslaved person like Magdalena arrives in a community when the water in the basin is at its lowest level. Inside the lock, she is slowly lifted up by the rising waters, as the traits of freedom and belonging gradually flow in. At the top, the upper lock opens, and she passes through into society.

The ambiguity arises because slave status is not an intrinsic attribute of anyone. It is a human artifice: a tag or a label that is affixed to a body to serve as a principle of classification. The tag is attached by means of performance, sets of actions and behaviors embodied in both enslaver and enslaved as a habitus.[8] These performances are seen and evaluated by observers, thereby generating information that is further disseminated and calibrated by the medium of talk. What is crucially important is that the tag is capable of falling off, especially in societies where slavery was not necessarily marked by race.[9] In such a world, the performance of domination must be endlessly reiterated if slave status is to be maintained.

Peire was well aware of the need to argue that any claim he possessed to Magdalena's person derived from his own performance of mastery. His problem lay in the fact that Magdalena could make claims of her own through performance. With this, we return to the question of what may have been going on beneath the surface between 1406 and 1408. Legal behavior is itself a performance. This is true in any society where litigation is a subject of spectacle, perhaps notably so in later medieval Marseille, where the courts of law met in outdoor stalls located in front of the Palace, in the very heart of the city.[10] Every time Peire summoned Magdalena to court, he afforded her another occasion to appear in public not only as a respectable married woman and moneylender but also as a legal actor with a presence and a voice. Anyone pausing for a moment to enjoy the spectacle would have had the opportunity to evaluate her speech, her posture, her clothing, all the attributes that define someone as one of us. Any information gathered by those present subsequently percolated through the city in the form of talk. A second audience, just as important, consisted of the judges and notaries of the court. Standing before them, Magdalena could play the role of the poor but honorable woman oppressed by the machinations of the rich and the powerful. Magdalena's appearances in court steadily eroded the very claims that her antagonist made against her.

———

The case of Magdalena Coline and Peire Huguet is one of several thousand disputes preserved in the judicial archives of late medieval Marseille. The archives comprise a series of fat registers left by three courts of first instance and two appellate courts, nearly five hundred in all before 1500. Each register is typically several hundred pages in length. The richness of the series lies not in the overall volume, which is exceeded by judicial archives elsewhere, but in the manner in which the registers faithfully preserve, in chronological order, detailed notes on the proceedings.

The layered series of suits that set Magdalena Coline against Peire Huguet and vice versa, encompassing a half-dozen pleas and appeals in all, stretched out over a period of two years from the 16th of August 1406 to the 3rd of September 1408. Put together, they constitute one of the longest running disputes found in any of the records from Marseille. It all began when Hugonin de lo Chorges appeared before Johan Raynaut, a judge of one of the lesser courts of first instance, to file his claim. About a month after the initiation of his suit and Peire's countersuit, all went quiet for half a year. The dispute flared up again on the 8th of March 1407, when Peire Huguet appeared before Antoni de Raude, the judge of the other lesser court, and accused Magdalena of theft. A week later, Peire transferred the theft claim out of the hands of Antoni de Raude and annexed it to his original countersuit, thereby resuscitating the whole affair. His witnesses were heard in April of 1407. In May, following a setback, Peire had the suit transferred to the Palace court, the major court of first instance, over which presided the *viguier* or chief administrative officer of Marseille, Mathieu de Bella Valle, and in his absence a lieutenant named Elziar Autrici. In July, witnesses for Magdalena and Hugonin were heard. Late that month, the lieutenant ruled that both parties had failed to prove their claims, a decision that Peire immediately appealed. The appeal, which opened before the judge Guilhem Arnaut on the 16th of August, dragged out for three months, ending on the 19th of November with a ruling in Magdalena's favor.

8 PROLOGUE

Two months later, on the 26th of January 1408, Peire Huguet, undaunted by the setbacks, launched a second lawsuit, this time claiming that Magdalena had failed to demonstrate the reverence and honor that freed slaves were bound to display toward their former masters, known as "patrons" in Roman law. Testimony on the new set of claims was heard before the judge of the Palace court, Hugo Vincens, in February and March. A brief entry in the transcript for April indicates that there was some hope of arranging a concord between the disputing parties. On the 28th of May, those efforts having evidently failed, Peire submitted an expert legal opinion, known as a *consilium*, prepared by a doctor-of-laws at Aix-en-Provence named Antonius Virronis. In a ruling issued on the 9th of June, Hugo declared that Peire's case was defective. Peire appealed this verdict, appearing once again before the judge of the first appellate court, Guilhem Arnaut, to press his claims. Having lost patience with Marseille's judiciary, however, Peire simultaneously petitioned King Louis II for a ruling in his favor. The favorable royal response was filed on the 21st of August, and a week later, the first appellate judge ruled in Peire's favor. But when Magdalena herself sought an audience before Louis II, the king had a change of heart and issued a letters patent in her favor. On the 3rd of September 1408, the king's ruling was entered into the proceedings of the appellate court, and the matter was finally stilled.

As it happens, none of the proceedings heard before the three courts of first instance has survived the passage of time. A complete record of the long-running dispute, however, was faithfully preserved in two registers of the first appellate court. Coming in at more than three hundred pages in toto, the two cases together constitute one of the most voluminous records of any dispute found in Marseille's archives. When launching an appeal, an appellant had to submit a fair copy of the prior proceedings, including a copy of the sentence issued by the judge of first instance. The transcript, sealed by the originating judge, was subsequently bound into the register of the appellate court. On two occasions in 1407, as we have seen, Peire had taken steps to change the venue. In both cases, he was similarly obliged to submit a transcript of the hearings made before the prior judge. Like a matryoshka doll, the fair copy of Peire's first appeal includes transcripts embedded inside transcripts.

Though rich in detail, the record lacks explicit information of the kind we might hope for to study slavery not as a system of laws but as a set of performances. Paleontologists and archaeologists speak of taphonomic processes, highly variable from site to site, that degrade and alter the skeletons and artifacts that find their way into the soil. When documents are made, a similar kind of taphonomy strips out much of the meaning, leaving only the fragments of information that are capable of hardening in the form of text. Historians have long been aware that when action is represented as text, the resulting record lacks the behavioral clues and emotional expressions that provide social life with its meaning. Imagine a pottery jar used for storing wine or condiments that has been shattered, fragments strewn across a broad debris field, contents volatizing into the air, seeping into the soil, leaving barely a hint of their passing. Centuries later, all that remains are the scatterings of potsherds bearing faint traces of chemical compounds. Many sherds are missing, some damaged, others of doubtful provenance. With a great deal of patience, it is possible to gather the handful that survives and cautiously piece them together, using informed imagination to fill the many gaps. Through careful residue analysis, one can reconstitute some sense of the contents, and thereby restore a semblance of meaning.

The sherds of evidence are pretty much all that survives of the lives and doings of the participants in the drama, apart from any bones they may have left in the soil, traces of ancestry preserved in the DNA of their unwitting descendants, and any microscopic fragments of hair or skin that they may have inadvertently shed on the documents. Fortunately, the archive that preserves those sherds is robust. Between 1378, the year of the papal schism, an event that triggered the cascading series of events that brought Magdalena to Marseille, and 1423, the year of the great sack of Marseille by the Aragonese fleet, an event constituting a brutal rupture in the city's timeline, hundreds of registers left by public notaries, law courts, hospitals, churches, merchants, the city council, and other institutions have survived. Virtually all were kept on sturdy rag paper, made in molds whose dimensions were typically around 44 centimeters by 31 centimeters.[11] Folded into gatherings and sewn up as registers, this paper resulted in registers some 31 centimeters high and 22 centimeters wide, although for some types of business, notaries created narrow registers half this width. The page length of these registers varies considerably. Few are shorter than a hundred pages. Not many exceed a thousand pages. Collectively, they preserve a good deal of information.

Patterns emerge when the surviving information is read across its totality. From those patterns, it is possible to acquire intuitions about the city and its people, intuitions that are essential for understanding the story of Magdalena, her enslaver Peire Huguet, and the friends, neighbors, and enemies who play various roles in the drama. Everywhere, acts and conflicts arising from relationships of debt tell us how deeply credit was woven into the fabric of society. Everywhere, we find women occupying positions not only as wives and daughters but also as merchants, lenders, borrowers, buyers, workers, and a host of other roles or activities. In records from the years around 1400, immigrants are distinctly visible, much more so than they are in records from the period before 1350. To judge by their origins, most of these immigrants arrived by choice, at least to the extent that any immigration induced by poverty or warfare can be said to be voluntary. Maidservants came to take positions in domestic service. Laborers struggling to make do in the small communities of Upper Provence migrated to the great port in search of more secure livings. Skilled artisans and practitioners of various trades filled the niches left vacant by the episodic outbreaks of plague after 1348. But some of the immigration was decidedly involuntary, as vividly attested by the slave sales whose numbers spike grotesquely in the second half of the fourteenth century.

Along with the patterns it reveals, the documentary field preserves hundreds of thousands of notarial acts commissioned by many thousands or even tens of thousands of unique individuals between 1380 and 1423. Acts involving the persons of the drama are scattered broadly across this mass. On their own, these acts are typically small and uninteresting. Here, we find a chance reference to the location of someone's house. There, a sentence refers to an act of debt collection pursued against a familiar name. Only a few sherds of evidence, such as the one preserving the scene of the brothers Huguet gloating over the spoils of war in 1388, are dense with information. These rare survivals contribute significantly to our ability to reconstruct the drama. Meaning accumulates as all the sherds are brought together and fitted into the reconstruction.

The durable fragments preserve only the thinnest residue of behavior and emotion. But even so, the experiential dimension is not completely lost. In certain passages, it is frozen within the matrix of the text, taking the form of subtle and contemptuous delays, the filing of excitable and sometimes incoherent arguments, and elsewhere in the nooks and crannies of legal forms and procedures. As one reads and rereads the texts, the passages begin to thaw, and in thawing, they release traces of the odors and scents of human experience. The records arising from Magdalena's lawsuit and Peire's countersuits are particularly rich in the tantalizing nimbus of human experience.

Thanks to the existence of this nimbus, I can say with some certainty that Peire Huguet was enraged by the lawsuit filed against him in August of 1406. An odd shift in the pacing and nature of Magdalena's court appearances in the spring of 1408, when things were looking bad for her, points to a stomach-churning anxiety. Similar intuitions take shape as one reads and rereads the documents in the case. But I can't explain where any of these intuitions come from. Some of the claims made in this book derive from what Michael Polanyi has called "tacit knowledge," a type of knowledge that makes it possible for an archaeologist specializing in faunal remains to classify fragments of bone found at an ancient campsite by taxon and instantly distinguish cut marks from chance scratches.[12] Such intuitions are not grounded in evidence. They cannot be taught. Following Arlette Farge, one acquires such knowledge only by patient doing and slow reading.[13]

What this means is that the believability of the drama as told derives from a familiarity with the fragments and processes used to reconstruct it. It is only by having a feel for the meaning and fittingness of those fragments that one can pursue the sort of informed imagination that is needed to bring such stories to life.[14] Since so much relies on plausible reconstruction, and since so much resides on the decidedly nebulous end of what Tiya Miles has described as "the hazy space between 'probably' and 'certainly,'" it is more than usually necessary to attend to the manner in which meaning can be extracted from the reluctant fragments.[15] Following the aesthetic that informs the Pompidou center in Paris, where the structure and the conduits are exposed for all to see, the story conveyed in this book is one in which the drama is interleaved, in places, with the story of the fragments.

———

Although the protagonist of the story is a Mediterranean woman who had once been enslaved, this book is not about Mediterranean slavery per se. Among other things, the remarkable growth of the field since the early 2000s has had the effect of showing that the phenomenon it purports to describe cannot easily be encompassed by the familiar label. To take the most obvious point, it is problematic to describe the phenomenon as "Mediterranean" when a sizable majority of the enslaved, after 1300, were Tatars, Ruthenians, Russians, Circassians, Greeks, and other peoples of the lands surrounding the Black Sea. After 1380, these were joined by a growing number of Africans from the Sudan and the western regions of the continent. "Mediterranean slavery" is a term of convenience. It is not a term of analysis.

Following recent developments in the historiography, the subject is best thought of as the northwestern circuit of a large, amorphous, pan-Afro-Eurasian network of slaving practices.[16] The interconnectivity of this network is attested by the fact that Mongol women show up in European records at the same time that Slavic women appear at the Mongol court in China. In the networks to the south, long-standing practices of trade and tribute brought Black Africans into households and courts across the Islamic world. A trickle of enslaved Africans, later growing into a stream, also flowed into the cities of Italy, Provence, Spain, and the Mediterranean islands. The emerging global framework of interpretation has shattered the once-dominant custom of explaining Mediterranean slavery solely with reference to its ancient antecedents in Greece and Rome. It remains important, of course, to attend to ancient history. As we shall see, Magdalena Coline was nearly undone in 1408 by the continuing force of a Roman legal provision dredged up by Peire Huguet's astute lawyer. But in most respects, the slavery practiced in Mediterranean Europe is best understood if we don't try to trace its roots back to Rome.

Beyond that, the most interesting aspect of Magdalena's story lies not in what it can tell us about her life in servitude. All that we can say about her life before 1399 is that it was probably typical. The interesting part takes place later, when she enters the stage as an autonomous actor: a respectable married woman and house mistress; a moneylender who gave her grateful clients access to coin when it was needed; a plaintiff and defendant appearing on the legal stage, speaking in her own voice.

It is tempting to explain Magdalena's passage beyond slavery in terms of her own agency, framing her as a solitary heroine who wrested freedom from a hard and implacable master and a local community coldly indifferent to the plight of a member of a despised class.[17] We are saved from the perils of romance by the fact that this is not what happened. It is true that Peire played the role of the hard and implacable master to perfection, but things were different where the local community was concerned. Reading between the lines, it becomes clear that almost everyone in the neighborhood of the Lansaria, in the years between 1406 and 1408, was on Magdalena's side. In some cases, being on her side was only a matter of expressing indifference to Peire's claims of ownership. In other cases, especially during the first trial, the support she received from friends and neighbors was concerted and active.

Inexplicable rulings by members of Marseille's judiciary indicate that even the legal establishment was kindly disposed to Magdalena's cause or, alternatively, hostile to Peire's. Judges bent the law in her favor, sometimes to absurd degrees. A case in point is the dramatic ruling issued in June of 1408 by the judge of the Palace court, Hugo Vincens, when he declared that Peire's lawsuit was procedurally defective. The defect supposedly arose from the fact that the records of the case did not include a copy of the instrument confirming that Magdalena's lawyer had the power to act on her behalf. In Hugo's creative interpretation, responsibility for this lapse lay with Peire, not Magdalena. It was a most convenient finding, allowing him to evade a judgment based on the otherwise incontrovertible evidence that had been submitted by Peire.

Here we arrive at the crux of the matter. Both community and law had turned on one of their own, even though it meant favoring a displaced woman of Muslim origins. This is not what we might have predicted, given decades of scholarship that has charted the growing intolerance afflicting the societies of western Europe. In the thirteenth century, Latin Christendom began to develop a suite of techniques for labeling whole classes of people. Marking technologies operated with special force in religious and social spheres, where they were used to identify Jews, Muslims, Romani, and other aliens deemed undesirable.

Enslaved people, at the point of seizure or sale, were also identified by means of labels, including ethnic origin, religious affiliation, and skin color. That would seem to have made them ripe for marking and exclusion. But as

THE SPOILS OF WAR 13

the case of Magdalena reveals, these labels did not necessarily become indelible stains that clung to enslaved people or their children for life. William Chester Jordan describes a similar phenomenon in his study of Muslim converts to Christianity who settled in northern France in the thirteenth century and dissolved into the Christian population.[18] Europe's capacity to absorb Muslim converts and former slaves offers a vivid example of the general paradox addressed by Miri Rubin: a society that was progressively excluding could at the same time be capable of assimilating.[19]

Here, three amendments are essential. First, the instinct to assimilate, as Patrick Wolfe has pointed out, should never be confused with benevolence.[20] The history of the Indigenous children in Australia, Canada, the United States, and elsewhere who were stolen from their families and assimilated into settler societies provides a painful and vivid demonstration of what can be the violent and violating aspects of assimilation.[21] The critiques of the thesis of Frank Tannenbaum, according to whom the Americas were divided into two zones, one of which favored the integration of freed slaves and the other that did not, add further insights into this matter.[22]

Second, we must avoid the temptation to generalize from the particular situation of Marseille. Afro-Eurasian slavery comprised a suite of traits that varied across its range. In the regions that eventually became southern France, practices of slavery were notably thin on the ground in comparison to other zones of the Western Mediterranean basin. Even in Marseille, which may have had a higher slave population than anywhere else in Provence and eastern Languedoc, the local people weren't used to dealing with the slaves and slave owners in their midst. Lacking the habitus of those who lived in a world where the social fact of slavery was more vivid, some may have found it difficult to distinguish a nominally free but otherwise dependent housemaid from her enslaved counterpart. Judges like Hugo Vincens were unversed in the laws and statutes that elsewhere defined slavery as a normative practice. This is what slavery was like in the borderlands of the practice. It doesn't mean that this is what slavery was like elsewhere.

Third and finally, there is a matter of typology. It is tempting to describe Provence as a "society with slaves" rather than a "slave society." But the supposed clarity brought by typology is an illusion. As Noel Lenski has pointed out, the variable practices of slavery cannot be contained in the conceptual baskets that have been designed to hold them. Part of the reason, as several distinguished historians have pointed out, is that slavery constantly moves in the flow of time.[23] To search for the common and stable set of traits is a noble but futile quest.[24]

Typological classification, therefore, obscures the variation that exists in the society it purports to describe. Across Marseille in the second half of the fourteenth century, and especially in the 1370s and 1380s, it is not hard to find institutions, events, and even people that are at variance with the norm. These decades, for example, saw the sudden emergence of a new occupational group, that of "slave broker," which appears in contracts of sale in the 1380s and just as quickly disappears.[25] One gets the distinct impression that the social fact of slavery was solidifying, though only in some circles, not in others, and not durably. If we typologize the practices of slavery in Marseille, such cases, and the trends they participated in, become unfamiliar and out of place, rather than becoming elements of the living fabric of the city.

At a structural level, the case of Magdalena Coline offers insight into swirling currents of thought and practice regarding slavery that coexisted in a single locality where no one could possibly know what the future held in store. At the personal level, it allows us to see how a singular woman managed to navigate the passage from enslavement to freedom. The story is compelling not because it was typical. It is compelling because it was possible.

1

Practices of Slavery

IN THE THIRTEENTH CENTURY, in concert with the Christian conquest of Iberia and the rise of the Mongol Empire, something noteworthy happened to practices of slavery across Eurasia. Slavery itself, in its various forms, has been around for a long time, from at least the late Upper Paleolithic era. Surveying the Afro-Eurasian world in 1200, a phenomenon that most observers would be inclined to call slavery can be found in regions stretching from the Korean peninsula to the Iberian peninsula and across Africa and the Near East.[1] In the Western Mediterranean basin, the Castilian and Aragonese military expansion against the Almoravids and the Almohads in al-Andalus, beginning in the eleventh century, produced a steady stream of captives. In the thirteenth century, this stream grew significantly in volume, as the pace of conquest accelerated.[2]

Thousands of miles to the east, the Mongol expansion, which began around 1200, had an even more profound effect, altering slaving practices across the entire Eurasian landmass. The Mongol conquests enslaved countless folk, feeding the slaving networks that stretched across Eurasia.[3] As the realm grew, the structures characteristic of that vast empire accelerated communication and commercial exchanges, binding the center with its satellite polities into an amorphous whole. Many things moved with ease along the routes promoted during the Mongol peace: goods, diseases, information, and peoples from all walks of life. By the last quarter of the thirteenth century, a growing number of the peoples enslaved in the greater Black Sea region and the Eurasian steppes were being sent westward. Beyond Constantinople, the traffic forked south and west, feeding existing markets across the Mamluk Sultanate and Europe.[4]

On the European shores of the Western Mediterranean basin, the rhythms and patterns associated with practices of slavery are faithfully registered in the region's extensive archival record. These records act as a seismograph, capturing signals generated by perturbations in the broader human ecosystem. From the eleventh century, the rumbling noise generated by the capture and enslavement of Muslims in Iberia could be heard as a steady low hum, one that rose distinctly in pitch with the string of victories by Castilian and Aragonese forces

15

against their Almohad rivals in the early thirteenth century.[5] In 1239, as reverberations from the Aragonese conquest of Valencia a year earlier rippled across the Western Mediterranean basin, references to captive Muslims begin to appear in significant numbers in sources outside Iberia, notably in Genoa, whose archives are among the earliest and best preserved (figure 2).[6] The Christian conquest of Menorca in 1287, which led to the removal of the entire Muslim population and the enslavement of those unable to pay the redemption fee, had a similar effect.[7]

In the first half of the thirteenth century, the enslaved peoples who surface in European sources outside Iberia were typically Muslims who had been seized in al-Andalus. A strange new signal appears in 1233, the date marking the first known reference in Genoese sources to an enslaved woman from the greater Black Sea region.[8] The proportion of Black Sea slaves in Genoese records grows in the last quarter of the thirteenth century and becomes progressively stronger in the first half of the fourteenth.[9] It leaps in the decades after 1359, following the civil war that shattered the Golden Horde.[10] Thenceforth, the slaves passing through the hands of the Genoese and the Venetians came primarily from the Black Sea.

The ascendance of the eastern trade is marked even in Iberia. As conquest gave way to border skirmishes between Christian kingdoms and the Nasrid state in Granada, the source of captives dried up. But the demand for slaves in Iberia was not changed by the declining traffic in Mudejar slaves. As a result, after 1350, the proportion of Eastern slaves rose significantly in Iberia, as Tatars, Ruthenians, Russians, Greeks, and other easterners filled the market.[11] Everywhere, the traffic in slaves seized in the Black Sea region, Greece, and the Slavic lands reached its height in the early Timurid era, in the decades around 1400, before entering a phase of stasis and eventual decline later in the fifteenth century. Practices of slavery gained ugly new life in the sixteenth century: in Europe, with the rise of galley servitude and the growing enslavement of Black Africans in Spain and Italy; abroad, with the horrors that set in across the Atlantic Ocean.

Slavery is present as a potential in any human society.[12] Like degrading gender asymmetries, social hierarchies that generate injustice, violence practiced in the interest of power, all the poisonous forms of "us versus them" thinking, it is one of a host of scourges that can plague the human condition. In any moment or phase, that potential can be activated or deactivated to one degree or another, following logics that are particular to the circumstances of the day. Slavery is thus constantly being reinvented "in novel ways and to particular strategic ends," as Joseph Miller has put it.[13] When we spin out the implications of this perspective, it becomes meaningless to locate the "origins" or "roots" of medieval slavery in the practices of the ancient world. It is equally

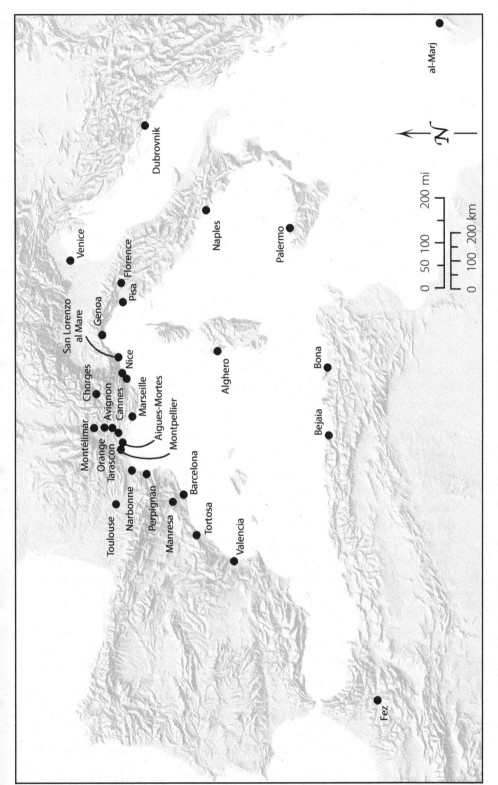

FIGURE 2. The Western Mediterranean basin, with places featured in the text. *Credit:* Scott Walker.

meaningless to imagine a handoff from medieval slavery to the systems of slavery practiced in the Atlantic and Indian oceans, the Ottoman world, Korea, China, and elsewhere in the early modern period. The persistence of certain elements associated with the practice of slavery, such as words, laws, and literary tropes, provides the illusion of continuity, deceiving observers into thinking that such tracing is possible and brings understanding. But it does not. In every world-historical configuration scarred by the practice of slavery, the practice itself is a constant reinvention, in much the same way that the ripples in a streambed, remade following episodes of spate and periods of drought, are unique in their particular configurations while broadly similar in form. Our duty, as historians, is to explore the variation. In so doing, it becomes possible to understand why the ripples ceaselessly return.

The forms of slavery practiced in Mediterranean Europe between the thirteenth and fifteenth centuries merit our attention not because the region served as a waystation on the road passing from ancient slavery to the early modern Atlantic slave trade, but because study of the period helps us understand the protean nature of slavery. What the study reveals, again and again, are shifting trends and moving distributions rather than stable norms. To take a notable example, the principal geographical source of those enslaved in Europe gyrated like a weather vane from decade to decade, often in keeping with geopolitical events happening far away.

In Palermo, on the island of Sicily, the gyrations of the weather vane are particularly visible. Up to 1310, the population of enslaved people consisted predominantly of Spanish Mudejars and North African Muslims. Over the next half-century, the source shifted to Greece, before swiveling to the lands above the Black Sea, as enslaved people of Tatar origin filled the markets. By 1400, the provenance of slaves was turning once again: a plurality of the enslaved people, more than 35 percent, were Black Africans, trafficked across the desert by Muslim traders through Barqah, a site in the modern state of Libya. The proportion of Black Africans in the enslaved population rose to 43.7 percent after 1440.[14] Grosso modo, the patterns in Palermo describe trends across the Mediterranean, with significant variation from region to region. The distributions that track similar trends in gender ratios, prices, and ages are equally unstable, their centers shifting restlessly back and forth across the plot as they dance to the rhythm of time.

To attend to distributions rather than norms frees us from the need to issue *ex cathedra* statements that purport to isolate some inner essence or quality of a given practice. Practices of slavery in medieval Mediterranean Europe allowed for the assimilation of slaves—except when they did not. Attitudes toward the enslaved were generally not racist—except when they were. Most of the enslaved were women—except in the many regions where sex ratios were more balanced. The tendency to search for norms obscures the fact that some of the most interesting phenomena are those that appear in the margins of the distribution, such as the anonymous woman, 28 years of age, who was described as "black" in a record from Marseille in 1359, a century before Black Africans became common in the city's records pertaining to slavery.[15]

The Topography of Servitude

The demographic data that have been generated in the many studies of Mediterranean slavery are fragmentary and highly skewed toward Latin Christendom. Even so, they are enough to give us a sense of the scale of the phenomenon. According to Monica Boni and Robert Delort, data available from Venice and Genoa suggest that each city was importing 2,000 slaves from the Black Sea region per year in the later medieval period, for a total of 4,000.[16] This figure aligns with an estimate proposed by Michel Balard, who used Genoese fiscal records from the Black Sea port of Caffa to suggest exports of slaves in the range of 3,200 per annum in the last quarter of the fourteenth century, though dropping to no more than 600 per year in the middle of the fifteenth century.[17] In the Iberian circuit, the population of enslaved people, formerly derived from Iberian Mudejars, gradually gave way to a population skewed toward Eastern slaves, many of whom were supplied by Venice and Genoa. But the enslavement of Muslims never ceased, and as the rise of Ottoman power began to restrict the Black Sea trade, growing numbers of enslaved men and women entered the Iberian circuit from sub-Saharan Africa and the Canary Islands. In the absence of hard data, it is plausible to suggest that the traffic in the Iberian circuit matched that of Venice and Genoa, and if so, the combined traffic across both circuits may have totaled 8,000 enslaved people per year.

Where the Byzantine, Ottoman, Mamluk, and Berber states are concerned, it's all guesswork. The sources point to the ubiquity of the practice. Shaun Marmon cites a proverb of the poet al-Ghuzuli that is relevant to this: "a slave is he who has no slaves."[18] In addition to military duties and domestic chores, slaves served as doormen, stable hands, and entertainers, and it appears as if most reasonably high-status households were well supplied with slaves. An observation by the Venetian trader Emmanuele Piloti suggests that the Mamluk sultan alone was purchasing 2,000 slaves per year, though undoubtedly this is exaggerated.[19] For the sake of having some numbers to think with, let us assume that the traffic in the Eastern Mediterranean and North Africa was at least as voluminous as that practiced in Latin Christendom. If so, we can hazard a guess that the total annual traffic across the Mediterranean basin and surrounding lands amounted to 16,000 enslaved people, bearing in mind the constant fluctuations from decade to decade.

It is helpful to compare this to later centuries. For Europe between 1500 and 1650, primarily in the Iberian and Italian peninsulas, Salvatore Bono has proposed an annual traffic of 15,000 African and Turko-Arabic captives, declining to 2,500 per year until 1700 and then 1,500 per year across the eighteenth century.[20] At the height of the Atlantic slave trade in the eighteenth century, by contrast, the annual trade in African captives ranged from 36,000 to 80,000, sometimes spiking to over 100,000. As the comparison reveals, the volume of the slave trade in the medieval and early modern Mediterranean, judging by the present state of knowledge, was distinctly smaller. But as noted earlier, the Mediterranean was one sector in a larger system that stretched across Afro-Eurasia and the Indian Ocean, the size and scope of which are currently unknown, especially for the medieval period.

If we were somehow able to represent the topography of Afro-Eurasian slavery in the form of a heat map displaying the variable density of enslaved populations, the corner of the map that depicts western Mediterranean Europe would appear as a dappled canvas of hot spots and cool zones, with the intensity of the shading waxing and waning over the years and decades. Down south, in Sicily and southern Italy, the colors would be warm. A similar tint would extend across the Balearic islands, Catalonia, and Valencia.[21] In Barcelona, around the year 1424, slaves comprised 10–18 percent of the population; in Palermo, the figure may have been as high as 12 percent, and in Mallorca, possibly as much as 16–19 percent in the last quarter of the fourteenth century.[22] Nowhere was the distinction between slavery and freedom a cornerstone of the social order, two sides of an indivisible coin where each constituted the other.[23] Even so, slavery was an active presence in the warm zones of the map, enough to have generated one of those complex things described by Émile Durkheim: a social fact, omnipresent to the mind, defined not so much by law or by material signs as by a shared set of norms and expectations embedded in bodily comportments, patterns of speech, and habits of thought.

Further north, on our theoretical heat map, the tints applied to cities such as Genoa and Perpignan are markedly less saturated. At the outset of the fifteenth century, the enslaved population in Genoa, the northern Italian city with the highest enslaved population, hovered around 2,000 and declined rapidly to around 800 after 1450. Since Genoa's population ranged between 50,000 and 80,000, this suggests an enslaved population between 2.4 and 4.1 percent.[24] For Perpignan, Élodie Capet has assembled some 530 slave sales and related notarial acts between 1350 and 1500. These represent but a fraction of the slaves in the city, and the percentages there are probably similar to those found in Genoa.[25] The map would be tinged by ever-cooler tones as one moves both north and inland. The enslaved populations of Florence and Pisa barely reached 1 percent, a figure that likewise holds for the Catalan town of Manresa in 1408.[26] Along the coast of French Languedoc and Angevin Provence, enslaved people appear in proportions so small that it is impossible, in our current state of knowledge, to come up with an estimate. Beyond that zone, slaves, or at least those named *sclave* or *sclavi* or similar words to distinguish them from serfs, disappear entirely.

Interesting questions arise when we approach the topographical variation as a question to be explained. To speak of "Mediterranean slavery," after all, is to flatten out the striking variation between the many zones. The variation has not gone unexamined in the scholarly literature. The prominent role played by Genoese and Venetian merchants and slave traders, for example, helps explain why those cities had more slaves than, say, Pisa or Lucca. The presence of Mudejars, coupled with the omnipresent fear of capture and enslavement by Muslim corsairs, may help explain why slavery was so robust in the Crown of Aragon and Sicily. These and other factors combined in complex ways to create the dynamic relief of Mediterranean slavery.

Zooming back, a wide-angle view of Europe as a whole reveals something equally important. Stretching across the entire north, from Iceland and Scandinavia to the British Isles and the societies of the Great European Plain stretching across France and Germany and beyond, the map reveals zones that were growing cooler even as the Mediterranean was warming up. The societies of the north had abounded in slaves in the centuries following the Iron Age. Enslaved people show up in early medieval texts ranging from laws and annals to saints' lives and sagas and also, dimly, in the archaeological and genetic record. As Michael McCormick has shown, the slaves exported to the Islamic world constituted a significant proportion of the merchandise that circulated in the early medieval European economy.[27] Yet slavery, as distinct from bonded labor, faded dramatically everywhere across northern Europe. Though there remains significant debate about the timing, pace, and the causal factors involved, the overall trend is well known, and scholars tend to agree that slavery waned in England, northern France, and Germany in the eleventh century.[28] In Scandinavia, the trajectories were different, and in Russia, even more so.[29] Nowhere in Northwest Europe, though, do we find the growth trajectory that defines practices of slavery in the Mediterranean. Even as Mediterranean regions were undertaking a pivot toward the new system of commercialized slavery, the lands in the north charted a different course.

Between them lay a broad borderland, a zone where the social fact of slavery was an ambiguous or uncertain thing. In the later Middle Ages, the borderland ran straight through Languedoc and Provence. At present, we have only a limited idea about where that border ran, how or when it oscillated, and what it meant to the men and women of the region, in part because the ongoing presence of slavery on French soil has been somewhat neglected as a subject of historical inquiry. In fourteenth- and fifteenth-century Provence, we can find slave owners in cities and towns as far north as Avignon. But that is where it ends. Reportedly, no slaves have been found in the records of Orange, a small city north of Avignon. Slaves are equally unknown in the records of Lyon, to date.[30] Further research in the region's archives will make it possible to define the contours of the borderland with greater precision than we have now.

In certain regions of the postmedieval world, it is possible to draw a line on a map and declare that slavery existed on one side of that line and not on the other. That is because the postmedieval world is a world of states with defined borders and sets of positive laws that distinguish citizens from strangers and the free from the enslaved. In the case of slavery in the nineteenth-century United States, the Mason-Dixon line served this function. In the fourteenth century, a border possessing a similar cartographic exactitude appears to have separated the Crown of Aragon from the Kingdom of France. Slaves making a bid for their freedom certainly thought so, as attested by the angry letters sent by Aragonese magistrates to French officials in Toulouse demanding the return of fugitive slaves.[31] But there was no such line to be found in greater Provence. The utility of the topographical metaphor lies in the way that it can suggest how a society with slaves, generally hugging the Mediterranean coastline and stretching up the Rhone valley, gave way imperceptibly to a society where slavery was a foreign practice.

As Orlando Patterson has pointed out, it is essential to attend to the places on the map where slavery did not attain structural significance.[32] The very existence of the borderland creates its own set of research questions. Among other things, it provides a setting in which we can ask whether the topography of the fact of slavery mirrored a similar topography in the social fact of slavery.

Slavery and Gender

The topographical variations of slavery can be measured not only in terms of proportion but also in terms of gender. Up to the eleventh or twelfth century, gender differences in slavery were not marked, since conflicts and raids along the frontier between Christian and Muslim states in Iberia, Southern Italy, and Sicily led to the enslavement of women and men in roughly equal proportions.[33] Enslaved men were especially prevalent among those reduced to slavery by Aragonese and Castilian aggressions in the twelfth and thirteenth centuries. By the later thirteenth century, however, a significant gender imbalance begins to appear in the Italian circuit. Hundreds of references to slaves in notarial registers from Genoa between 1239 and 1300 demonstrate that women constituted 61–64 percent of the slaves.[34] Around the same time, in Dubrovnik, on the Dalmatian coast, it was even higher, at 89 percent.[35]

According to the sample gathered by Henri Bresc, Palermo was marked by distinctive fluctuations in gender ratios. Around 1300, when the traffic was still tilting west and south, to the Muslim world, women predominated, constituting 64 percent of those appearing in slave sales. Between 1310 and 1359, Bresc describes a phase dominated by slaves of Greek origin. During this phase, the proportion of women sold in Palermo dropped to 45.5 percent. As is true elsewhere in Europe, a new phase featuring Tatar slaves was inaugurated in 1360, and the proportion of women rose again, to 61 percent.[36] Elsewhere in the Italian circuit, the growing gender imbalance across the fourteenth century is even more visible. In Florence, data from the *Registro degli schiavi* from the years 1366 to 1368 show that 203 of the 222 slaves registered were women, that is, more than 90 percent. The catasto of 1427–1428 shows an even higher proportion, 98.4 percent.[37] In Genoa across the fifteenth century, 86 percent of the slaves were female, with the percentage rising from 72 percent in 1413 to over 97 percent in 1458.[38]

One explanation that has been offered for the growing proportion of enslaved women lies in the growing demand for domestic labor in patrician households.[39] Most of that demand was met by young women who immigrated from the countryside and entered domestic service. As Dennis Romano has shown for Venice, however, the labor of enslaved women also contributed to satisfying the demand.[40] In Genoa and Florence, it is common to find households with one or just a few female slaves, often providing domestic labor alongside free women.

Across the Mediterranean zones of Latin Christendom, the comparative data collected by Charles Verlinden and Sally McKee suggested that sales of female slaves in Christian sources were four times more common than sales of male slaves.[41] In the scholarly literature, an understanding that later medieval slavery was largely feminine in nature has been accepted since the mid-nineteenth century.[42] These data, however, were collected in the period largely before the historical community had fully appreciated the massive evidence available in Aragonese archives. Thirteenth-century charters from Barcelona indicate that women, making up 57 percent of the enslaved population, were only slightly more numerous than enslaved men.[43] The balanced gender ratio persists through the next two centuries. In fifteenth-century Valencia, according to Debra Blumenthal, men and women were equally represented among the slave population.[44]

Male slavery, in short, was a robust and important component of the Mediterranean slave system, and enslaved men become increasingly more prevalent in the sources as the observer moves west and south, from the northern Italian to the Iberian and Sicilian circuits. The topography of male slavery is interesting partly for what it says about labor. Although male slaves in al-Andalus and elsewhere in the Muslim world often served as domestic servants or soldiers, in Christian Iberia many of them also performed manual labor of a sort that would have been familiar in the ancient world and the early modern Atlantic, such as working in the mines, chopping wood to feed the furnaces, laboring in the agricultural sector, working in the coral trade, and even performing a service as trumpeters.[45] We find labor of the male slave-gang type elsewhere in the Mediterranean. Philippe Bernardi cites a dramatic example involving one of the towers of the papal palace in Avignon whose foundations were set in place in 1341 through the labor of twenty male "Saracen" slaves, a gift from Alphonse of Castile to the pope.[46] In southern Italy, male slaves, including slaves from sub-Saharan Africa, continued to be used in the agricultural sector in the later Middle Ages.[47]

There was a noticeable divergence in the point of origin of female and male slaves, especially in the fourteenth and fifteenth centuries. The fact that ethnic labels were routinely attached to slaves at the point of sale has been a matter of some interest for historians since at least the middle of the nineteenth century, as these labels appear to make it possible to describe the swirling currents of the later medieval trade.[48] The need for labeling arose from the fact that not everyone could be legitimately enslaved; hence the ethnic labels served to guarantee the fact that the captive had been lawfully enslaved.[49] As Hannah Barker has astutely pointed out, though, the important legal function of ethnic labels means that we should doubt the literal accuracy of any given label, since raiders and traders had an incentive to lie.[50] Bearing this caveat in mind, we should use ethnic labels cautiously, assuming no more than an approximate accuracy.

As noted above, most of the enslaved women from the late thirteenth century onward were of Eastern origin, having been kidnapped and enslaved in the region of the Black Sea. The enslaved men, by contrast, continued to come largely from al-Andalus, the Maghrib, and, from the fifteenth century onward, from sub-Saharan and Western Africa. In Palermo in the period 1440–1460, the percentage of enslaved men described as "black" was strikingly high, 71 percent, a trend matched in Barcelona a few decades later.[51] Bresc reports an ominous correlate to this trend: a pathetically reduced number of manumissions given to Black slaves. Mediterranean slavery, in short, was becoming racialized along gender lines, with cascading social consequences for the enslaved people.

Running through the literature on practices of slavery in Mediterranean Europe is a tension between scholars who emphasize the labor performed by enslaved people and those who focus on the prestige and even the power that could be derived from the ownership of slaves. The tension between slavery perceived either as an economic institution or a social one is characteristic of the broader field. The dispute is based on the reductionist assumption that slavery needs to be "explained" primarily in terms of a single factor, where the other is rendered as subsidiary. This is not helpful. Among other things, there is nothing more prestigious than the spectacle of having others do work for you. For some analytical purposes, it may be legitimate to distinguish between the work demanded of laboring slaves and the symbolic performance that a slave offers simply by being. But it is essential to flip everything around and look at it from the perspective of the enslaved, for whom these distinctions made little difference. Here, what is interesting from the perspective of gender is the fact that both male and female slave owners derived prestige from the presence of slaves. Dowry contracts make it clear that some high-status women expected to acquire domestic slaves as part of their passage into married life. Navigating the streets, as Nevan Budak has pointed out, a woman would carefully position her slaves around her, with the slaves preceding the cortege in Italy and trailing it in Dubrovnik.[52]

A Marginal Phenomenon?

During the 1930s, in the shadows of war, the great historian Marc Bloch set to work on his magnum opus *La société féodale*. Ever curious, Bloch became intrigued by the question of how and why ancient slavery had come to an end in Europe, since it had a bearing on the question of serfdom. He drafted a paper setting out some of his preliminary thoughts on the matter. Bloch was killed by the Nazis before he had a chance to consider it further, but the manuscript was discovered among his papers after the war and published in the journal *Annales* in 1947.[53] The trajectory, as it appeared at the time to Bloch, was stark and simple. The ancient world of Rome had been full of slaves, and practices of slavery persisted well into the Germanic era of the early Middle Ages. Yet modern Europe no longer tolerated slavery on its own soil, with some rare exceptions. To Bloch, this was a remarkable transformation, which he described as one of the greatest that humanity had ever experienced. How was one to explain such a monumental shift?

With the benefit of hindsight, Bloch's rendering of the history of slavery seems curiously inattentive to things that had taken place beyond European soil in the early modern era. Yet where medieval scholarship is concerned, his description of the medieval transformation had a galvanizing effect on the field. In 1985, writing an homage to Bloch, Pierre Bonnassie surveyed the abundant scholarship on the passage from slavery to serfdom that had developed over the previous four decades. The literature, unsurprisingly, was characterized by profound disagreements among scholars concerning the causes of the transformation. Yet there was general agreement about the timing, for most participants in the debate agreed that ancient slavery was well and truly gone by the onset of the feudal era, in the eleventh century, if not earlier. Bonnassie himself located the extinction in the turn from the tenth to the eleventh century.[54]

To anyone who sought to describe the decline and fall of Roman slavery, the massive evidence collected and published by Charles Verlinden between 1955 and 1977 was more than a troublesome anomaly, for it threatened to undermine the beating heart of the argument, namely, that ancient slavery had collapsed under the weight of its own inefficiency as a form of labor mobilization. Juliane Schiel and Stefan Hanß describe an additional mental obstacle in this way: "How could slavery be part of what is thought to be the cradle of today's Europe?"[55] It is hardly surprising, therefore, that Bonnassie dismissed the slavery of the later Middle Ages as "a marginal phenomenon which really only affected the large Mediterranean ports."[56] The phrase aptly summed up the widespread indifference to Verlinden's findings that characterized much of the field at the time. Some of the indifference came from scholars, like Bonnassie, who were ideologically committed to the extinction narrative. But resistance also came from historians who were committed to an equally powerful though rather different narrative, one that insisted upon rupture. In a widely cited 1995 article, Robin Blackburn, like Bonnassie, insisted upon the decline or withering of ancient slavery, but he did so in order to emphasize the gruesome novelties of New World slavery: starkly racial, capitalist, consumer oriented—in effect, utterly without precedent.[57] In Blackburn's model, it was necessary to treat the forms of slavery practiced in the medieval Mediterranean as insignificant.

The understanding of Mediterranean slavery as a marginal phenomenon has generated a certain amount of resentment among those who study it. Reading the recent literature, you will find any number of variations on the statement recently made by Ivan Armenteros and Mohamed Ouerfelli:

> Slavery in the medieval and early modern Mediterranean is often considered to have been a marginal phenomenon, not comparable to the deportation of millions of African slaves toward the Americas. In effect, it has been asserted that both before and after the blooming of the traffic in black slaves and its impact on colonial America, slavery in the Mediterranean was limited to the importation of a small number of men and women destined primarily for household tasks and, along with this, had a limited capacity to affect the structures of production that made use of enslaved labor. One finds this image repeatedly in the historiography.[58]

No one has any desire to claim relevance for a subject by claiming equivalence in pain and ugliness. What matters, then, is not so much whether the practices of slavery in the Mediterranean were objectively as gruesome as those characteristic of Atlantic and Indian Ocean slavery and Ottoman slavery from the sixteenth century to the nineteenth century. What is interesting is why some scholars used to find it necessary to trivialize it in the first place.

Two different arguments stand out. The first of these, as noted by Armenteros and Ouerfelli, is the economic relevance of slave labor. This lies behind a central aspect of Bonnassie's argument. Ancient slavery, he claimed, was a mode of production, built into the economic fabric of ancient society, and lasting, according to Kyle Harper, through the long fourth century.[59] Medieval slavery, by contrast, was artisanal and domestic, and therefore epiphenomenal, since it supplied labor that could easily be supplied by existing labor channels. Several historians have been inclined to rebut Bonnassie and others who argue for the economic insignificance of Mediterranean slavery by claiming that slave labor mattered to the growth of the European economy.[60]

These interventions are well intentioned. Even so, by virtue of accepting Bonnassie's implicit measure of labor value, they obscure the fundamental problem with his argument, a problem so glaring that it hardly needs rebuttal. From the 1970s, following the pathbreaking work of Ester Boserup, a great deal of effort has been put into measuring both the value and the volume of unpaid women's labor. What this literature has shown is that what is often dismissed as "women's work" is itself a form of labor, even though it is largely invisible to metrics such as GDP.[61] Beyond that, enslaved women suffered from rape and other forms of sexual exploitation that can be theorized as labor. Enslaved women who gave birth to their masters' children were sometimes sold abroad so that the children could be raised in their fathers' houses without the embarrassing presence of their mothers.[62] A clearer instance of coerced reproductive labor is difficult to imagine.

Second, Mediterranean slavery is sometimes dismissed as a kind and gentle form of slavery by comparison to its ancient and Atlantic counterparts. Some of the most abundant evidence for late medieval slavery, paradoxically, resides in the ubiquitous acts of manumission. These acts take the form of contracts of manumission as well as testamentary manumissions. Manumissions were not quite what they appear at first glance, since they often came with strings attached. But even so, the practice points to the existence of what Alan Watson has described as an "open slave society," and the rate at which manumission was practiced suggests that the phenomenon was normal enough.[63] The manumission of women, in turn, was often associated with coerced sexual and reproductive labor, since women who bore their enslavers' children were sometimes eligible for manumission. This brings us back to the prominence of enslaved women in Mediterranean Europe. Here, the literature at times takes on a lurid quality, suggesting how masters sometimes fell in love with their enslaved concubines. The unstated implication is that well-treated slaves were content in their subjection and happy to wait until their masters deigned to free them. The point here is not to deny that some masters may have felt affection for their enslaved concubines. The point is that no one ever thought to ask the women what they thought about any of it. Debra Blumenthal's vivid description of the anger and frustration experienced by a formerly enslaved woman whose enslaver, the father of her children, sent her love letters, provides a reminder of the importance of attending to both sides of the question.[64]

It is difficult to avoid the conclusion that medieval Mediterranean slavery was trivialized because the enslavement of women was somehow seen as less violating than the enslavement of men. As recent scholarship on the lives of enslaved women in the Black Atlantic has painfully demonstrated, this is no longer a stance that needs rebutting.[65]

Slavery as a Social Fact

The postulated existence of a borderland running along the edges of Mediterranean slavery and passing through southern France invites some of the most important questions asked in this book. First, how did men and women in the borderlands construe the social category of slave? How did they recognize and treat the slaves among them, and how did they interact with former slaves following manumission? Second, to what degree did practices of slavery depend upon the assent of the community? Was slavery embedded in Provençal society, treated as a normal or ordinary thing, or was it instead understood as an alien practice?

Lying behind these questions is an important premise, namely, that much is missed if we approach slavery only as a system of laws and transactions. As argued earlier, it is also a cultural or social system embodied in attitudes, gestures, comportments, and dispositions.[66] Unsurprisingly, the sources pertaining to Mediterranean slavery have little to say about the cultural understandings of slavery. As noted earlier, in the slave sales, manumissions, and fiscal accounts that constitute the bulk of our evidence, enslaved men and women appear as little more than representations or legal abstractions. But it is important to think very carefully about what these documents are telling us. The sources upon which we rely were once living elements of the worlds that generated them. The very processes that brought them into being contributed to the social fact of slavery. Contracts and records, in other words, do more than merely reflect a status quo. They were also an instrumental part of how slavery was created and known. In every act we have before us, therefore, we need to be alert to the presence of the members of the community who, though silently off-stage, are actively participating in the systems of classification and objectification upon which slavery depends.

2

Slavery in Marseille, 1248–1491

ONE OF THE OLDEST collections of acts pertinent to the study of medieval European slavery was assembled by a local historian of Marseille named Jean-Anselme-Bernard Mortreuil in the 1850s. After his death, his notes, including transcriptions of 112 documents, were donated by his widow to the Bibliothèque nationale de France. A century later, between 1955 and 1977, the sample was significantly extended by the great Belgian historian, Charles Verlinden, who added eighty-seven records to those discovered by Mortreuil. Since 2019, I have had the privilege of working with a talented team of historians searching for new records pertaining to slavery in the archives of Marseille. Sampling registers unexamined by either Mortreuil or Verlinden, we have added thirty-seven records.

The result of these three tranches is a reasonably random corpus of acts consisting of about one hundred and fifty slave sales, several dozen manumissions of various types, and a variety of other records, including sightings of enslaved people in court documents and acts concerning the marriages of formerly enslaved women. By the standards of the records available from cities elsewhere in the Mediterranean, this is a feeble amount: there are thousands of such acts from Barcelona alone. But it is sufficient for the goal of this chapter, which is to establish a sense of the practices of slavery in the city.

Slavery Comes to Marseille

The chronological distribution of the slave sales has some interesting features. Rendered musically, as a somber orchestral symphony, the distribution begins in 1248 with a crash of cymbals so loud and jarring as to make one wonder whether the percussionists responsible for it had simply missed their cue. The notes in the measures that follow over the next century are played so softly that the audience has to strain to hear them. After 1350, the dynamics change abruptly. During the second movement, lasting until 1390, a crescendo mounts steadily over the decades before reaching its disturbing climax in the 1380s. The third and final movement, from 1390 to 1491, introduces ominous new melodies.

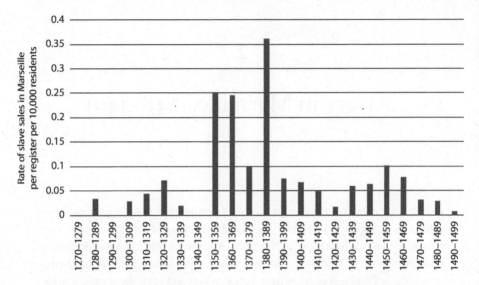

FIGURE 3. Rate of slave sales in Marseille per notarial register per 10,000 residents, 1270–1499. This figure, which indicates the relative frequency of slave purchases, serves as a proxy for changes in the slave population in later medieval Marseille. The total number of known notarized slave sales per decade has been divided by the number of notarial registers extant from that decade to arrive at a rate per notarial register. The rate is then represented as a ratio per 10,000 inhabitants, to account for the decline in population from ca. 25,000 in 1300 to ca. 10,000 in 1500. The figure excludes the anomalous register of 1248. There are no notarial registers extant between 1250 and 1269. *Source:* Marseille slave database.

Leaving aside for now the startling and anomalous crash at the outset, the distribution follows one of the four classic narratives of historical writing, one that describes the rise and fall of some phenomenon (figure 3). As we contemplate the dramatic spike in slave ownership that characterizes the second phase, from 1350 to 1390, dozens of questions to which we do not have answers spring to mind. Were the growing number of enslaved people in the city treated by the locals in a manner similar to the way in which they treated ordinary housemaids or servants? Or were enslaved people considered an altogether different kind of person? Was it easy to tell the difference, and if so, what were the behavioral cues or visible signs that facilitated the act of recognition? Was one supposed to respect the members of the growing class of slave owners in one's midst, or did one treat them as obnoxious social climbers? What did members of the family feel when a paterfamilias brought home an enslaved woman, took her to bed, and sexually violated her? For the female domestics in the household, did the acquisition of an enslaved housemaid induce a sense of relief, as in "there but for the grace of God go I"?[1] What kinds of signs triggered the complex processes that might lead to an act of manumission, in a world where few people had prior experience with the curious alchemy that could turn a slave into a free person? Did people understand an act of manumission as an act of kindness, a reward for long and faithful service? Or was it understood instead as an act of cruelty inflicted on an elderly woman or man who, late in life, had lost value and become a financial burden?

And so on. All these questions are even more compelling when viewed the other way around. There was little that would constitute hereditary slavery in this world. As a result, the newly enslaved had to learn how to negotiate a status that had been imposed upon them. How did one know how to act like a slave, when needed, if there were few people from whom to learn such things? How did one disentangle one's condition from that of a recent immigrant who hasn't been absorbed into local culture and society? How did one leverage community opinion against an abusive master? How did one plan?

These and questions of a similar nature would have arisen for anyone who experienced the rapid acceleration in the number of enslaved people between 1350 and 1390. Some people may have confronted these questions explicitly. But others may have experienced these questions phenomenologically, as problems of social life that one handled intuitively. In all cases, people had to make up their own solutions and then enter the complex, never-ending social dialogue by means of which all of us unconsciously and habitually tune our own reactions to those of others, where the goal is to arrive at a rough sort of harmony. That harmony, if it ever does occur, is what we call a set of norms. As those norms emerge, they ease the burden of thinking. Thinking is tiresome. Norms simplify the demands of social life. They allow us to respond to most triggers and events in ways that are automatic and embodied. But in new or changing conditions, norms emerge slowly, and until they do, all is unsettled.

The Anomalous Register of 1248

Let us return to the middle of the thirteenth century, at the outset of the first movement, and consider the anomalous register of 1248. When geologists and paleontologists search for images to describe the splintered nature of the evidence upon which they rely for their reconstructions of the pathways of ancient life, they sometimes reach for the metaphor of a great library whose holdings have been nearly obliterated by the passage of time and decimated by moments of spectacular destruction. In a famous passage in *On the Origin of Species*, Charles Darwin described the geological record "as a history of the world imperfectly kept, and written in a changing dialect; of this history we possess the last volume alone, relating only to two or three countries. Of this volume, only here and there a short chapter has been preserved, only here and there a few lines."[2] But the image works just as well the other way around, from geology to archival science, for one of the best ways to appreciate the vagaries of the surviving written record is to compare the archive to a sedimentary deposit, bent and torn by the violence of ancient orogenies, then thrust above the waters and exposed to the relentless erosion of rain and stream and wind, such that, with the passage of time, all that is left for the historian are little more than broken outcrops.

In the case of Marseille, one of these fragments, as spectacular and unique as the Burgess Shale, is the 1248 register of the notary Giraud Amalric.[3] It is the first of its kind: the oldest notarial register surviving from the Occitan-speaking lands in what is now southern France, antedating the second oldest register from Marseille by nearly three decades. It is also the last of its kind, since the notarial registers that survive from Marseille after 1277 lack the volume of contracts that characterizes the Amalric register. In the space of five and a half months, between March 14 and July 29, 1248, Giraud recorded 1,031 acts, sometimes a dozen or more in a single day. A considerable majority of these concern commercial and monetary transactions of various kinds. Had this register not survived, we might have looked upon Marseille in the mid-thirteenth century as a sleepy backwater, not the hub of Mediterranean commerce that we know it to have been.

One of the most unusual features of the register stems from the fact that it preserves eleven slave sales. We can attain a sense of why this is so peculiar by comparing the figure to the total number of all slave sales recorded in the twenty-eight notarial registers extant before 1300. Many thousands of acts are to be found in these registers. Only one of them, a single act from July of 1287, is a slave sale.[4]

The enslaved people identified in the eleven sales in the 1248 register were all described as "Saracens." From this, we can deduce that they were Andalusi in origin, part of the ripple of slaves emanating from the conquered lands of al-Andalus in the decades following the fall of Valencia. Seven of the acts identify the cities of origin of the sellers. Two merchants were from Tortosa, and a third from Valencia. Four were from cities located along the Occitan coast: Narbonne (in two cases), Montpellier, and Cannes. This suggests how the passage from origin to destination sometimes proceeded by way of intermediate stages, with slaves passing through two or more hands. All eleven of the enslaved individuals bore names characteristic of Muslims: Aissa, Ali, Atzona, Azmet, Fatima, Marieme, and Motqa. Nine were women.

Was this set the result of a single freak wave that crested briefly in Marseille around 1248? Or was it a symptom of the mid-century city's enduring

SLAVERY IN MARSEILLE, 1248–1491   33

engagement in the slave trade? I believe it to be more the former than the latter, though the question is open. The basis for the claim that the large number of references to slaves is an anomaly lies in the fact that 1248 was an unusual year, a year of crusade, the first of two launched by King Louis IX of France against Muslim sultanates in Egypt and Tunis.[5] Although Louis himself did not sail from Marseille—the fleet departed in late August from the French port of Aigues-Mortes—Marseille supplied twenty ships with equipment and crew.[6] Several latecomers to the crusade, moreover, departed directly from Marseille. Earlier that year, as preparations for the crusade were ramping up, merchants from all over the Western Mediterranean basin would have flocked to Marseille to get in on the action. The intense activity is reflected in the enormous volume of acts recorded in the Amalric register. In addition to their cargo, merchants and ship captains often brought additional goods to sell on the side, including slaves. The unusual presence of the slaves, in this interpretation, was a product of an unusually high level of commercial activity.

We know that at least some enslaved individuals were present in the city in the mid-thirteenth century, since there are several sightings mentioned in sources other than sales. A single contract of manumission in the Amalric register, from April of 1248, is particularly revealing.[7] Through this act, freedom was bestowed on a formerly enslaved woman known as *Alazacia bastisata* ("Alazacia, a baptized woman"). Likely of Muslim origin, she seems to have converted to Christianity, since Alazacia is a typical Provençal name. She was freed along with her son, Johannet. The person responsible for the act, Guinarda, the wife of Johan Ermini, also left Alazacia a bed-set consisting of a corded frame, a mattress and bottom mattress, a pair of sheets, a blanket, a bedspread, and a pillow. The act notes that Alazacia slept on this bed, suggesting a transition from domestic slave to live-in maid. Another reference is found in a curious entry in a register of the court of first appeals from 1264, when a judge's original order to seize an enslaved woman as a pledge for a debt owed by her master was overturned on appeal.[8]

But such references are rare. Elsewhere, the silence is deafening. Marseille's statutes, compiled in the 1250s and updated from time to time, include only a single and highly ambiguous reference to slaves.[9] This stands in stark contrast to Iberian and Italian law books in which the matter of slavery is treated at some length, a degree of attention that speaks to the omnipresence of enslaved people in those worlds. Likewise, no references to slaves have been found in the extensive record of the deliberations of Marseille's city council before 1381.[10] The indifference of Marseille's administrators and legislators suggests that although enslaved people were present in the thirteenth and early fourteenth centuries, their numbers were too insignificant to merit attention.

The Tatar Phase

Approximately one hundred and seventy notarial registers, created between 1277 and 1348, have survived from Marseille. Collectively, they preserve in excess of 17,000 acts, using the very conservative multiplier of one hundred acts per register. Among these acts, there are eleven known slave sales, less than a tenth of 1 percent of the total number of acts, a figure that provides further evidence for the marginal status of slavery in the city. Nine mention the provenance of the enslaved. Greece was the favored source, as indicated by the seven individuals described as Greek or Byzantine in origin, including two Greek men, Petrus and Jorgius, who were sold together in a single act. Two acts name "Saracens," and a final one identifies the slave's provenance as "Barbary."

No sales survive from the 1340s, and at the end of the decade, the coming of the Black Death in 1348 briefly disrupted any commerce in slaves. In 1353, the series of slave sales restarts abruptly, with no fewer than four acts of sale. One of them conveys the first reference, in Marseille, to a Tatar individual. Her name was Duncia, otherwise known as Catarina, and her provenance was identified by the adjective "tartaress."[11] Somewhat confusingly, the act says that Duncia was "a Greek or a slave (*gregam sive sclavam*)." Owing to the predominance of enslaved Greeks in the first half of the century, it is likely that "Greek" had temporarily become a shorthand for referring to all slaves, regardless of origin.[12] A few months later, a second woman identified as "tartaress" appears in a slave sale.[13] From this point forward, the adjective vanishes, and notaries switched to expressions of provenance based on ethnonyms and toponyms derived from the word "Tartary."

What did this word mean to Western observers at the time? As lexicographers have noted, "Tartar" is an amalgamation of two etymologically unrelated words. The first derives from "Tatar," the name of a Turkic-speaking people in central Asia who were conquered by the Mongols in the early thirteenth century and incorporated into the expanding Mongol Empire.[14] Subsequently, the name was used indiscriminately to describe the Mongols. The second is "Tartarus," an ancient word for the netherworld. In a long genealogy rooted in a body of literature known as the Wonders of the East, "Tartarus," in the thirteenth century, came to be associated with the Mongols, partly owing to a vague awareness of the existence of the Tatar people and partly because of the inclination to link the Mongols with the legions of Satan. For all practical purposes, the word "Tatar" and its variants was a catch-all term gesturing toward any individual from the lands of the Mongols.[15]

Over the next fourteen years, as the number of sales accelerated, two more Tatar women appeared in slave sales, alongside others said to have been from Bulgaria, Barbary, Circassia, and Greece. Then, in March of 1367, the trickle of

Tatars swelled into a flood, a wave that struck Marseille about a decade after it reached Genoa and Palermo.[16] To date, some sixty-two slave sales have been found to have occurred from 1367 to 1390. Fifty-six of these identify the supposed origin of the enslaved person. Two were from Ruthenia or Russia (*de Rossia*). One was from Bejaia, a prominent city in North Africa, and another from Pantelleria, a small island between Sicily and what is now Tunisia, as well as a Turk and a Bulgarian. The remaining fifty were Tatars. So common were sales of Tatars that the two phrases typically used to describe their provenance—"of the race of the Tartars (*de genere Tartarorum*)" or "from the lands of Tartary (*de partibus Tartarie*)"—acquired the characteristic qualities of boilerplate text, so routinized that notaries didn't think much as they pushed pen across paper. Three acts added a layer of geographical precision, indicating that the individual in question was "from the lands of Tartary, in *Rossia*." Slavery's second phase, in Marseille, was massively and insistently a Tatar phase.

The Tatar phase ended almost as abruptly as it began. In 1394, we find a sale of a man named Aly, from a place called "Annaba" (today Bona, in Algeria). From this point forward, and throughout the third phase, which lasted from 1390 to 1491, slave origins once again become diverse. People of Tatar origin continued to pass through Marseille for another seventy years (the last one in 1462), but North Africa returned as a prominent source of slaves, often with carefully wrought designations of place such as Algeria, Bona, Fez, Mauretania, and Tunisia. People from *Rossia*, which roughly corresponds to present-day Ukraine, appear for the first time without the qualifier "Tartar," along with a single person identified as Abkhaz and another described as a Goth. Between 1458 and 1491, five of the nineteen known sales brought in individuals whose origins were placed in "Mont de Barcas" (today al-Marj, in Libya). All five were described as "black (*nigrus, nigra*)." They joined six other individuals also described as "black," for a total of eleven. Only three sales from this last segment refer to individuals described as "white (*albus, alba*)."

One of the many distinctive features of the Tatar phase, from 1350 to 1390, lies in its highly skewed gender ratio. Across the entire span of the sample, from 1248 to 1491, 70 percent of the enslaved people were women. The average, however, hides a significant variation over time. In the Tatar phase, 87 percent of the sales involved women. In the third phase, in sharp contrast, the gender ratio was balanced, with men slightly outnumbering women (33 to 31).

The striking acceleration in purchases of slaves in the second phase is of a piece with what we know about trends elsewhere in the Mediterranean. As many observers have had occasion to note, the second half of the fourteenth century marks a significant turn in practices of enslavement across Latin Christendom. Since the turn is chronologically associated with the Black

Death of 1348, it is natural to wonder whether there was a relation of cause and effect.

In 1911, the Russian economic historian Maxime Kowalesky was the first to propose a causal link between the two phenomena, at least in the case of Spain, where landowners had experienced a decline in revenues from their tenants and were thus prompted to revert to unfree labor. According to Kowalesky, this threatened a return of the Roman system of slave labor, prompting peasant and worker revolts.[17] In 1955, Iris Origo independently arrived at a similar conclusion, suggesting that the acceleration in Tuscany in the second half of the fourteenth century was occasioned by labor shortages and rising wages, although the matter was of little interest to her and was limited to four lines in her article.[18] The wage thesis has proliferated in recent scholarship.[19]

The wage thesis figures prominently in the work of those who feel that late medieval slavery has been overlooked because of its supposed economic irrelevance.[20] It is easy to appreciate the attraction of the thesis, for it helps buttress a more general interpretation according to which the enslaved people were used for more than merely ornamental purposes.[21] There is little doubt that the enslaved were put to work in later medieval Mediterranean Europe, and, for that reason, the phenomenon has to be influenced to some degree by wage rates. A persuasive case linking the Black Death and wage growth to the acceleration in slavery has been offered by Roser Salicrú i Lluch, a leading historian of slavery in the later medieval Crown of Aragon.[22] Outside the Crown of Aragon, however, the wage thesis runs into some headwinds.

First of all, wages were rising all over Europe, yet slavery remained largely confined to cities and large towns along the Mediterranean coastline and thinned out dramatically in the countryside. Moreover, there were stark variations in the numbers of slaves from one city to the next. The wage thesis cannot easily explain any of this variation. Second, as Charles Verlinden pointed out in his rebuttal to Kowalesky, the second half of the fourteenth century stands out for the striking predominance of women among the enslaved.[23] Wages were rising in every sector of the economy, not just in those that involved women's labor. In those regions of Mediterranean Europe where the post-plague gender ratio was distinctly skewed toward women, the wage thesis does not easily work unless it can be demonstrated that the wages primarily or partly associated with women's labor—the carting of wood and water, cleaning and washing, food preparation, sewing, sex work, and wet-nursing, among other tasks—were rising more rapidly than wages in sectors of the economy that primarily involved men's labor.

Alternatively, the wage thesis has to be able to demonstrate that the supply of life-cycle housemaids, prostitutes, and concubines had become so severely restricted that recourse to enslaved women was the most logical alternative.

No convincing argument has been put forward to date. Finally, the wage thesis is demand driven, and hence Eurocentric. It is insensitive to the geopolitical events in the region of the Black Sea that help explain why the emerging cohort of enslaved people, for some decades, predominantly consisted of Tatars.[24] It is supply, not demand, that explains the prevalence of Tatar women in post-plague Europe.[25]

The point is not to dismiss economic considerations. It is to insist that slavery was and is a complex and over-determined phenomenon. The Black Death led to rising wages, and in some regions, notably the Crown of Aragon, changing wage rates had an effect on the population of enslaved people, as argued convincingly by Salicrú i Lluch. But we are not dealing with a reductionist and one-size-fits-all argument that applies willy-nilly across the Mediterranean. The explanation for the growing number of Tatar slaves must take into consideration the political discord in the Golden Horde, together with the late fourteenth-century expansion of Ottoman power in the regions around the Black Sea. It needs to consider the demand for male slaves in the Eastern Mediterranean as mamluks and janissaries. Also important is the collapse of some industries and the shuttering of markets, leading to a dramatic uptick in the search for alternative sources of revenue through piracy and other nonstandard forms of economic activity, the intriguing thesis proposed by Dominique Valérian.[26] Finally, any explanation that links the arrival of plague with the growing population of enslaved people has to consider other changes wrought by the plague. The mortality changed the availability and size of housing stock and altered domestic spaces. It accelerated patterns of immigration, notably from the countryside to towns and cities. Most significantly, it scrambled the system of signs that individuals in any society use to mark social status. Wages were not the only thing affected by the arrival of plague.

Vectors

Careful attention to the buyers and sellers of slaves in the sample from 1248 to 1491 reveals four distinct vectors: internal transfers, where buyers and sellers were residents of Marseille; imports, where the seller was identified as a foreigner; exports, where the buyer was a foreigner; and external transfers, where two foreign merchants, simultaneously present in Marseille, used local notaries to transact their business. In practice, these divisions are not as neat and tidy as the schema suggests, nor is it easy to classify any given act with certainty. To take an example, an act involving a Marseille merchant who had just returned from abroad and was undertaking to sell a slave to a compatriot could be classified as an import, but the acts don't provide any way to distinguish the situation from one in which a resident of the city, for whatever reason, decided to sell a slave to someone else. In similar fashion, any internal transfer could mask an export. By way of example, in 1354, a cooper from Marseille sold an enslaved Tatar woman named Lucia to a Marseille merchant named Johan Aycart. This was one of three purchases of enslaved women made by Johan between October 1353 and March 1354. Although it is faintly conceivable that the merchant was acquiring domestic workers for his house, it is far more likely that he was planning to sell all three women abroad.[27]

But even if the resulting information is noisy, the patterns tell us something important. The default setting is to imagine a situation where every slave sale was an import, the result of a stepwise transaction taking a captive from an origin to a destination. A Tatar girl is taken in the steppes and sold to a Genoese merchant in Caffa. From there, she passes through one or more hands before ending up in Marseille, where she is stuck for the remainder of her days. Although this surely happened from time to time, the sale and resale of slaves was an ongoing phenomenon. Craig Perry has aptly described this as the "churn."[28]

The places of origin for the foreign merchants involved in the thirty-six imports are diverse, with four sellers from Savona in Italy, three each from Barcelona, Genoa, and Narbonne, two each from Montpellier and Tortosa, and fifteen additional locales attested just once, including the city of Aix-en-Provence and the town of Apt in the interior of Provence. The nineteen external transfers, involving foreign merchants selling slaves among themselves while in Marseille, are the fewest in number. Coupled with imports and exports, they reveal how the port of Marseille was an active center for transshipment. Merchants from all over the Western Mediterranean basin passed through the port, and along with their bulk cargo, they sometimes brought one or more slaves to sell, often to the locals, but also to other merchants in transit.

Of all the categories, exports are the most arresting. In nearly a third of the acts (46 out of 151), a resident of Marseille was selling an enslaved person to a foreign buyer. The cities or regions of origin of the buyers are as diverse as those involved in imports, although the geographical profile is different. Among other things, Marseille was a major supplier to merchants from Mallorca, as evidenced by seven sales. Cities in the hinterland of Provence were an important market, led by Avignon, the destination of the captive in five cases. Merchants from Barcelona (five sales) and Genoa (three sales) also figure among the foreign purchasers. Four slaves were sold to merchants from Venice. In no case can we say that the captives were going to end up in the city of residence of the merchants in question, since the merchants may just as well have been acquiring them to sell at the next port of call.

Acts are usually silent about the circumstances that bring them into existence. A few of the exports, however, include formulae that cause us to sit up and take notice. The gist of the clause was to forbid the purchaser from ever selling an enslaved woman back to anyone from Marseille.[29] A typical instance is found in an act from 1382, in which a woman named Catherina de Rabesio made arrangements to sell her enslaved woman, a Tatar named Cita, to a buyer from Perpignan, in the Crown of Aragon. The exclusion clause was particularly detailed: it specified that the purchaser must not resell Cita in Provence or anywhere in the realm of France, Genoa, Pisa, or Sardinia. If the condition should be violated, Cita could be taken back by the seller and presumably resold.

What prompted such clauses? Although the evidence from Marseille is too fragmentary to answer this question categorically, the grim fate suffered by an enslaved woman named Lucia provides a clue.[30] The episode involves the machinations of a slave owner named Jacme Baudry, described by Charles Verlinden as a man who had achieved the very summit of odiousness. Jacme acquired Lucia around 1368 and subsequently fathered several children by her. Thirteen years later, in February of 1381, he arranged to sell her to a merchant from Alghero, in Sardinia. Almost immediately, however, something happened to change his mind. Canceling the initial sale, he chose instead to manumit her, though on the condition that she leave Marseille and hire herself as a maidservant in Alghero. The context suggests that Jacme had every intention of raising the children as his own but felt that their mother's presence would prove to be an embarrassment.

The presence of children, then, may be the key. The situation dimly visible in Marseille is amply confirmed by the more persuasive evidence found elsewhere. As Corinna Peres has argued, "cutting the ties between the slave and her child was a way of reducing ... social and legal stigma and increasing the chances of integration into the father's society."[31] Slave owners may have had other motives to sell their slaves abroad, of course, and we should not assume that all exports of enslaved women arose from a desire to separate mother and child. Even so, the practice speaks volumes about the social or emotional complications that occurred when enslaved women gave birth to children fathered by the men of the household. Fathers formed attachments to their children and wanted to raise them as their own.

It is important to recognize that such attachments would not have formed if it was normal to enslave the children born to enslaved women. Such enslavement could and did happen. There are two known cases from Marseille, one of which we have already considered: the manumission of young Johannet with his mother Alazacia in 1248. We shall consider the next case shortly. But the rarity of these cases, coupled with the prevalence of exports, suggests that most Massiliote men intended to raise their children as natural offspring, and took steps to sell their mothers abroad lest their presence create an embarrassing reminder.[32]

40 CHAPTER 2

The Slave Owners

From the ensemble of sources deriving from practices of slavery, it is possible to get a sense of the social or professional identity of the slave owners in Marseille. This survey reveals that slave ownership was possible across a considerable range of socioprofessional groups.[33] To the extent that we can sort members of the many occupational groups and professional cohorts into broader groups corresponding to major sectors, such as animal husbandry, legal services, seafaring professions, and so on, we can say that most of these sectors are represented at least once among slave owners. The noteworthy exception is the clergy. Although priests, deacons, canons, monks, nuns, friars, and other members of the secular and regular clergy constitute around 10 percent of the approximately 7,200 unique individuals with known occupations identified in a sample from Marseille in the mid-fourteenth century, no member of the clergy is identified in any source as a slave owner.[34] Since slave ownership is occasionally found among members of the clergy elsewhere, this may be one of the distinctive features of practices of slavery in the borderlands.[35] Several women are found among the slave owners but no Jews, apart from a cryptic reference in a 1248 contract indicating that a Jewish merchant of Marseille was taking steps to acquire a slave.

But even though it was possible for slave ownership to be diverse, in practice it was distinctly skewed. In this regard, the profile of enslavers in Marseille contrasts with the profiles found in nearby Genoa and Barcelona, where slave ownership extended well beyond the ranks of the elite.[36] In Marseille, men identified as merchants accounted for 50 percent of all slave owners, despite constituting no more than 7 percent of the city's population. Members of the landed or titled nobility were also prominent, owning slaves at a rate twice that of their demographic presence. The other side of this is that although nearly a quarter of the population was identified as a laborer (*laborator*), a status group that could include unskilled manual laborers, wealthy peasants, and everyone in between, the number of laborers who owned slaves was less than 2 percent. In other sectors, notably the leather trades, building trades, and food provisioning, the gap between the demographic importance of the sector and the rate of slave ownership among members of the trade group was less stark but nonetheless noteworthy. None of the city's bakers or confectioners, for example, became a slave owner, at least in the records available to us. Many of these trades had high labor demands. The fact that slave ownership, sector by sector, was not proportional to the demographic weight of that sector represents another challenge to the wage thesis.

In Marseille, wealth and social status were the most important correlates of slave ownership; of this there is no doubt. Three-quarters of the slave owners in Marseille were merchants, members of the nobility, bankers, or members of legal professions. Of the remainder, members of trade groups oriented to the sea were distinctly more likely to own slaves than members of trades oriented to agriculture or craft production. Individuals described as "mariners" or seamen are a case in point, for that group accounted for slightly more slave owners than their demographic weight would suggest. More granular analyses are also suggestive. The members of the occupational groups appearing in the set of slave owners included a butcher, a carpenter, a cooper, and two rope-makers, occupations that were linked to the maritime industry. In addition to wealth and social status, then, access was an important factor in determining slave ownership. Individuals were more likely to acquire a slave if they knew another slave owner or were connected to the commercial networks through which slaves circulated. Among trades oriented toward maritime activity, it is likely that slave ownership was normalized, and became more approachable, through contact with practices of slave owning elsewhere in the Mediterranean.

In sum, patterns of slave ownership in Marseille are more susceptible to explanations that invoke prestige consumption and access than explanations grounded in rising wages. But the goal of this chapter isn't so much to debate causes. It is to consider consequences. Where prestige consumption is concerned, one of the primary consequences of the growing presence of slaves lies in the way that slaves could serve as a tool for marking elite status or aspirations for social advancement. This, in turn, raises the question of whether the growing presence of slavery may have sparked an instinct to regulate access to slave owning.

Regulatory instincts were widespread in medieval European society. To take a pertinent example, the Italian communes, from the late twelfth century onward, began to pass legislation regulating access to clothing, jewelry, and other articles of prestigious consumption. The custom soon spread.[37] Although sumptuary laws, as they are called, were motivated by multiple factors, one of the most prominent motivations sprang from a desire to govern the signals that displayed one's position in the social hierarchy. To my knowledge, the extant body of medieval sumptuary legislation contains no laws governing access to slave ownership. In a sense, it is a curious oversight, though one that can be easily explained if we consider that enslaved people were not nearly as easy to acquire as, say, fine clothing, golden crowns, and the other types of items commonly targeted by sumptuary laws. In the absence of formal sumptuary laws, though, we might expect that access to slave owning was increasingly governed by a set of implicit norms, calibrated through conversations rather than explicit laws, that emerged to regulate the unsettled new world.

Access to the market was almost entirely unregulated, except to the important extent that the high cost of slaves ensured that only the wealthier could afford them. But even in the absence of sumptuary laws governing slave acquisition, the ongoing act of slave ownership could be open to tacit forms of community regulation. Since personal honor was one of the coins that gave individuals access to prestige and resources, the honor claims of men and women were constantly being assessed by their compatriots to determine whether they were worthy of distinction. Slave ownership was one of the claims that could be fed into the social algorithm that determined the distribution of honor. In other words, people noticed.

Though this claim lies in the realm of the strictly hypothetical, it is important to think through it here, for two reasons. The first lies in the fact that although historical sources are necessarily biased toward the kinds of behaviors that sediment most readily in writing, this should not lead us to imagine that other behaviors are any less important to the stories that we want to tell. This stance does not mean that we can simply make it all up, and this is the second reason for why the speculation is helpful. The case of Magdalena Coline and Peire Huguet offers exactly the kind of scenario we would have requested if we wanted to see whether it was possible to get at the unspoken things. The drama concerns a social climber with an unpleasant disposition who acquired a slave only to have her taken away by those who felt he was undeserving of the honor that, in this society, was normally accorded to people who owned slaves. It is also the story of a woman who learned how to activate community opinion against her enslaver and thereby ease herself out from under his thumb.

Lives Beyond

As the acts of export reveal, many of the enslaved who arrived in Marseille were subsequently sold abroad. For those who remained, one of two fates awaited them: death in servitude or manumission. The former is not easy to track. To date, I have only found a single reference to the death of a slave in Marseille, one that occurs in the account book of Laureta Bonaffazy in the year 1404. A laconic entry, in Laureta's dialect of Occitan, reports an expenditure of 11¼ gros occasioned "when the slave woman died (*cant mory l'esclava*)."[38]

Manumissions, which are distinctly more visible, took one of two forms: testamentary manumissions, by means of which an enslaved person was manumitted by the decedent in a last will and testament, and acts of manumission, which can be found on occasion in notarial registers. Fourteen testamentary manumissions have been found so far in Marseille's archives (with two slaves freed in one of the testaments).[39] Typically, the clause freed the enslaved person and provided the individual with a nest egg. By way of example, in 1359, a woman named Catharina, described as the "servant and slave" of Nicolau Grifen, was freed by a clause in his testament. She was given ownership of a house,

SLAVERY IN MARSEILLE, 1248–1491   43

a vineyard, and a bed worth 100 s.[40] In 1361, during the second outbreak of plague, the enslaved Elena was freed by a pious legacy in the testament of the merchant Peire Austria; she received 25 florins for her marriage and three yards of cloth worth 2 florins per yard, as well as a bed worth 10 l.[41] In 1395, the merchant Julian de Casaulx, who had been deeply involved in the slave trade over the preceding two decades, manumitted his enslaved woman, Magdalena, with a substantial legacy of 50 florins, equivalent to the average sale price for a slave. In the same testament, he freed a male slave named Johan Martin, though without a legacy, which strongly suggests that the legacy given to Magdalena was intended to serve as her dowry.[42] Of the fifteen individuals manumitted by way of testament, all but two were women.

Nineteen notarial contracts of manumission have been found to date. Most were given unconditionally, although several included requirements of service for one or two more years. A particularly interesting case concerns an enslaved man named Johan de Brandisio in June of 1372, who was manumitted by the recently widowed Lady Raynauda Ode on the condition that he serve her for an additional year.[43] Mortreuil indicates that on the same day, Johan married a local woman and received some land and a small monetary legacy of 15 l. A generation later, his son, Esteve de Brandisio, became a prominent figure in the city, suggesting that Raynauda or another member of the Ode family continued to offer him the patronage he would have needed to make his way in society.

Contracts of manumission are relatively uncommon relative to sales: we have more than 150 sale contracts from Marseille compared to 33 manumissions of both types. From this, it would be natural to assume that the majority of enslaved people died in servitude. Yet this assumption is problematic. First, as we have seen, a considerable number of slave sales were resales, inflating the number of sales relative to manumissions. Second, there was another way to manumit enslaved women, since Roman law granted a tacit manumission to formerly enslaved women who married with the permission of their masters, obviating the need for a formal manumission. We shall return to this in a later chapter, since it has a bearing on the status of Magdalena Coline following her marriage in 1399.

If manumission was relatively common, then it becomes important to ask whether enslavement had a typical duration. As Corinna Peres has demonstrated, documents preserved in the Datini archive show that the practitioners of slavery carefully distinguished between two categories of slaves: those who could be enslaved for life and those who were enslaved for a limited duration.[44] The latter category is associated with situations in which slaves had the ability to gradually pay down their purchase price and thereby acquired the condition of a *statuliber* or conditionally freed slave.[45] The sparse evidence from Marseille provides no grounds for estimating the typical duration of servitude. Thanks to the work of Michel Balard, however, we have some sense of the situation found in nearby Genoa.[46] On the basis of an extensive set of slave sales, Balard has determined that the average age for male slaves at the moment of purchase ranged from 14 to 18 years of age, and for female slaves, from 16 to 20 years, bearing in mind that the age at sale does not necessarily reflect the age at the original acquisition.[47] The average age at manumission for men, in turn, was 28 years, and for women, 32 years. As this suggests, men were typically held in servitude for ten to fourteen years and women for twelve to sixteen years. It is important to bear in mind that although these might be the typical durations, slave owners were not necessarily bound by customs or expectations.[48]

Catherina of Tartary

In January of 1376, when Magdalena Coline was a young girl with little inkling of what fate had in store for her, another woman, Catherina of Tartary, entered Marseille's notarial record in a noteworthy way. We catch sight of Catherina when she makes an appearance in a contract of manumission from that year, in the act of purchasing her own liberty.[49] As many historians of slavery have pointed out, whenever one considers data, it is important not to lose sight of the people who lived and suffered. A life compressed into the space of several hundred words can hardly be said to be a life at all, but even so, the act is dense with information. The elements we can scrape from it capture fundamental truths about the patterns of enslavement in Marseille across the fourteenth and fifteenth centuries. Let us consider what the act tells us about Catherina's life and experiences and use the story to help make sense of the overall patterns and trend lines considered in this chapter.

At some point in time before 1376, a distinguished Massiliote merchant named Raymon de Syon acquired a slave. Three decades earlier, it would have been unusual for someone in his position to think of doing so. In a sample of several thousand notarial acts and a substantial body of court records and other documents from 1337 to 1348, a corpus that contains references to thousands of men, women, and children, I have found references to only two slaves in a population consisting of upward of 20,000 people. Even allowing for the fact that slaves are much less visible than other actors, it is hard to imagine that slaves amounted to any more than a tiny fraction of a percent of Marseille's population. But starting in the 1350s, the prospect of acquiring a household slave was becoming distinctly more thinkable. For whatever reason, Raymon found the idea an appealing one.

No trace of an act of sale for Catherina has survived. Given the fragmentary survival of records, we shouldn't expect to be able to link any given manumission to a prior sale; indeed, it is uncommon to be able to do so. There is no reason to assume, in fact, that the original sale would have been recorded in the notarial archives for, as a merchant, Raymon or one of his friends or agents could easily have acquired Catherina abroad. Elsewhere in the archive, we occasionally find evidence of purchases made abroad. At some point in the early 1400s, for example, a merchant from Valencia named Jacobus Martini, doing business on the island of Cyprus, sold an enslaved woman named Crussi, described as a Tatar, to Petrus Cathalani of Alghero. The original transaction was oral, lacking even a private handwritten note from one of the parties. We only hear about it because, in June of 1404, the two men appeared before a notary in Marseille, since the seller wanted to convert the original oral transaction into written form.[50]

The only record preserving a reference to Catherina—or to be more accurate, the only record that we know of, because any of the dozens or hundreds of sightings of people named "Catherina" in records after this date just might be her—is the contract of manumission from 1376. Contracts of manumission are often surprisingly dull and annoyingly pious documents, dominated by boilerplate text describing the master's gracious acknowledgment of the many years of faithful service and the enslaved person's pathetic gratitude for the gift of liberty. Though Catherina's manumission has some (not all) of this language, it is strikingly different in other ways.

Unusually, the act begins with an explanatory preamble. Such preambles were inserted into notarial acts on the rare occasions when something about the series of events leading up to the act fell so far outside the bounds of the ordinary that an explanation was considered necessary. What we learn is that Catherina had been impregnated by Raymon's son, Monet, and had given birth to a son. She swore to the truth of this by taking an oath on the Holy Gospels. After the birth, Raymon arranged to sell her to someone described as a "foreigner, from far-distant lands."[51] Here, the language of the preamble becomes extremely vivid, for the notary tells us that Catherina, "spitting upon the sale and refusing to change lords or to serve a different lord," took herself out of Raymon's control and fled to ecclesiastical sanctuary. One of the curious features of slavery as practiced in Mediterranean Europe is that slaves, in some circumstances, could be asked to consent to their own sale.[52] Catherina, whether wittingly or unwittingly, had found a way to exercise that right.

Negotiations ensued. According to the settlement that was hammered out, Catherina agreed to purchase her freedom for 28 florins. The payment was to be made in annual installments of 4 florins over a period of seven years, due on the Feast of Saint Michael, the 29th of September. By way of a down payment, or perhaps earnest money, Catherina handed over a single florin to Raymon. The act stipulated that the manumission would not be complete until the sum was fully paid; until that time, she was forbidden to leave Marseille. No explicit provision was made for her lodging. Though it is hard to describe any of this as a happy outcome, it probably seemed better to Catherina than the alternative scenario, one in which she would have been separated from her child and sold abroad.

Among the manumissions discovered to date in Marseille, this is the only one in which the master insisted on receiving monetary compensation. Most of the contractual manumissions in the Marseille sample are complete and un-conditional, which is also true of the majority of the testamentary manumissions. Several included conditions of various types, notably the requirement of a period of continuing service, typically lasting two to four years. Others, as we have seen, required the freedwoman to leave the city, never to return. A very odd manumission from 1367 required that the freedwoman, Catharina, refrain from hiring herself out as a housemaid while in an unmarried state (*sine marito*). Should she refuse and pursue such employment, the act stipulated that her former master could receive her domestic services in return for half the agreed-upon wages.[53] But in no other case do we find a condition in which a newly manumitted woman was required to compensate her master.

What explains the unusual condition—unusual, that is, for Marseille, since the requirement to purchase liberty is common elsewhere? It is quite possible or even likely that Raymon was a vindictive man and wanted to hold Catherina beneath his boot to the fullest extent possible. But along with this, it seems likely that the manumission, following local expectations, was premature. There are two clues. First, the price of her manumission, 28 florins, was about half the sale price for a young Tatar woman at this time. Second, the period of continuing indenture, seven years, was half the typical period of servitude, judging from the data assembled by Michel Balard. We can hazard a guess, then, that Catherina arrived in Marseille seven years earlier, in 1369. By 1376, she had worked off half the original sale price.[54] The premature manumission came about when Raymon's young son, reaching the age of sexual maturity, impregnated Catherina. Following the birth of the child, the boy's father, perhaps ashamed by what had happened and unsettled by the realization that he was now related by blood to his own slave, arranged to sell Catherina abroad, the event that triggered Catherina's flight to sanctuary and her resulting manumission.

One of the most noteworthy features of Catherina's flight to sanctuary concerns the timing. To our knowledge, she did not flee when Monet first impregnated her, nor did she mention the birth of her child as a factor. The triggering event, instead, was the proposed sale to a foreigner. The mystery lies in how she learned about ecclesiastical sanctuary. Ecclesiastical sanctuary was a well-known device for gaining leverage in certain kinds of negotiations. But it was a stratagem typically used by men who had either committed acts of violence or fallen into terminal bankruptcy, not by an enslaved woman who had recently arrived from the steppes.[55]

SLAVERY IN MARSEILLE, 1248–1491   47

Reading between the lines, it is likely that Catherina benefited from a group of well-wishers who were uneasy about her predicament. Hints as to the existence of this unseen group are found in Raymon's suggestion that she had been taking things from him and spiriting them out of the house. But if so, where had Catherina been storing the items? The implication is that she had friends or contacts beyond the household who were willing to help out. Being impregnated by Monet de Syon was apparently not problematic enough for her to play the sanctuary card. But the prospect of her being sent abroad was another thing entirely. The notary tells us, gratuitously and therefore meaningfully, that Raymon's friends and family had gotten involved in the negotiations, urging him to grant Catherina the boon of manumission.[56] It is not hard to imagine that someone from this same circle had told her how to use sanctuary as a lever. The point here is that Raymon appears to have crossed a moral line, leading to pushback from neighbors, friends, and kin.

It is likely that Raymon had the last word. The historian Charlie Steinman, who has closely considered this sad case, has argued that a young man and former slave named Martin Fabre, manumitted in 1394, was Catherina's son, now 18 years of age. Steinman's analysis relies on the fact that Monet de Syon, now known by the adult name Raymon, was included on the witness list of Martin Fabre's manumission, where he was identified as the boy's *patruus*, a Latin word that normally means "paternal uncle." If Steinman is right, the word was used here as a euphemistic nod to what everybody knew, namely, that Monet was the boy's father. In this scenario, Raymon de Syon senior, bowing under the pressure placed on him, had canceled Catherina's sale and granted her a manumission. Rather than raising the boy as a natural child in his house, however, he had instead given him as a slave to the Fabre family.

In the annals of slavery in late medieval Marseille, the story of Catherina stands out for the unprecedented degree of insight that a single act can provide on a single life. It is possible and even quite likely that similar stories lie behind the sales and manumissions of other women, such as Cita, who was sold to a slave owner in Perpignan under conditions that would never allow her to return to Marseille, or Lucia, who had to abandon her children and take employment as a domestic servant in Alghero, but if so, we shall never know it. Yet however unique the act, Catherina's experience was utterly typical of her generation. She was a Tatar woman arriving at the height of the Tatar phase. She had been acquired by a well-to-do merchant whose trade was oriented toward maritime commerce. She had been sexually exploited by at least one of the men of the household, and an attempt had been made to sell her abroad.

Catherina chose to defy her enslaver and did her best to leverage a less awful outcome for herself. It is important to not lose sight of this aspect of the case, because although the deck had been stacked against her, Catherina played her hand with uncommon skill. Somehow, she had acquired resources, consisting not only of the single florin she was able to pay Raymon at the time of the manumission but also language skills and cultural literacy. She also seems to have acquired a group of well-wishers who supported her against her enslaver.

Magdalena Coline started out in an entirely different place. She was the only woman of North African descent known to have been enslaved in Marseille, since all the other enslaved North Africans were men. She came via capture rather than sale, which created a situation, down the road, where Peire Huguet had no written instrument to prove her legal condition. But in many other respects, her own trajectory, and in particular the manner in which, over the years, she insensibly became embedded in the community, closely matched that of Catherina.

3

Peire the Privateer

IN 1938, for reasons grounded in its understanding of the rite of baptism, the Church of Latter-Day Saints began a campaign to microfilm family records from all over the world. I first became aware of the project in 1991, as a graduate student pursuing doctoral research in the departmental archive of the Bouches-du-Rhône, in Marseille. At the time, the archive was located in a former Jesuit chapel on the rue Saint-Sebastien, in the southern part of the city not far from Castellane. In the spring of 1991, the staff photographer kindly allowed me to use the splicing machine available in his laboratory to assemble the filmstrips I had taken over the preceding three weeks into microfilm. The photographer introduced me to an agent of the LDS, ensconced in the bowels of the church, who was patiently filming an endless selection of the archive's holdings.

The film, I imagine, was eventually sent to Salt Lake City, where the records were indexed and entered into a database. Less than a decade later, the LDS launched the first version of an online genealogical research tool that allows users to research their genealogies.[1] Former residents of the Bouches-du-Rhône can be found in the present-day version of the search tool. But if any records from medieval Europe were collected by the LDS during the campaign, they have yet to be indexed. A search for anyone with a variant of the name "Peire Huguet," born in Marseille around 1350, will come up empty.

Fortunately, there are plenty of sources we can use to track him down. Although Marseille's notarial and administrative records from the centuries before 1500 are not ideally suited for genealogy—the survival of records is patchy and the information less consistently pertinent—it is distinctly possible to locate individuals and reconstruct family trees. Dowry acts, last wills and testaments, estate inventories, and related documents provide abundant information. Other records make it possible to link names with variant spellings and disambiguate individuals of the same name. The life histories of prominent and long-lived individuals are especially easy to trace.

The earliest sighting to date of Peire Huguet, Magdalena's former master, occurs in a record from the year 1381. He makes dozens of appearances over the next three decades, up to 1413. As the contexts reveal, he was a prickly man, quick to use the courts to pursue injuries or debts. The vastness of Marseille's notarial holdings means that more sightings will almost certainly come along in time. These will contribute additional details to the life history of someone who probably would have wanted to be remembered for his moments of fame rather than his enduring infamy.

In some although not all of these records, Peire is described as a shipwright. Shipwrights and other craftsmen prominently associated with maritime business, such as caulkers, carpenters, oarmakers, and coopers, were ubiquitous in Marseille, the most consequential port along the stretch of Mediterranean coastline between Aigues-Mortes and Genoa. Under the Angevins, Marseille's shipyards, over the course of the fourteenth century, had turned increasingly to the production of warships.[2] In the Mediterranean, with its variable and dangerous winds, galleys manned by oarsmen had been favored since antiquity as engines of war, as they could make passage across the seas by means of both wind and oar.[3] Various clues indicate that Peire did wield an adze from time to time, or at least worked with those who did. In a contract from 1391, he joined with several other investors to build a type of ship known as a *destreria*.[4] Unlike his fellow shipwrights, though, Peire was not content with building ships. He wanted to command them. Over the course of the 1380s, his restless ambition drew him into a world where profits were made by harrying Muslims and other enemy ships on the high seas. The crucial decade of early 1380s saw him turn from shipwright to privateer.

An Obscure Lineage

To find anyone in an archive, it is helpful to know something about how names were made locally. By 1400, all patronyms, in Provence, had long since been converted into stable surnames. In most cases concerning men, records refer to individuals by two names, a given name and a surname. For women, it is somewhat more common for the surname to be omitted, although such cases are usually accompanied by a reference to the woman's father or husband, as in "Bertomieua, the wife of Peire Huguet." A few unusual individuals were known only by a single name, such as a member of the Knight Hospitallers who appears often in the records around 1400 bearing the singular name "Talabart."

Surnames that formed as patronymics around the given name *Hugo* are not uncommon in the city of Marseille in the fourteenth and fifteenth centuries. In notarial registers and administrative documents, we find dozens of individuals bearing the Latinized surname *Hugonis*, which literally means "of Hugo" or, by extension, "the son of Hugo." In the vernacular version of the same name, the genitive was not used: thus, someone known in Latin by the common name *Petrus Martini* would have been known, in Provençal, as *Peire Martin*. For women's surnames, in both Latin and Provençal versions, the stem was feminized by the addition of an "e" or an "a." By way of example, Peire Huguet's daughter-in-law, whose acquaintance we shall make later on, was called *Hugoneta* or *Hugona Huguete* in Latin.

In all such names, the letters "et," appearing in the middle of a given name or a surname, constitute a diminutive. The given names of most of the children who appear in records include an "et," as in *Hugoneta*. Variants appear where the phonetics made them necessary, as in *Andrivetus*, the diminutive of *Andreas*, or *Peyretus*, the diminutive of *Petrus*. The spelling of men's names typically lost the diminutive when they came of age, though it could persist as a nickname or a sign of affection. Women's names, by contrast, often preserved the diminutive into adulthood.

The Latin form *Hugueti*, therefore, literally means "[son] of little Hugo." It may have come into existence some two centuries earlier, when given names, across the region, first began to pass into surnames. We can imagine a scenario where a man who had clung to the given name "Huguet" into his adulthood had a child who took his father's given name as his surname. But for all we know, the spelling may have been an affectation, or even a mistake that somehow endured. Whatever its origin, the surname *Hugueti/e* is exceedingly rare in the sources from Marseille between the 1330s and the 1430s. Records from the 1340s and 1350s, which contain references to about 13,000 unique people, yield only half a dozen sightings of individuals bearing the surname. The only individuals with the Huguet name between 1380 and 1430 were Peire, his brother Johan, his son Lazaret, and their wives. In the 1390s, the occasional notary, perhaps bemused or taken off guard, accidentally wrote *Petrus Hugonis* when he should have written *Petrus Hugueti*. These slips attest to the highly unusual nature of Peire's surname.

The first sighting of a member of the family Huguet occurred in 1341, when a merchant named Peire Huguet appears among the witnesses to a dowry act.[5] His social or professional obscurity, though, is suggested by the fact that one otherwise searches in vain for his name in the relatively rich body of records from the 1340s. But he did survive the Black Death of 1348 and appears to have done well for himself, for he next shows up as a member of the city council early in the fall of 1350. In the opening pages of the register of council deliberations for that year, he was named as one of the representatives of the administrative quarter or *sixain* of Accoules to the committee charged with the task of chasing prostitutes out of respectable neighborhoods.[6]

A few weeks later, he shows up again in the records of the city council, this time in rather different circumstances. On the 26th of September, a man named Peire Calafat submitted a petition to the council concerning the killing of his brother, Antoni Calafat.[7] The murderer was Peire Huguet, who was seized by officials of the bishop's court and imprisoned in the royal jail on their orders. This was a matter of some concern to the council: Peire, as a layman, did not fall under the criminal jurisdiction of the bishop. Accordingly, the council resolved to send an ambassador bearing an indignant letter to the bishop. An entry made a few days later briefly records the nature of the bishop's temporizing reply. The matter then disappears from the council's records.

Peire Huguet also disappears for a short while, perhaps to make peace with the victim's family and rebuild his reputation. Soon after, though, we spot another person bearing the Huguet surname. In 1354, an individual named *Perrotus Hugueti* appears briefly as the respondent in an aborted lawsuit initiated by a merchant over a small debt of 3 florins. A year later, a Perrotus shows up as a witness in a notarial act.[8] The given name *Perrotus* is not Provençal in origin; it almost certainly points to someone of foreign origins.[9] Given the similarity of the given names, the rarity of the surname *Huguet*, and the fact that both names are associated with merchants, it is distinctly possible, even likely, that *Petrus* and *Perrotus* are one and the same individual. If so, it suggests the intriguing possibility that Peire Huguet himself was an immigrant, which would explain the rarity of his surname.

In 1357, Peire Huguet appears again in the deliberations of the city council, this time not as an evictor of prostitutes or murderer but instead as the author of a letter on a matter pertaining to the nearby town of Allauch.[10] His final appearance in records sampled to date was occasioned by his purchase of some cloth from the shop of a distinguished draper named Marques de Favas at some point before October of 1373. His name, and the amount of the invoice, were entered into the shop cartulary, and because the debt remained unpaid at the time of Marques's death on the 3rd of October of that year, it was copied out in the inventory made of the decedent's estate by his widow, Lady Catharina.[11]

What was the relationship, if any, between Peire or Perrot Huguet the merchant and Peire Huguet the shipwright? Happily, there is no need for guesswork. The first unambiguous reference to the younger man occurs in a notarial act that took place on the 2nd of September 1381. In this act, the principal actor was called "Peire Huguet of Marseille, son of the late Peire."

Using this and other clues, we can begin to compile a reasonably full portrait of Peire Huguet the elder, though it is important to acknowledge the guesswork. When he first appears in the records of Marseille, he was a decidedly obscure man, kinless in a world where family was important. The rarity of his surname and the phonetic similarity between "Peire" and "Perrot," coupled with the foreign provenance of the latter, suggest foreign origins. This possibility is amplified by the fact that he was a merchant, a profession that would not have been easy to enter in the absence of a well-placed father and supportive kin group. It is easier to imagine that Peire the elder had entered the guild elsewhere and immigrated to Marseille, perhaps serving as a local factor for a merchant company, perhaps because some legal trouble back home encouraged his extended absence. Given that Peire the elder was mature enough to have witnessed a notarial act in 1341, he would have been born at least two decades earlier, around 1320. In his late twenties, amid the social vacuum left by the ravages of the Black Death, Peire wed a local woman, and by virtue of inserting himself into local society, he ascended to the city council in 1350.

His social ascent, however, was abruptly curtailed by the murder of Antoni Calafat in September of 1350. It is not easy to know whether there was a relationship of cause and effect here, since homicide, at the time, did not necessarily produce the sort of stigma it would today. What is striking, though, is that the rate of references to Peire the elder fades at a life stage when, at least for prominent and successful individuals, those references should be accelerating in number. At this distance, we cannot know whether the life experiences of his father had any influence on Peire the younger. But it is possible to imagine that Peire's burning ambition was formed in the crucible of his father's failure to make good.

Peire the Privateer

Between 1381 and 1387, Peire the younger makes a handful of appearances in notarial acts. Since he was the only Peire Huguet, the notaries who recorded his name had no concerns about the possibility of ambiguity. Partly for this reason, they usually didn't bother attaching identity labels such as occupation, parentage, or residence, labels that were not uncommonly added to other, less distinctive names. On one occasion in these early records, Peire was described as a shipwright. Curiously, in 1384, a notary attached to one of the law courts made the mistake of calling him a "caulker."[12] The error was understandable, since members of both occupations were involved in building and servicing ships.

Although shipbuilding was an honorable profession, it wasn't a particularly distinguished one. Few shipwrights appear among the ranks of the great and powerful in Marseille. The fact that Peire Huguet the elder, a merchant, could do no better than place his son and namesake in the trade speaks to his inability to make a name and fortune for himself. But although Peire the elder may have apprenticed his son in a trade that required manual labor, it is distinctly possible that he also provided him with the resources that would, in time, allow him to grow beyond the status of shipwright. In the earliest sighting of Peire Huguet the younger, in 1381, we see him not in the act of making a ship, but owning one.[13]

The ship in question, bearing the Latin name *Sanctus-Urbanus*, was a type of war galley known as a *panfilus*, or "panfilo" in modern Italian. In September of 1381, the galley was docked in the port of Berre 30 kilometers to the northwest of Marseille. To minimize risk, shipowners often did not own ships outright. They preferred instead to invest in shares, typically one-third to one-quarter, and distribute those shares across several galleys. In this instance, Peire owned one-third of the *Sanctus-Urbanus*. The names of the other two shareholders, one of whom was a resident of Berre, are unfamiliar, and clearly not part of Peire's world.

The act in question was a procuration by means of which Peire named three friends or associates to act as his legal representatives. The three procurators were charged with the task of selling the galley for a price that Peire hoped would come to 166 florins and 8 gros, that is, one-third of the value of the galley. A plausible scenario is that Peire Huguet the elder had died fairly recently, leaving a share in the panfilo to his son, who had decided to sell it.

Five months later, in February of 1382, the *Sanctus-Urbanus* makes another appearance, in a context that clearly indicates that Peire, ultimately, had chosen not to sell the panfilo. Instead, he made it a going concern. In this act, Peire joined with two other men with equal shares in the galley to hire a mariner to captain the ship for a period of time.[14] As a warship, the panfilo, with twenty-four banks of oars, was on the small side; the great galleys in Marseille's harbor typically had twenty-nine banks of oars, and the smaller galiots had twenty-six or twenty-seven. This suggests that the panfilo may have been useful for its agility or speed, not its fighting strength. The pursuit of lucre figures prominently in the act, which specifies that the captain will receive a quarter of any profits with the remainder distributed evenly among the three investors.

It is easy to discern the reason for Peire's change of heart. Further to the south, tensions were mounting. Pursuing the crown of Naples, Charles of Durazzo had assembled an army in the fall of 1381 and descended on the southern regions of the Italian peninsula, making war against his cousin, Johanna of Naples. With conflict looming, a war galley could be put to profitable uses. In 1382, Peire was poised to make the leap from shipwright to privateer.

Peire's Partners

In the acts arising from Peire's activities before 1387, the contours of a network of business partners and investors gradually come into view. Some of Peire's associates, such as the draper and nobleman Isnart de Sant Gilles, remained a presence in Peire's life for several decades. Others, including the merchant Antoni Gracian, were present for only a decade or so. In one of the earliest acts, from 1381, Antoni appears as one of three individuals named to negotiate the

PEIRE THE PRIVATEER 55

sale of Peire's share in the *Sanctus-Urbanus*, although we know that ultimately the share was not sold. Antoni was one of Peire's close neighbors and clearly a trusted associate. His departure from Peire's life a decade later came about in the most unusual of circumstances, because Antoni was murdered in April of 1391 by yet another long-term associate of Peire, Jacme Limosin.[15]

One of the most prominent of the men who appeared in the early records that pertain to Peire was a mariner named Antoni de Lueys. Confusingly, Antoni had a cousin who was also named Antoni de Lueys, and since the two men were very nearly the same age, the notaries almost always disambiguated the two men by adding their professions to the identity clauses, "mariner" in the case of Peire's associate, "master oarmaker" in the case of the other. Both men make an appearance together as investors, with Peire, in a third share each of the panfilo *Sanctus-Urbanus*. Clearly, the shares belonging to the previous two part-owners had been bought out by the two Antonis. Subsequent acts in the coming years indicate that Peire and Antoni the mariner formed a tight and trusting partnership.

An act from April of 1387 contains some of the earliest inklings of the partnerships Peire established with other men. The act reveals that Peire owned a share of a galley named *Sancta-Catherina* together with Johan Bellissens, Jacme Limosin, and Antoni de Lueys.[16] But privateering was an expensive line of work, requiring additional investors. According to the terms of the act, therefore, the shipowners were forming a society with Martin Elie and Bertomieu Simondel, representatives of a broader group of investors that included Isnart de Sant Gilles. The merchant Bertomieu Simondel shows up elsewhere as one of Peire's financiers: an act from some years later indicates that on the 6th of May 1387, Peire contracted a debt to the merchant in the amount of 166 florins and 8 gros, a precise figure that almost certainly indicates an investment in a third share of a galley appraised at 500 florins.[17] The nobleman Johan Bellissens also appears around this time as both an investor and one of Peire's creditors.[18] These private loans indicate that, unlike some of the other shipowners and captains, Peire was unable to supply the necessary capital on his own.

By 1387, Peire the privateer had assembled a robust network of partners and investors. Not all of these relationships were positive. Late in the year 1384, for example, he had a falling out with his partner Jacme Limosin over some matter related to a galley in which the two men each had a share. Jacme Limosin was another shipwright-turned-privateer and one of Peire's closest neighbors in the Lansaria. Other members of the Limosin family were also enmeshed in Peire's activities; among other things, Jacme's brother, Guilhem Limosin, had purchased shares in one of the galleys that participated in the expedition to Naples. Yet some dispute arose between the two men, and on the 24th of December 1384, Jacme went to court and acquired an order against Peire.

In the text of the judge's order, Peire was required immediately to surrender to Jacme "all the equipment of the galley shared by Jacme and Peire in common."[19] The tension between the two associates foreshadows the shape of things to come. Peire was good at making partners, who recognized his energy and talent. He was less good at keeping them.

In 1387, the clouds of war were gathering, as the courts of queen and pope began to lay plans for invading Naples. Having turned himself into a shipowner and privateer, Peire was positioned to profit from the impending turmoil. The notaries of the age had an intuitive feeling for matters of dignity and worth. Those who met Peire in the months leading up to the expedition to Naples saw that something had changed. In October of 1387, a few weeks after Peire had an audience with Queen Marie in Avignon, he finally broke through: a notary named Antoni Audebert, drawing up an act of procuration for Peire, for the first time in the known record accorded Peire a title of distinction, selecting "honorable man (*honorabilis vir*)" as the honorific most appropriate to the occasion.[20] The procuration took place in Peire's neighborhood, just outside the portal of the workshop of his trusted associate, the merchant Antoni Gracian. The witnesses included Antoni and the shipwright Jacme Limosin, whose differences with Peire had evidently been smoothed over. As good fortune smiled on the Angevin cause, and plans were being laid for an expedition to Naples, Peire was on the brink of a rapid social ascent.

The Women of the Family Huguet

From references made many years later, we learn that the elder Peire Huguet married a woman named Gassenda. They had two children who survived into adulthood, Peire the younger and Johan. Peire was almost certainly the elder. Gassenda lived well into the 1390s, and may have been approaching 70 years of age at the time of her death. We catch a glimpse of her once or twice in association with Magdalena Coline, in the act of giving her hand-me-down clothing.

In records from the 1380s and 1390s, several sources identify a woman named Bertomieua as the wife of Peire Huguet the younger. A chance reference floating in a sea of miscellaneous entries in a court register from 1412 gestures toward a dowry act from 1 April 1374 that gave Peire rights in a plot of land.[21] It is very likely that this was Bertomieua's dowry, which points to the day of their wedding. Very soon afterward, Bertomieua gave birth to a son whom they named Lazaret. The boy's name was a somewhat unusual choice. In the generation of Lazaret's grandfather, the name was exceedingly uncommon. By the later fourteenth century, though, it had come into fashion: the name "Lazarus" is scattered across the records with growing frequency. Its use, however, was favored by some of the members of the city's upper crust. The fact that Peire chose such a name for his son provides a hint about his aspirations as a social climber.

In the few acts in which Bertomieua makes an appearance, we get the distinct impression of a retiring woman lacking any desire to mix things up in public. On several occasions, she makes a nameless appearance, identified simply as "the wife of Peire Huguet," as if all life and color had been drained from her by her overbearing husband. It is difficult to know what lay behind these moments of unnaming. Did Bertomieua, eyes cast down, tell notaries "I am the wife of Peire Huguet," or did notaries express a quiet contempt for her mousy demeanor by silently dropping the given name from the record? On those occasions when the notaries deigned to acknowledge her given name, they did not provide her with a surname, calling her "Bertomieua, the wife of Peire Huguet." Though it is probably not something they thought about a lot, notaries gave surnames to people who carried some distinction relative to others in their walk of life. They gave surnames to people whom they considered capable of being autonomous legal actors. They did not give surnames to enslaved people, nor to wives they found to be unremarkable.

Bertomieua comes to life on only two occasions, once in the middle of the 1380s, when she makes a brief appearance in a lawsuit, and once, at the very end of her life, when she did something nice for Magdalena. The first of these concerns us here. In 1385, Bertomieua made a cameo appearance in a lawsuit involving an inheritance. The lawsuit itself has not survived in the court registers, but it left a record in the form of a notarized arbitration.[22] In the table of contents at the beginning of this register, the act is identified as "A compromise on behalf of the wife of Peire Huguet and the husband of Moneta Durante." Bertomieua's only role in this garden-variety inheritance dispute was to grant her husband the authority to act as her procurator. From the act, we learn that her maiden name was Durante. The Duranti/e family name is a relatively common one and therefore hard to trace, but no one holding the given names of her father or grandfather appears with any distinction in the previous generation or two. Bertomieua, like her husband, was almost certainly of modest origins.

Like his brother, Johan Huguet appears frequently in acts from the years surrounding 1400. In records from the 1380s and 1390s, the younger of the two siblings comes across as star-struck by his dashing older brother and prone to being led astray against his better judgment. In his early decades, Johan was prickly about small debts owed to him, appearing regularly in court to insist on payment rather than granting delays or forgiving the loans, which were otherwise common practices.

Johan's wife, Alaseta, appears to have been the stabilizing force in his life. Alaseta had been born and raised in the village of Ceyreste, located several dozen kilometers to the east of Marseille, just north of La Ciotat. Since her father, Bertran Colin, was still living there in 1403, it is likely that Alaseta had left Ceyreste in her youth and immigrated to Marseille as a domestic servant.[23] There, probably in the early 1370s, she met and married Peire Bertran. Since one of the members of the Bertran family in 1393 was a master oarmaker, it is likely that Alaseta's in-laws had connections to Marseille's maritime communities, a likelihood confirmed by the fact that no fewer than four shipwrights bearing the surname Bertran were active in the 1340s and 1350s. Alaseta and Peire Bertran had two children, Hugoneta and Peyret. Following the death of her first husband, Alaseta married Johan Huguet, bringing a sizable dowry of 300 florins. They first appear as a married couple in November of 1392, though it is possible that they married a year earlier, in 1391.[24]

In May of 1393, Alaseta and Johan took out a loan of 100 florins to provide a dowry for Alaseta's daughter, Hugoneta.[25] In a manner that skirts the edge of what was allowable under canon law, Hugoneta was getting married to her stepcousin, Lazaret Huguet, and the dowry was being paid to Johan's brother, Peire. Lazaret could have been no older than 19 at the time of his marriage. If we assume that Hugoneta was similar in age, then she would have been born by 1375 at the latest. Since Hugoneta appears to have been the older of the two siblings, their mother, Alaseta, was probably born around 1355. Perhaps because of Alaseta's age—she would have been in her mid- to late thirties at the time of her remarriage in 1391 or 1392—perhaps owing to Johan's infertility, the couple never had any surviving children of their own.

In the 1380s and early 1390s, the fortunes of the brothers Huguet were bound together, and the marriage between Lazaret and Hugoneta would seem to have made those bonds even more solid. Yet to all appearances, Johan's wife Alaseta gently inserted an oar between her husband and his brother, and across the 1390s, she slowly and patiently pried them apart. Although Johan never became disloyal to his elder brother—we catch a few glimpses of them acting together as late as 1412—Alaseta appears to have largely succeeded in her efforts to displace Peire as the gravitational center of Johan's orbit.

She and Johan appear several times in subsequent records from the ensuing decades, acting together in a comfortably conjugal way. They survived the plague of 1401 and the dramatic sack of the city by the Aragonese fleet two decades later, in 1423. One of the very last sightings of any figures in the dramatis personae occurs when the two of them made an appearance on the 28th of May 1429. On that day, Johan Huguet and his wife, now known as "Lady Alasacia," appeared together before a notary to hire a stonemason to repair a house of theirs located in the plaza of the Vivaut.[26] At the time, the couple, nearing the end of a long and adventurous life together, must have been in their mid-seventies. The scene is a poignant one: an elderly couple investing in a ruined landscape and helping to bring the city back to life. In drawing up the clause whereby Alaseta was identified, the notary clearly saw in her the type of force or presence associated with a remarkable woman. He did so in two ways: by granting her the title of "lady" and by dropping the diminutive from her name.

Early in life, under the influence of his charismatic elder brother, Johan had done some unsavory things. The lawsuits he filed for petty sums suggest a grasping, untrustworthy character. His marriage to Alaseta, a strong-willed widow with two children, turns out to have been his salvation. As we shall see, there was no such redemption in store for Peire Huguet. The women in his life had other things in mind for him.

4

The Expedition to Naples

IN THE WORLD BEYOND THE LANSARIA, in the halls and palaces of the great, other things were afoot. On the 27th of July in the year 1382, Queen Johanna of Naples, in the thirty-ninth year of her tumultuous reign, was smothered to death on the orders of her cousin and rival, Charles of Durazzo.[1] Her body was displayed in the church of Santa Chiara in Naples for a week before reportedly being dumped in a well. With the queen's assassination, the simmering dynastic conflict between the two rival branches of the Angevin dynasty turned into open warfare, unsettling the peoples who lived along the shores and on the islands of the Western Mediterranean basin for decades to come. The prize was worth fighting for: rule over the sprawling Kingdom of Naples, a piecemeal realm that encompassed the city of Naples, the lands of southern Italy, the county of Provence, and dynastic claims to Sicily and Jerusalem. Yet more was at stake than the crown of Naples. All Christendom lay in the balance, for the Angevin contenders each backed the claims of rival popes. If that were not enough, looming in the background were the imperial ambitions of the Kingdom of France in the Western Mediterranean, and the equally powerful ambitions of the Crown of Aragon.

With war on the horizon, Marseille's naval yards shifted into a higher gear, and investors poured funds into provisioning the fleet of galleys that lay in the harbor. Though the land assault on the Kingdom of Naples was already underway, control of the sea-lanes between Provence and Naples was essential for communications and for the rapid movement of highly placed persons.[2] Like other powers of the time, neither the Avignonese papacy nor the Valois Angevins had a standing navy manned by a permanent corps of officers and enlisted sailors. When a navy was needed, they went out and found one. They did so by negotiating military service with teams of investors who owned galleys and took responsibility for furnishing them with crew, officers, and armaments. The economic incentives were considerable. In addition to direct payments, the investors and their captains were guaranteed a share of the spoils of war.

THE EXPEDITION TO NAPLES   61

In the fall of 1387, the time was ripe for launching a naval expedition to Naples. Four Massiliote galleys were hired, and they joined forces with two Neapolitan galleys to make up a flotilla of six ships. One of the Massiliote galleys selected was *La Stella*, captained by Peire Huguet. War is an occasion for both destruction and profiteering. In the expedition to Naples, the political objectives of Pope Clement VII and his Valois Angevin allies were inextricably entwined with the piratical motives of the galley captains and their men. As events would show, Peire was among the most piratical of all.

The Revolt of Provence

Late in the month of June of 1380, Queen Johanna of Naples, pressured by the Avignonese pope, Clement VII, quietly adopted Louis I, the Duke of Anjou, as her heir.[3] The younger brother of King Charles V, Louis was a scion of the Valois dynasty of France. Following the death of Charles V in September of 1380, Louis served as regent during the minority of Charles VI. Any dynastic claims he had to the throne of Naples were exceedingly tenuous, and by rights, the throne should have descended to Johanna's younger cousin, Charles of Durazzo, as Johanna herself acknowledged, having named Charles as her heir in 1373.

Yet there had been no great affection between Johanna and Charles of Durazzo. Charles's father, Louis, had launched a rebellion against Johanna in 1362 and died in Johanna's prison when the rebellion was quashed. Additional tensions arose in the wake of Johanna's fourth and final marriage to Otto of Brunswick in 1376. But dynastic duty might have prevailed over mutual dislike had not the papal schism of 1378 abruptly changed the political landscape. Johanna's decision to favor the claims of Clement VII angered the Roman pope, Urban VI, who excommunicated the queen, announced a crusade against her, and stripped her of the crown, instead throwing his support behind Charles of Durazzo. Johanna's fateful decision to back Clement VII locked her into the French camp to which Clement himself was attached. The price of their support was the nomination of Louis I as her heir.

In the fall of 1380, when news of the adoption reached Charles's ears, he assembled an army and marched on southern Italy.[4] In June of 1381, Pope Urban VI crowned his champion king of Naples. In July, Charles defeated Otto of Brunswick and triumphantly entered the capital city. Johanna held out for a month, vainly hoping that her new allies would come to her rescue, before capitulating in August, whereupon she was imprisoned by Charles. Louis I began making his own preparations for war, first in the hopes of making a rescue, and then, once news of Johanna's death reached him in 1382, to make good on his claims to the throne. That same year, he launched an assault, making his way down the peninsula at the head of a massive army to engage Charles in battle.

62 CHAPTER 4

Simultaneously, a fleet of twenty galleys financed by Pope Clement VII and Louis I departed from Marseille to harry the enemy in Calabria and Sicily.[5]

The nomination of Louis I as heir to the throne of Naples had not been well received in Provence. In 1368, while serving as lieutenant-governor of Languedoc, Louis had allowed mercenary troops under the command of Bertrand du Guesclin to plunder Provence, alienating the townsfolk and the nobles of the county.[6] For a time, loyalty to Queen Johanna prevailed over the county's intense dislike for Louis. But when news of her demise filtered into Provence, with the cause of death rumored rather than known, only Marseille and Arles declared obedience to Louis I. A larger union of cities and great lords, led by Aix-en-Provence, entered into open revolt, siding with Charles of Durazzo.[7]

Louis I died in 1384 while campaigning in Apulia, leaving it to his widow, Marie of Blois, to pursue the Valois cause as regent during the minority of their son, Louis II. Where the support of Provence was concerned, Louis's death no doubt helped the cause. Even so, the situation was bleak. Having cemented control of southern Italy, Charles was so confident that he left Naples to pursue dynastic claims to the throne of Hungary. But he had not reckoned with the formidable Marie, who came to Provence in the spring of 1385. Starting in August of that year, she began to travel through the county, slowly and painstakingly making peace with her rebellious subjects. Thanks to the firsthand account preserved in the journal of Marie's chancellor, Jean Le Fèvre, bishop of Chartres, we have intimate details about her patient diplomacy.[8]

In 1386, Charles was assassinated in Buda, leaving a son and heir, Ladislas, who at the time was only a boy, nearly the same age as Louis II. Charles's untimely death came at a crucial moment, as Marie's careful diplomacy had begun to win back the rebels. As news of his death reached his remaining supporters, they gradually fell back into Marie's camp. In October 1387, she and her counselors staged a royal entry into Aix featuring the 10-year-old Louis II, providing a powerful symbolic conclusion to five years of open revolt. Provence was once again securely in the Valois camp.

Simultaneously, plans were being made for a maritime expedition to Naples, to be launched from Marseille. Pressure for such a move had been mounting since at least 1384, when powerful Neapolitan lords alienated by Charles of Durazzo came to Marie's court, beseeching her to retake Naples. After confirming his control of Naples, Charles had fallen out with his patron, Urban VI, and had even imprisoned the pope. In July of 1387, Otto of Brunswick returned to Naples, inducing the queen-regent, Margaret of Durazzo, to flee with her son Ladislas to the castle at Gaeta, a hundred kilometers or a day's sail north of Naples.[9]

To judge by the journal of Jean Le Fèvre, interest in Naples had been growing since 1386, as a stream of Neapolitan supplicants requesting confirmation

THE EXPEDITION TO NAPLES   63

of their rights and privileges began to appear at Marie's court. The first inkling that an expedition was being contemplated appears in August of 1387, in the wake of Otto's conquest of Naples in July, when Marie received letters from allies in Genoa urging the queen to arm galleys and send them to the capital city.[10] Shortly after, a Neapolitan delegation reached Avignon to plead with the queen. Jean Le Fèvre describes their entreaties in some detail:

> On the 24th day [of August], Madame attended a mass in Avignon before the grave of the cardinal of Luxembourg, and dined at the house of the Monseigneur of Embrun, and there, after a period of rest, the ambassadors from Naples explained their mission under four headings: the moment had come to take possession of the city of Naples; they pleaded for the king to go there; they asked for galleys and the funds needed to support them; they asked that an embassy be sent from the king of France to the Genoans and the Florentines.[11]

The next day, the 25th of August, the ambassadors spoke urgently in council about the need to send galleys and money to Naples, mentioning a figure of 50,000 florins and asking the queen to solicit the pope for a contribution. On the 4th of September, the queen and pope announced that they would each contribute 15,000 florins and would make arrangements to take the Italian counts to Naples by galley, with the funds being transmitted separately by means of letters of exchange.[12] On the 25th of September, Jean reports that the anxious Italian counts renewed their pleas before the queen. Two days later, she reiterated her promise to supply 15,000 florins by the 15th of October.[13]

Now that Provence was back into the Angevin camp, it made sense for Marie to turn her attention to Naples. To judge by the silences in the journal of Jean Le Fèvre, however, she never became significantly involved in the preparations underway for the expedition to Naples. It is easy to appreciate why she would have been unwilling to countenance the idea of sending 10-year-old Louis II into the nest of vipers that was Naples, and in any event she was ill-disposed toward Otto of Brunswick.[14] Planning was entrusted instead to the count of Cerreto.[15] The entries in Jean Le Fèvre's journal from November and December give no sign that the court was even aware of the existence of the December expedition.

In the fall of 1387, as Naples leaned ever more strongly into Marie's camp, the stream of supplicants seeking confirmation of their grants grew more intense. They came from Naples, Averso, Capua, and elsewhere in the kingdom of Naples. Day after day, Marie confirmed the grants of her supplicants and stripped the rebels of their rights. She was also kept busy taking care of the fallout from the rebellion of her Provençal subjects, forgiving injuries and confirming grants. One of the most interesting grants and concessions occurred

64   CHAPTER 4

on the 29th of September 1387, when Peire Huguet of Marseille came to Marie's court to request confirmation of grants formerly made to him by King Louis I.[16] These supplications indicate that Peire had received an office or privilege in the city of Naples. Marie confirmed this grant together with several others, including the right to bear arms in the counties of Provence and Forcalquier. Peire was also exempted from certain gabelles and transit tolls.

The historian Édouard Baratier has discovered a range of documents identifying the prominent Massiliote shipowners who participated in assembling a squadron of twenty-some galleys that had been sent in the summer of 1382 to aid in the conquest of the Kingdom of Naples.[17] All the familiar names appear, including one of Peire's investors, Johan Bellissens of Narbonne, who was named treasurer of the squadron. But Peire Huguet was not among them. The grants made to him by Louis I, in all probability, had been made after this point in time.

Louis' death in the fall of 1384 put an end to the campaign he had been undertaking in southern Italy and temporarily halted any plans for assembling another fleet of galleys. Early in the summer of 1385, however, new plans were being laid down, and in June of that year we see Peire Huguet in the act of contracting with the papal curia to provide naval services.[18] Together with Peire Enguayte of Mallorca, a shipowner who appears on Baratier's list of great men in 1382, Peire Huguet contracted to supply the curia with two good galleys, subtle, fully furnished with the accouterments of war. The two shipowners were to undertake a good war against "Bartolomeo, pretender to the apostolic seat, and Charles." To pay the crew's wages, each of the two investors received 1,600 florins per month, and they undertook to serve for a minimum of two months, although both agreed to continue their service beyond that at the agreed-upon figure for as long as necessary.

What Peire did over the next few months is not clear, but it is hard to imagine that he didn't pursue the adventure with vigor. The profit, to him, would not come from any wages he received. It would come from any plunder he took and hostages that he could sell back to the curia. Beyond that, a successful voyage surely would have bolstered his reputation as a servant of the crown, and news of his service to the papal and Angevin cause would have spread. When he made his way to the Angevin court in Avignon to remind the queen of the favors he had formerly received from her husband, one would expect that he was given a warm welcome.

The Dogs of War

In November of 1387, preparations for the assault began in earnest in Marseille. On the 23rd of that month, a group of men, including Peire Huguet's closest associates, convened in the workshop of Peire's house on the street of the

THE EXPEDITION TO NAPLES 65

Lansaria. The objective was to arrange for the sale of Peire's share of an un-named galley, probably the *Sancta-Catherina*, with all its appurtenances, to anyone wishing to buy it.[19] The act itself is not unusual: investments come and go, and people change their minds. It is the witness list that gives one pause. Those present included Lord Peire Olivier, the vicar of the church of Marseille, and Franciscus Comitis, identified as "the porter of our lord the pope." As the presence of both men suggests, the papal curia was interested in sorting out the matter of Peire's galley. It is unclear whether Peire was upgrading his equip-ment or raising the capital needed to invest in the impending expedition. What is clear is that Peire had made a bid to join the expedition as one of its captains.

The following day, the 24th of November, witnessed the making of three acts that shed more light on the preparations for war.[20] The acts, executed by Laurens Aycart, Marseille's most distinguished notary at the time, took place in the house of the mariner Antoni de Lueys, located on the embankment of the port. In the first of these, the shareholders of the *Sancta-Catherina* ap-pointed Antoni to serve as the galley's captain for the upcoming expedition.[21] When we first saw the shareholders of the *Sancta-Catherina* seven months earlier, in April of 1387, the group had included Johan Bellisens, Jacme Limo-sin, Peire Huguet, and Antoni de Lueys. But now, Johan Huguet had acquired the share owned by his brother. In the second act, we learn that whereas the *Sancta-Catherina* had formerly been under the command of Peire Huguet, he was now transferring his command to *La Stella*, which was also being armed for the upcoming expedition.[22] As we learn elsewhere, *La Stella* had been the property of the papal curia in 1384.[23] Two years later, the curia sold its shares in the galley to Massiliote investors, Peire among them. The third act indicates that a Massiliote nobleman named Jacme Martin would lead the expedition as admiral of the fleet and owner and captain of a galley named the *Sanctus-Georgius*.[24] Elsewhere, we learn that Bertomieu Aymeric was to be the captain of the fourth Massiliote galley.

The financing of war, in the later Middle Ages, was a complex, pay-as-you-go affair. The major powers in any conflict—princes, popes, and pretend-ers alike—provided the money needed to pay the crew's wages. But shipowners were expected to pay for furnishing the ships with armaments and provisions and for undertaking repairs and maintenance. In compensation, they received a pro rata share of the spoils of war.

Rich details about the furnishing of galleys are provided by a series of papal acts from 1384 to 1385 now preserved in the Bibliothèque nationale de France. Many of these acts concern galleys owned or provisioned by Massiliote ship-owners and investors.[25] A rubric at the outset, dated 1384, informs us that the acts concern engagements made by the papal chamberlain "with those who intend to lead galleys and galiots in the service of the Roman church and lord Louis, king of Jerusalem and Sicily." The provisions listed in the contracts are relatively standard, where the variables concern the size of the warships and the amount of funding provided by the papal curia. Invariably, the contractors were not to harass any allies of the pope—Genoans, Pisans, Venetians, and Catalans were commonly listed, although other nationalities were added from time to time depending on the nationality of the contractor—unless they were assisting the enemy. The size of the warships varied from larger galleys, with twenty-nine banks of oars and three men to each bank, to the smaller galiots, which could have as few as twenty-three banks of oars and two men to each bank. It was expected that the oarsmen would be Catalans, Spaniards, and Sicilians. The contractors had to furnish the warships with crossbowmen, ranging from fifteen to forty in number, and a suite of officers, including pilots, constables, scribes, trumpeters, and surgeons. From one of these acts, we learn that Peire Huguet's future command, *La Stella*, was provisioned with thirty-five crossbowmen, near the upper end of the range.[26] Each galley was also expected to have one or two cannons with the necessary powder and shot. Contractors also had to supply masts, sails, armor, weapons, shields, and chests of quarrels for the crossbows.

The profiteering was very closely regulated. All plunder had to be divided evenly between the papal curia and the contractors, with the expectation that careful accounts would be kept of each and every item of plunder, whence the need for the scribes. Some of the contracts specifically excluded clothing, vestments, and equipment from the papal share; these were instead to be divvied up among the members of the crew who took them.[27] Special provisions were made for notable captives, who were to be assigned to the papal curia or the king for an amount not exceeding 2,000 florins, where the price would be negotiated according to the value of the person.[28] The papal curia provided monthly stipends to cover the wages of the crew; these figures ranged from 1,500 to 2,000 florins per month. Since no provisions were otherwise made for the contractors, it is clear that they were expected to profit from the spoils of war. The enlisted men, in addition to their wages, would be motivated by the prospect of seizing valuable clothing from their victims.

As a profit-making enterprise, war was and is a fickle institution, rife with risk and uncertainty. The way to manage risk is to distribute it across multiple stakeholders. Owing to the existence of commenda contracts and marine insurance policies, we know that there was a long history of managing risk in the maritime world of Mediterranean Europe.[29] Where the impending expedition to Naples was concerned, if calamity should strike one of the captains and shareholders, there was a risk they would be left with losses that outweighed any profits from the spoils of war.

So it is not surprising to learn that Peire had another plan for minimizing his exposure to risk. This involved making a separate partnership with Antoni de Lueys. According to the terms of this partnership, revealed in an act from a few years later, they promised each other to place their earnings in a common pool and share the proceeds equally. Such matters were not entered into lightly. To bind their partnership, Peire and Antoni came together in the church of Saint-Laurent to exchange solemn oaths.[30] Perched on a hill above the western edge of the port, the church of Saint-Laurent is one of the few edifices from the fabric of medieval Marseille to have survived to the present day. Six centuries ago, the church was the center of the devotional practices of the community of fisherfolk and mariners who lived just below, along the harbor, in the *sixain* of Saint-Jean. Standing before the altar of Sainte-Catherine, the two partners promised one another that once the voyage was complete, they would share and share alike the profits accruing to each of them. In order to make an accurate reckoning, they promised to account for their earnings in the ships' cartularies, kept by ships' scribes. War, like any business, demanded accurate accounts.

The Expedition to Naples

The four Massiliote galleys joined with two galleys supplied by Niccolò Sanframondi, the count of Cerreto, to form a flotilla of six ships. Some days later, the flotilla set sail for Naples and soon arrived in the vicinity of Gaeta, a day's sail north of the Bay of Naples, to which Margaret of Durazzo had fled after the fall of Naples. There, they spotted a galley from Pozzuoli, the ancient Roman grain harbor to the north of the Bay of Naples (figure 4).

A faithful narrative of what transpired has been preserved in the *Cronicon Siculum*, a history of the Kingdom of Sicily whose anonymous author recounted events that unfolded in southern Italy in the fourteenth century. The narrative accords in almost every respect with stories told in three additional sources. "On the 10th of December," reports the chronicler,

> the count of Cerreto, admiral of the realm, returned from Avignon with five galleys and a galiot, four of which were Provençal. . . . On the day they arrived near Gaeta, they took a Pozzuolan war galley with the bishop of Pozzuoli and some of the best men of Pozzuoli. Around the hour of vespers, they took another war galley with men from Castellammare, Sorrento, and Positano whose captain was a Genoan, along with many Genoan confederates. In this galley they discovered 3,000 florins in coin and jewels worth 25,000 florins.[31]

At the time of his capture, the wealthy bishop of Pozzuoli, Francesco III, was an ally of the Roman pope, Urban VI, and therefore eligible to be plundered

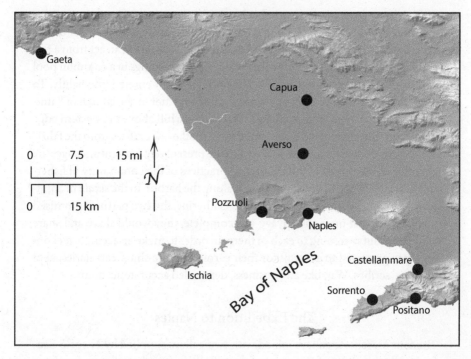

FIGURE 4. The Bay of Naples, ca. 1400. *Credit:* Scott Walker / Dan Smail.

and ransomed.[32] The *Cronicon Siculum* does not explain why the second galley, with its Genoese captain, was eligible for plunder, but it is safe to assume that the galley belonged to the sphere of influence of Urban VI or the house of Durazzo. One possible explanation was that the galley was bringing succor to Margaret of Durazzo in Gaeta when it was taken, for Margaret was known to be facing serious financial constraints.[33]

From other sources, we learn further details about the second of the two warships. According to firsthand witness testimony, the Angevin squadron had captured the galiot that evening off the coast of the island of Ischia. The galiot was captained by Corrado Doria. The distinguished Italian historian Enrico Basso, who has considered the identity of Corrado Doria, has suggested that he may have been the son of Pietro Doria, the admiral of the Genoese fleet who was killed by the collapse of a fortification at the Battle of Chioggia in 1380.[34] If so, Corrado was a scion of one of Genoa's most distinguished families. Why he was acting in the service of the house of Durazzo is not clear.

When the flotilla finally arrived in Naples, representatives of the Valois Angevins took the royal share of the spoils seized from both galleys, and the ship captains took theirs. It is worth pausing for a moment to consider the value of

THE EXPEDITION TO NAPLES   69

the gold coins and jewels taken from the galiot of Corrado Doria. First, given the fact that the royal or papal outlay for hiring warships came to no more than 2,000 florins per month, the half-share pertaining to the curia that came from the galiot alone, at 14,000 florins, easily allowed the curia to recoup its investment. The remaining 14,000, divided among the captains of the six warships, came to 2,333 florins each, so even a quarter-share in one of the galleys would have yielded a profit of over 500 florins. Any profits from the spoils of the bishop's galley, including the ransom of his person, would have added even more.

Second, the wording used by the anonymous author of the *Cronicon Siculum* suggests, indirectly, that the curia's share was derived from treasure alone. Other movables and furnishings, loosely described as "clothing, vestments, and equipment," were understood to belong to those who, by their industry, managed to seize them. The ability to profit in this way beyond any wages has long been known to be one of the inducements for enlisted men to engage in military or naval campaigns.

Let us return to the *Cronicon Siculum* to pick up the narrative. The next day, soldiers seized the tower of Mergellina, held by troops loyal to Margaret. Thirteen of Margaret's men were hanged. A celebration followed, including a procession in honor of the Avignonese pope Clement VII, a mass in the church of Sant'Aniello a Caponapoli, and, on the 15th of the month, the raising of the standards of both Clement and Louis II in the city of Naples. The Valois Angevins had achieved victory.

Late in December of 1387, the Massiliote galleys continued their journey to the south. As we learn elsewhere, however, Peire Huguet and his galley were not among them, Peire having defied the order given to him by the vice-regent to range southward with the flotilla, to the Amalfi coast.[35] According to a subsequent report, while on his way back to Marseille, he harried Genoese and Neapolitan craft, seizing ships and plunder amounting to more than 400 florins in value.[36] But the profiteering of the brothers Huguet had already begun weeks earlier, in secret. At the outset of the voyage, Johan Huguet had stationed himself on the *Sancta-Catherina*, the galley captained by Antoni de Lueys in which he had a quarter-share. When the flotilla seized the bishop's galley off the coast of Gaeta on the 10th of December, the men of Antoni's galley, Johan among them, set about to plunder the unfortunate bishop. This is what Johan supposedly did:

> When they were near Gaeta, they came across a galley from Pozzuoli in which there was a bishop. Johan Huguet, the brother of Peire, who was in the galley that Antoni was captaining, plundered a chest belonging to the bishop in which there were 40 ounces of *carlinos*, and many jewels worth 400 florins and more.

Since this was treasure, it was Johan's duty to bring the chest back to Antoni's ship so that the contents could be duly entered into the ship's cartulary by the scribe. But Johan did no such thing. Instead, he spirited the chest and its contents away to the galley captained by his brother, where Peire appropriated it for himself, bypassing his own scribe.

That evening, a similar thing happened following the capture of Corrado Doria's warship. While the galiot was being plundered,

> Johan Huguet, the brother of Peire, took a certain amount of the plunder, worth 200 florins, from the galiot and placed it in a doublet, and beyond that, he took a silver jug worth 18 florins . . . The said Johan transferred the 200 florins, the doublet in which they were hidden, and the silver jug to the galley of the said Peire Huguet, who was fully aware of what was going on. When they were back in Marseille, Johan passed over all these things and the money to Peire, counting it out on his dining table.[37]

Again, it was perfectly legitimate for men to pursue their own profit by stripping their victims of clothes and equipment. But for anything that could be counted as treasure, notably the 200 florins and the silver jug, the plunderer had a duty to report the find to the ship's captain and scribe. The dissimulation practiced by Johan—hiding the booty in an article of clothing, a legitimate target of private plundering—suggests that he was aware that his actions had crossed a line.

We have already had a chance to visit the lurid spectacle where the brothers Huguet were gloating over the loot displayed on Peire's dining table early in 1388. We shall return to this scene a final time because it matters how we know it. The descriptions of the sequence of events arising from the plundering of the two warships quoted above were provided by none other than Antoni de Lueys, in arguments he put forward in 1391 in a bitter lawsuit that set him against his former partner, Peire Huguet. It was bad enough for Johan and Peire to have defrauded the curia. But that was not Antoni's affair: the curia could decide for itself whether to pursue this violation. What mattered to Antoni was the violation of the oath that he and Peire had sworn before the altar of Sainte-Catherine in the church of Saint-Laurent to share any plunder earned from their own private despoliations. Peire's lust for plunder led him to betray one of his closest associates.

The End of Angevin Patronage

Late in the year 1387, Naples was set to welcome its new king. Yet nearly three years passed before Louis came down to Naples to claim his throne, in August of 1390. Throughout his ill-fated reign, Naples was never more than a beachhead

THE EXPEDITION TO NAPLES 71

in an unsettled land, caught between the ominous presence of the Aragonese in Sicily and the growing imperial threat of France.[38] For a time, Urban VI's animosity toward Charles of Durazzo and the young Ladislas of Naples denied them the support they needed. But Urban died in 1389, and the new pope, Boniface IX, restored papal support for Ladislas, crowning him king of Naples in 1390.

Early in the 1390s, as the Valois Angevins were desperately clinging to Naples, opportunities for royal service arose on several occasions, and Peire was among the investors and captains who benefited from Angevin patronage. In February of 1393, he and two other investors pooled their funds to construct a massive new galley, the *Sanctus-Johannes-Evangeliste*, and furnish it with two hundred oars.[39] A series of related acts from February of 1393 indicate that the Duke of Bourbon, on behalf of the royal courts of both France and Naples, was planning another campaign to the Kingdom of Naples, and that Peire was to join the mission.[40] Two years later, a notarial contract provides further clues about Peire's ongoing service to the crown. In this act, Peire acknowledged a debt of one hundred florins to Bertomieu Simondel, one of his most prominent financiers. This debt was on top of the existing debt of 166 florins and 8 gros that he had incurred in 1387. Bertomieu's willingness to sink even more capital into Peire's privateering business is an indication that some investors, as late as April of 1395, still considered him a good bet.

Yet Peire's inability to repay Bertomieu was a sign that things were going awry, as Peire repeatedly extended his existing debts in order to finance new missions. As a business model, this was not necessarily a problem, given the immense profits that could be made at sea. But after 1395, ominously, there are no signs that Peire participated in any further military ventures. The reason for this may be found in the fading prospects of his patrons. In 1390, when the just-crowned Louis II took the throne in Naples, the future must have seemed bright. By the middle of the decade, however, dark clouds were gathering. With the death of Clement VII in September of 1394, tensions arose between France and Avignon, leading to the withdrawal of French royal support for Louis II.[41] In 1399, the ascendant Ladislas, having made peace with his own fractious nobles in southern Italy, recovered Naples. Louis II continued to style himself as the king of Jerusalem and Sicily and spasmodically pursued his claims in the Kingdom of Sicily. But for figures like Peire Huguet, the days of easy profits were gone.

The loss of Angevin patronage from 1395 forward was a serious blow to Peire's fortunes. It undoubtedly informed the decision that Peire and his partners made in May of 1398 to sell their interest in the *Sanctus-Johannes-Evangeliste* to the commune of Nice for the immense sum of 2,025 florins.[42] Peire's share would have come to just over 500 florins. The only clue suggesting that Peire continued to harbor ambitions as a sea captain and privateer after this date can be found in an elliptical phrase from the records of the deliberations of Marseille's city council in August of 1401. The passage records how the council sent a complaint on Peire's behalf to an official in Toulon, alleging that his claims had been dismissed and that Peire himself had been threatened.[43] As this suggests, he was still engaged in some kind of maritime activity, though the episode was probably commercial rather than military in nature. By 1395, Peire's days as a privateer were over.

5

Magdalena Comes to Marseille

ALL WARS GENERATE REFUGEES, and this one was no exception. Among those set adrift by the expedition to Naples in 1387 was the young woman we know as Magdalena Coline, who happened to be taking passage on Corrado Doria's galiot through the Bay of Naples when it was seized by the Angevin flotilla. Before her first direct appearance in the record in 1399, everything that we know or surmise about Magdalena is based on the faintest and most fragmentary allusions. Let us pull on the threads of evidence that connect us to Magdalena's past and see what we can make of them.

Off the Roads of Naples

In February of 1408, a ship's scribe by the name of Aycart Vedel, sworn in as a witness in the second trial launched by Peire Huguet against Magdalena Coline, sat down before a notary of the Palace court of Marseille to give his testimony. The notary asked him to provide testimony on a set of claims that formed the heart of Peire's case. The scene comes easily to the imagination: a middle-aged scribe, perhaps a little nervous, swept up into a trial that was something of a cause célèbre in the city, asked to testify about events that had taken place many years ago. The notary read out each of the claims in the local vernacular and jotted down Aycart's responses in the form of rough notes on paper. Later, he edited the transcript for the judge's consideration, converting Aycart's remarks into the third-person singular, reducing the mass into crisp and efficient summaries, and translating the entirety into Latin.

To begin, the notary asked the scribe to say all that he knew about the moment when Magdalena had been given to Peire as a slave. This is how Aycart's response was rendered in the resulting deposition:

> Interrogated and diligently examined on the first of the articles of proof, he swore on his oath that around twenty years ago, he was serving as an assistant ship's scribe on a war galley captained by the late Antoni de Lueys.

73

The galley was making its way toward the Kingdom of Naples in a flotilla under the command of the count of Cerreto, along with several other war galleys, in order to make war on the king's enemies. The flotilla came across a certain war galley commanded by the Genoese captain, Corrado Doria, who was making war on the king's allies, and captured the galley. On it, they discovered the aforesaid Magdalena, along with a male slave (*reperta fuit predicta Magdalena cum quodam sclavo*).

Later, the witness heard from the people in those galleys that the count of Cerreto, together with Jacme Martin, Antoni de Lueys, and Bertomieu Aymeric, the captains of the galleys, determined that Magdalena should be given as a slave to Peire Huguet as part of his share of the spoils, and that the male slave, likewise, should be given to Antoni de Lueys as part of his share. Afterward, the witness repeatedly saw Magdalena in Peire Huguet's galley, where he held her as a slave. And Peire took her home with him when he returned to Marseille in his galley.[1]

The episode narrated here is also described, with slight variations, by four other witnesses. One of them, the shipwright Guilhem Limosin, who had given his testimony a few days earlier, noted that he had received an injury during the battle itself.[2] Weak and feverish, he did not attend to much of what was going on, but did recall having heard that Magdalena had been given as a slave to Peire. A third witness said that the events had taken place not twenty years previously but eighteen; otherwise, his testimony corroborated the sequence of events.

If Peire was an artist, sketching events that unfolded in December of 1387, witnesses such as Aycart Vedel and Guilhem Limosin served as the pencils with which he drew the lines and filled in the shading. The scene off the roads of Naples comes vividly to mind: the six galleys descending on the galiot of Corrado Doria; the sharp struggle, resulting in the injuries to Guilhem Limosin; the perquisitions through the bowels of the ship, seizing gold, silver, and other items of plunder. But some of the most interesting features of the resulting sketch reside not in what Aycart and Guilhem and the others said, but instead in what they left out. It is from the things not said, in other words, that we catch faint glimpses of who Magdalena was and where she may have come from.

In the later Middle Ages, when captives were taken in war, the law of the church, known as canon law, permitted the enslavement of any infidels, that is to say Muslims and other non-Christians. At a stretch, it was permissible to enslave Orthodox Christians as well, although the practice was legally problematic and caused some nervousness.[3] What was prohibited was the enslavement of Roman Christians, with the curious exception of Sardinians, whose resistance to Aragonese control made them eligible for the slave market, and the young children from the lands of the Adriatic, known as *anime*, who were seized and sold in Venice in a condition that approximated enslavement.[4] In both Italy and Iberia, prospective purchasers were attentive to the origins of slaves since any sale could be voided should a slave be able, at a later date, to demonstrate that she had been illegally enslaved.[5] Yet the picture sketched out by Peire's witnesses treats it as wholly unremarkable that Magdalena was seized as booty and handed over as a slave. The question is why.

The record is almost completely silent on this matter. The reason for this lies in the simple fact that all forms of human communication rely on oceans of implicit information. Testimony in lawsuits, to consider the relevant domain here, typically skips over everything that was understood to be ordinary, expected, and obvious. It focuses instead on that which is variable or unique. If those present off the roads of Naples on that December day, ranging from august commanders to sailors, shipwrights, and ships' scribes, could take it for granted that Magdalena was enslaveable, it is almost certainly because when they first came across her, Magdalena looked, acted, and spoke in some way that observers instantly recognized as "not one of us."

An arresting feature of the testimony in the second trial lies in something else that the five witnesses did not say. In his own testimony, the ship's scribe, Aycart Vedel, casually mentioned the presence of a male slave. It stands to reason that an accountant would carefully recall such a detail. But neither he nor the other four witnesses explicitly declared that Magdalena was already enslaved at the time she was seized. Since it should not have been possible to enslave a woman of the Roman faith, this silence raises the tantalizing possibility that a free Muslim woman taking passage on Corrado's galiot was seized in a just war and lawfully reduced to slavery. Muslim men did travel on Christian ships from time to time, and any of them may have brought wives, daughters, or servants.

But as it happens, a clue found in the records of the first trial points to the likeliest scenario, namely, that she had already been enslaved. The testimony here concerning Magdalena is curiously thin and insubstantial, consisting of just a few lines from two witnesses, including Guilhem Limosin, who also testified in the second trial. In the first deposition, however, Guilhem provided a crucial line of hearsay evidence that is missing from his second deposition.

Since the context is important, let us peek ahead once again to matters that will be considered more closely in chapter 10. In April of 1407, as the first trial was heating up, Peire named nine witnesses to attest to his claims regarding Magdalena's slave status. In his overweening pride and confidence, however, he made no effort to coach them beforehand. Starting on the 6th of April, a small stream of witnesses began to appear before the notary of the court to give testimony. A few days into the depositions, however, things were going terribly wrong, for the witnesses were not responding satisfactorily. Putting their heads together, Peire and his lawyer hastily assembled a set of additional claims, the first of which ran as follows:

> Magdalena was given as a slave to Peire by the count of Cerreto and the nobleman Jacme Martin and other great men who were at the time on the voyage with the count of Cerreto going toward the region of Naples. [It was] in the galley of Corrado Doria, an enemy of the crown, in which she was captured.[6]

In his response to the initial set of claims, the shipwright Guilhem Limosin had denied any knowledge of Magdalena's slave status. Pressured to tell the truth by this more precisely formulated query, he told the court what he knew:

> Next, on the first of the additional claims, he said that what is contained in it is true. Asked how he knows, he said that he had been serving in the galley whose captain was Antoni de Lueys; the witness owned a share in the galley and was present when Magdalena was taken in the galley of Corrado Doria. Jacme Martin and Antoni de Lueys and the other captains, whose names he does not remember, apart from that of Bertomieu Aymeric, the captain of the other galley, gave the said slave to Peire as the portion and share coming to the said Peire. All the people on Corrado Doria's galley were saying to the witness that she was the slave of their own lord, a certain lord who was related to Corrado Doria and was, as was said, the admiral of Sicily, and Magdalena's master.[7]

This testimony contradicts a line in the deposition Guilhem provided in the second case, ten months later. In the second deposition, his lack of certainty about Magdalena's status was explained by the notary in this way: "Although Guilhem was present at the taking of the vessel, he was badly wounded and for a long time was oppressed by his wounds and the fevers that followed. For this reason, he could not know for sure whether the lord count of Cerreto and the other captains gave Magdalena to Peire."[8]

Though there are any number of explanations for the discrepancy, one possibility is the following. When the question was sprung on Guilhem the first time around, he was under pressure to tell the truth and later felt guilty about throwing Magdalena under the bus. The ensuing interval provided plenty of time for him to reconsider the events that had taken place twenty years ago. In February of 1408, he told enough of the truth to avoid any recriminations by Peire, but dropped in a clue that would allow the judge to discount his testimony if he was so inclined.

Let us assume that the first deposition was truthful. If so, then Magdalena had already been enslaved when she was taken with the rest of the spoils of war from Corrado Doria's galiot on the 10th of December of 1387. She was enslaved, moreover, to someone described as the admiral of Sicily, whose men, serving under Corrado Doria, were transporting treasure across the Bay of Naples.

Amazigh Origins?

As we have seen, things were going badly for Peire and his lawyer in April of 1407, as witnesses called in the first trial were proving reluctant to attest to Peire's claims regarding Magdalena's slave status. It must have been with a sigh of relief that they heard Guilhem Limosin, attesting to the first of the additional titles, blurt out the truth about Magdalena's status, since that provided the two witnesses required by Roman law to prove a claim made in court. We shall have an occasion later on to consider the rest of this fascinating set of claims.

For now, however, let us consider the second of the additional titles formulated by Peire and his lawyer in April of 1407, for the claim provides a vital clue as to Magdalena's possible origins:

> Next, [Peire] intends to prove that the said Magdalena and other Saracen women who are taken from the region of Barbary have a great difference with Christians inasmuch as they have certain marks, made with fire, on the arms. And he held her as a slave for a period of ten years and more, in the manner in which other lords owning slaves are accustomed to holding and possessing them. Word has spread throughout the city of Marseille that Magdalena was and is the slave of Peire Huguet, and that she carried herself as the slave of the said Peire.[9]

In a dispute whose transcripts extend over more than three hundred pages, this is the only trace of evidence we have about Magdalena's place of origin.

The historian Elizabeth Casteen, who has considered the statement noted above about the women having marks on their arms, is undecided as to whether the mark referred to was a brand or a tattoo, though she suspects the former.[10] But the logic of the phrase clearly points to the latter—that is, if by "brand" we mean a mark deliberately applied to an unwilling recipient. Peire Huguet himself understood that the marks were characteristic of "Saracen women who are taken from the region of Barbary." That's what made them different from Christians. Elsewhere, there is little evidence suggesting that slaves in Christian Europe were routinely branded.[11] William Phillips, following the work of Aurelia Martín Casares, indicates that most of the references to slaves bearing *hierros* or "marks of iron" in sources from early modern Spain refer to tattoos characteristic of some peoples from North and West Africa. Those who were actually branded were typically unsuccessful fugitives. Any brands, moreover, were typically applied on visible places such as the face rather than the arms.[12]

It is highly likely, then, that the mark to which Peire was referring was a tattoo customarily applied to girls or women in Magdalena's homeland. If we accept this claim, the comment suggests that Peire himself engaged in slave-raiding among the Amazigh peoples of North Africa and was familiar with the appearance of the women enslaved as an outcome of those raids. For him, it was a matter of common knowledge: Muslim women have tattoos on their arms. The tattoos once widely practiced in Amazigh culture are not in fact produced by fire, as Peire seems to have thought, but instead by a method that today involves the use of a needle, kohl powder, and wood ash.[13] But an inexperienced observer might have easily mistaken them for burn scars.

As a legal matter, the claim was a nonstarter: it fizzled out within days and never appeared again in any of Peire's arguments. Only three witnesses, all of whom were men, provided testimony on the new set of claims. All three men denied having any knowledge about the appearance of Magdalena's arms. This is not surprising, for although anyone could have learned about the tattoos via hearsay, most men not living in the house probably would not have had an occasion to observe a woman with unclothed arms.[14]

Nothing in the record provides any direct evidence that Magdalena was from North Africa, and we should briefly consider the possibility that Magdalena, like the vast majority of enslaved women in Marseille around 1400, was originally from the greater Black Sea region. But if this were so, it is nearly inconceivable that Peire would not have known it, and it is difficult to imagine what he could have gained by lying. Given what we know or can cautiously assume about the Amazigh custom of tattooing, his comment to the effect that Muslim women seized in slave raids in Barbary typically have "marks, made with fire, on the arms" indirectly corroborates his claim regarding Magdalena's Amazigh origins. It is wildly improbable that he would have added such an observation had he not known about the practice and, for that matter, had not seen the marks on her arms.

Tugging the thread constituted by this exceedingly faint clue, we can begin to pull back the veil that obscures Magdalena's life history before she was seized off the roads of Naples in 1387. Let us begin with her age. Slavers at this time tended to target children or teenagers, on the theory that individuals brought into slavery at a younger age adjusted more easily to their condition.[15] Sale contracts and administrative records of various types sometimes record the age of the enslaved, but these documents are unreliable sources for determining the typical age at the point of seizure, which could have taken place months or years earlier. Especially valuable, therefore, is the median age of 14 that Hannah Barker has calculated for a sample of 221 slave sales in Tana between

1359 and 1363, because the purchases were made when notaries arrived in Tana with the first wave of Venetian merchants.[16] The orders for slaves found in the Datini registers, as Corinna Peres has shown, indicate that the desired age range fell between 8 and 16 years, with individuals in their early teens considered optimal.[17]

According to Guilhem Limosin, Magdalena had already been enslaved at the time she was seized in December of 1387. If she were around 15 years of age at the time, which is little more than a random guess, she could have been born as early as 1372. This would fit with the fact that she got married in 1399, at the putative age of 27, for such an event would have been less likely had she been significantly older. Is it possible that she was younger than this? The reference to the marks on her arms provides a tantalizing clue—that is, if we accept the hypothesis above that Peire's words point to Amazigh tattoos. As Cynthia Becker has suggested, tattoos among modern Amazigh women are associated with the onset of puberty.[18] If the custom was also associated with puberty in the fourteenth century, then Magdalena could not have been born later than the year 1375 or so.

To what kind of family was she born? Once again, we need to peer ahead, to clues that appear in the trial transcripts from 1406 to 1408, in order to see back into Magdalena's past. In August of 1408, in a desperate bid to salvage her case in the face of a spectacular setback, Magdalena, aided by her faithful lawyer, Bertran Gombert, drafted a petition and submitted it to King Louis II in his court in Aix-en-Provence. In one of many phrases that leap out of this document, a single line describes Magdalena as a woman "born of free parents."[19] It is possible that this sort of phrase normally appears in such petitions and therefore it may have been recommended by the astute Bertran. But it is also possible that the phrase found its way into the record because Magdalena herself had said it, and that she said it because she had been born into a respectable family.

Her Amazigh origin, if we choose to accept the reasoning above, is somewhat unusual, given the fact that the trade in the region in the later fourteenth century was dominated by enslaved Tatar women who had been abducted in the region of the Black Sea. North African Muslims accounted for less than 3 percent of the traffic flowing through contemporary Palermo, for example.[20] But we do know that by the 1380s, in conjunction with the slow emergence of a system of hostage-taking leading to redemption, reciprocal slave-raiding was taking place on both shores of the Western Mediterranean basin.[21] The reference made by Peire to "Saracens who are taken from the region of Barbary," as we have seen, indicates that he was aware of slave-raiding activity on the North African coast. Perhaps he had done some corsairing himself in the early 1380s.

Though we do not know what these raids were like on the African side, records preserved in Marseille's archives offer details on the reverse raids undertaken by Muslim corsairs and the ransoms that were subsequently arranged. Let us consider just one of dozens of examples from Magdalena's day. In 1407, the ecclesiastical court of Marseille initiated an inquest into the actions of a cleric in minor orders named Raymon Felip. The cleric was accused of aiding and abetting Muslim slave raiders or ransomers. Some time earlier, Raymon had been captaining a ship sailing the seas east of Marseille. Off the Ligurian coast, near the town of San Lorenzo, he spotted a flotilla of Muslim corsairs bearing down on him. Realizing that he and his crew had no chance of escape, he instead negotiated with the corsairs, offering to help them seize Christian captives from San Lorenzo. Although the details of how he accomplished this are not provided, the accusation makes it clear that several dozen men, women, and children were then seized from San Lorenzo, with Raymon's assistance, and conveyed into the power of the corsairs.[22]

Given the ubiquity of cross-Mediterranean slave-raiding, it is plausible to assume that Magdalena had originally been taken captive by Christian raiders. This brings us to the admiral of Sicily, identified by the shipwright, Guilhem Limosin, as Magdalena's first enslaver. Guilhem had been present at the taking of Corrado Doria's galley and was wounded in the attack. Nonetheless, as revealed in his deposition in the first trial, he had time to converse with the men on Corrado's vessel, who told him that Magdalena was the slave of their own lord, the *admirallus* of Sicily, whom they described as a relative of Corrado Doria. Who was this individual?

Earlier in the century, two members of the Doria family, ancestors of Corrado, had sported the title "admiral of the Kingdom of Sicily."[23] In the *Cronicon Siculum*, the count of Cerreto was also described in one location as "the admiral of Sicily," though possibly in error.[24] As Enrico Basso has suggested, however, perhaps the most intriguing candidate is Manfredi Chiaramonte (d. 1391), the count of Modica, described in the annals of Genoa in 1388 as "admiral or *armiragius* of the Kingdom of Sicily."[25] Nowhere in the extensive genealogies of the Doria family is there any indication that Manfredi and Corrado were related, as reported by the men on Corrado's galiot.[26] What strongly favors the identification, however, is the indisputable fact that Manfredi bore the title "admiral of Sicily" in the late 1380s.[27]

A good deal is known about Manfredi, who was one of the most powerful lords of Sicily in the second half of the fourteenth century. There is no indication in his biography that he had ever been seized and ransomed by the Valois Angevins. It is not difficult, however, to imagine a scenario explaining why Magdalena was in transit on Corrado's galiot in 1387 in Manfredi's absence. By 1387, it is likely that Margaret of Durazzo, who was desperate for support, was already in an alliance with Manfredi Chiaramonte. We know that her efforts at wooing him bore fruit in August of 1390, with the marriage of her son,

MAGDALENA COMES TO MARSEILLE 81

Ladislas of Naples, to Manfredi's daughter, Costanza, who brought with her an enormous dowry. On this theory, the galiot captained by Corrado Doria, with its treasure, was a diplomatic gift sent by Manfredi to Margaret. Such a gift would fit the logic of a political theology according to which royal authority was buttressed by the display of sovereignty over infidels.[28] In this scenario, Magdalena and the unnamed male slave had been included with the rest of the gifts. Intriguingly, Manfredi is known to have had interests in North Africa, for he led an attack in 1388 on the island of Djerba, off the coast of modern-day Tunisia, in response to daring raids undertaken by a fleet of Muslim galleys that had been harrying Christian lands over the last year or two and seizing many captives.[29] It is distinctly possible that Magdalena had been seized in one of the skirmishes leading up to this assault. If so, it seems very likely that she had only recently come into Manfredi's control when she was taken by Peire Huguet in 1387.

It is worth commenting on the social standing of Magdalena's first master. The leading candidate, Manfredi Chiaramonte, was an aristocrat of the highest order, a major landowner on the island of Sicily and future father-in-law of Ladislas of Naples. But even if the "admiral of Sicily" who appears in the testimony of Guilhem Limosin was not Manfredi but instead a member of the Doria family, he would nonetheless have been someone of very high standing, an intimate of the Aragonese court, able to pick and choose among the enslaved women he acquired for his entourage. This, in turn, may say something about Magdalena herself: about her birth, her bearing, perhaps her beauty.

Of all the fragments of evidence relevant to Magdalena Coline's early biography, one of the most curious, and the last we shall consider here, concerns her surname. As we have seen, notaries almost invariably mentioned the surnames of their male clients, at least at the first reference. But with women it was different. No-name and inconsequential women, like Bertomieua, the wife of Peire Huguet, were rarely afforded surnames—or rather, we know that they were no-name and inconsequential because they weren't afforded surnames. With both age and widowhood came a growing respect, in the form of more regular use of surnames, especially for women of distinction who were granted the title Na or Domina. It comes as little surprise to learn, therefore, that enslaved women were invariably known only by their given names, either their names from birth or, far more commonly, the names conferred on them at the moment of baptism. In this regard, Magdalena Coline is unique. She was regularly identified with the surname "Coline" during the first and second trials. Even more strikingly, she bore the surname "Coline" at the time of her marriage in 1399, even as she was pivoting from enslaved to free status. It was a name, in other words, that had already been attached to her while enslaved.

Where did the name come from? It was not Peire's surname. If Magdalena had been the widow of someone named Colin in 1399, it is almost certain that the dowry act would have mentioned this, or that the name would have surfaced during the trial. It was the maiden name of Alaseta Huguete, the wife of Johan Huguet, and it is conceivable that Magdalena borrowed the name from her, though hard to imagine why. What seems more likely is that the name is a phonetic echo of her former name in the Amazigh tongue, either a family or tribal name or a given name, which was subsequently rendered as "Coline" by notaries as they tried to make sense of what Magdalena was saying to them.[30]

With these fragments, let us sketch out a conjectural portrait of Magdalena before she was Magdalena, bearing in mind the tenuous nature of the evidence. Around the year 1372, in a city or town somewhere in North Africa, a girl was born to free Amazigh parents and was given a name phonetically similar to *Colina*. At the onset of puberty around 1385, the elder women of her community marked her arms with the tattoos characteristic of her people. For those who lived along the coast of Mediterranean Africa, this was a dangerous time, unsettled by the squabbling of royal dynasties across the sea and near-constant acts of slave-raiding and hostage-taking by Christian corsairs. In the troubled years of 1386 and 1387, as slave-raiding was heating up in the Western Mediterranean basin, the young woman was abducted and enslaved by corsairs in the service of Aragonese interests, who fed her into a circuit of exchange that brought her into the entourage of the admiral of Sicily, probably Manfredi Chiaramonte. In December of 1387, currents that arose from diplomatic gifts or war finance brought the fifteen-year-old Magdalena onto a small galiot working its way across the Bay of Naples toward Gaeta. There, owing to the inscrutable operations of fate, she fell into the hands of Angevin privateers and was dragged off to Marseille as the slave of Peire Huguet.

In the House of Peire and Bertomieua

Once Peire Huguet abandoned the expedition to Naples shortly after the seizure of the galiot of Corrado Doria, he spent some days privateering in the Bay of Naples and points north before returning to Marseille. Assuming the winds were favorable, *La Stella* and its crew probably returned to harbor in January of 1388, bringing Magdalena Coline back with the rest of the loot.

It is difficult to imagine the nature of the welcome she would have received from the members of the Huguet household. One of the claims made by Iris Origo in her 1955 study of female domestic slavery in Renaissance Florence is that Florentine wives were hostile toward the female slaves brought home by their husbands, since they knew how common it was for those husbands to turn the women into concubines.[31] By 1388, the women of Marseille had come to know slavery as more than a theoretical possibility, since enslaved Tatar women had been arriving for several decades. By the late 1380s, the spate was

MAGDALENA COMES TO MARSEILLE   83

easing, leaving a number of enslaved women scattered across the city in the houses of merchants, lawyers, notaries, and people oriented to the sea. But even though the sight of an enslaved person had become somewhat familiar to the local population, it is hard not to assume that Magdalena's arrival came as a bit of a surprise to Bertomieua. Peire had not set out to acquire a slave. No one participating in the assault on Naples could have anticipated coming across an enslaved woman on one of the enemy's warships. Still less could Peire have expected that any slave would have been allotted to him as a spoil of war.

But even if we know nothing about the scene where introductions were first made, we know where it took place. Thanks to a record of ground rents paid to the royal chancery in 1411, we can locate Peire and Bertomieua's house with some precision. At the time of their rise to power in the twelfth and thirteenth centuries, the counts of Provence had acquired the lordship of several hundred houses throughout the city, including most of the houses located along the harbor. Property owners paid an annual *census* or "rent" to their lords. Every year, accordingly, officers of the treasury went door-to-door, collecting the rents owed from householders. Records of these payments were subsequently listed in the treasurers' accounts, and several of these registers have survived the passing of the years.

For reasons lost in the obscurity of time, the royal treasurers in Marseille customarily organized rent payments by *insula*, or city block. On page after page of the account books, one finds a rubric naming the insulae, followed by a neat column listing the names of the householders on the block and the amount of rent paid by each. Some of the names given to the blocks derived from durable features of the landscape, such as churches or markets. In other cases, the insulae were named after their most prominent residents, and these names were prone to change. Some of the names given to insulae could survive a generation or two after the death of the eponymous individual. Others changed more rapidly.

One of the account books has survived from the years during which Peire Huguet was active. In this register, from the year 1411, we catch a glimpse of an insula in the midst of being renamed. Along the harbor, just west of the plaza of the Shipyards, an insula had long been named for Antoni Martin, a prominent figure from an earlier generation. In 1411, the name still clung, but the names of two new people were now beginning to crowd their way into the title. The entry in 1411 accordingly reads "The insula of Antoni Martin, Bertran de Brachio, and Jacme Limosin, the carpenter."[32] The very first name on the list of householders was Peire Huguet. Since the notaries who worked for the royal treasury tended to proceed from east to west, it is very likely that Peire's house was located on the eastern end of the block, abutting the plaza of the Shipyards (figure 5).

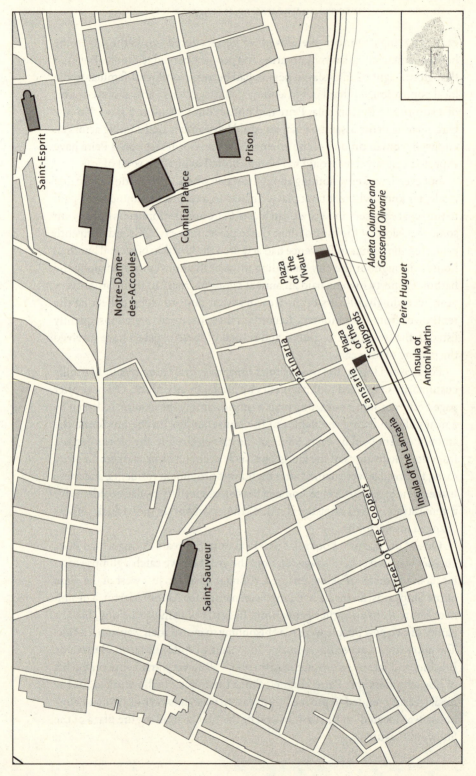

FIGURE 5. The neighborhood of the Lansaria. *Credit:* Marc Bouiron/Scott Walker/Dan Smail.

Notarial sources provide further details about Peire and Bertomieu's house. In November of 1387, as the clouds of war were gathering, a notary came to the house to draw up a legal contract. In the location clause at the end, the notary placed the house on the Lansaria. Since the houses on the insulae in this area of the city were only one deep, this description indicates that the principal entryway was located on the Lansaria, with the back of the house abutting the strand. The act was drafted in a space described as a shop, perhaps a workspace filled with the tools of the trade and the shavings left by the operations of the adze.

Marseille's archives have not yielded an inventory of the contents of Peire's house, so we have to turn elsewhere to glean insights into the kind of domestic space where Magdalena lived for fifteen years. Although the maritime-oriented neighborhoods of Marseille's western quarter are poor in surviving inventories, we do have inventories from the estates of two fishermen who lived in the vicinity. The first of these describes the estate of a well-to-do fisherman, Andrea de Garda, who died on the 7th of June 1394. In his last will and testament, Andrea named as his universal heirs the members of his family who survived him—his wife, Hugueta, their two children, and his stepson—but he failed to make provisions for the children's guardian. In early July, therefore, his widow appeared in court to have herself named as guardian. The inventory that resulted from the proceedings reveals that Andrea's house was situated in the far western corner of the port, near the church of Saint-Jean, close to the site where the imposing Fort Saint-Jean now stands. The ground floor of the building was occupied by the shop of the fisherman, Johan Engles. Andrea lived with his family in the four-room house located on the two floors above the shop. Their living space comprised a kitchen, a hall, and two bedrooms.

The other inventory, listing the contents of the estate of the fisherman Johan Martin, was compiled in dramatically different circumstances. Though the story departs from the main thread, it is worth going into detail for the color it brings to the portrait of the neighborhood that Magdalena had joined three years earlier.

Toward nightfall on Sunday, the 16th of April 1391, Johan Martin was having words with a merchant named Antoni Gracian, a neighbor and close associate of Peire Huguet, down by the water's edge.[33] At issue was the lease of a fishing vessel, which the fisherman had rented from the merchant some time earlier but was now returning to its owner. As the dispute grew heated, a small crowd formed. Angered by something Johan said, Antoni made a gesture toward his knife, which many men at the time carried in sheaths on their belts. The peaceably minded Johan drew back his cloak and said to the bystanders words similar to this: "This man is trying to kill me, but take note, all of you, that I carry no knife." He then stepped back three paces.

At that moment, along came Johan's son-in-law, none other than the shipwright Jacme Limosin. Jacme had had many interactions with Peire Huguet over the years and was one of the four galley captains involved in the expedition to Naples. Presumably, Jacme had also been enriched by the spoils of war. In the 1390s, he was emerging as one of the most notable residents of the Lansaria. Two decades later, in 1411, his name became part of the city's mental topography. We don't quite know how personal names were attached to insulae, but we can assume they were given in recognition of some role the individual played as a community leader or *capo di famiglia*.

Outraged by the threat to his father-in-law, Jacme grabbed Antoni by his clothing and spoke some threatening words. In his fright, the merchant drew his knife and stabbed Jacme in the arm, and then, stepping back, fell off the low quay into the waters of the harbor. Enraged, Jacme, his own knife drawn, leapt into the water and stabbed the stricken man, piercing Antoni's right side with what the record describes as a "terrible blow" that penetrated to his vitals. Antoni died instantly.

Horrified onlookers drew the body from the water, the knife still in the wound. Poignant testimony describes how the tearful nephew of the dead man clung to his uncle's body. Neighbors, Peire Huguet among them, carried the corpse across the strand to Antoni's house, located on the insula of Antoni Martini a few doors down from where Peire lived, and laid it out on a bed. There, five surgeons, including the barber-surgeon Nicolau de Sala and two Jewish surgeons, Ferrar Marvan and Mosse Salves, came to inspect the body, probing the wound and turning the corpse over to make sure there were no additional wounds behind. The notary Guilhem Baiul arrived, and several neighbors, including Peire Huguet, were asked to identify the dead man.

In the meantime, Jacme fled with his father-in-law to sanctuary in the cathedral church of La Major. Jacme was subsequently prosecuted for the murder and interrogated by the notary. When asked whether he hated Antoni, he responded, "Not at all, I held him more as a friend than an enemy."[34] His sudden anger had risen when Antoni had insulted him, using the unforgivable epithet *ribaut*.[35]

Although Johan Martin struck no blow, the criminal court charged him with being an accomplice in the murder and issued several citations to him to appear in court. All were met with silence. We soon learn the reason why. Gravely ill with fever, Johan had remained in sanctuary for five or six weeks, attended by a priest named Guilhem Valencia. In his testimony, the priest described how he had nursed the sick man with sugar and water. In the meantime, the court moved against Johan's assets in order to hold them as collateral, and following normal procedure, the treasurer drew up an inventory of the estate. At the end of the inquest, Johan was assessed a heavy fine of 200 l. for

MAGDALENA COMES TO MARSEILLE   87

contumacy and sentenced to banishment. On the 6th of July, having recovered his health, Johan lodged an appeal.

As we learn from the inventory, Johan's house was located on the street of the Coopers, which ran parallel to the Lansaria to the north and west. The layout was nearly identical to Andrea's—a hall, kitchen, two bedrooms, and a storeroom. Given the circumstances, the inventory is more rudimentary than most. Part way into the kitchen, after listing a basin and a cauldron, the notary decided not to bother with further details and simply wrote "and other kitchen furnishings." No clothing was found, nor any portable valuables. This suggests that members of the family, mindful of the impending arrival of the sergeants of the court, had quietly spirited things out of the house before the inventory was made.

With these two inventories in hand, we can derive a composite portrait of the domestic space that may have met Magdalena's eye when she was brought to the city in January of 1388. In those years, a stone house owned by someone of middling status in Marseille's maritime neighborhoods typically consisted of five rooms distributed across two floors. The main living space was the hall, furnished with a dining table on trestles and seating in the form of benches and chairs. Weapons and armor of various descriptions were kept in the hall. Andrea's house tilted toward the martial end of the spectrum: in addition to owning seven shields, three crossbows, and four swords, he had two fencing swords. Other miscellaneous items were stashed in the hall, ranging from chests and coffers full of clothing and jewelry, as attested in Andrea's inventory, to barrels of salted fish. A touching entry in the inventory of Andrea's hall identifies a crib located next to the dining table.

A fully furnished bed was found in each of the two bedrooms in Andrea's house. In Johan's, by contrast, a single room supposedly held three beds, although one can reasonably suspect that the sloppy notary who was responsible for compiling the inventory placed the bed identified as "furnished for the servants" in the main bedroom rather than where it really belonged, in the bedroom next door. The servants' room, if that is what it was, also included a number of miscellaneous items, among them twelve empty barrels used for storing salted fish. Both estates included several fishing nets, but whereas Andrea had three fishing boats, Johan only had one. Although both men owned a vineyard, only Johan's house included any wine-making equipment. Finally, both estates included a second house, which may have been used for rental equipment or storage. In times of plague, people die, but houses and things do not. Over the four decades stretching between 1348 and 1390, the population of Marseille had been reduced by half, and as real estate and household goods made their way down the braided channels of inheritance, they piled up in the estates of the survivors.

The material profile of Peire and Bertomieua's house was probably very similar to the profile we can derive from these two inventories, bearing in mind that Peire was not a fisherman. Among other things, there is no indication that Peire had used any proceeds from his share of the spoils of war to buy the house next to his and combine the two into one. When fortune smiled, people did not respond by enlarging their houses, in part because they knew that fortune was a fickle creature. Instead, to judge by Andrea's inventory, they bought fancy clothes and accessories and stuffed them into exotic chests and coffers. Alternatively, they invested in more fishing boats or plots of land or hired additional housemaids and servants to help out with all the work that needed doing.

To someone who may have spent time in the palace of the admiral of Sicily, a five-room house on the Lansaria might have seemed rather small and cramped. The Huguet family consisted of Peire and Bertomieua, their teenage son Lazaret, and probably Peire's mother, Gassenda. It is not unlikely that there was another servant or one or more journeymen shipwrights, since references to live-in servants in the Huguet household appear in later documents. The bed in Johan Martin's house that was "furnished for servants" suggests that all the servants shared a single bed. Servants' rooms, however, are rarely identified as such in household inventories from Marseille, and when they do appear, we are typically reading the inventory of an exceedingly well-to-do house. Here and there, we find a kitchen furnished with a bed frame or a sleeping pad. It is conceivable that Magdalena bedded down there or perhaps somewhere else in the nooks and crannies of the house.

Magdalena had probably been baptized by the time she arrived in Peire's house. Though she was at least nominally Christian, it is impossible to know where she would have placed herself on the indeterminate spectrum of belief and practice that stretched between the poles of "Muslim" and "Christian." But if her original seizure had taken place around 1386, as proposed above, then it seems unlikely that she would have been habituated to a Christian landscape by the time of her arrival in Marseille. Differences in sonic environment strike everyone who travels to the lands of other faiths, whether it is the sound of the muezzin in Muslim lands or the ringing of church bells in Christian ones. Peire's house lay four streets to the south and a little east of the nunnery of Saint-Sauveur. Slightly further away stood the churches of Saint-Laurent and Notre-Dame-des-Accoules with their own bells. No doubt the neighborhood of the Lansaria was suffused with some of the many sounds and signs that are routine in Christian devotional practice, including prayers, Sunday services, and alternating feasts and fasts.

Along with this, articles of Christian devotion may have been present in the house. Here, there is less need for guesswork, because devotional items, as objects, were listed in household inventories when present. To judge by the inventories, a great divide separated the practices of elites and ordinary folks in late medieval Marseille. In the houses of ordinary folk, it is not uncommon to find paternosters or rosary beads, typically made of amber, coral, or silver. But there was little beyond that. The more prestigious devotional objects, such as crucifixes, retables, and paintings of the Virgin Mary, were found almost exclusively in the houses of the very rich.[36]

And what of the devotional practices of the maritime community of ship-wrights, fishermen, and mariners in Marseille's western neighborhoods? Today, the churches that once serviced the needs of those who went to sea sometimes preserve votive plaques commissioned by the grateful survivors of storms and shipwrecks. Such plaques fill the inner walls of the basilica of Notre-Dame-de-la-Garde, perched on the summit of the hill south of Marseille's harbor. Similar plaques may have once been mounted in shrines located in the churches of Saint-Jean and Saint-Laurent, but if so, they are now long gone.

As noted earlier, we have surprisingly few inventories from Marseille's western neighborhoods; at present, only the inventories of Andrea de Garda and Johan Martin offer insights into the material world of the city's maritime community. As it happens, Johan's inventory lacks any mention whatsoever of devotional objects, although the circumstance of its production makes us doubtful of its reliability as a source for material culture. Thanks to the attentive work of the widow Hugueta de Garda, the inventory of Andrea's estate is much more detailed. Like those of many reasonably well-to-do people in his status group, his inventory includes a set of paternoster beads, in this case made of amber. The beads were found in a great painted chest of Neapolitan design located in the hall of Andrea's house. In drawing up the list of the contents of the chest, Hugueta started with the clothing and accessories, beginning with her late husband's cloak and his marvelous purple houppelande, furnished with a hood and lined with rabbit or squirrel fur, and ending with a lady's hood, made of a purple fabric, and another lady's hood in a ruby-red cloth. Following that, she turned to all the fancy dress accessories belonging both to her and her late husband, including two gold rings studded with pearls, a silver crown, and two silver belts. The beads were found here, amidst all the bling.

To judge by this evidence, any Muslim, current or former, who entered the house of Peire and Bertomieua would not have had much occasion to encounter Christendom in a material form. It is doubtful that the newly arrived Magdalena would have found herself confronting crucifixes on the wall or panel paintings standing on a chest in the corner. The scenes painted on a Neapolitan chest could have been devotional, but such chests more typically displayed secular images, including scenes from romances. Inside the house, the Christian experience would have been heard and felt instead through the contemplative recitation of the Our Father and other prayers, perhaps accompanied by the soft clicking of the beads. Outside, along with the bells, reminders of the devotional environment were conveyed in the blasphemous curses invoking God and the saints uttered by men locked in mortal combat along the quay.

There is almost nothing we can say with any confidence about Magdalena's early years in the house of Peire and Bertomieua. It seems improbable that she was not sexually abused by Peire, although only his knowledge of the tattoos on her arms provides any insight into the likelihood of this. She almost certainly wore the drab service clothes characteristic of maidservants and, at least in the early years, probably had only one set of them. Enslaved people, in the urban environment of Mediterranean Europe, were not laden with chains and confined to the house. They moved about the neighborhood, displaying few, if any, outwardly visible signs of their legal status. But the fog that obscures any direct knowledge of those early years is a thick one. Only by the end, in 1399, when Magdalena re-emerges into the light of the record as a changed woman, can we once again pick up the threads of speculation about what may have happened to her in the interval.

6

The Wheel of Fortune

IN JANUARY OF 1388, following the successful expedition to Naples, Peire Huguet was nearing the summit of his fortune. This simple shipwright had carved out a career for himself as a privateer in royal service, rising up the ranks to rub shoulders with the high and mighty of the realm. His services to the crown in 1387 earned him the gratitude of Niccolò Sanframondi, the count of Cerreto, who awarded those services by granting him a slave woman formerly belonging to the admiral of Sicily. In May of 1391, we find Peire's name listed with others who belonged to the city's governing hierarchy, for like his father before him, he had landed a place on the city council.[1] It was a position he would hold for nearly two decades.

In records from the 1390s, the notaries of the city, with their uncanny feel for the signs of distinction, occasionally granted him titles even better than "honorable man," as he was called in 1387. By July of 1390, some notaries had taken to calling him a *providus vir*, a Latin expression that denotes a careful gentleman, wise in the ways of the world. The first known reference to his newfound status appears in an act drafted by Peire Calvin, one of Marseille's most distinguished notaries.[2] The need for the act arose because two men, a master and his serving man, had received an advance of 25 florins on their wages for participating in the assault on Naples. The monies paid to the two men were carefully noted by the ship's scribe in the cartulary dedicated to the expedition. But for some reason, the two men declined to join the expedition. Peire initiated proceedings against them and had already recovered about a third of the amount owed, but the men were having difficulty raising the rest of the money. By means of the act, the *providus vir*, Peire Huguet, graciously and with benignity agreed to extend the due date for the remainder until the feast of All Saints. In another act from February of 1393, Peire, along with some other investors, was named a *discretus vir*, or "a gentleman of distinction."[3] The notary, drafting Peire's identity clause, originally added the profession "shipwright" after his name. Upon reflection, though, or perhaps prodded by his client, the notary then drew a line through the words *magister assie*. Peire had left his old life behind him (figure 6).

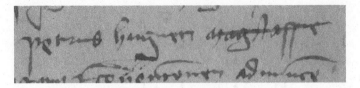

FIGURE 6. The changing identity of Peire Huguet. Following Peire's name, the notary had originally written "shipwright (*mag[ister] assie*)." In a nod to Peire's new status as a *providus vir*, he then drew a line through the phrase to delete it. Source: ADBR 355 E 76, fol. 205r.

The heady days did not last. Already by 1390, those in the know were probably muttering about the manner in which fortune had bestowed its favors on someone unworthy to receive them. His true character was familiar to anyone with knowledge of the loot that Peire, conniving with his brother Johan, had secreted from the general reckoning of the spoils of war in 1387. Others had had problematic dealings with him. For a decade, the wheel of fortune had smiled on this ambitious upstart. But all of that would soon change.

A Litigious Man

Across Europe, the thirteenth century witnessed the elaboration of an extensive set of legal and administrative practices, among them secular courts of law that attracted an ever-growing share of the market in disputation. By 1400, courts of law were intimately familiar to just about everyone. The extent of the business ranged from family courts that handled guardianship procedures to hearings where plaintiffs could initiate lawsuits against those from whom they claimed to have suffered injuries. By far the most common types of acts, outstripping both criminal cases and lawsuits by orders of magnitude, derived from simple cases of debt collection and related claims. Creditors of various stripes merely needed to submit a plea and sufficient evidence to the court to begin proceedings. Marseille's municipal archives preserve an extensive array of registers containing thousands of such acts.[4] Coupled with the equally extensive records left in registers of lawsuits and appeals, these records provide an intimate sense of the landscape of judicial practice in the city.

At present, the volume of information far outstrips our capacity to encompass it. But if we were able to systematically track the activities of unique individuals and link those individuals to the equally impressive residue of court actions that are found in the registers of the notaries, interesting patterns would emerge. What we would find is that the proclivity for judicial action was distributed unevenly across the population. Some individuals, such as the

THE WHEEL OF FORTUNE 93

fisherman Johan Martin, were peaceably minded and ready to forgive injuries and insults. These people appear rarely in the judicial records. To look ahead to a person whose acquaintance we shall make in a later chapter, Auruola de Jerusalem, one of the most prominent female moneylenders of the 1380s, never appears in any of the extant records concerning debt collection, despite issuing hundreds of loans. Since it is vanishingly unlikely that she was repaid each and every time, forgiveness of debt was part of her business model.

Others, though, were quite prickly and quick to use the courts in pursuit of what they perceived to be injuries. An instance is provided by the barber-surgeon, Nicolau de Sala, one of Marseille's most prominent individuals in the 1390s and 1400s, distinguished enough to have had an insula named for him. Nicolau was one of the barber-surgeons called to probe the death-wound of the merchant Antoni Gracian in 1391, and we shall meet him again, since he plays a prominent role in the lawsuit that Peire Huguet launched against Magdalena Coline. But whenever Nicolau was not seeing patients or inspecting corpses, he was likely to have been found in court. He appears dozens of times in court records stretching across two decades, and since these registers are but a fragment of the original body, the dozens of textual sightings indicate hundreds of court appearances. We find him constantly wrangling with people over sums of money that were often ridiculously small. As these instances reveal, Nicolau was an irritable man, swift to pursue claims against debtors. Those who knew Nicolau's character, in turn, had not the slightest compunction about pursuing him for the debts he owed them. Turnabout is fair play.

Peire Huguet was a decidedly litigious man, if not quite in the same league as his near-neighbor, Nicolau de Sala. One of the first references to Peire's court-related activity, from August of 1384, is the one in which he was erroneously described as a caulker by the notary of the court.[5] Nine months later, in May of 1385, a procurator working for Peire appeared in court, pursuing small debts of one gold franc owed by each of three men.[6] A court crier was sent to seize pledges. From one, he took three items: an unidentified tool used by carpenters known as a *siment*; a tub nominally used for washing dishes; and an adze. From the second, he seized a sword, and from the third, an anvil. The first and third of these involved the seizure of tools used by people to make a living. Such cases, when we find them, indicate coercive or punitive intentions on the part of the creditor.

A few years later, in the spring of 1388, Peire was caught up in a lawsuit with the royal court. In May of that year, he appears briefly while hiring procurators to pursue actions.[7] In June of 1388, the probable need for the procurators comes to light: a fragmentary entry in the register of the court of first appeals reveals that Peire had lost the lawsuit and was now pursuing an appeal. He abandoned the appeal immediately, perhaps realizing that the case was hopeless, perhaps because grounds for a settlement had been reached out of court.[8] Although neither record offers any clues about the matter of contention, it is likely that the matter arose from the assault on Naples six months earlier. In the month of August, yet another dispute broke out, this time pitting Jacme Limosin, one of the leaders of the expedition to Naples, against the captains of the other three Massiliote galleys, including Peire Huguet and Antoni de Lueys. The matter concerned the profits from the expedition and may have been occasioned by revelations made in the case heard a few months previously. In this instance, the matter was steered away from the courts of law and into arbitration.

In October of 1388, Peire hired yet another procurator to pursue further legal action against the royal court and its allies.[9] According to the preamble of the contract, the galley *La Stella* was in port and fully prepared to serve in another expedition to Naples. But the money needed to complete the arming of his ship had not yet arrived, and Peire's newly appointed procurator was authorized to pursue the count of Cerreto and a cardinal of the apostolic chamber for breach of contract.[10]

A few years later, Peire was at it again: a brief entry in the court register from January of 1391 indicates that he was pursuing someone for a debt of 8 florins.[11] The crier seized a cask full of wine. Several weeks later, the victim of the plunder, Antoni Robert, made an appearance in court, and we learn that once again, Peire was using the courts to pursue a man who had served under him.[12] A short while earlier, Peire, acting in the service of the royal court, had assembled a body of one hundred mercenaries to pursue an adventure in Montélimar, a town on the Rhone River to the north of Avignon. Antoni Robert was one of their number. Peire claimed that he had given Antoni an advance of 8 florins on his wages, but when the troops arrived in Avignon, the mercenary declined to serve and absconded with the advance. Antoni, for his part, declared that he never received the promised advance, adding that he had fallen ill and was unable to serve. Several days later, Peire received authorization to sell the cask at auction to the highest bidder, indicating that he had proven his claim.

In the meantime, on the 13th of January, Peire launched a third case against one of his men.[13] This time, the dispute involved a seaman named Nicolau who had joined the crew of a galley jointly owned by Peire and another individual named Antoni de Surda. According to Peire, the seaman had taken leave from his post without Peire's permission. The seaman retorted that he had in fact been granted leave by the knight, Guigo Flote, and was prepared to prove this by means of a document. Nicolau, who had been jailed on Peire's request, was released from prison, and Peire was condemned to pay the expenses arising from the trial. Unhappy with the ruling, Peire appealed the case to a higher court, though the outcome has been lost.

THE WHEEL OF FORTUNE 95

From these cases and another considered earlier in this chapter, we can assemble a portrait of Peire as employer. At various points between 1388 and 1389, in the course of three separate military adventures, at least four men had declined to serve under Peire Huguet. One of them may have gone so far as to feign an illness in order to avoid service. From this alone, it is impossible to say that Peire was incapable of inspiring loyalty in his men; such defections may well have been typical of mercenary service. But we can say with confidence that Peire was not the sort of commander willing to chalk up such defections to the cost of doing business. Instead, he readily engaged in legal fisticuffs with the men who served under him.

There would be little point to reciting the endless train of petty suits and pursuits involving Peire that unfolded over the next two decades. It does bear noting that Peire's brother, Johan, also made numerous appearances in court, if not at quite the same rate as Peire. The brothers Huguet clearly were cut from the same cloth, bristling at slights and perceived injustices, swift to use the courts against their enemies, incapable of letting bygones be bygones.

Falling Out with Antoni de Lueys

In the years after 1384, as Peire was pivoting to his new status as a privateer and a *providus vir*, his brittle sense of dignity led him to act against his underlings, in a manner that would have seemed faintly shameful to more decent men. But he also tangled with men of his own rank. The 1385 lawsuit pitting him and his associates against his former associate and neighbor, Jacme Limosin, offers the first clue we have to suggest that he did not necessarily hold faith with his own business partners.

On the 14th of February of 1391, Peire filed a lawsuit against a partner, the mariner Antoni de Lueys, who had stood shoulder-to-shoulder with him for at least a decade. According to the terms of the contract to which the two men had bound themselves before the altar of Sainte-Catherine in the church of Saint-Laurent, each owed the other a half share of their profits from the expedition to Naples in 1387. According to Peire, Antoni had earned more than 600 florins, which had been faithfully entered into the ship's cartulary by the scribe. On many occasions, Peire said, he asked Antoni to hand over half of his proceeds, but his partner had refused to do so.

Antoni immediately countersued, arguing exactly the same thing. But whereas Peire's claims were vague and indecisive, the narrative laid out in Antoni's countersuit was devastating. As seen in a previous chapter, Peire and Johan were accused of having removed coin and valuables worth 600 florins and keeping it for themselves. On the journey back to Marseille, the brothers engaged in further actions of dubious legality, plundering several Genoese and

Neapolitan sailing barks in the seas off the Italian town of Civitavecchia, acquiring an additional 400 florins. This constitutes the loot that the two brothers laid out on Peire's dining table early in the year 1388 in order to undertake the reckoning and gloat over the haul.

Curiously, Antoni did not sue Peire for the entirety of his share of the thousand florins that Peire had supposedly seized. Instead, Antoni only claimed 300, since he was concerned that the seizure of the barks did not conform to the laws of just war, and in any event would have been strictly forbidden by the terms of the contract that Peire had made with the papal curia. Had Antoni accepted a half-share of the 400 florins to which he was technically entitled, he could have become liable for reprisals from the Genoese. He had repeatedly asked Peire for his share of Peire's legitimately gotten gains, with no success.

Since the two men each demanded 300 florins from the other, it seems odd, at first blush, that they should have disagreed about anything. To appreciate the bone of contention, one has to reconstruct those moments over the preceding four years during which the two partners may have met and angrily demanded of the other that he should fulfill his part of the bargain. Peire clearly had gained access to the cartulary kept by the ship's scribe on Antoni's galley. He could point to the spot on the page that contained the reckoning of Antoni's private profits, beyond the share doled evenly out by the curia. But Antoni, in his turn, could do no such thing. Thanks to the fraudulent activities of the brothers Huguet, the cartulary of Peire's galley evidently showed a net profit of zero. Antoni must have heard rumors of Johan Huguet's doings, though, and used that as a basis for refusing to settle the accounts.

Although nothing connects the actions launched in February of 1391 to the series of lawsuits that unfolded during the spring and summer of 1388, it is likely that they were all of a piece. A plausible reconstruction runs as follows. In the months after the flotilla's return to Marseille, news of Peire's dealings gradually leaked out. In May or June of that year, the royal court got wind of it and successfully sued Peire. An inkling of this is found in the counterclaim made by Antoni de Lueys in February of 1391. The narrative provided to the court, in the section that referenced the plunder seized from the galley of Corrado Doria, included the phrase: "it was discovered that Johan Huguet, the brother of the said Peire, took 200 florins from the total value of the plunder found in the galley."[14] The passive construction of the verb suggests that Antoni himself had not made the discovery.

Recognizing that Peire was an entrepreneur of doubtful propriety, the count of Cerreto and the papal curia then refused to follow through on a contract they had made with Peire to finance a second mission, leading to the lawsuit that Peire filed against them in the fall of that year. Meanwhile, reverberations from Peire's actions had shattered the bond of understanding that had formerly united the captains of the Massiliote galleys, causing Jacme Limosin to launch a suit against Peire and the others in August of 1388. At the time, Antoni stood by his partner. If so, it must have been shocking to him that Peire should repeatedly approach him over the ensuing months, demanding a share of Antoni's loot. It is easy to imagine Antoni's riposte: "But what about all the lucre you fraudulently took for yourself?"

It is somewhat difficult to know what to make of Antoni's accusations. If Peire had really absconded with 600 florins, it was not Antoni alone who suffered. It was the fleet as a whole, since ship captains were supposed to report all their plunder to the count of Cerreto to be evenly divided among the principals. The implication is that the royal curia had already made its own reckoning with Peire and that Antoni had been willing to let bygones be bygones if only Peire would leave him in peace. But once Peire sued him, all restraints were removed.

The intimacy of the detail provided in Antoni's narrative of the events is typical of cases that almost invariably succeeded in court. The details indicate that Antoni had access to some very well-placed informants who were willing to testify to the shenanigans of the brothers Huguet. One of these informants must have included a mole placed in Peire's house, since someone had witnessed the reckoning of the loot laid out on the dining room table. Unsurprisingly, Peire took the sensible route and allowed the case to go to arbitration. On the 9th of December 1391, the two parties met before a notary and agreed to submit to the ruling of two arbitrators, distinguished citizens of Marseille named Guilhem de Sant Gilles and Bernat de Berra.[15] So far, no trace of their ruling has been found, meaning that it is impossible for us to fact-check Antoni's assertions. Regardless, it is almost certain that at least some of the details of the accusations had filtered out into the city's gossip networks. If so, it is easy to presume that some of the reputational luster Peire had so industriously burnished had begun to rub off.

The Abyss of Debt

The falling out of Antoni and Peire marks the point where the wheel of fortune, with Peire lashed to one of its spokes, began its inexorable decline. For a decade, the two men had been tightly bound together. After 1391, the two men fell apart, never to reconcile, and Peire was the worse for it.

After 1391, we begin to hear about Peire's lingering debts, although at the outset, the signal is faint and hard to isolate from his other doings. In the previous years he had taken out numerous loans, since privateering, as a business model, required a great deal of start-up capital. Buying shares in galleys was costly enough, since a quarter-share of one of the big galleys cost upward of 500 florins. Beyond that, there were all the furnishings and armaments.

Contracts from later years attest to the capital Peire had had to sink into equipment and armaments. A sale credit from April of 1395, for instance, indicates that the cost of furnishing a galley with forty pavises, a type of tall shield, came to at least 20 florins. A single sail cost as much as 100 florins.[16]

The loans needed to fund these enterprises begin to appear in the record in the 1380s, as Peire became a privateer. In addition to those considered earlier, we hear of a loan that Peire took out from the nobleman Guilhem Giraut in July of 1390.[17] A faint clue suggesting that Peire was financially stretched first appears in September of 1391, when his creditor, Johan Bellissens, appeared before a notary acknowledging a debt of 25 florins to another man.[18] Not having the funds to pay off that loan, he transferred to his creditor half of a debt of 50 florins owed to him by Peire. But it's not easy to know, from this act alone, whether Peire was beginning to look at his account books with a worried frown.

Three weeks later, another contract in the same notarial register records a curious set of transactions related to Peire's dispute with Antoni.[19] When the suit was joined back in February, the two parties were required to offer pledges for the fee that was charged for opening a lawsuit. In the act, the treasurer belatedly acknowledged having received from Antoni a crown of silver and pearls worth 10 florins and noted that whenever the court fees were paid, he would return the pledge to Antoni. The contract also states that Peire Huguet promised to pay the necessary fees when required, and, in a curious phrase, left two crossbows "as a reminder of his commitment (*pro memoria dicte assignationis*)." Since the value of two crossbows was considerably less than 10 florins, these were not pledges so much as memory aids. The act took place in the house of the city's viguier, and one is left with a very strong impression that it was associated, in some way, with the ongoing arbitration.

In the space left beneath the act, a note was entered in a different hand and in noticeably darker ink. The entry was dated 24 November 1394, and it indicates that Antoni de Lueys had redeemed the crown held in pledge all this time. This in no way implies that the arbitration took that long to settle. It merely means that Antoni had other uses for his coin and saw no need to redeem the pledge for several years. Significantly, no entry indicates that Peire's debt had ever been canceled. Once again, we see the faint signs of insolvency.

One of the last scenes suggesting persisting investor confidence in Peire occurred in 1395, when the financier Bertomieu Simondel advanced 100 florins to Peire on top of the existing unpaid debt of 166 florins and 8 gros that Peire had incurred eight years earlier, in May of 1387, for purchasing a share in a galley.[20] Tellingly, the 1395 contract shows no sign of having been canceled in the notary's register. A year or two later, Bertomieu went to his grave without having been repaid by Peire. Peire's debt passed into the hands of Bertomieu's brother, Esteve, who then sold it to another of Peire's investors, the draper Isnart de Sant

Gilles, in 1405.[21] Debt instruments were usually sold at a discounted rate, when original creditors had lost hope of repayment. The sale of such instruments was almost invariably a sign that debtors were in serious financial straits.

With Peire's reputation as a privateer fading, his lingering debts began to surface. In January of 1398, the debt of 100 florins that Peire had owed to the nobleman Guilhem Giraut since July of 1390 popped up, having been included in the dowry of 1,000 florins that Guilhem assigned to his daughter, Dalphineta, for her marriage to Johanet de Sarciano.[22] Later that same year, in November of 1398, an ordinary sale credit appears in a register of the notary Peire Calvin.[23] In it, Peire Huguet acknowledged a debt of 34 l. and 9 s. to his neighbor and close associate, the draper Isnart de Sant Gilles. Though the source of the obligation is not specified in the act, various clues suggest that it had come about because Isnart had supplied fabric for the wedding garments for the marriage of Lazaret Huguet to his stepcousin Hugoneta five years earlier and had not yet been repaid.

This particular act is surprising. In normal circumstances, purchases such as this did not need to be notarized. Drapers entered details about new orders in their shop cartularies and expected their clients to pay the bills.[24] Five years on, though, Peire had still not honored the invoice. In 1398, alert to Peire's growing financial troubles, Isnart decided to secure the debt by means of a notarial contract. When people like Isnart did this, it's not because a notarial act was more legally binding than a line entered in a shop cartulary. All private cartularies were considered valid legal instruments in the eyes of the court. The notarization of a debt was useful for two unrelated reasons. First, as we have seen, notarized contracts, like bills of exchange, could circulate as value-bearing notes. With a legal instrument in hand, Isnart could sell the debt to another investor or pass it along to his heirs. Second, the notarization of a contract was a public affair, requiring the presence of witnesses and thereby generative of talk. To notarize a shop debt was to expose the debtor in the eyes of the community and increase the pressure to repay.

The parties convened in the house of Hugoneta's stepfather, Johan Huguet, which is one of the clues suggesting that the debt had arisen from Hugoneta's wedding clothes. Rather than appearing himself, Isnart sent his factor to represent the interests of the firm, though it is not clear whether this was a symptom of his anger over the affair or, alternatively, his uneasiness about putting the squeeze on a friend and neighbor. Peire agreed to pay the sum owed and the due date set was the upcoming Lent, several months hence. The act bears no marks of cancellation and the debt was probably never paid.

The notary who drew up the act was Peire Calvin. In 1390, Peire Calvin had been one of the first to bestow the honorific *providus vir* on Peire Huguet. In 1398, things had changed. The fortunes of the Angevins had taken a turn for the worse, and Peire's privateering business was in tatters. Peire's partner and neighbor, Isnart de Sant Gilles, had chosen to put him through the public humiliation of being subjected to the notarization of a shop credit. The label *providus vir*, in short, no longer suited the broken man who stood before the notary. Contemplating the turn of the wheel of fortune, Peire Calvin dropped *providus vir* and restored Peire's old title of *magister ascie*. Peire Huguet, after flying high for a decade, was once again a simple shipwright.

Sitting on a Man

Prior to the arrival of British colonial rule, as the Africanist Judith Van Allen pointed out in a famous 1972 article, the Igbo women of southern Nigeria were significant actors in the domains of politics and markets. From time to time, whenever a presumptuous man got out of line and did something that offended women's privileges, the women would sit on him. "Sitting on a man," Van Allen wrote,

> involved gathering at his compound, sometimes late at night, dancing, singing scurrilous songs which detailed the women's grievances against him and often called his manhood into question, banging on his hut with the pestles women used for pounding yams, and perhaps demolishing his hut or plastering it with mud and roughing him up a bit ... The women would stay at his hut throughout the day, and late into the night, if necessary, until he repented and promised to mend his ways. .... No man would consider intervening.[25]

It is no surprise, therefore, that when the tax policies of the British colonial administration irritated Igbo women in 1929, they chose to sit on the warrant officers who were the instruments of the offensive tax policy. The women heightened the shame of their protest by removing all of their clothing apart from their loincloths, smearing their faces with charcoal or ash, and carrying symbols representing the powers of the female ancestors.

Though the world's customs vary a good deal, most women are familiar with the idea that although it may be possible to put up with a disagreeable man for a while, there comes a moment when enough is enough, and it is time to sit on him. Taking off your clothes and singing ribald songs is one way to do it. Marseille's women, in the decades around 1400, went about things differently. Quite a few of them, acting alone, used stones and staves to strike and thereby shame the men who had offended them in some way. Those who had less stomach for violence could do much the same thing by using the forms of coercion and humiliation made available by the courts of law. When circumstances warranted it, women filed lawsuits against the men who had offended them. In dozens of such lawsuits across the fourteenth and early fifteenth centuries, witness groups consisted primarily of women, and women provided

THE WHEEL OF FORTUNE 101

the most damning testimony. This was a very effective way to sit on a presumptuous man in late medieval Marseille.

Between 1400 and 1403, in a coordinated one-two punch, Peire was sued first
by his sister-in-law, Alaseta Huguete, and then by his daughter-in-law, Hugoneta.
On the 12th of July 1400, Alaseta, acting in her own name though with the consent of her husband, Johan, appeared before a notary to launch a dispute against
her brother-in-law.[26] The act consisted of a procuration by means of which she
named the jurist Jacme Peytamin to represent her in court for a lawsuit that she
was proposing to launch against Peire Huguet or his son over the nuptial garments supplied by the boutique of the heirs of Guilhem de Montels.

The act provides little information about the source of the dispute, although
various clues allow reasonable speculation. The invoice that Peire had owed to
Isnart de Sant Gilles, coupled with Alaseta's lawsuit, suggest that several years
earlier, Peire had taken responsibility for paying the cost of Hugoneta's nuptial
garments. Johan and Alaseta had assigned to Peire a dowry for Hugoneta valued at 200 florins, of which at least 100 florins consisted of cash. The nuptial
garments, clearly, were paid from the cash component of the dowry, leading
to a situation where the garments then formed part of her trousseau. The
family commissioned the garments from the two drapers' shops. In both cases,
Peire had failed to pay the bills.

In 1398, as we have seen, Isnart de Sant Gilles moved against Peire, publicly
converting the entry in his shop cartulary into a notarial act and thereby sending a stern message to his errant neighbor. But the boutique of the de Montels
family went about things differently. Having lost patience with Peire, they initiated proceedings in court. A court crier was sent not to Peire's house but instead to Hugoneta's place of residence, where he seized the nuptial garments.
It was a stunning act of public shaming.

In October of 1402, Peire's growing insolvency flared up, here taking the
form of a brief entry in the registers of the deliberations of the city council
indicating that he was being pursued for unspecified debts by the treasurer of
the episcopal court.[27] In January of 1403, in an unrelated move, two notaries,
Laurens Aycart and Pons de Scalis, seized pledges worth 10 florins from him.[28]
It is quite likely that these were the pledges that Peire had left for the unpaid
court fees associated with his 1391 lawsuit against Antoni de Lueys: among
other things, the names of the two notaries were identical to those listed in
1391, and the fee, 10 florins, was the amount charged to Peire.

But the worst was still on the horizon. In November of 1403, a brief entry
in the records of one of the lesser courts indicates that Hugoneta, joining her
mother in the act of sitting on Peire, had opened proceedings against her
father-in-law.[29] On the 28th, she appeared personally at court, and the entry
made by the notary indicates that she was repeating a request she had made

earlier. The register opens abruptly on the previous folio, on the 26th of November, and from this it is clear that one or more quires have been lost. Regardless, it is easy to determine what brought her into court in the first place, for the notary went on to write that the judge ordered Peire to immediately pay her 10 l. for the necessary aliments and a further 10 l. on the feast of Christmas. Should he protest these payments, goods equal in value to her dowry of 200 florins would be seized from him. As this indicates, Hugoneta had initiated proceedings to recover her dowry from the insolvent estate of her father-in-law.

Peire, as one might have expected of someone so litigiously minded, appeared in court to protest the decision. No trace of the corresponding action in court has surfaced, and the dispute between the two moved to arbitration. Happily, we know what happened this time, thanks to a notarial act from the 21st of December which recorded the decisions of the two arbitrators.[30]

Two men, Peire de Serviers and Raymon Aymes, served as arbitrators. They were described as common friends of Peire and Hugoneta, and indeed they were. We shall run across Peire de Serviers again soon enough, since his wife, Blacassia, appeared off-stage on more than one occasion during the first trial between Magdalena and Peire. The notary Raymon Aymes, in turn, was a long-time associate of Peire's. He had been one of the investors in the galley *Sanctus-Johannes-Evangeliste* and had worked closely with Peire for a period of time stretching from 1393, when they launched the galley, to 1398, when it was sold to the commune of Nice. Yet this long association left little room for sympathy. The ruling handed down by the two arbitrators, four days before the feast of Christmas, required Peire Huguet to return 50 florins to Hugoneta immediately and to repay the remaining 150 florins in the form of annual alimony payments of 20 l., equivalent to 12½ florins. It was a total victory for Hugoneta and a crushing defeat for Peire.

If one thing emerges with startling clarity from these sorry episodes, it is this. Peire's penchant for untrustworthy dealings was not limited to betrayals of his close business partners. It extended even to women from his own family. In the preceding years, it is not difficult to imagine mother and daughter exchanging angry words about their high-handed brother- and father-in-law, and putting pressure on their husband and father, Johan, to do something about it. But Johan was a person of indifferent resolve. All the strength of character in their house lay with his wife, Alaseta. In 1400, the dam that held back her anger was finally breached, and after bullying her husband into granting the necessary legal permission, she took her brother-in-law to court. After a decade of indignation, Alaseta had finally lost patience.

7

Magdalena Gets Married

ON A FEW OCCASIONS IN THE late 1380s and the 1390s, we catch glimpses of Peire, standing with other men on the doorstep of his house on the Lansaria, making contracts in the presence of a notary. It is hard not to feel the silent presence of Magdalena as she passes by on her errands or observes them from the doorway. She is gathering information in the way that all people do, naturally and unconsciously, noting the patterns of interaction and the style of clothing, hearing tones of voice and the scratching of quills on paper. Like anyone in this world, she is alert to the signs of dominance and deference, the greetings and honorifics, the courtesies that lubricate social exchange. All this information gradually flows into her without any conscious effort on her part. Day after day, the layers of experience slowly accumulate, forming oceans of implicit knowledge about how the world works in this unfamiliar land.

From time to time, it may have occurred to her to wonder what it meant to be called a slave. Although medieval legal categories inherited from Roman law nominally divided everyone into categories of free and enslaved, no one in the world of medieval Europe, apart from kings, princes, and popes, was ever really free, at least in the modern sense of the word, where being free means freedom from coercion and dependence.[1] It could even be said with some justice that high rank brought with it a significant loss of freedom. Those of high social rank, or at least those with any conscience, were burdened with sets of duties owed to dependents. When we speak of freedom in this age, we are referring to the capacity to engage in autonomous action.

The ability to act autonomously was a quality that came in degrees. Enslaved individuals and serfs had very little autonomy of action; household servants and other dependents probably only a little more. Autonomy increased as one moved along the spectrum from dependents through wealthy farmers, artisans, urban elites, members of the nobility, bishops, princes, and eventually to popes and kings. As Magdalena became familiar with this spectrum, she may have wondered where she herself was located. Peire and members of his household may have called her a slave, but the clothes she wore were almost certainly no different from the clothes worn by free housemaids. The orders conveyed to her by her mistress, Bertomieua, were probably no different, in form and tone of voice, from the orders that mistresses everywhere across the city gave to their servants. It is possible that signals denoting her status were conveyed to the omnipresent body of watchers who silently noted where she slept or saw that Peire claimed sexual access to her in a manner that would have been less permissible with an ordinary housemaid. Such signals may once have been apparent to contemporaries, though they have long since been lost to us.

Amidst everything else, Magdalena couldn't have failed to notice how writing worked in this land, and how writing intersected with autonomy of action. By 1400, those capable of autonomous action, men and women alike, regularly interacted with the written word. The degree to which they did so serves as a convenient proxy for their degree of autonomy. Every respectable household kept a cartulary recording the daily business of the household. For more important business, ranging from major life events such as marriages and funerals to loans and legal actions, notaries were called upon to lend publicity to the action and thereby give it the force of law.

These documents, in the form of instruments made of paper or parchment carefully folded into convenient flat wads or rolled up and tied with string, were gathered and stored in sacks and chests or loose piles. Household inventories often include references to these domestic archives. They are omnipresent in the houses of the well-to-do; rare and scattered in the houses of the less well-to-do. Everywhere, the visible signs of distinction included access to and storage of the written word. In a feedback loop, the ceremonies of notarization, which included a carefully managed distribution of honorifics to the actors involved, generated documents whose visible storage further cemented an actor's claim to be the sort of person capable of engaging in legal action in the presence of a notary.

In the decade that followed her arrival in Peire and Bertomieua's house, Magdalena, in keeping with her legal condition, left no trace in the surviving record. Unlike the situation for most enslaved women, not even a contract of sale accompanied her into the house, no legal instrument that Peire might have been able to place alongside Bertomieua's dowry and all the other family papers that typically filled the domestic archive. The absence of any appearance in the written record, perhaps more than anything else, was both a sign and a symptom of her enslaved condition.

In the year 1399, on Sunday, the 24th of August, as the church bells tolled vespers to summon the monks and nuns to evening prayers, Magdalena finally entered the historical record—and did so with a splash. She was in the act of

MAGDALENA GETS MARRIED 105

getting married.[2] The groom was a master shipwright named Johan Petre, an immigrant from the town of Sluis, in Flanders. The bride, named "Magdalena Coline," was identified as the *pedicequa*, or housemaid, of Peire Huguet. In the part of the identity clause where point of origin was sometimes inserted, she was described as being "also of this city of Marseille (*etiam dicte civitatis Massilie*)." It was a small but significant phrase, indicating that she was perceived as being one of us. Standing in the hall of Peire Huguet's house, with their hands touching the Holy Gospels in the manner of the Christian faithful, Johan and Magdalena affirmed their intention to bring the marriage into effect.

The notary responsible for the act, Reynier Nicolai, was nearing the end of a fairly undistinguished career and would be dead in a few years' time. He was well known to the Huguet family. Twenty-five years earlier, in April 1374, he had drawn up the dowry contract for Bertomieua at the time of her marriage to Peire Huguet, when the shipwright was a 24-year-old nobody. At a symbolic level, it is noteworthy that Reynier had been called in to notarize Magdalena's marriage.[3] Reynier did not rank among the greats of Marseille's community of notaries. Perhaps awed by the company into which he had been summoned once again, perhaps out of recognition of the solemnity of the occasion, he chose to describe Peire as a *providus vir*. If Peire had known that this was one of the last occasions when the honorific would be conferred on him, he might have savored it more.

Magdalena's dowry was assembled and granted to Johan Petre by Peire Huguet himself. It had three components. First was a cloak and a houppelande, in a slate-blue fabric that was one of the signature colors in Marseille at the time. Next was a bed, furnished with a mattress, a good bolster, two coverlets, and two pairs of sheets. Common friends reported that the garments and the bed together were worth 20 florins. The third item was rent-free lodging in Peire's house for a period of six years, together with some cash, that was valued at another 20 florins, for a total of 40 florins. As dowries go, this one was peculiarly stingy, for Peire had given her very little that actually cost him anything. By all appearances, he had consented to, or arranged, a marriage between his housemaid and a shipwright who worked in his yard. The couple settled into the spare bedroom, perhaps alongside the rest of the servants. Presumably, they slept in a bed that was now hers.

The marriage changed Magdalena in many ways. Among other things, by virtue of entering the record, she finally becomes directly visible to the gaze of the historian working six centuries after her time. But even more tellingly, through the alchemy of notarization, she had become visible to the people in her own day. After nearly twelve years of obscurity, she had become a legal person.

Why Now?

Why did Magdalena's marriage take place when it took place? And why did it happen at all?

All forms of historical explanation are located on a spectrum that runs from the explicit actions of individuals to the nudging influence of structures or patterns. Individuals are proud. It is they who fall in love, grow angry or indignant, and feel the weight of injustice. Their subsequent actions explain much. At the other end of the spectrum, structures determine landscapes of possibility, providing the nudges that make some outcomes more likely than others. Magdalena's marriage happened because certain people made it happen. But it also happened because there were structures of expectation in force that normally encouraged masters to manumit their female slaves and marry them off after a decent interval of time.

At the near end of the spectrum of explanation, we can imagine several actions or events that may have triggered the marriage. It would have been normal enough, for example, for a Christian man who had impregnated his slave to marry her off to one of his dependents, for this allowed him to avoid the duties of paternity and covered his shame with a veneer of decency. In a different vein, we can't discount the possibility that Johan Petre was attracted to his employer's enslaved housemaid and she to him. Johan was a master shipwright, not an apprentice. It is not inconceivable that he had some political capital to bring to bear in such negotiations. For immigrants like Johan, marriage was an instrumental aspect of the passage from foreigner to local.

One thing we know for sure is that the marriage didn't just happen. People made it happen. Let us consider closely the opening paragraph of the act:

> In the year of the Lord above, on Sunday, the 24th of the month of August, at vespers. Let it be known to all etc. that a marriage was arranged that united, through words of the present consent, Master Johan Petre of Sluis, from the region of Flanders, a shipwright, now said to be a resident of Marseille on the one hand, and Magdalena Coline, a housemaid of the *providus vir* Peire Huguet, also of the city of Marseille on the other—that is, in the wake of negotiations of several common friends of the same parties.[4]

One of the most intriguing features of the dowry contract is found in the final sentence above, in language suggesting that negotiators had gotten involved. Phrases referring to "common friends" can be found from time to time in dowry contracts, but they are more characteristic of the language associated with settlements, including contracts of arbitration and acts of peacemaking. Reynier Nicolai, the notary responsible for Magdalena's dowry, did not use the phrase in either of the two dowries that appear later in the same register.[5] Evidently, the phrase was not one he normally deployed when drawing up dowry contracts. The expression sometimes appears in other dowry contracts from Marseille, one example being that of a dowry contract from April of 1355. What makes that act noteworthy is the context, for the wedding had been hastily arranged by common friends to resolve a vendetta that had arisen between two families following a homicide.[6]

The presence of the clause suggests that the marriage resulted from a negotiated settlement. If so, who were the rival parties, and what was the nature of the dispute? Of the many possibilities, the likeliest begins with this presumption: Peire's wife, Bertomieua, had just died, and on her deathbed, she insisted that Magdalena, after nearly twelve years of service, be launched into a new phase of life. From evidence presented in the first trial, we know that Bertomieua had left Magdalena a legacy of 10 l., the equivalent of 6¼ florins. Peire's wife evidently had some affection for her enslaved housemaid or at least felt duty-bound to provide for her future. In this hypothetical scenario, the marriage was triggered by Bertomieua's impending death.

The picture that subsequently emerges fits neatly into our understanding of the chronology of events and the personalities of the parties involved. Following Bertomieua's death, Peire failed to honor his late wife's wishes. As we learn in the first trial, his shortcomings as an executor extended to the point of refusing to pay Magdalena the legacy that was owed to her. Upon observing Peire's reluctance to marry her off or manumit her, neighbors and friends put pressure on Peire to do the right thing. Honoring Bertomieua's memory, they insisted that it was high time that Magdalena be married.

Why should the people of the Lansaria have sided with an enslaved housemaid against their own neighbor and kinsman? Perhaps they were more loyal to Bertomieua than they were to Peire. But this is also where the structural considerations come to bear on the possible explanations for the why and the when. The societies that surrounded the greater Mediterranean basin were generally inclined toward the assimilation of the enslaved rather than their permanent denigration and exclusion. Magdalena had already served Peire for nearly twelve years. On this theory, the neighbors felt that she had done her time.

Structure and agency, then, fall neatly together. In the months leading up to the wedding, people who lived in the neighborhood of the Lansaria had begun to notice that Magdalena had moved some distance along the spectrum that ran from servitude to freedom. In 1399, we can imagine a woman approaching 28 years of age, an attractive marriage prospect for a recent immigrant from Flanders. Bertomieua's impending death, in this hypothesis, was the triggering event.

Dowry Makes Free

The following day, after the ceremony and the consummation, had Magdalena Coline become a free woman? The question hovers tantalizingly in the air as we read the details of the contract. Our intuition is that she must have been free, because what could possibly induce a free man to marry an enslaved woman? As it happens, however, the situation was deceptively complex.[7]

Canon law held that a valid marriage arose when two parties freely exchanged vows of present consent. The condition of one or both of the parties had no bearing on the validity of the marriage. The great subtlety lay in the matter of defining what was meant by "consent." In causa 29 of his *Decretum*, the twelfth-century canonist Gratian considered situations in which a person had consented to a marriage according to a belief that turned out to have been mistaken.[8] Under what kinds of conditions, he wondered, could error of belief be sufficient to nullify the consent? Servility of condition figured prominently in the scenarios he considered, along with chastity and poverty. In the opening scenario, Gratian considered a case in which a woman had exchanged vows with a man of servile condition who had dissimulated his identity, pretending to be the free man of noble birth to whom she had promised her hand. In this case, the woman could be excused from her vows, because she had been misled as to the identity of the person to whom she had given her consent. As Gratian put it, "error as to person occurs when one thinks someone is Virgil when he is Plato." He came up with a practical scenario involving an error as to person. If one were to sell a field to Marcellus, and a second person named Paul should arrive, claiming he was Marcellus, and purchase the field, it is clear that the sale should not be valid. Error as to person, by analogy, was also sufficient for invalidating a marriage.

But this was not true of every error that one might commit while consenting to a marriage. Gratian considered a case where a woman married a pauper, thinking him wealthy. According to Gratian, that would be like buying a barren field or a vineyard, supposing it to be fruitful. The purchase may have been made in error but the error, in this case, does not cancel the sale. Likewise, he wrote, a man might marry a prostitute, thinking her virginal and chaste, only to discover his error later. In such a case, he cannot send her away and take another. These cases concern errors as to fortune and quality, and such errors could not be taken to invalidate a marriage.

What about errors as to condition, when a person consented to a marriage with someone servile? If the consent had been given in full knowledge of the servile condition, there were no conditions under which the spouse could subsequently be repudiated. But what about the case where a woman marries a man whom she thought to be free, only to discover afterward that he is servile?

"Many arguments," Gratian wrote, "prove that the woman cannot lawfully leave the slave." But having considered both sides of the matter, he concluded that error as to condition was indeed sufficient to invalidate a marriage. "When one is deceived as to person or condition, one need not adhere to the one through whose fraud one was deceived."[9]

Marriages between free and servile were perfectly valid in canon law, in other words, as long as the status of the slave was not fraudulently hidden. Magdalena did not need to be free to contract a valid marriage with Johan Petre. The marriage, in turn, did not automatically convey upon Magdalena the free status of her husband, unlike the manner in which marriage to the citizen of a modern state would normally put a spouse on a path toward citizenship. But Magdalena's marriage involved more than her vows. It also came with a dowry provided by her master, Peire Huguet, and this implied his consent. And his consent made for an entirely different situation.

The common law of medieval Europe derived from the body of civil law assembled by the Roman emperor Justinian and his jurists in the second quarter of the sixth century. A provision in Justinian's Code declares that "If anyone gives his female slave in marriage to a free man and gives her a dowry in writing—which is a custom only among free persons—the female slave shall become a Roman citizen."[10] Justinian's jurists were alert to a delectable type of fraud that could be occasioned by a marriage between the free and the enslaved. A slave owner, not being fully transparent about the legal status of his slave woman, could marry her to an unsuspecting free man and thereby ensnare the poor devil in a tangled web of dependency—something that might well describe Johan Petre's situation. A clarifying provision made in Justinian's Novels, therefore, explicitly declared that whenever a master had taken steps to arrange a marriage involving his slave woman, the woman shall receive *tacitam libertatem*, that, is, freedom by implication.[11]

A legal textbook from the twelfth century gives us some sense of how this provision of Roman law might have been understood in a medieval context. *Lo Codi*, compiled in the Rhone Valley or nearby in the third quarter of the twelfth century, was a collection of legal commentaries based on the first nine books of the Code. Originally drafted in Occitan, the text was later translated into Latin and several vernaculars. A number of laws in the text have a bearing on slavery, including this provision concerning marriages between the enslaved and the free: "If anyone shall have given his slave woman in marriage and shall have given her a dowry, this slave is made free, since a marriage cannot be made except between free persons, and when a lord gives her in wife to another, it is understood that he intended her to be free."[12]

Lo Codi had no legal authority whatsoever; among other things, the understanding that marriage can exist only among free persons ran spectacularly afoul of canon law. Beyond its legal failings, the text was obscure in its own day and, by 1400, had long been superseded by legal commentaries that were far more authoritative and robust. Even in its own day, it is best understood as a kind of students' "cheat sheet" to the principles of Roman law rather than as an authoritative body of positive law.[13] It is relevant here because the thinking that appears in Lo Codi may reflect certain attitudes that were baked into Occitan-Provençal customs governing marriage, and that the assumptions of Magdalena's neighbors in 1399 drew on that reservoir of custom.

As it happens, an understanding similar to that conveyed in Lo Codi resurfaced less than a century later, in the *Siete Partidas*, the law code for Castile assembled by Alfonso the Wise and his jurists. The law, entitled "A slave can be freed by reason of marriage," made no mention of the dowry; it followed the Novels in declaring that a slave who has married a free person becomes free as long as the master is aware of the marriage and offers no opposition.[14] The later medieval statutes of Genoa addressed an identical scenario. One of the statutes, entitled "That slaves marrying among themselves are not thereby released from the power of the master," declared that two slaves who married one another shall not ipso facto be free, even if the marriage should take place with the consent of the master, unless the master were to explicitly acknowledge that they should be free.[15] This stands to reason: a master might well want to encourage marriages without wishing to lose his slaves. But to this, the legislators appended a second paragraph governing marriages between enslaved and free persons: "If, however, a lord shall have given his consent to a marriage between a slave man or slave woman and a free or freed man or woman, by virtue of that consent he or she is understood to be freed from the power of the lord or lady, though the duty to honor a patron still applies." The statute included the suggestion that freedom arrives by implication: it is *understood* that marriage with a master's consent brings freedom.

As it happens, Marseille's statutes are utterly silent on matters pertaining to slavery. In the absence of any clarifying local statute or ordinance, however, it is reasonable to suppose that the provisions described in law codes from contemporary Genoa and Castile and outlined in Lo Codi and the Novels would have applied in Marseille. What this suggests is that on Monday morning, Magdalena had gained freedom by implication in the eyes of the positive law.

To think about the question of her legal condition solely from the perspective of the positive law, however, is not the only way to go about it. By the time of her marriage in August of 1399, Magdalena had been serving Peire for nearly twelve years. A decade and more is a long time. It is time enough for a young person, at least for one who is so inclined, to learn how to speak the local language, to absorb the local mannerisms and ways of carrying oneself, and to learn the rules of the social game. By the time of her marriage, in other words,

Magdalena looked and acted like a member of local society. It is true that Peire never stopped thinking about her as his slave. But it wasn't up to him alone to define her legal condition. The community of the Lansaria, consisting of those who interacted with Magdalena on a daily basis as she went to fetch wood or water or undertook other tasks outside the house, also had a say in the matter. If in their eyes she was free, then she was free, regardless of what the positive law might have said or whatever Peire might have thought.

Several additional elements of the dowry contract offer grounds for arguing that the contract included what I shall henceforth call a tacit manumission. To begin with, the contract explained the granting of the dowry using this language:

> And for the purpose of more easily bearing the burdens of matrimony for this same person, as is customary, the aforesaid Peire Huguet, acknowledging the good and faithful service accorded to him by the said Magdalena, and out of reverence for God, moved by piety and a sense of duty to remunerate the aforesaid services accorded to him by the said Magdalena, in good faith and for himself and his heirs. . . .

The ensuing passage then laid out the dowry that he had assigned to Magdalena's new husband. Like computer programmers today, notaries rarely invented lines of text if they could copy pertinent clauses from other contracts and paste them where needed. Tellingly, the clause that refers to Magdalena's faithful service was borrowed from a formula that appears in contracts of manumission. In the eyes of the notary, the contract may not have been a manumission in a technical sense, but it was near enough as made no difference.

A second clue is provided by the word the notary used to identify Magdalena's occupation, pedicequa. This word, derived from classical Latin, is made by joining the word for "foot," *pedis*, with the verb "to follow," *sequeri*. In a literal sense, the combination refers to "one who follows on foot." Where a male servant was concerned, the word can be rendered in English as "footman." When it is used to refer to a woman, the best translation might be "housemaid" or "scullery maid." The word "pedicequa" is relatively rare in records from Marseille. Enough instances survive, though, to indicate that "pedicequa" typically refers to a free Christian housemaid or kitchen maid, many of whom were immigrants from the countryside. The few women to whom the label was assigned have characteristically Provençal names, quite unlike the narrow range of Christian names typically given to slaves.[16] The case we considered earlier of the Tatar woman, Catharina, who was manumitted by her master in 1367 on the condition that she not hire herself as a housemaid while unmarried offers an interesting exception, since the act spoke of hiring herself out as a pedicequa.[17] Though normally applied to local Provençal women, in other words, the word "pedicequa" could also be used to describe the occupation of a foreign-born freedwoman.

A record emanating from Marseille's criminal court in 1380 offers unambiguous support for the idea that local people distinguished between slaves and pedicequas. The brief case records the successful prosecution of a pedicequa named Biatris de Bosqua, alias "Columbana" or "the Little Dove," who had attacked a *sclava* or slave woman named Maria, whose master was a shoemaker.[18] In her defense, the pedicequa Biatris declared that the slave woman had insulted her and refused to allow her to enter a walled field. A surgeon called in to examine Maria reported that the injuries she suffered were not lethal. As this case indicates, observers made a careful distinction between servants and slaves. This being the case, no one present at the making of Magdalena's dowry contract would have missed the significance of the use of the word "pedicequa" to describe Magdalena's condition.

What did Magdalena understand about her own condition following her marriage? We have already had occasion to peek ahead to the supplication she made to the court of Louis II in 1408, and we shall be considering this extraordinary scene in more detail in a later chapter. The same document preserves another phrase, so vivid that one can almost hear the words issuing from her mouth, informing the king that Peire Huguet "married off the said Magdalena not as a slave but as a pure, free woman, and contributed part of her dowry."[19] And although it means engaging in a certain amount of pedantry, knowing the Latin word is essential to an accurate reading of the passage. The word used in the text, *liberam*, does not mean "freedwoman," that is to say, an enslaved woman who has been released from bondage. Had Magdalena or her counsel intended the former, they would have used a word such as *libertina* or *manumissa*. The word used unambiguously means "free woman." Written this way, the passage both denied that Magdalena had ever been a slave while at the same time hinting that even if Magdalena had been a slave, his assent to the marriage freed her.

To sum up, almost everyone present at the marriage of Magdalena Coline and Johan Petre in August of 1399 would have considered her free status to be a settled matter. As a matter of positive law, Peire had tacitly manumitted her by assigning her a dowry. Phrases inserted in the act by the notary indicate that he took it for granted that the dowry was effectively a manumission. All who heard the use of the word "pedicequa" rather than "sclava" would have taken that as a sign that Magdalena was a dependent but free housemaid. But even though Magdalena acquired a husband, she had not acquired a formal contract of manumission. She did not have a legal instrument that she could file away and brandish before anyone who might question her condition. Seven years later, as Peire prepared his countersuit against Hugonin and Magdalena, he was able to say with a straight face that Magdalena had never been manumitted.

Had anyone pointed to the existence of the dowry, of course, Peire might have found himself on shaky grounds. Here, things get interesting. At the very top of Magdalena's dowry, in the blank space that had been left before the opening lines of the contract, a notation indicates that at some later date, the notary Peire Calvin made a full copy of the dowry. He did so in a form known to local historians as an *extenso*, that is, an extended version of the act. The making of an extenso, though common enough, was not routine. It is not implausible to suggest that during the first trial, Magdalena's lawyer had investigated the matter of her dowry in order to determine the conditions under which she had been married and asked Peire Calvin to ferret out the act.

If so, it is remarkable that Magdalena and her lawyer never chose to enter the dowry act in court as evidence for her free status. And even though it means erecting another hypothesis on an already shaky foundation, it is worth considering why that might have been the case. The answer is obvious. Any use of the dowry contract to argue for Magdalena's free status would make sense only if she and her lawyer were prepared to admit that she had in fact been previously enslaved. But such an admission would have exposed her to legal peril arising from the tangled skein of arguments into which Peire and his lawyer had inexorably drawn her. According to Roman law, as we shall see in chapter 11, freed slaves were duty bound to honor their patrons. Among other things, this duty normally prevented freed slaves from acting against their patrons in court. This is exactly what Magdalena had done. It was exceedingly perilous for her to launch any argument that would require her to acknowledge her former status as a slave.

Manumission and Marriage

How common was it for an enslaved woman to acquire a tacit manumission via marriage to a free man? The question has a bearing on the means by which women undertook the passage from slavery to freedom.[20] Some women acquired free status through contracts of manumission or testamentary manumissions. An unknown proportion of them, however, did so via the tacit manumission that came with marriage to a free man, obviating any need for a formal contract. It is exceedingly unusual, admittedly, to find a dowry act in which a master provided a dowry for his former slave woman. In the archives of Marseille, Magdalena's dowry is a rare exception. As it happens, nowhere in the act is there any mention of her enslaved condition. Even if other such acts existed, in other words, we would not easily be able to recognize what was going on.

But even though the manner of the passage is hard to follow, it is still possible to get a sense of the population of formerly enslaved women who had

114   CHAPTER 7

TABLE 1. Names given to enslaved women in Marseille, 1248–1491. Seventeen additional names appear only once.

Name	Frequency
Catherina	29
Lucia	16
Maria	13
Marguerita	10
Magdalena	8
Cristina, Christiana	7
Elena, Erena	7
Aissa	4
Anna	4
Cali	4
Cita, Sita	3
Atzona	2
Fatima	2
Johannina	2
Marta	2

Source: Marseille slave database.

dissolved into the free population. The archival visibility of a small number of formerly enslaved women arises because some of them, as Steven Epstein and many others have discussed, bore distinctive names. Though references to the condition of slavery disappear, those distinctive names remain.[21]

From slave sales, we can assemble a list of the names characteristically given to female slaves in Marseille (table 1). Catherina, Lucia, Maria, Marguerita, and Magdalena are among the most common. Women of Greek origin often kept their names and appear in records with distinctive names such as Elena or Helena and Theodora. Some of these names, of course, were also given to Provençal girls, which means they can't be used for identifying freedwomen. The given name "Catherina," for example, was especially common in Provence, and "Maria," although less common, was nonetheless a local name. But some names associated with enslaved women were rarely given to Provençal girls, to judge by dowry contracts. In records from the decades around 1350, before the acceleration in slaving practices that took off in the last quarter of the fourteenth century, the names Lucia, Magdalena, and Marta, and the Greek names Elena and Theodora, are rare or absent. Whenever we encounter free women bearing these names, we can legitimately entertain the possibility that they had arrived in the city as slaves.

MAGDALENA GETS MARRIED 115

In Magdalena's day, one of the most interesting candidates was a woman named Elena, the wife of Nicolau Yscla, a weaver. The couple ran a commercial practice involving almonds, wool, salted sardines, and probably other bulk merchandise of a similar nature.[22] Between 1388 and 1403, Elena appeared at court on several occasions, pursuing overdue debts and in turn being pursued by her own creditors.[23] In 1395, her husband went bankrupt, and Elena hired procurators to retrieve her dowry from his estate.[24]

"Elena" is one of the ambiguous names, for a single dowry from the year 1349 features a woman bearing the name. Though she may have been one of the Greek women who arrived as slaves in the city in the first half of the fourteenth century, it's also possible that she was a local woman.[25] With the name "Magdalena," however, there is no ambiguity. Across a sample consisting of 300 dowry acts and more than 6,300 other notarial acts from the years 1337 to 1362, there is not a single reference to a woman named Magdalena. It is exceedingly likely, therefore, that all women named "Magdalena" found in records from later decades were current or former slaves.

In a sample of archival sources consulted from 1380 to 1465, I have come across twenty sightings of women named "Magdalena" (table 2).[26] Several of these point to the same individual. Since most lack the clues needed to link records with confidence, it is difficult to say how many unique individuals there may have been, although it is likely that the number was fifteen or fewer. Seven were identified in at least one record as having been enslaved, three of whom were manumitted. Eight appear only as free actors.

The collective experiences of women named Magdalena attest to the role that marriage played in the manumission and assimilation of former slaves. Seven of the nine women appear as wives. Though the observation is partly tautologous, it is nonetheless worth pointing out that some of the married women show signs of having entered society as legal actors and members of civic and religious communities. Magdalena Ruffe, for example, had become a landowner. The Magdalena who married the peasant Bertomieu de Sosquiers in 1412 provided her own dowry of 20 l. She went about the task of paying the dowry to her new husband at a leisurely pace, taking just over a year to complete the transaction. It is faintly possible that this woman is Magdalena Coline, now on to her third husband. If so, one can theorize that because her capital was tied up in her moneylending business, it took time to liquidate enough assets to pay the dowry.

One of the most interesting sightings is that of Magdalena, the wife of Guilhem Frayre, whom we catch in the act of drawing up her last will and testament. The burial preferences and pious legacies she selected were typical for people of the era. She wished to be buried next to the grave of her first husband and requested that her body be carried to the cemetery of Saint-Martin

TABLE 2. Women named "Magdalena" appearing in a sample of records from Marseille, 1382–1465

Name	Inferred Status	Date	Context	Source
1. Magdalena	Enslaved	5 February 1382	In this act of sale, Magdalena, described as being from Tartary, is being sold by Julian de Casaulx to Isnart Bonafos, a slave broker.	ADBR 351 E 52, fol. 263v
2. Magdalena	Enslaved	12 June 1388	In this act of sale, the enslaved Magdalena is being sold by Bernat Martin to Jacme Trelhe.	BnF NAL 1325, p. 133
3. Magdalena Coline, enslaved by Peire Huguet; married to Johan Petre (1399–1401); married to Hugonin de lo Chorges (1401–?)	Enslaved, then freedwoman	1387–1408	Appears indirectly and directly in multiple contexts between these dates.	ADBR 3 B 858, 3 B 861
4a. Magdalena	Enslaved	29 April 1390	In this act of sale, the enslaved Magdalena, 30 years old and described as Ruthenian, is being sold by a merchant from Savona to Mathinet Ruffi, a merchant of Marseille.	ADBR 355 E 45, fol. 15r-v; duplicate 355 E 298, fols. 68r-69v
4b. Magdalena Ruffe	Freedwoman	7 October 1405	Magdalena, the wife of Lois Laurens, acknowledges owning a plot of land. The linkage with 4a is suggested by her surname, since it was not uncommon for newly manumitted slaves to be given their former masters' surnames.	ADBR 351 E 137, fol. 51r
4c. Madalena, married to Lois [surname blank]	Freedwoman	1409	Madalena paid a fine of 50 s. for having committed adultery with a vagabond, Johan de Scorcia. It is probable though not certain that she is the same as the wife of Lois Laurens in 1405 (4b, above).	ADBR B 1944, fol. 8v
5a. Magdalena	Freedwoman	1 January 1395	Magdalena is freed by testamentary manumission by Julian de Casaulx.	BnF NAL 1325, p. 166
5b. Magdalena	Freedwoman	23 September 1395	Magdalena receives a 50-florin legacy from Julian de Casaulx. In the act, she is described as the "slave (serva)" of Julian, although she had already been manumitted.	BnF NAL 1347, fol. 50v
6a. Magdalena	Enslaved	26 August 1411	Magdalena, formerly known as Avvegaxia (Latin for Abkhazia, a region in the Caucuses), appears in an act of sale. At some earlier point in time, she had been sold to a Marseille slave broker by a Venetian merchant. In the notarial register, this act of sale immediately precedes the act identified in 6b.	ADBR 351 E 706, fols. 84v-85v

6b. Magdalena, enslaved, abducted by the Aragonese	Enslaved	4 October 1424	Magdalena had been seized by the Catalans during the sack of Marseille in 1423, and Johan Maximi is taking steps to recover her by naming procurators to act for him.	ADBR 351 E 706, fols. 83r-84r
7. Magdalena, wife of Bertomieu de Sosquiers, urban peasant	Freedwoman	30 November 1413	Her husband acknowledges receipt of a dowry of 20 l., as promised in a dowry act from 26 November 1412.	ADBR 351 E 108, fol. 34v
8. Magdalena, wife of Guilhem Frayre	Freedwoman	26 March 1414	Magdalena is drawing up her last will and testament. She had previously been married to Mitrius Vermelhi.	ADBR 355 E 67, fol. 230r-v
9a. Magdalena, wife of Andrea Augier	Freedwoman	10 October 1424	Testimony offered by three witnesses concerns items that had been stolen from Magdalena's house.	ADBR 3 B 158, fols. 21v-22r
9b. Magdalena, wife of Andrea Augier	Freedwoman	1424–25	A settlement arising from the purchase of a house belonging to Magdalena and her husband by Jacme Clarian of the village of Allauch.	ADBR 351 E 272, fols. 117v-118r
10. Magdalena, wife of Peire Johan	Freedwoman	30 October 1424	Peire, gratefully acknowledging the services provided to him by his wife Magdalena, donates all his goods to her after his death, reserving some funds to pay for pious legacies. This unusual act, equivalent to a last will and testament, was of a type also used to make grants to concubines.	ADBR 351 E 315, fol. 3v
11. Magdalena of Septèmes	Freedwoman	19 January 1425	She was arrested for failure to pay a debt, having no goods that could be seized in compensation.	ADBR 3 B 158, fol. 104v
12. Magdalena, wife of Johan Juvenis, laborer	Freedwoman	20 August 1425	Jacme de Sarda, a laborer from Gardannes, owed Magdalena 12 florins arising from a loan; the debt is now paid. He is described as Magdalena's brother.	ADBR 351 E 289, fol. 107v
13. Magdalena, wife of a Spaniard named Johan de Villemonte	Freedwoman	27 July 1434	Magdalena was named the heir of Maria, the wife of Gilh de Portugalhi, for services rendered. One of the executors of Maria's estate, Peire de Barreria, had once brokered a slave sale.	ADBR 355 E 97, fols. 46r-47r
14. Magdalena Limosine, a sex worker	Freedwoman	1441	Magdalena, described as a femina falhita or "fallen woman," was fined twice by the criminal court.	ADBR B 1949, fols. 28v and 31r
15. Magdalena, enslaved	Enslaved	4 April 1465	Magdalena, described as "black," is being sold by a seaman of Marseille named Dominic Bertoli to Esteve Prior, a merchant of Nice	ADBR 355 E 112, fol. 1r

accompanied by four candles each weighing a quarter of a pound. A sung mass in her memory was delivered on the evening of her death, and she added provisions for thirty additional masses. She also left 10 l. to the religious confraternity to which she belonged, the "Lumenaria of the Body of Jesus Christ." All the rest of her possessions she left to her husband and his heirs. The testament shows no great wealth but demonstrates how a formerly enslaved woman, if that indeed is what she was, could enter society by way of marriage and civic piety.

This survey of women named Magdalena also has elements that are distinctly grimmer. In 1409, Madalena, the wife of a man known only as "Lois" (probably Lois Laurens), appeared before the treasurer to pay a fine of 50 s. for having had sex with a vagabond. The dry and lifeless entry in the accounts reveals nothing of the context. If this Madalena is indeed identical to the Magdalena from *Rossia*, purchased by a merchant in 1390, which is exceedingly probable though not certain, she would have been middle-aged at the time of her arrest for adultery. It is likely that she had been married and manumitted a few years before 1405, when she shows up as the owner of a plot of land. In 1409, she had the financial wherewithal to pay the fine, suggesting a degree of financial solvency. What gives one pause is the status of her sex partner. Was the sex consensual? If so, what explains the attraction? Alternatively, had she been raped? If so, it is possible that her former status, with the stigma of licentiousness often associated with slavery, prompted the court to view the event as adultery rather than rape.

Without minimizing these grim notes, social integration via marriage was the more typical pathway. In light of this, Magdalena Coline's marriage in 1399 was thoroughly in keeping with the standards and mores of the day. Having done her time in servitude, she was manumitted through the simple expedient of marriage. The testamentary manumissions explored in chapter 2 give us an inkling of the sense of duty that some former masters may have felt toward their enslaved housemaids, though we need to bear in mind the formulaic nature of these expressions of pious charity. The sense of duty could be prompted either by conscience, as suggested by the testamentary manumissions, or by the insistent prodding of friends and neighbors, which is almost certainly the context that best describes how Magdalena got married.

Forgetting

One of the most striking features of the acts concerning married women named Magdalena is located not in what they say but what they do not say. Not once do they indicate that the actor had formerly been a slave. On some level, the reticence is regrettable, since it forces us to engage in speculation. But on a different level, the reticence, if that is indeed what it was, is significant in its own right. It tells us how memory of the condition of slavery was forgotten.

References to former slaves do appear from time to time. A vivid instance is found in a 1384 act by means of which a Marseille stonemason named Jacme Nigri donated a house to his wife, Theodora, in the event that she should outlive him. No particular reason was given for the donation, other than his affection for her and the gratitude he felt toward her for the many services she had freely provided to him.[27] To the Provençal ear at the time, the name "Theodora," being Greek in origin, would have seemed distinctly foreign. The act itself tells us nothing about her. Yet it turns out that Theodora's former condition had not been entirely forgotten.

Starting in the later fourteenth century, notaries in Provence found it useful or fashionable to attach tables of contents to their registers. Once the register for the year was complete, they took a separate quire of paper, drafted brief rubrics summarizing each of the acts, and then listed the corresponding folios. Using the Latin preposition *pro*, meaning "for" or "on behalf of," the rubrics typically designated the beneficiary of the contract, such as a creditor in the case of a loan or the purchaser of a house. Theodora, in this case, was the beneficiary of this particular contract. In the act of drafting the rubric, the notary added a detail that was not present in the act itself (figure 7). For reasons known only to himself, he wrote the rubric in this way: "For Theodora, formerly a slave, fol. 145."

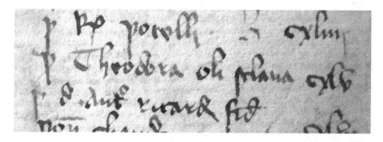

FIGURE 7. "For Theodora, formerly a slave." *Source:* ADBR 351 E 39.

As this indicates, when drafting legal contracts, notaries were inclined to enter information about condition only in situations where it was pertinent to the matter at hand. In the vast majority of acts involving former slaves, their condition was legally irrelevant, whence the absence of any references. An exception that tests the rule comes from 1423, where we find one of the rare references to a woman's prior enslaved condition. The act, a contract of procuration, describes a marriage that had taken place between Johan Blanc, a shoemaker, and the recently deceased Marta, described as the former slave of two brothers, Franses and Esteve de Poncilionis.[28] Some years earlier, the two brothers had given Marta in marriage to Johan and had provided her with a respectable dowry of 60 florins. The need to mention her former condition arose because a clause attached to the dowry held that if Marta should die without issue, the dowry would revert to the two brothers. They were now taking steps to make good on that claim.

The former status of Theodora appeared in the table of contents, on this theory, because the table had no legal relevance. It was a convenience for the notary himself, and was unlikely to have been seen or used by anyone except the notary himself and his apprentices and successors. The reference to her condition may have formed part of some mnemonic, a device that helped him remember the circumstances of the act, but it also could well have been a casual reference about which he didn't think twice.

A former condition of enslavement became irrelevant in the wake of a marriage or a manumission and therefore was forgotten to the law. But as the case of Theodora indicates, memory could linger on. This possibility of lingering memory raises an important question. When enslaved women were assimilated via marriage, how long did the memory of their former condition linger in the minds of contemporaries? Did some people, in the spirit of charity, work to forget? Did others, in the spirit of malevolence, cling to the memory? Only faint clues speaking to any of this survive in the record, but it is worth pausing to consider the fragments that do.

The most important observation to be made is that the condition of enslavement did not enter the lexicon of insult in medieval Marseille. The lexicon of insult comprised a number of expressions, most of which were local expressions derived from the culture of insult widely shared across Europe at the time. Since insults were considered verbal assaults, they were prosecuted like other kinds of assaults.[29] One of the delightful qualities of the records in Marseille is that, in the spirit of accuracy, many notaries chose to write the insult in the local vernacular rather than translating it into Latin. As a result, we have a rich sense of the Occitan words that people hurled at one another, including a good many suggesting that the victims were persons of uncertain parentage. This is not the place to undertake a complete accounting of the insults. The relevant thing is that among the hundreds of insults found in Marseille's records, only one refers to the condition of enslavement. It was far worse, evidently, to be called the son of a whore than the son of a slave.

The single exception, as it happens, is exceedingly interesting. It appears in one of the registers of the notary Guilhem Barban. One day, in July of 1393, Guilhem made several short entries arising from a criminal case being heard before the court. A woman named Peyroneta de Stela accused Laureta, the wife of Lois Chaupin, of having said the following words to her: "Get lost, captive, since if it were not for me, you would be a whore."[30] In the next accusation, Peyroneta then accused Maria, a slave in the Chaupin household, of having called her "a whore of the Catalans." This was immediately followed by a third denunciation against a woman named Jaumona Ausier.[31]

MAGDALENA GETS MARRIED   121

Though the context is obscure in the extreme, here is a plausible scenario, one that hinges on the fact that in the Crown of Aragon, slaves were often called "captives," rendered as *caytieva* in eastern Occitan. Some years earlier, Catalan merchants had sold the enslaved Peyroneta to Lois Chaupin, a situation that led Laureta to suggest that she had "saved" Peyroneta from the brothel. At some point, Peyroneta married and acquired both the surname "de Stela" and her freedom, but the memory of her servitude lingered on, at least in the Chaupin household. Especially noteworthy was the insult delivered by Maria, the woman who had replaced Peyroneta as the enslaved maidservant in the Chaupin household, for she called Peyroneta "a whore of the Catalans." This insult carries more than a hint of the expectation that enslaved women purchased from Catalans were normally used as sex slaves.[32]

However striking, this incident is distinguished by its singularity. For the most part, the Magdalenas, the Elenas, and the many untraceable Catherinas and Marias and so on all disappeared without leaving any trace apart from the distinctive names borne by some of them. What this suggests is that in August of 1399, most of the people in the neighborhood of the Lansaria, or at least those who were disposed to view their fellow human beings with charity, would have launched into the process of forgetting Magdalena's origins.

On the morning of the 30th of August 1399, it is easy to imagine that Johan and his new bride were equally bent on forgetting—on Magdalena's side, perhaps desperately so. The forgetting may have come easily for Johan, for as a recent immigrant, he would have had limited experience with Magdalena as a slave. In the normal course of events, Magdalena might have dissolved invisibly into the free population. Catching a glimpse of her in a later act, we might never know that Magdalena the moneylender, wife of Johan Petre, had once been enslaved to Peire Huguet.

But fate had yet another cruel blow in store for her. Two years after the marriage, Johan was dead. The details and the dating are unclear in the extreme, since we pull them from a close and speculative reading of a claim made by Peire years later, in 1406. We shall have an occasion to visit this argument soon. What we do know is that the plague, after a period of quiescence lasting a few decades, had broken out again. A riveting passage in a court case involving the barber-surgeon Nicolau de Sala offers piercing insights into the devastations wrought by plague as well as insights into the dating. In July of 1402, the judge of the court of first appeals issued a ruling against Nicolau, for the latter had failed to pursue an appeal in a timely manner, having allowed six months to elapse without action.[33] When Nicolau finally appeared in court, in August of 1402, he explained that the delay had been occasioned by the plague which "was now ravaging the city" and had brought about the death of his daughter. As he went on to explain, "every father is duty-bound to serve his children in sickness and in death." For this reason, he had neglected his legal case and begged to be excused. It was a poignant moment, one of the few instances where we catch a glimpse of the human dimension of this otherwise disagreeable and cantankerous man. We can't be sure that Johan Petre too died of plague, but its presence in the city in 1401–1402 suggests a very likely cause.

The bed and the clothing that the newly widowed Magdalena had received in dowry, at least nominally, were still hers. She still had a roof over her head. But with the death of her husband, she abruptly entered a state of considerable legal ambiguity, under the authority of someone who may have been bullied into marrying her in the first place and was never fully persuaded that the marriage had freed her. She had probably lost the two women who may have provided some cover, namely, Peire's mother, Gassenda, and his first wife, Bertomieua. Worst of all, she had lost her husband, a key element in the system of signs by which she was known to be free.

8

Magdalena the Moneylender

IN THE MANY LEGAL ARGUMENTS made by Magdalena Coline and Peire Huguet and their lawyers over the course of two years, there was precious little they ever agreed upon—except, that is, for one thing. Both parties agreed that Magdalena lent money. Amid the realms of uncertainty occasioned by the documents in the case, this is one of the things we can be sure about.

In August of 1406, the shoemaker Hugonin de lo Chorges appeared before one of Marseille's lesser courts, claiming that his wife, Magdalena Coline, had lent money to Peire Huguet on two separate occasions a "long time ago." It couldn't have been all that long ago, in fact. Among other things, it is hard to imagine Peire borrowing money from his enslaved housemaid before her tacit manumission in August 1399. The overall sum claimed by Hugonin, 6 florins, was not insubstantial, equivalent to a month or two of wages for an unskilled laborer. When Hugonin took Magdalena to wife, shortly after Johan Petre's death late in the year 1401, the supposed debt was still unpaid. The right to claim it came to Hugonin because Magdalena, as she compiled the dowry for her new husband, included the credit among her assets. Hugonin claimed that Peire was asked repeatedly to repay the debt but to no avail. We cannot be certain that the debt attributed to Peire was genuine, of course, but it is likely the claim held at least a germ of truth. It would be strange indeed if Magdalena had invented the whole thing, pursuing the fantasy so far as to deceive her own husband.

For his part, Peire was even more insistent on Magdalena's status as a lender of money. In the first phase of the dispute, one of his most important arguments, first mentioned in the unformed plea he lodged in August of 1406, hinged on the following claim:

> He said that Magdalena, while still a slave woman in the possession of Peire Huguet, among other things that she had stolen from his house, took 30 florins in order to make loans to various people in the city, with Peire unaware and ignorant of what was happening, despite the fact that she

124   CHAPTER 8

knew, or must have known, that those 30 florins and whatever profit that could be made from them, if any, pertained to the said Peire by his rights as her master.[1]

A few weeks later, his astute lawyer, Johan de Ysia, massaged the rambling complaints lodged by Peire at the outset of the countersuit into a reasonably coherent set of legal claims. During the interval, the size of the capital supposedly deployed by Magdalena swelled from 30 to 50 florins. Though this touches on matters considered more closely in chapter 10, it is worth considering the articles of proof presented by Johan de Ysia here because several of them provide crucial insights into Magdalena's life as a moneylender:

First, he intends to prove that the said Magdalena was a slave woman of the said Peire Huguet for many years. He held and possessed her as a slave for many years, and rumor of this has worked all across the city of Marseille among neighbors and people in the know.

Next, he intends to prove that Magdalena, while living in Peire Huguet's house, him being unaware and ignorant of what was happening, lent to many and various persons sums of money amounting to 50 florins and more. Word of this circulates . . .

Next, he intends to prove that Magdalena, after having taken her first husband in marriage, lived for two years in the house of Peire Huguet, at his expense. During those two years, Magdalena consumed food provisions provided by Peire Huguet to the amount of 20 florins in value. Word of this circulates . . .

Next, he intends to prove that the food provisions commonly consumed by a single person comes to 10 florins per year.

Next, he intends to prove that Magdalena promised to pay Peire for the food provisions through the work that she did during those two years, [labor which she instead] appropriated to herself.

Next, he intends to prove that whatever a slave man or slave woman acquires while in servitude, she acquires for the master to whom she is enslaved. Word of this circulates . . .

Next, he intends to prove that each and every claim made is public knowledge.[2]

Johan de Ysia's claims allow us to assemble a picture of Magdalena's early career as a moneylender, bearing in mind that details may have been twisted to suit the argument. Magdalena had begun lending money while she was still enslaved, in the years before her marriage to Johan Petre. Following her first marriage, Magdalena and her husband remained in Peire's house and continued to dine at Peire's table. Johan Petre may not have needed to pay for his food and drink; provisions for his board may have been included in the contract governing the labor he provided in Peire's shipyard. But Magdalena's food and drink was another matter. From the moment of her marriage, she ceased working as a housemaid under orders. Instead, "having appropriated her labor to herself," she supposedly promised to compensate Peire for her board. Implied, though not stated, is that the wherewithal to pay was going to come from the revenue generated by her moneylending business.

How could this possibly have happened? When Magdalena came to the city in the year 1388, she lacked resources of any kind other than the education she may have acquired from her parents, the street-smarts learned during her period of servitude to the admiral of Sicily, and any skills she had gained as a domestic worker. Within a decade of her arrival in Marseille, she had launched herself into the career of moneylending. "Everyone talks about this," as Peire's lawyer put it. It was an astonishing transformation.

A host of questions spring to mind. By what means had she assembled the necessary capital—as much as 50 florins, if Peire's lawyer is to be believed? Who, if anyone, helped her undergo this transformation? What does it even mean to be a moneylender—no less, a female moneylender—in a city in Provence around the year 1400?

Magdalena's activity as a moneylender was instrumental to her pursuit of freedom. The trade gave her the financial assets she needed to attract the attention of a respectable shoemaker and marry him, the dramatic event that allowed her to move out of Peire's house in 1401 or shortly after and escape his sphere of domination. More important, the connections with associates and clients that she assembled over the years provided her with something even more valuable. She acquired social capital, a type of human asset consisting of the family, friends, and others who have access to their own resources and are willing to help out when needed.

Money and Credit

The world of later medieval Europe was suffused with the concept of money. It is difficult to exaggerate this claim. Money-thought permeated the consciousness of actors in a multitude of settings ranging from domains where we might expect to find it, such as keeping accounts for shops, households, municipal offices, royal courts, and commercial firms, to domains where such thought might seem less relevant, such as justice and devotional practices. The concept of money, as a result, is ubiquitous in the massive bulk of Provençal archival material, suffusing thought and action in virtually every domain of activity visible in the records. It permeates notarial contracts, the vast majority of which concern, in some form, directly or distantly, the movement of money.

The bulk of civil litigation also involved money in some form, given how the injuries described in almost every claim had to be expressed in monetary terms for them to be comprehensible to the law. At first blush, the records of sentences issued by criminal courts may appear to involve behavior, such as insults and violations of municipal ordinances, that do not concern money. Even so, apart from a very few blood sanctions and public humiliations, the penalties assigned were almost always expressed in monetary terms. Great rent registers recorded rents owed and payments received, and the account books of hospitals and private households, in similar fashion, recorded income and expenses in minute detail.

If one were to read only sources such as these, the impression one would receive is that of a world not just defined but obsessed by money. It can be something of a relief, therefore, to turn to a different body of sources such as statutes, ordinances, and council deliberations, for money is less omnipresent here. Even so, it is never far from the scene. Statutes and ordinances, for example, occasionally set penalties defined in monetary terms, such as the penalty recommended for anyone inconsiderate enough to allow a pig to run free in the city of Marseille, defined whimsically as a single *obol* to be paid for each of the pig's feet.[3]

Money was important because it was the conceptual tool used to track imbalances in human relations. As Joel Kaye has argued, medieval society was deeply concerned about balance, or rather the imbalances that continually troubled social harmony.[4] Restoring equilibrium was therefore viewed as the duty of those who were responsible for the maintenance of good order. Imbalance took many forms, only some of which involved money in some way. But regardless of the medium, money was understood as one of the principal metaphors for describing how an imbalance could be corrected by means of a flow. In practical terms, this meant converting non-fungible injuries into injuries that could be expressed in monetary terms. Such habits of thought are vividly displayed in the law codes and legal habits of Europe in the early Middle Ages which list, sometimes in minute detail, the sums to be paid for injuries ranging from homicide to cutting off a little finger. The purpose of such payments was to restore the equilibrium that had been upset by the injury. Gifts to God, the saints, and the church worked to restore the imbalance generated by original sin. All these transactions were defined in monetary terms.

By the later Middle Ages, thanks to the records that become available, it is possible to acquire an intimate sense of how people actually used money. One thing that becomes clear is that in this society, as in our own, much of the money in circulation never materialized in a form that you could put in your pocket. It existed instead in the form of symbols marked on paper or parchment or, alternatively, in memories and habits of value assessment. This system did include some tangible money, which took the form of coins made of gold, silver, and various base metals. This kind of money was essential for the operations of the system as a whole; among other things, it provided a baseline for determining how value was construed.

Unlike our own world, though, there was never enough money available in liquid form. Persistent debt, as a result, was ubiquitous, not because people lacked wealth, but because they lacked coin. Imagine a power grid producing a fraction of the electricity needed to power a city. Rolling blackouts afflict most of the neighborhoods most of the time. When the power comes back on in your neighborhood, you use it to complete the tasks that have piled up. Being mindful that it will soon turn off again, you prioritize the important ones first. Debts, in similar fashion, could linger for months or years in the dark because debtors lacked liquidity. When cash came in, the urgent debts were paid off first. When pressed, debtors lacking the necessary cash could devise workarounds, such as transferring a credit owed by someone else or settling debts through payments in kind. Because money was in short supply, it was aggressively in demand. This is why it cost so much to gain access to coin. This is why interest rates in medieval Europe were so high, and why moneylending was such an essential and profitable business. In such an economy, the people who lent coin performed a hugely important service. Through their actions, they facilitated the workings of an invisible hand that constantly moved money around the circuit so that it could reach the places where it was most in demand.

Despite the important function played by moneylenders, moneylending was not an occupation in Marseille. People who appear in the city's notarial and administrative acts are routinely identified by the name of the occupation with which they were most commonly associated. We have already run across a number of these professional labels—shipwright, housemaid, notary, barber-surgeon, and so on—and there were dozens more. But nowhere in the city's records will you find a person identified as a "moneylender" (e.g., *fenerator*) or even a "Lombard" or a "Cahorsin," words that appear elsewhere in Europe as names for moneylenders. The closest label is "moneychanger" (*cambiator*), someone who took a fee for converting foreign coin into local coin and vice versa. Yet the two practices are different. Moneychangers sometimes lent money, but so did many other people, ranging from merchants to parish priests. Many of the moneylenders in Marseille and elsewhere in Provence were Jewish, but even those Jews most deeply involved in lending money were never called "moneylenders."

In the landscape of practice where an occupation is not actually an occupation and anyone can participate, everyone's degree of involvement can be located somewhere on a spectrum running from "deeply involved" to "very occasional." In medieval Marseille, those most deeply involved with money-lending have left abundant traces of their activity in notarized loan contracts, the single most common type of notarial contract from the era. In Magdalena's day, one such was Julian de Casaulx. We have already met Julian, since on his deathbed in 1395, he had freed one of Magdalena's namesakes. His activities are particularly easy to trace because, unusually among his peers, Julian commissioned the distinguished notary Laurens Aycart to maintain a casebook composed solely of the acts generated by Julian during the last two decades of his life, between 1378 and 1394.[5] Julian was one of dozens of creditors whose names crop up repeatedly in the sea of notarial documentation. Though Jewish lenders are prominent in notarial records, the majority of these lenders, like Julian, were Christian.

Loans secured by means of a notarized contract helped moneylenders gain access to the enforcement available through the law courts should a debt fall into arrears. But not all loans were secured in this way. Shopkeepers routinely issued shop credit, using their cartularies to list the debts owed to them. Many loans were secured by nothing other than word of mouth, where the security was generated by the custom of transacting all such loans in the presence of friends and neighbors. The formulaic phrases recited on these occasions amounted to a liturgy governing the process whereby a loan was offered and accepted. Access to the law was granted to all creditors, regardless of the device used to record or secure a debt. Everyone could expect the courts of law to assist with the task of enforcing payment of a debt owed. Possession of a notarial instrument might simplify the process, but even hand-loans secured only by word of mouth were defended by the courts as long as the creditor could find two witnesses willing to attest to the existence of the debt.

One of the most important qualities of debt is that it can serve the interests of power. In the vast literature on the history of credit and debt, typified here by the work of the anthropologist David Graeber, the observation is something of a banality, since it is taken for granted that debt is a device for coercing labor.[6] Such interpretations are funneled through an image of society divided into haves and have-nots. But although Graeber's two-tier model works when it comes to explaining the forms of coercion in modern society, it is far less suitable when it comes to explaining what his book is nominally about, namely, how credit and debt operated in earlier eras. The two-tier model is an especially inapt way to characterize the complex webs of credit and debt that shaped local society in medieval Europe. In this web, credit was not monopolized by a dominant class. Even housemaids and freedwomen could get into the business. In such a world, the withdrawal of credit may have been a fiscal transaction, but it was simultaneously a moral sanction.

The Neighborhood Pawnbroker

Many of the loans we encounter were secured neither by means of notarized contracts nor by entries in shop cartularies and the like. They were secured instead through pledges left as security, the system commonly known as pawnbroking.

Professional pawnbroking, when regulated by local officials, is visible to historical analysis. Not nearly as visible, however, are the activities undertaken by moneylenders who were located toward the "less involved" end of the spectrum. We catch a glimpse of unregulated, small-scale, neighborhood pawnbroking from time to time in judicial records and sources such as household account books. By way of example, let us consider several loans that appear in a register of household accounts kept by one of Magdalena's contemporaries, Laureta Bonaffazy.[7] Laureta's husband, Peyret, had died in October 1403, and Laureta was named as guardian for their three children. For the next few years, Laureta kept the books associated with her household's wine-making business, carefully recording all the revenues and expenses in her beautiful and evocative dialect of Occitan. When she remarried in 1407, a partial set of her accounts was recopied by a family friend and bound into the records of the court that processed the routine transfer of the guardianship out of Laureta's hands. Among the 174 expenses recorded during her first year of managing the estate, three involved transactions whereby Laureta paid to redeem items that Peyret had left in pledge for loans. Although these entries were not dated, they probably occurred in January, August, and September of 1404. Laureta was in some financial difficulty, and the spacing of these intervals suggests that every now and then, she was able to scrape together enough cash to redeem some treasured object.

> Item mays per rezeme i quolar d'arjent que era ha mans de Monon de Sion, i florin, v gros, ii quarts
>
> Item mays hay paguat a Berenguoya per i basinet que avya en guaye de mon marit, ii florins
>
> Item mays avem paguat a Floret lo causatier per i calssas que li devya Peyret de que avya en guaye i quoltel verat d'aryent, i florin, v gros, ii quarts

> *Next, to redeem a silver necklace which was in the hands of Monet de Sion, 1 florin, 5 gros, 2 quarter-gros*
>
> *Next, I paid Berenguoya for a basnet helmet which she took in pledge from my husband, 2 florins*
>
> *Next, I have paid Floret, the tailor, for a pair of breeches; Peyret owed him this, for which he had in pledge a silver knife, 1 florin, 5 gros, 2 quarter-gros*

The debts listed first and third are identical, suggesting that in both cases, Peyret had borrowed a single florin, a nice round sum, and had agreed to pay interest of 5 ½ gros, or 45 percent. The third entry arose from a shop credit, although in this case the tailor accepted a nice silver knife in pledge rather than relying solely on an entry written in his shop cartulary. The second entry is perhaps the most interesting, since it alerts us to the existence of a woman in the neighborhood, perhaps a friend or acquaintance, who was involved in the business of lending money on pledges. Since Peyret had died the previous October, these loans had been outstanding for some months. The silver knife, in particular, may have reposed in some corner of the tailor's workshop for a year or more. Given the fact that Peyret, not Laureta, had taken out the loans, it is even possible that she was alerted to the existence of the debts only when the creditors, having heard no news for a while, ventured delicate inquiries.

The existence of these loans is known to us only by the freakish survival of Laureta's account book. This raises two important questions. First, how common were such small-scale and unregulated neighborhood loans? Second, how can we learn more about them? A partial answer to the second query, which may bring us back to the first, springs from a suggestion above: pledges had to be stored, sometimes for long periods of time. For this reason, they show up in estate inventories from the period.[8] In such records, pledges take one of three forms. The first of these consists of entries recording the existence of items left in the house in exchange for loans. Such entries carefully identify the items in question and the names of the original owners, that is to say, the debtors. Occasionally, they list the amount owed. The second is much the same except that it goes the other way around, recording items belonging to the estate that were out in pledge at the time of the compilation of the inventory. In both cases, it is unclear how the compilers of inventories knew what to record. Though it is likely that people who lent money on a small scale committed the facts to memory, it is also possible that items in the house bore labels containing the necessary information. The larger the operation, the more likely it was that writing was involved.

Before turning to the third type of clue, let us consider what happened should a debtor fail to redeem a pledge. In similar cases handled by the courts, the creditor was expected to sell the item at auction, keep the principal and interest, and return anything over that amount to the debtor. But it seems unlikely that these rules applied to the informal pawnbroking practiced by the kind of people listed in Laureta's account book. Instead, one imagines that abandoned pledges were left to gather dust or absorbed into a household's array of usable things. Many inventories exhibit items found in rooms where they do not belong or are juxtaposed with completely unrelated items in random assemblages. To the extent that at least some of the out-of-place items were pledges that had arrived in the house via neighborhood lending and were slowly being re-absorbed among the living goods, inventories suggest that the scale of neighborhood lending via informal pawnbroking was sizable. This is the third type of clue.

Given the existence of the practice, it is easy to imagine how an individual like Berenguoya could have entered into the business of pawnbroking. Anyone with coin to spare, a reputation for honesty, and a place to store pledges for indefinite periods of time could easily enter into the practice on the "very occasional" side of the spectrum. In the absence of a banking system, people flush with cash for whatever reasons—a good year for the wine vintage, a substantial legacy, a profitable business—had no choice but to find a place to park their surplus wealth. There wasn't nearly enough coin available to make it possible to store wealth in that form. Numerous options presented themselves. One could brighten up the dining table with the purchase of jeweled goblets or silver spoons. One could purchase property or invest in some commercial venture. Toward the end of his life, Julian de Casaulx started mopping up ground rents. Sheets and tablecloths, woven from durable linen, made excellent investments. The point is that small people with surplus assets amounting to no more than a few dozen florins could do worse than occasionally lend money on the side. The fact that pledges were left meant that the risk was low, and the high interest rates of the day ensured that the profits were good.

Women Lend Money

In the city of Marseille in the later Middle Ages, women owned a not-insignificant portion of the available wealth. Inheritance customs, practiced across the county of Provence, ensured that daughters typically received a sizable portion of their parents' wealth, both in the form of a dowry and through inheritance. The wealth that daughters received from their parents or family, regardless of how it was received, was typically bundled into a dowry whenever they married or remarried. What this meant, in practice, is that the assets that they nominally owned fell under the control of their husbands or fathers-in-law. In certain circumstances, a dowry could come back into a woman's direct control, as in the circumstance we have already seen where Peire, the holder of his daughter-in-law's dowry, was verging on insolvency, and Hugoneta successfully sued him to recover the dowry. Such claims for dowries are surprisingly common; they constitute around 11 percent of the lawsuits found in Marseille's judicial archives.[9] In addition, a woman who outlived her husband was sometimes named life heir and/or given management of the estate as guardian for the couple's children. As a result of this, it is not uncommon to meet women, typically older women and widows, who were directly managing their assets.

As a class, women were not as wealthy as men. A variety of records from Marseille suggest that women owned or controlled 20–30 percent of the city's household wealth. To take the example provided by a rent register kept by the hospital of Saint-Jacques-de-Gallicia from these decades, 21 percent of the properties in the hands of individuals were owned by women.[10] In some admittedly rare cases, access to financial assets made it possible for women to go into business on their own. In Magdalena's day, one of the most renowned of these was a formidable businesswoman named Resens Cambale, who ran a shop under her own name.[11]

But Resens Cambale was unusual. Far more typical would have been the experience of women such as Laureta Bonaffazy. Laureta's husband, Peyret, was a member of one of the city's distinguished if decaying families, whose surname was known in Latin as *Bonifacii*. Peyret didn't have an occupation per se; he wasn't a shoemaker or a shipwright capable of earning an income. Instead, he operated a wine business. When Peyret died in October 1403, therefore, Laureta stepped in to manage the business.[12] Most of the family's income was derived from the wine produced on their farm, known as a *bastide*. The bastide also comprised a grove of filbert trees whose nuts were gathered in the fall and sold. Occasionally, Laureta's servants collected and sold firewood. In addition to this revenue from the land, the family collected an annual lease rent from a house in the city as well as two small ground rents. All told, Laureta's annual revenue during the three fiscal years of her management ranged from 93 to 100 florins, equivalent to perhaps $50,000 in today's currency.

Unfortunately for Laureta, money flowed out faster than it came in. She bought food for the household and clothing for herself and the children. She paid to repair a broken door hinge and to furnish the donkey with fodder, shoes, harness, and baskets for carting the grapes and firewood. She paid taxes and various fees for professional services. But above all, she periodically hired men and women to help with the many tasks associated with running a wine business, ranging from pruning and hoeing the vines and harvesting the grapes to the ugly task of scraping out the great barrels every fall. No one would have placed Laureta in the socio-professional category of lady merchant, but even so, she was involved in all the work of managing the estate. Importantly, Laureta was hardly unique. As we learn from the evidence of estate inventories and proceedings for guardianships, her situation would have been familiar to many women in Massiliote society at the time.

Across the three years of her administration, Laureta was barely scraping by. We see no evidence that she invested the profits from the wine business, no doubt because there were no profits to invest. But for other women, life was better, and the presence of surplus cash meant that they were placed in the fortunate position of figuring out where to hold it. For many, the solution lay in moneylending.[13] As Kathryn Reyerson has demonstrated for nearby Montpellier, women were recorded as lenders in 7.6 percent of a sample of 384 loans.[14] Sarah Ifft Decker has shown that Jewish women appear not infrequently as moneylenders in Catalan villages.[15] One of the interesting features of her work is that many of the women had living husbands, indicating that it was not necessary for a woman to be widowed in order to be an economic actor. In Marseille, we find much the same phenomenon. Records are replete with Jewish women who were active moneylenders.

Christian women are equally visible. One example shall serve for many. During the 1380s, one of Marseille's most prominent moneylenders was a woman named Auruola de Jerusalem, who had married into one of Marseille's most distinguished families.[16] Auruola was a businesswoman with a diverse portfolio. In addition to running a draper's shop, she speculated in real estate. Alongside these activities, Auruola made at least fifty loans between 1380 and 1389 and doubtless many more. Another nine debts in her favor were configured as sale credits, but a suspicious uniformity in the structure of these acts suggests that these, too, were voluntary loans. The loans ranged in value from 3 to 30 florins, typical of bridge loans or consumption loans. Several were nominally issued by her husband, Pons, but these contracts indicate that Pons was acting in his wife's name, using Auruola's personal money.[17]

Several features of the loan profile point to the fact that Auruola's lending had a charitable dimension. Ten loans were issued to widows, and the list of debtors includes several recent immigrants and a substantial number of peasants or unskilled laborers. Early in 1386, when other sources indicate the existence of a tight credit market, she launched what can only be described as a lending spree, issuing dozens of loans in the space of a few months. Only a quarter of the loans she issued were repaid within the assigned deadline, typically three months to one year. Thirteen were overdue by more than a year.[18] More than 20 percent provide no indication of having been repaid at all. Abundant records arising from legal proceedings for debts survive in Marseille's archives from the period in question, and in them we find numerous cases of creditors moving against their debtors. Nowhere in these records, however, do we find any actions initiated by Auruola, suggesting that she systematically declined to pursue unpaid loans.[19]

Initially, it seems peculiar to suggest that moneylending could be a virtue. Here, it is important to bear in mind that the familiar rhetoric of moneylending as an evil, a rhetoric that fills the text of papal bulls, Franciscan sermons, and other moralizing texts, is wholly at odds with the practice of moneylending on the ground. Such rhetoric consistently deceives the many historians who lack archival experience. In the neighborhood, moneylending was a charitable activity, and the women and men who lent money were respected members of society.

Magdalena Learns How

Magdalena did not lend money on the security of notarized loans. Among other things, she never figures as an actor in any of the thousands of loan contracts that survive in the city's archives from the era, nor does she appear in court records that describe the proceedings that arose from debt collection. This is what we should expect to find: the ambiguity of her legal condition, coupled with the small scale of her practice, would have made lending through notaries nearly unthinkable. All the clues point to the fact that Magdalena was a pawnbroker.

As noted above, the logic of the arguments made by Peire Huguet's lawyer indicate that Magdalena had already begun lending money before her marriage to Johan Petre. There is no reason to doubt this claim, and it is not one that Magdalena had any interest in contesting. As it happens, some positive evidence indicates that the claim was true. In April 1407, witnesses were interrogated by a notary of the court and asked to attest to the truth of the claims made by Peire's lawyer. One of them was a woman named Guillelmeta Romanete, who was asked to say what she knew about whether Magdalena had lent money to many and various persons. This is how she answered:

> On the second article, she said she knows little about the matter except to the extent that Magdalena lent nine gold florins to the witness's husband. Asked when this happened, she said that it was her impression that this happened at least nine years or so ago. There was also another time, around ten years ago. She doesn't know what pledges were left.[20]

Working back from the date of her deposition, Magdalena was already lending money in April of 1397, more than two years before her marriage.

How much can we rely on Guillelmeta's words here? She was almost certainly in a position to have direct knowledge of the matter. At the end of her deposition, Guillelmeta revealed that she was Peire's stepdaughter, for, as she explained to the notary, Peire had taken her mother as his wife. We don't know when Peire married her mother, Guillelmona, although if his first wife died shortly before Magdalena's marriage in August of 1399, as postulated above, then he could have remarried as early as 1400. Daughter Guillelmeta was already married by this point and probably living in the neighborhood of the Lansaria.

The dates are another matter. It is always wise to be careful about giving too much credence to the passage of time as described in witness testimony. In the later Middle Ages, folks didn't think about time, especially calendrical time, the way we think about it now, and they certainly didn't have access to the kinds of resources that make it easy for us to remember dates and events. But the inexactitude that characterizes almost all witness testimony about time works in favor of the idea that Magdalena was already lending money while still enslaved, for witnesses typically underestimated, rather than overestimated, the passage of time. To take one example among many, one of Peire's witnesses, testifying in April of 1407, declared that Magdalena had been captured at sea "fifteen or sixteen years ago." His guess was off by at least three years, since the events in question had taken place in December of 1387, nearly twenty years earlier.

How had an enslaved housemaid acquired the necessary capital? Peire, as we have seen, had an answer to this: she stole it. He intimated as much in his initial plea, in August 1406, where he claimed that she had filched 30 florins. Curiously, although his lawyer changed the sum to 50 florins, he said nothing about how she acquired it. So obviously there was disagreement among the two men.

An explanation for the lawyer's caution is suggested by the verbs Peire used to describe how Magdalena acquired the capital. At the outset of the trial, he was strangely reticent about deploying the suite of words that normally appear in court records whenever someone accused someone else of theft. Typical verbs, in such contexts, are *abstulit* or *furtavit* ("she stole . . ."), and these are sometimes accompanied by adverbs such as *furtive* or *secrete* (". . . and she did it furtively"). Peire's initial claim used the plain-vanilla verb *habuit*, "she had." His argument ran like this: "While serving as Peire Huguet's slave, among the other things she took from his house, she *had* 30 florins for lending to certain people in the city." Here and later in the first trial, the more theft-like word *extraxit* ("she took," "she removed") also makes an appearance, though this word hardly amounts to a full-throated accusation of thievery. We find the verb *extrare* in other suits from the period in contexts that are distinct from simple theft. By way of example, a recent widow, kicked out of her late husband's house by his unfeeling heirs, might take a few things from the house without their permission. The heirs would then accuse her of "extracting" the things. In such contexts, the word doesn't point to theft so much as "she took something from me under a false pretext and I will show that she was wrong to do so."

Five of Peire's witnesses, including Guillelmeta Romanete, confirmed that Magdalena was a moneylender:

> On the second claim, she said she knows little about the matter except that it is quite true that Magdalena lent 20 florins to her husband. Asked about the time, she said it was at least seven or eight years ago (*testimony of Gabriella Baussane*).
>
> On all of the claims, he agreed with everything that his wife just said (*testimony of Antoni Baussan, Gabriella's husband*).

On the second claim, he said he knows little about the matter except that he heard from Antoni Baussan that Magdalena had lent Antoni some money, though he doesn't remember the amount (*testimony of Nicolau d'Ays, butcher, Peire's brother-in-law*).

On all the claims, she said just what her son said (*testimony of Rayneria d'Ays, Nicolau's mother*).[21]

None of them paid the slightest heed to the suggestion that Peire was unaware of what was happening. This stands to reason. Pawnbroking required the lender to store pledges for indefinite periods of time. In businesses of any size, lenders used tags or kept ledgers providing descriptions of the items in pledge, the names of the owners, and the size of the loans. Failing that, as in cases where the lender was unable to read and write, they needed witnesses. Pawnbroking could not be done on the sly.

Furthermore, moneylending of any kind was impossible without a clientele and a reputation. How did Peire imagine that Magdalena, operating on her own and in the shadows, could have been able to get the word out to potential clients? Pawnbroking required debtors to hand over items typically worth considerably more than the size of the loan. What would induce someone to entrust a valuable garment or a silver knife to an enslaved housemaid in exchange for cash worth a third as much? If Magdalena had indeed been trying to lend money surreptitiously, as Peire claimed, potential clients would have noticed the secrecy and stayed away out of fear that she had done precisely what Peire had accused her of: stealing from her master.

Peire's claims of furtive lending and his hints of stolen capital, in other words, are hollow. The need to make this absurd claim was imposed by the legal quandary in which he and his lawyer found themselves. The point is this: according to Roman law, any slave can work on the side with the master's permission, and the profits of this labor formed the slave's *peculium*, capital that the enslaved person could subsequently use to purchase his or her freedom. The only way for Peire to claim that all the income derived from Magdalena's business belonged to him was to declare that he had not given his consent.

Peire's initial hesitation when it came to calling a theft a theft, and his lawyer's outright refusal to include the claim in the formal legal positions, is one of the levers we can use to pry open the mystery of how Magdalena was able to begin lending money in the first place. Use of the word *habuit* suggests that she "had" the money, and from this we can infer that the money was "had" from the hands of one of her mistresses, either Bertomieua, Peire's first wife, or Gassenda, Peire's mother. We can conjure a scenario in which Bertomieua herself engaged in small-scale neighborhood pawnbroking. A record from November 1397 provides a precious clue suggesting that this supposition may be true, for an unnamed wife of Peire Huguet, almost certainly Bertomieua, appeared in court to receive a tablecloth that had been seized from one of her debtors, a woman named Perrussella, in compensation for a small debt of 14 s., about half a florin.[22]

Let us run with the idea that Bertomieua was a small-scale pawnbroker and see where it takes us. Needing assistance with the work or perhaps motivated by a sense of charity and duty toward her enslaved housemaid, Bertomieua introduced Magdalena into the trade at some point in the 1390s, as soon as the latter's command of eastern Occitan was good enough. Magdalena could have assisted in several ways: greeting clients at the door, taking messages, minding the stock, running errands, and so on. It is even possible that she was taught to read and write in order to help manage labels and paperwork. Once Magdalena had gained experience, Bertomieua might have given her money to lend on her own, under the aegis of House Huguet, allowing her to keep some of the profits for her peculium. This neatly explains how Magdalena "had" the money.

The suggestion that Magdalena developed good relations with the women of Peire's household during the 1390s helps us make sense of a curious interlude in the first trial, an interlude involving Peire's late mother. As noted earlier, the first trial opened in August of 1406 and moved along briskly until the 12th of September, when the proceedings came to a sudden halt. The dispute resumed six months later, on Tuesday, the 8th of March. Curiously, it did not initially resume exactly where it had left off, in the court of Johan Raynaut. Instead, Peire appeared before the second of the two lesser courts in order to lodge a different claim. In it, he claimed that after the death of his lady mother, Gassenda, Magdalena "extracted" two garments belonging to her. One of them was a beautiful houppelande, made from a multi-colored fabric known as medley and coated, if the wording is correct, with a kind of varnish or wax to make it shine. The other was a cloak also made of medley. Each garment was worth 6 florins, perhaps $3,000 in today's currency. The final element of Peire's argument is that as co-heir to his lady mother, both garments pertained to him.[23]

This side-suit was soon abandoned and we learn about it only because the transcript got swept up into the bigger case. But Peire was not finished with his wild claims about thievery. A few weeks later, in April of 1407, he asked an ironsmith to testify to his claim that Magdalena had once taken a rod to the smithy in order to have it reworked into a turnspit. The smith was rather befuddled by this claim and so are we. What on earth would this prove?

Although Peire grumbled about Magdalena's thievery, he never made a serious attempt to prove any of his claims. It is possible that the aborted lawsuit in the second of the lesser courts, together with the idiotic claim about the rod taken to the smith, were just legal stunts. Both episodes make a great deal more sense if we assume that Peire was merely trying to plant the seed of the idea of theft in the judge's head. But even if this was the case, it is difficult to imagine that Peire's argument was entirely bereft of substance, at least where the garments are concerned. Although there are several possible scenarios, the most likely is that mistress Gassenda had given the garments to Magdalena. This would have been a perfectly normal thing for a mistress to do for a serving woman.

The plausibility of this suggestion is bolstered by a passage that appears in the initial version of Peire's argument. There, Peire claimed that the houppelande, today, "would be worth 6 florins if it were in the condition in which it was during his mother's lifetime." The implication is that in 1406, Magdalena was still wearing the houppelande, and the value had deteriorated somewhat over the years. Of the cloak we hear no more; perhaps she sold it to assemble the capital she needed for pawnbroking. If she did wear the houppelande from time to time, perhaps someone had brought this to Peire's attention, leading to a hastily filed lawsuit that was abandoned once he learned that the garments had been a gift.

Though it might seem far-fetched to imagine Magdalena as an apprentice, and a well-dressed one at that, in an informal pawnbroking business run by her mistress, it was common enough to teach enslaved people a craft to profit from their labor and, perhaps, to prepare them for life beyond slavery. Admittedly, many of the cases we know about involved enslaved men receiving some kind of formal apprenticeship, not enslaved women. Even so, there is no reason to think that women could not receive such attention. An act from 1318, discovered by Anselme Mortreuil, describes just such a situation, since the enslaved woman who features in the act, Anna, was being placed as an apprentice in a weaver's shop.[24]

It is likely that Peire's mother, Gassenda, died in the 1390s. None of the witnesses in the trials of 1406–1408 had anything to say about her, suggesting that any memories of her had long since faded. Bertomieua may have died shortly before Magdalena's marriage in August of 1399. If these women helped prepare Magdalena for a trade, their patronage had probably come to an end by 1399. Before leaving this world, however, they had done what they could to set their housemaid on her way in life, providing her not only with capital, consisting of several valuable garments and a legacy of 10 pounds, but something even more valuable: access to their own network of clients and the know-how needed to run a successful moneylending business.

9

Alaeta and Her Friend

IN AUGUST 1399, a group of friends and neighbors came together to negotiate the terms of Magdalena's marriage to Johan Petre. The need would have been apparent to anyone who wished her well. With the death of both Gassenda and Bertomieua, the two women who had served as a buffer in the Huguet household and had provided for her with clothes and cash were gone, and Magdalena was alone and friendless. By 1399, Peire's days as a privateer were over, and financial tensions setting him against the women of his family were mounting. It is easy to imagine what effect the impending collapse of his fortune might have had on his temper, and who better to bear the brunt of his irritability than his enslaved housemaid. Those who stepped in did so in order to secure a husband for her. There wasn't any question, apparently, of marrying her off to a poor but respectable laborer or artisan who lived elsewhere. Peire, presumably, objected to the idea of her leaving his control. Fortunately, there was someone at hand, perhaps working in Peire's shipyard and already living in his house, who was willing to take Magdalena as wife.

Two years later, Johan Petre was dead. But this does not mean that Magdalena was bereft of supporters and well-wishers. That unseen people were looking out for her is attested by her second marriage to Hugonin de lo Chorges, an immigrant shoemaker from the village of Chorges in Savoy. In August 1406, Peire raged against this man, describing him as Magdalena's "alleged husband," from which we can infer that she had married Hugonin without Peire's consent. As a point of law, she was a free woman and free to marry whom she liked. As a point of custom, it was deeply offensive to one's patron to marry without his consent. It could not have been easy for Magdalena to walk out of Peire's house. No trace of the circumstances in which she married Hugonin have survived. Even so, it is impossible to imagine that she found a suitable husband and negotiated the terms of the dowry without the intervention of supporters. The scenario that comes most readily to mind is one in which her well-wishers banded together to get her out of the clutches of that awful man.

Who were these friends, and from what circles were they drawn? The likeliest candidates are found among the individuals, two dozen or so, whose names are scattered in and about the testimony provided in the first trial. All these people lived in the vicinity of the Lansaria or participated in the social circles in which Peire and his family and dependents moved. Only a few of them may have been involved in the negotiations that led to both marriages. But even if we cannot precisely identify Magdalena's well-wishers, we can at least explore the reservoir from which they were drawn.

Of those who may have been the most well disposed toward Magdalena, the two likeliest candidates are Alaeta Columbe and her friend, Gassenda Olivarie. In April of 1407, as we shall see, the two women stuck their necks out to support Magdalena's cause, offering testimony that abruptly short-circuited Peire's case. That they did so at some personal risk is suggested by the fact that their testimony brought shame on the brittle and litigious figure of the barber-surgeon, Nicolau de Sala, who was their neighbor in the plaza of the Vivaut, located just east of the Lansaria. Alaeta and her friend have a remarkable personal history. It is worth taking a diversion from the thread of the narrative to consider this history, because their relationship offers an object lesson in the nearly invisible networks of female solidarity that suffused Massiliote society. That network gradually solidified against Peire over the 1390s and early 1400s and was partly responsible for bringing about his eventual ruin.

Magdalena's Network

On the 12th of April 1407, Peire appeared before the judge of one of the lesser courts in order to add some additional claims to those presented the previous fall. Throughout the first trial, a dissatisfied Peire was constantly tinkering with his own arguments, adding things here, dropping things there, changing crucial details, and so on. He must have been a nightmare of a client to work with. In April of 1407, as testimony was being taken, things were clearly going wrong for him, which is why he and his lawyer hastily put together a new set of four additional claims. We have already looked at one of these: the claim, discussed in chapter 5, that Magdalena's status as a "Saracen" could be proven by the marks on her arms. The third of the four claims is one of several he made about Magdalena's supposed thefts. It interests us here for what it reveals about Magdalena's potential networks of support:

> Next, he intends to prove that the said Magdalena, serving in the house of the said Peire Huguet, plundered him and deposited the item stolen in a certain coffer in the house of Antoni Baussan. And on the pleas of a number of ladies, namely, lady Blacassia de Serviers and lady Alayeta de Sant Gilles

and Gabrielleta, the wife of the said Antoni [Baussan], Peire declined to expose to the court the theft that the said Magdalena had made from the house of the said Peire. The loot is commonly valued, on his oath, at one franc and more.[1]

Once again, Peire scrambled to find words to describe what Magdalena had done. One of the words he settled on, to judge by the Latin translation selected by the notary, was *depredata fuit* ("she plundered him"). The verb, from the classical Latin *depraedari*, is an unusual way to describe a theft. According to the dictionaries, it means something like "plunder" or "despoil" or "to carry off booty." In other words, it's something that is done by Vikings or highwaymen, not housemaids. The other word was *furtum*, used in the passage in both of its contemporary meanings, the action, "theft," as well as the article stolen, "loot." This passage contains the strongest language ever used by Peire to describe Magdalena's putative theft.

The value attributed to the loot, expressed in terms of a coin that occasionally circulated in Marseille, is bizarrely low, for a single franc was worth perhaps half a florin. It is difficult to imagine anyone being seriously impressed by such a loss. The value is so out of keeping that it is safe to assume the existence of a scribal error. All becomes clear if we suppose that the notary inadvertently wrote *unum* where he should have written *centum*, or "one hundred," because 100 francs in some currencies was equivalent to 50 florins. This is exactly the figure that Peire's lawyer had used to describe the amount of capital Magdalena had assembled for her lending business.

According to the tale told by Peire, three women intervened in the matter, pleading with him not to denounce Magdalena to the criminal court. Two of them, Blacassia and Alayeta, were identified as *domine*, a word that paralleled *providus vir* and was typically reserved for women of high social standing and/ or for businesswomen and moneylenders. We shall meet them again shortly. The third, Gabrielleta, was the wife of Antoni Baussan. Peire knew Gabrielleta and Antoni quite well, so well, in fact, that he asked them to provide testimony on his claims *against* Magdalena. When he presented his new claims on the 12th of April, both Gabrielleta and Antoni had already testified, a few days earlier, on the first set of articles. As Peire may have already known, Gabrielleta's testimony was not helpful to his cause. She acknowledged that Magdalena had lent money to her husband seven or eight years ago but declined to confirm any other accusations.

If there was any truth to Peire's claim, then, three prominent women had sought to intervene with him on a matter involving a woman serving in his household. This, in itself, is worth lingering over, for it implies the existence of a network of support offered by the women of the neighborhood. One of them, Gabrielleta, had supposedly gone so far as to give Magdalena access to a coffer in her house for storing the loot—or so Peire claimed. This raises the intriguing possibility that after the death of her mistress Bertomieua, Magdalena had started running her pawnbroking operation out of the homes of friends and neighbors.

Beyond that, it is important to look more deeply into the matter of the dispute. After all, we only have Peire's word for it that Magdalena had "plundered" him. In the administrative documents from the era, the word *depredari* carried a very strong connotation of a legal action, the seizure or distraint of goods for the purpose of debt collection. The process of distraint was commonly glossed using words drawn from the Latin stem *preda*, which used to mean "loot" or "plunder." By 1400, however, it had come to mean something quite different, namely, "distrained article" or "pledge." On this reading, Peire's use of the word *depredari* inadvertently suggests that she may have seized the article in question as a pledge for a debt owed to her, perhaps as a form of private distraint. One runs across acts of private distraint from time to time in the records from the era and in most cases, the action was interpreted by the victim as theft.[2] The women, then, may have intervened to make sure that a misunderstanding should not end up as the subject of expensive litigation.

Three months later, other potential members of Magdalena's network came to light. In July of 1407, the articles of proof that Hugonin de lo Chorges had presented to the court eleven months earlier were finally brought before witnesses.[3] Two women, Antoneta Poncie, the wife of Jorgi Pons, and Catherina Limosine, the wife of the shipwright Guilhem Limosin, were called to testify to Hugonin's claim that Peire, on two occasions, had borrowed sums of money totaling 6 florins from Magdalena. Their depositions are curious in the extreme. Both women responded at length to the first claim but said little or nothing about the remaining points. What is more, nothing in their testimony indicated that Peire himself owed the debts. Instead, the verbal acknowledgment of debt was attributed to his second wife, Guillelmona. The case is so weak that it becomes necessary to try to explain why Hugonin and Magdalena could not have done better than this. A distinct possibility is that potentially favorable witnesses had been scared off or suborned by Peire. A second possibility is that the evidence was weak because there was no real need to prove the claims in the first place. On this reading, Hugonin and Magdalena were also pulling a legal stunt, that of filing claims known to be unprovable merely to make it possible for Magdalena to be seen in court arguing them.

In each of their responses to the first article, Antoneta and Catherina described an exchange that had supposedly taken place three years earlier, in July 1404. They had witnessed the exchange in the storeroom of the house of

Peire's close associate and investor, Isnart de Sant Gilles. Present in the store-room were the two witnesses, along with Guillelmona, the wife of Peire Hu-guet, and two women whom we have just met, namely, Isnart's wife, the lady Alayeta de Sant Gilles, and the lady Blacassia, wife of the nobleman Peire de Serviers. Then came Magdalena, bearing articles of clothing in her arms. An-toneta recalled seeing only a single garment, known in Occitan as a *rahondon*, made of a black woolen fabric and bearing arms depicting a lion in fine gold. Catherina remembered two garments. The first of these she identified as a *rihandon*—the shift in the notary's spelling of the word indicates his lack of familiarity with the garment—made of a dark brown fabric known as burnet, bearing arms with a lion in fine gold, and along with that, a small child's houp-pelande made of silk. Both witnesses agreed about what happened next: Mag-dalena handed over the garment or garments to Guillelmona, saying "I hold you to be pledged for this, in the amount of 6 florins, which you owe me." Guillelmona responded, saying "We shall certainly repay you," to which, ac-cording to Catherina, she added ". . . when the harvest comes in." Catherina also noted that lady Blacassia whispered to her something along the lines of "those garments are not worth one florin," a type of disclaimer typically made in testimony arising from acts of moneylending.

It was normal for a pawnbroker to accept a pledge in exchange for coin. One of the oddities of this passage is that it describes a kind of reverse pawn, where Magdalena was passing one or two garments over to Guillelmona and declar-ing her indebted for the value of the garments. The implication is that Guil-lelmona needed a bridge loan and borrowed the garments with the intention of placing them in pawn elsewhere or selling them at auction. What is not clear, in this scenario, is why Magdalena had no cash to lend, or why she herself had not chosen to sell the garments. There is an important side note: if the statements by the witnesses were true, and if we accept 1404 as the date of the transaction, then Guillelmona had chosen to borrow money from her hus-band's former slave. She must have known about his unhappiness with the manner in which Magdalena had slipped out of his grasp, and yet she still, supposedly, chose to have dealings with her.

Let us return momentarily to the date on which this transaction supposedly took place. According to the calendar elaborated in the previous chapter, Hu-gonin and Magdalena were married in 1401 or 1402, after the death of Johan Petre. This almost has to be the case, since Peire reported that Magdalena lived in his house for two years after her marriage in 1399. But the witnesses were testifying about a debt that should have been incurred *before* Magdalena's mar-riage to Hugonin, given that the debt was included in the dowry. It is hard to know how to resolve this inconsistency, unless the two witnesses badly un-derestimated the passage of time. The inconsistency disappears if we note that neither witness asserted that the exchange was the same as the one to which Hugonin and Magdalena referred in the first article of proof. On this reading, the well-intentioned witnesses were doing their best to help Magdalena by saying something, anything, that might leave the judge with the impression that a member of Peire's household, and by extension Peire, owed something to Magdalena.

These passages are fascinating for what they collectively reveal about the social circles in which the now juridically free Magdalena was moving. In particular, the testimony places Magdalena in the company of two women who belonged to the upper echelons of Massiliote society, notably Blacassia de Serviers, who was married to Peire de Serviers, an exceedingly illustrious citizen. These connections appear to have come about through Magdalena's activities as a pawnbroker. Also intriguing is the fact that one of the witnesses, Catherina Limosine, was the wife of the shipwright Guilhem Limosin, whom we recall as the witness who had confirmed Magdalena's enslaved condition in the first trial. Catherina's testimony may not have helped much in the end— the impression one gets is that Magdalena had placed her in an awkward position by asking her to comment on claims that were basically unprovable—but even so, she seems to have done what she could, perhaps against the wishes of her husband.

Alaeta the Highlander

One of the most dramatic moments in the first trial took place on Saturday the 16th of April 1407, when Alaeta Columbe and her friend, Gassenda Olivarie, appeared in court to offer testimony on Magdalena's behalf. A few days earlier, the barber-surgeon, Nicolau de Sala, had proffered testimony confirming Peire's claim that Magdalena had arrived in Marseille as his slave. Together with the testimony of the shipwright Guilhem Limosin, this gave Peire enough evidence to prove his claim. Nicolau de Sala was a distinguished man, and his testimony was especially damaging to Magdalena's cause. It is easy to visualize the anxious scene where Magdalena met with her procurator, Antoni Arnaut, to discuss how to respond. The solution they settled upon was to attack Nicolau's bona fides.

To launch the procedure, Magdalena came before the court that Saturday and dramatically announced that Nicolau was in a state of hatred with her. If proven, this would negate the probative value of his testimony. By way of proof, she asked the court to summon Alaeta and Gassenda to provide testimony about the hatred. Both women were described as "resellers" as well as former neighbors of master Nicolau, the latter being important because it explained how they knew such things. A crier was sent and the witnesses appeared that evening, at the hour of vespers. Unusually, they gave their testimony before the judge rather than before a notary. This is what they said:

> The said Gassenda Olivarie, a witness produced on behalf of Magdalena, swore on the Holy Gospel to speak the truth about the things on which she shall be interrogated, namely, about the hatred that master Nicolau holds for the said Magdalena. She said that on a day that she does not at present recall, the said Magdalena requested from master Nicolau certain blades called *razors* which she had given to him for the purpose of being sharpened or honed. This very master Nicolau told Magdalena that she could not have them unless she would go upstairs with him into his hall. This witness told Magdalena that she ought not to go upstairs, lest master Nicolau do something shameful to her. On account of this, she believed there to be a hatred between Nicolau and Magdalena. To the many other questions asked of her, she declared that she knows nothing more than that which she has deposed.
>
> The said Alaeta Columbe, a witness produced on behalf of Magdalena, swore on the Holy Gospel to speak the truth about the things on which she shall be interrogated, namely, about the hatred between the said master Nicolau and the said Magdalena. She responded that she knows nothing other than that one day, which she does not recall, when Magdalena asked for some blades called *razors* from the master Nicolau, which she had given to him for the purpose of being sharpened or honed, master Nicolau answered that she could not have them unless she would go upstairs to the hall of his house. Alaeta advised her not to go upstairs, lest master Nicolau do something shameful to her. On account of this, she believed there to be a hatred between Nicolau and Magdalena. To the many other questions asked of her, she declared that she knows nothing more than that which she has deposed.[4]

As we can infer from this, Nicolau had refused to deliver the razors unless Magdalena agreed to have sex with him. The two women reported that his enmity was born when he was publicly snubbed.

The testimony is remarkable on several levels, and we shall have occasion to revisit it in the next chapter. One of its most pungent features lay in the tacit suggestion that Magdalena was a woman of honor. In Roman and Christian moral discourse, servile women lacked sexual honor. Lisa Bailey writes of the early medieval assumption that "women in service were sexually compromised and that sex with them did not constitute a sin comparable to adultery," describing it as an idea that persisted well into the Middle Ages.[5] The logic deployed by Alaeta and Gassenda subtly reversed the syllogism: Magdalena was a woman of honor, therefore she could not be a slave.

146   CHAPTER 9

Who were these two women? Happily, we know a good deal about both of them. Alaeta Columbe was an immigrant to the city of Marseille originally from Aups, an ancient Roman town located in the highlands of the modern-day department of the Var, about 100 kilometers northeast of Marseille. She appears several times in notarial acts and other records from the 1390s and 1400s, where she was sometimes called "lady Alaeta" by the respectful notaries, or occasionally "lady Alasacia," using her first name without the diminutive. They also regularly assigned her the sobriquet *la Gavota*, meaning "the Highlander" (modern French *la Montagnarde*). In an act from 1405, these appear in combination to yield the expression *domina Alasacia Columbe alias la Gavota*, "lady Alasacia Columbe, otherwise known as the Highlander."

In records sampled to date, Alaeta makes her first confirmed appearance in 1390 or 1391, in a contract carrying the evocative title "A purchase of female goats and two-year-old goats and the formation of a business partnership for Alaeta Columbe."[6] From the very outset, then, Alaeta appears as a businesswoman with a connection to goats, a suitable occupation for a highlander with experience in the pastoral economy. Several contracts over the next fifteen years show that she specialized in the livestock version of sharecropping: she lent her goats to a goatherd for a period of a few years and would split the profits that accrued. In Provence, the contract was known as *gajaria*. In August 1399, for example, an act reveals that Alaeta lent a herd of goats to Monet d'Esparon of the village of Vitrolles, along with a loan of 20 florins.[7] Several years pass before we see the goats again, when Alaeta lent the herd to a recent immigrant from the village of Pennes and his two sons.[8]

Along with goats, Alaeta lent money from time to time. In September 1390, "lady Columba" appeared in court to pursue a small sum of money from one of her debtors, and although the abbreviated act does not provide a first name, it is likely that the creditor was Alaeta. Two years later, lady Columba appeared once again in court to pursue a small debt.[9] The small sums of money involved in both cases suggest non-notarized hand-loans. But Alaeta also provided larger notarized loans. In 1393, two men from Lambesc, near Aix-en-Provence, acknowledged receiving a loan of 20 florins from Alaeta.[10] This act, like others of the day, carefully names the coins that were handed over to the two men: gold shields, gold florins, silver gros, and some black money (*uchenis nigris*), coins minted in a base metal. She was partnered in the loan by a resident of the town of Auriol, and an act from later that year indicates that she hired a second resident of Auriol with the same surname to serve as her procurator. The latter act was executed in Marseille, in the house of a prominent moneylender.[11]

Several more acts involving the extension of credit pile up over the ensuing years and there is no point in reviewing all of them. The last glimpse of her as a moneylender took place in March of 1407, when a resident of the fishing village of Cassis acknowledged receipt of a loan of 27 florins from Alaeta.[12] Just over a year later, in June of 1408, Alaeta drew up her last will and testament. Whatever health scare induced her to do this, however, seems to have been a false alarm, since she appears in the fiscal year 1411–1412 in the act of making a rental payment on a house.[13]

Three features of Alaeta's business practices stand out. First, she took nearly all of her legal business to a notary named Antoni Lombart. In the register compiled by Antoni for the years 1390–1391, she makes one of her first appearances in the table of contents, setting up the business partnership involving goats. Here, he named her simply "Alaeta Columbe." But Antoni's respect grew as his dealings with his client deepened, and in 1393, when she next makes an appearance in one of his registers, he called her "Lady Alaeta Columbe, alias the Highlander." He continued to use the respectful title "lady" off and on during the ensuing years.

Second, most of the loans notarized for her by Antoni involved debtors who either lived in the countryside around Marseille or had immigrated so recently that they were still being identified by place of origin. As we have seen, she had a factor or procurator based in Auriol, and she also did business with individuals in a halo extending up to 45 kilometers from Marseille (figure 8).

Finally, Alaeta regularly did business with a lawyer named Honorat de Sant Gilles, the brother of the draper Isnart de Sant Gilles, one of Peire Huguet's associates and investors. Honorat's relationship with Alaeta first becomes visible in January of 1398, when she named him as her procurator and charged him with tasks related to pleading, demanding, recuperating, and receiving the debts owed to Alaeta.[14] A month after that, in February, Antoni Jay of Aubagne acknowledged a debt of 12 florins to Alaeta. A note appended to this contract indicates that the first installment of 5 florins was received eighteen months later, in August of 1399.[15] A second note, dated 6 September 1406, indicates that Honorat had been involved in securing the payment of the full sum on Alaeta's behalf. He also witnessed one of the goat loans, made in August 1399.[16] Like the notary Antoni Lombart, Honorat entered Alaeta's life as a trusted legal counsel for her moneylending business. But the relationship deepened and he became a very close friend.

Between 1390 and 1411, Alaeta was a significant figure in the community of moneylenders in Marseille, though she perhaps did not quite achieve the fame and distinction that came to prominent lenders such as Auruola de Jerusalem.

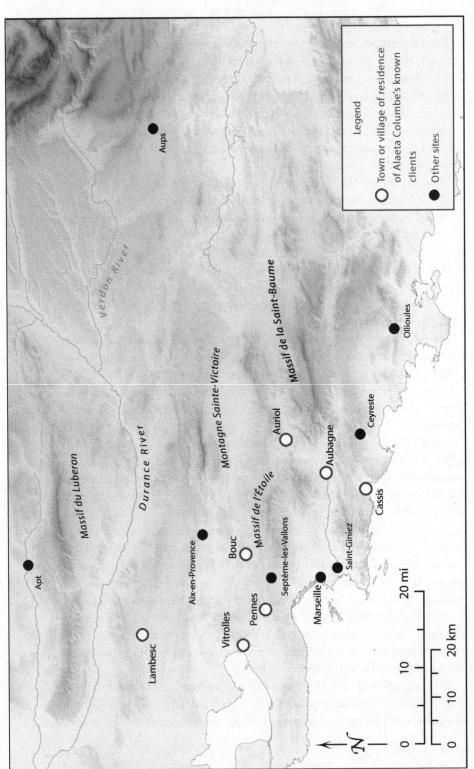

FIGURE 8. The business world of Alaeta Columbe. Alaeta was originally from the town of Aups, and her daughter had married a resident of Ollioules. *Credit*: Scott Walker / Dan Smail.

We get a glimpse of her on numerous occasions doing business with a number of men and relying on members of the legal profession to keep her legal affairs in order. On no occasion do we ever meet a husband. She was never described as "the wife of so-and-so." Even her 1408 testament, in a manner that is exceedingly unusual, lacked any reference to a husband. And yet we know from this same testament that she had given birth to several children, who in their turn had borne grandchildren. We even have an act from 1397 arising from the marriage of her daughter Johanneta to a resident of the village of Ollioules, near Toulon. The act is a quittance whereby her son-in-law acknowledged having received full payment of Johanneta's dowry of 60 florins.[17] The absence of any reference to a husband is so pointed as to cause us to sit up and take notice.

No clue about Alaeta's life prior to 1391 has surfaced to date in the archives of Marseille, and we are left to wonder what happened. Among the many scenarios, perhaps the most plausible is that she had left Aups around 1391 to escape a husband who was abusive or who could not tolerate her proclivities as a businesswoman. The reasoning is that if she had affection for a husband who had simply died, she would almost certainly have named him in her testament. It seems that she brought her capital with her and subsequently invested it in Marseille. Since her daughter married someone from Ollioules rather than Marseille, Alaeta clearly maintained some ties to her home region. The fact that she dowered Johanneta and eventually named her as her universal heir suggests an enduring affection between mother and daughter.

Setting Up House

Within a year or two of her arrival in Marseille, Alaeta met a fripperer, that is, a dealer in second-hand garments, named Gassenda Olivarie. The two women soon became intimate friends and business partners. Gassenda appears on two occasions in the late 1390s as a minor partner in Alaeta's moneylending business, and she also acquired credits arising from her own business.[18] But their firm friendship had been established earlier, in October of 1393. On the 30th of that month, the two women purchased a house formerly belonging to a blind laborer and his daughter (figure 9).[19] A telling phrase reveals that they purchased the house "with common funds (*de comuni peccunia*)." The price, 80 florins, was high for this period, since the loss of population caused by recurring bouts of plague had led to the abandonment of a number of houses in the city and a general decline in property values. The two women paid 50 florins in cash and promised to pay the remainder by Easter of 1394.

FIGURE 9. Rubric for a house purchase made by Alaeta Columbe and Gassenda Blanque. *Source:* ADBR 351 E 670, fol. 118r.

The house was located on a street known as the Baths of the Tannery, in the southeastern corner of the city.[20] Later, Alaeta and Gassenda moved to a more upscale neighborhood in the vicinity of the plaza of the Vivaut.[21] They appear together in a rent register from 1411 in the act of paying a ground rent owed on a house located in the insula of the Oven of the Shipyards, situated between the plaza of the Vivaut and the port (see figure 5 in chapter 5).[22] This house was located just a few steps east of Peire Huguet's house on the Lansaria. Alaeta and Gassenda lived together for the remainder of their lives.

From this sale and the testaments left by each of the two women, it is possible to work out some of the details of Gassenda's life.[23] She was the daughter of Monet Blanc and "lady H." At some point she married Bertran Olivari, although her husband had almost certainly died before 1393, since for the purposes of the house purchase Gassenda used her maiden name, "Guassende Blanque." To judge by her last will and testament, no children of hers survived into adulthood, since the act named two cousins as heirs. Where many widows would have remarried, however, Gassenda entered instead into a domestic relationship with Alaeta, who had immigrated to Marseille two years earlier and was similarly without a partner.

Alaeta died before Gassenda. The affection between the two women is amply attested by the provisions left for Gassenda in Alaeta's testament. The act, drawn up by Alaeta's faithful notary, Antoni Lombart, was entitled "The testament of Lady Alasacia Columbe alias the Highlander, of Aups." She was identified as the daughter of the late Bermon Columbi. Alaeta asked to be buried in the cemetery of the parish church of Saint Martin, and a sad phrase gives details about the location: "in the grave where the bodies of my children and grandchildren are buried." Details for her funeral services were left to the discretion of Honorat de Sant Gilles and Gassenda Olivarie. That she had become quite wealthy through her moneylending business is revealed by the fact that she left 100 florins to be used to purchase rents to sing perpetual masses "for my soul and the soul of Gassenda Olivarie." If we hazard a guess that pious legacies typically comprised about 10 percent of the value of an estate, at least in cases where the decedent had living heirs, then she was worth around 1,000 florins at the time of her death, enough to place her within the upper echelons of society at the time.

She made special and revealing provisions for the important people in her life:

> I give to Honorat, for his good services and in remuneration for those services, after the death of Gassenda Olivarie and not before, half of the house in which I live, located in the city of Marseille next to the plaza of the Vivaut, abutting the sea, the street of the port, and two streets. I leave to Honorat half of all my goats and half of all the fruits of those goats; the goats are currently being sharecropped by Laurens Motet of Bouc, as I declare. For the remaining goods and rights etc., I name as my heir my beloved daughter Johannona, wife of Jacme Olivari. I also wish that Gassenda Olivarie have the right to own and manage all my goods for as long as she lives, and she should not be required to do a reckoning of the assets at the end of her life.

Gassenda, in short, would be Alaeta's life-heir for the remainder of her days, a provision that guaranteed her financial security.[24]

The intimate relationship between Alaeta and Gassenda gives us insight into the testimony that they offered to Magdalena in the summer of 1407. One of the most striking features of the Alaeta-Gassenda network is that it does not seem to have overlapped with the first network, headed by Blacassia de Serviers and Alayeta de Sant Gilles. This is not unexpected. Alaeta Columbe was a proudly rustic person, a highlander oriented to the land, not the sort of person to rub shoulders with women who belonged to the city's mercantile elite. The only interesting link runs through her dear friend Honorat de Sant Gilles, given that Honorat was the brother of Isnart, one of Peire Huguet's investors and the husband of Alayeta. This exception aside, it appears that Magdalena had established herself in two distinct networks, both of which were involved to some degree in moneylending.

Alaeta and Gassenda were loyal enough to Magdalena to provide testimony that was bound to have angered two powerful men in the city, Peire Huguet and Nicolau de Sala. This indicates that their affection for Magdalena was stronger than might otherwise be inferred from the brevity of their court appearance on her behalf. Following the deaths of Bertomieua Huguete and Johan Petre, Alaeta may have stepped forward to provide Magdalena with support and resources of various kinds, perhaps even giving her access to her network of clients and supporting her by the weight of her own reputation. It is possible that Alaeta was involved in the negotiations that led to Magdalena's

152 CHAPTER 9

second marriage to Hugonin de lo Chorges. Although Hugonin was from the village of Chorges, a long way to the north of Alaeta's hometown of Aups, Alaeta was in tune with the immigrant community.

All this is entirely hypothetical. It is worth considering, though, because Alaeta's importance as a putative patron for Magdalena would derive from her complete financial autonomy. By 1407, Alaeta was a well-to-do woman, an immigrant who had parlayed her caprine expertise and her extensive rural connections into a profitable business. She had no need to show deference to anybody. Peire had injured one of her friends or clients. Alaeta, on this theory, made sure that he would pay for it.

10

A Roll of the Dice

WHEN HUGONIN DE LO CHORGES launched the lawsuit in August of 1406, it is easy to understand why the nettlesome Peire chose not to meekly accept the insult to his honor, responding instead with a vigorous countersuit. What is hard to understand is why Magdalena and Hugonin chose to provoke him in the first place.

In the summer of 1406, Magdalena was probably in her mid-thirties. It had been seven years since she had married and gained a tacit manumission. The death of her first husband in 1401 may have been a traumatic setback, but women she had met through neighborhood relations and her pawnbroking activities helped steer her into a second marriage with a respectable shoemaker. Faint clues provide fragmentary impressions of the household they set up. In June 1406, Hugonin took a young orphan as his apprentice for seven years. In the act, Magdalena's husband was identified as "Master Hugonin of Chorges, from Savoy, a shoemaker, now a citizen and resident of the city of Marseille."[1] He promised to teach the boy the shoemaker's trade, provide him with food, clothing, and shoes, and care for him in sickness and in health. A few months later, Hugonin acted as a witness to a notarial act involving another shoemaker.[2] Two years later, in August 1408, we catch a glimpse of a scene at the doorway to his house.[3] A crier had been sent to summon Magdalena for a court hearing. The door was answered by a male servant (*famulus*), perhaps the apprentice, perhaps another dependent member of the household, who informed the crier that Magdalena was not in. Household dependents were to be found in virtually every respectable household. Their duties included opening the door to visitors and attending to the words of criers. It is a telling insight. Magdalena had become a housemistress in her own right.

By 1406, she had made a life for herself beyond slavery. So why stir up the hornet's nest by launching a lawsuit against her former enslaver? Searching for answers to this puzzle, one imagines that Hugonin, tired of waiting for repayment of the debt given to him in dowry, must have been the responsible party. But Peire claimed that the author of the suit was actually Magdalena, and there is more than a germ of truth to this. Hugonin was a cipher. Having launched the suit in August 1406, he disappeared from the stage, apart from a perfunctory appearance in July 1407. This is unusual. In similar cases, husbands were often deeply involved in arguing cases that involved rights pertaining to their wives. Often, the case was argued by the husband, not the wife. One's impression is that Hugonin was uncomfortable in the limelight, perhaps a little embarrassed by the attention drawn to his wife, desperately hoping the whole thing would go away and leave him in peace.

We can imagine several scenarios that prompted Magdalena to launch the suit. Perhaps she had heard rumors indicating that Peire was about to move against her, in which case her lawsuit was a legal ploy to get in there first. If Magdalena were in her mid-thirties in 1406, she may still have been of childbearing age. Was she concerned about the juridical status of a future child? Nothing suggests that she ever bore a child, but even so, we cannot discount the possibility. Finally, in the absence of a formal manumission, Magdalena may have found it difficult to engage in legal business before any notary who was aware of her former status, unable to extend or take out loans, buy or sell land, compile a last will and testament, or even hire a procurator.

All these scenarios are possible and none of them excludes the others. But hovering over all of them was the profound matter of Magdalena's dignity. To get a sense of what her feelings about this may have been, let us revisit the doorway of the barber-surgeon, Nicolau de Sala, where Magdalena was waiting to collect some razors that Nicolau had stropped. Nicolau was familiar with Magdalena's past, for he had been present off the roads of Naples in 1387 when the enslaved Magdalena had been handed over as booty to Peire Huguet. Seeing her on the doorstep, in the company of his neighbors, Alaeta Columbe and Gassenda Olivarie, he said something like this: "You can have the razors, but to get them, you'll have to come upstairs with me." But the literal wording, whatever it was, is not what Magdalena heard. As LaKisha Michelle Simmons has observed, the word "upstairs," to an enslaved woman, refers to the "intimate and dangerous geographies" of domestic spaces associated with sexual violence.[4] What Magdalena heard, then, was this: "Once you were a slave with no sexual honor. To me, you're still a slave, never mind your pitiful shoemaker husband." Although the story told by Alaeta and Gassenda about the source of Nicolau's hatred may have been too good to be true, the social logic conveyed by the story is distinctly believable. The act of forgetting did not proceed uniformly across the social field: certain actors might prefer not to forgo memories when those memories gave them power over others. Some of the formerly enslaved women assimilated by the act of marriage may have been able to endure the persistent slights of people like Nicolau de Sala. But Magdalena, following this hypothesis, wasn't one of them.

By 1406, Magdalena was a free woman, clad in good clothes, married to a respectable citizen, a housemistress with a measure of authority over one or more dependents, a recognized moneylender who provided people with access to coin. She had passed fully along the spectrum that ran from enslaved to free. But as the reconstruction of the scene at Nicolau's doorstep suggests, her own enslavement continually gnawed at her, and the painful wound, only lightly bandaged by the passage of time, was opened afresh every time she suffered an insult. For that matter, in a city of 10,000 people, it seems likely that she would have run across her former enslaver from time to time on the streets, and we can only imagine what he said to her or how he looked at her on these occasions. In this view, the lawsuit was a high-stakes wager, a roll of the dice. The ultimate objective was to bring out the boil and, with any luck, lance it once and for all.

Magdalena Speaks

The plea filed by Hugonin de lo Chorges was registered in the court book on Friday the 13th of August 1406, and a crier was sent to summon Peire to appear within five days. On Wednesday the 18th, Peire appeared and dramatically announced his countersuit. On the 27th of August, a lawyer named Antoni Arnaut showed up in court, declaring himself to be the procurator for Hugonin and Magdalena. Over the next two weeks, the record preserves details about the procedural moves initiated by Antoni and by Peire's procurator, Johan de Ysia.

In the preceding chapters, we have already had occasion to explore some of these passages, such as the articles of proof presented by Johan de Ysia, which were essential for sorting out the matter of Magdalena's status as a moneylender.[5] The first phase of the trial was completed by the 12th of September. Strangely, the dispute fell silent for a period of six months. It is conceivable that proceedings were stilled in the hopes that common friends could arrange for a peaceful arbitration. If so, those efforts proved to be in vain. On the 8th of March 1407, the case exploded back to life when Peire lodged a new claim in the second of the two lesser courts. This was when he accused Magdalena of having stolen two garments worth 12 florins from his mother, Gassenda.

On the 9th of March 1407, Magdalena arrived at court bearing a copy of the last will and testament of Peire's wife, Bertomieua. This was her first known appearance before one of the judges of the case. The legal instrument recorded the details of the legacy of 10 l. that Bertomieua had left Magdalena.[6] Having seen the testament, the judge of the second court, Antoni de Raude, immediately ordered Peire to deposit the sum of 10 l. in escrow with a notary of the court. Peire responded that he did not have the money ready to hand but would return to the court on the 16th to fulfill the judge's order, which he did, leaving the money and receiving a receipt from the notary. Embittered by the judge's decision, however, Peire declared Antoni de Raude "suspect" a few days later, on the 11th of March. This procedural move allowed him to transfer the claims heard in the second court into the records of the suit he had begun making the previous fall, before the first court.

From this point forward, Magdalena appeared regularly at court to argue her case.[7] On the 13th of March, she lodged a routine objection to a procedural move. Following a two-week hiatus for the Easter holidays, she was present again on Wednesday, the 6th of April, to hear Peire's witnesses swear on the gospels to tell the truth, and returned a week later, on the 13th, to lodge a routine procedural objection about the testimony that had been received. On the 14th, she lodged another procedural move, and on the 16th, initiated her dramatic claim regarding the hatred of the barber-surgeon, Nicolau de Sala. The riveting testimony provided by Alaeta Columbe and Gassenda Olivarie was then followed by a pause lasting a month. On the 24th of May, Peire engineered a transfer of the case to Marseille's highest court of first instance, the Palace court, again declaring that the judge of the lesser court was "suspect." Magdalena appeared before the Palace court on May 25th, and after another long delay, reappeared on July 8th, in a curious episode where she was asked to estimate her value as a slave.[8] Magdalena and Hugonin then appeared together on the 12th of July, when the two initiated the brief phase of the trial where they attempted to prove that Peire owed 6 florins. This moment constituted Magdalena's final appearance in the first trial, for the judge issued his sentence a few days later, on July 19th. Both parties, he declared, had failed to prove the claims they had made the previous year (the record is silent on Peire's subsidiary claim of theft, made in March of 1407). But he did declare that Magdalena had proved Bertomieua's legacy of 10 l. and thereby confirmed the decision made earlier to transfer the deposit into her keeping.

Peire, as we have seen, appealed this ruling, and the appeal dragged on until November of 1407. On Magdalena's side, some of the burden of argument during the appeal was carried by her new procurator, Bertran Gombert. But on six different occasions between the 14th of October and the 12th of November, she appeared at court to argue some key points and make procedural moves. Her seventh and final appearance in the fall occurred on the 14th of November, as the appeal was drawing to a close, when she formally requested that the judge declare the appeal null and condemn Peire to pay her court costs for the previous year, amounting to 25 florins. The ruling, in Magdalena's favor, was issued around the 19th of November.

In the brief entries that record Magdalena's presence in court, little is said about what she said. Most of the references consist of pro forma procedural

A ROLL OF THE DICE 157

moves and objections. In many of these comments, she would have no doubt been coached on the formulaic expressions required by the circumstances. What speaks volumes, therefore, are not her words so much as her appearances. Between March and November of 1407, she was present at court on at least sixteen different occasions, sometimes twice on a given day. These are only the appearances we know about. At the time, Marseille's courts met out of doors, in booths located before the lower doors of Notre-Dame-des-Accoules, in the civic and spiritual center of the city.[9] She made these appearances before all three judges of the courts of first instance as well as the judge of first appeals, perhaps dressed in the luxurious houppelande she had either received as a gift (her story) or had stolen (Peire's) from his mother, Gassenda.[10] She could have invited her procurators to appear in her stead, but she did not. Magdalena and her legal team, I submit, were intensely aware of the value of having her appear at court. To argue a case in law was a powerful way to perform one's freedom.

Peire's Bind

When Peire learned that he was the target of Hugonin's lawsuit in 1406, he responded with a convoluted set of claims inspired less by their logical interrelatedness than by the hope that at least one of them might stick. The problem arose because Peire was caught in a logical bind of his own making.

From the outset of the first trial, Peire had argued, with a consistency that was otherwise rare for him, that Magdalena was still his slave. A phrase appearing in his initial complaint, presented to the court on the 18th of August 1406, is unambiguous: "she was never manumitted by Peire nor in his name."[11] In a narrow technical sense, this was true, since he had never provided her with a formal manumission.[12] To this he added the claim that Hugonin was her "alleged" husband, where the veiled suggestion was that slaves cannot marry without the permission of their masters.[13] Additional vituperations included the claim that she ought to be returned to her original condition of servitude "since she is not worthy of liberty."[14] When the trial restarted in the spring, one of the articles presented by Peire included the phrase "she was and *is* the slave woman of the said Peire Huguet."[15] As Alice Rio has pointed out for analogous situations from the earlier medieval period, we should read such statements not as descriptions of reality but instead as claims that attempt to create the very status that they purport to describe.[16]

Up to this point, judges had paid little attention to the claim of present servitude. But something happened in July 1407 that brought about a change. Following Peire's recusal of the lower judge, in late May 1407, there was a long pause before the case restarted in the Palace court in early July. During this time, the acts of the lesser courts were copied into the registers of the Palace court and read by the lieutenant judge, Elziar Autrici. Peire's assertion that Magdalena was still his slave caused Elziar to sit up and take notice:

> And the lord lieutenant ordered that the said Peire Huguet, the adversary party, be summoned to court by one of the criers of the present court that evening, at the time of vespers, to proceed with the case and also for the purpose of reckoning the value of the said Magdalena, given that he asserts her to be his slave (*suam esse asserit sclavam*) and established in his service, lest the rights of the court be damaged in any way on account of the fee.[17]

The claim of Magdalena's present servitude—the judge's use of the verb "to be" in the present tense leaps out of the passage—had raised doubts about the fee that had been collected when the suit was opened. This fee (*lata*), much like a writ in the English common law, was paid by every litigant seeking to open a cause against an adversary. Elziar was anticipating the possibility that Peire might be able to reinstate his mastery over Magdalena. Were that to happen, the fee charged should be determined on the basis of her value as a slave, not on other monetary considerations.

Three days later, Peire appeared at court and gave his reckoning of her value, which he set at 25 florins, to which he added a little dig by referring to Magdalena as "the said slave." It is understandable that he should lowball her value, since that would reduce the amount of the fee he would have to pay. In the curious scene that followed, Magdalena was then asked the same question. She chose to reckon the value of her person at 100 gold francs, the equivalent of at least 50 florins and possibly more than 100 florins, depending on which franc she meant. Finally, the judge, whose interest in the matter seems to have become prurient by this point, turned to Peire's lawyer, Johan de Ysia:

> And the said lord lieutenant interrogated the lord Johan de Ysia, procurator, as is claimed, of the said Peire Huguet, who was present, asking how much he would sell or price the said slave if she were his. The lord Johan, representing his client as above, on his oath, said that he would rather have the said Magdalena as a slave than 50 gold florins.[18]

It is hard to read this passage without imagining the men having a good laugh at Magdalena's expense, and it is significant that the lieutenant judge, perhaps unconsciously, had echoed Peire's reference to "the said slave" while posing the question to Johan.

Peire's claim of present servitude made sense on one level, given his hopes that he might be able to seize the profits of Magdalena's moneylending business on the theory that everything earned by a slave belongs to the master. The claim of present servitude, of course, placed him in the ridiculous position of suing his own slave. In addition, it seriously undermined the logic of the other argument that he had hoped to press, namely, that Magdalena had lived in his house for two years after her marriage to Johan Petre, partaking of food and drink provided at his expense and costing him more than 10 florins per year. It would be absurd to bill a slave for her food and drink.

What did his procurator, Johan de Ysia, think about his client's stubborn refusal to let go of his claim regarding Magdalena's slave status? Johan knew perfectly well that the best way to argue the case was to start from the premise that she was a freedwoman. Tellingly, whenever he appeared at court, Johan referred to her servitude in the past tense—that is, if we assume, as I do, that notaries were sensitive to these grammatical nuances and took pains to capture them. The first occurrence of this kind took place on the 1st of September 1406, when Johan presented the articles of proof to the judge. As noted earlier, these articles typically consist of a careful restatement, in the form of a tabular list, of the claims presented in narrative form in the initial plea or libel. The process of converting the narrative to a list was a tricky one, since it involved adapting the sometimes rambling free-form plea into discrete logical blocks and then adding the elements needed to make them viable at law and comprehensible to witnesses. At the very outset, Johan's language explicitly referred to "Magdalena, *formerly* the slave woman of Peire Huguet." A sentence or two later, he declared that "she *was* the slave woman of the said Peire," a phrase that appears again in the record of a hearing involving Johan that took place on the 12th of September. On the same day, Johan offered a new article: "Next, it was and still is commonly said in this city that the said Magdalena was and is Peire's slave."[19] Though the use of the present tense here appears to violate the suggestion that Johan acknowledged Magdalena's liberty, it does not. The argument he was proposing in this instance involved hearsay, not fact.

The Neighbors Vote

The first article presented by Johan de Ysia on the 1st of September 1406, as we have seen, ran like this: "First, he intends to prove that the said Magdalena was a slave woman of the said Peire Huguet for many years. He held and possessed her as a slave for many years, and rumor of this has worked all across the city of Marseille among neighbors and people in the know." Since Magdalena had been acquired as booty on the high seas, Peire lacked any written proof. The only way to demonstrate the truth of his claims, therefore, was to rely on the testimony of witnesses.

As we have seen, testimony was not heard until April of 1407. Peire initially called upon ten witnesses, consisting of three women and seven men. This witness group represented a mix of social backgrounds. Three of them were relatives of his by marriage. Two were dependents who worked in his house. Others were friends and neighbors. Given this situation, one might have expected them to support his cause. With one exception, however, they did not, instead offering testimony that was at best guarded and at times indifferent to Peire's claims. This is the impression one would receive from witnesses who favored Magdalena's cause but were nervous about confronting Peire publicly.

The empty responses occasioned by the first article are particularly revealing, and it is worth considering each of them in turn:

On the first and second articles, interrogated on his oath, he said and deposed that he knows nothing about the things contained in them. (*Testimony of Johan de Bellomonte, a laborer who had worked for Peire for a period of three months and lived in his house*)

On the first and second articles, interrogated on his oath, he said that he knows nothing about the things contained in them. (*Testimony of Johan Cochet, alias "Little John," a laborer who had lived in Peire's house for fifteen months while working for him*)

On the first article, she said she knows nothing about it, whether she [Magdalena] was truly a slave or not. (*Testimony of Guillelma Romanete, who declared that she was Peire's stepdaughter, since Peire had married her mother*)

On the first, [she said] nothing. (*Testimony of Gabriella Baussane*)

On the first article and, following that, on all the remaining articles, he said and deposed just as his wife Guillelmeta [*sic*] had testified. (*Testimony of Antoni Baussan, Gabriella's husband*)

On the first article, he said that what is contained in it is true. Asked how he knows, he said because when he was in the region of Naples, he saw that Jacme Martin and Antoni de Lueys, the patrons of a certain galley captained by the said Antoni de Lueys, gave the said Magdalena to the same Peire Hugoni, and they [*sic*] held her as a slave. Asked when this happened, he said. fifteen or sixteen years ago or thereabouts; more, he does not know. (*Testimony of Nicolau de Sala, barber-surgeon*)

He said and testified on his oath that he knows nothing about it except that he heard it said by many people in his neighborhood. (*Testimony of Nicolau d'Ays, butcher, brother-in-law to Peire Huguet and probably Guillelma Romanete's uncle*)

She said and testified on her oath on all the articles just what the previous witness, her son Nicolau d'Ays, had deposed. (*Testimony of Rayneria d'Ays, Nicolau's mother and Peire's mother-in-law*)

On the first article, he said that he knows nothing on it other than that, for many years, he saw Magdalena living with Peire Huguet; he knows nothing else on the matter. (*Testimony of Hugo de Relhana*)

A ROLL OF THE DICE   161

On the first article, interrogated on his oath, he said and deposed that he knows nothing about it other than that, for many years, he saw Magdalena living with Peire Huguet; he knows nothing else on the matter. (*Initial testimony of Guilhem Limosin, shipwright*)[20]

Leaving aside the testimony of the barber-surgeon, Nicolau de Sala, these depositions amounted to a collective refusal to participate in the act of defining Magdalena as a slave.

Considered from one angle, this collective refusal bordered on a lie. We can appreciate the nature of the untruth by taking a close look at testimony provided by the shipwright, Guilhem Limosin, whom we met in an earlier chapter. In his first round of testimony, Guilhem joined with others in denying full knowledge of her status. Yes, he admitted to having seen Magdalena often enough in Peire's house but could not say for sure whether she was a slave or not. In this case, Peire could prove that the witness was lying, because Guilhem had actually been an eyewitness to the dramatic events that had taken place twenty years ago, off the coast of Naples, when Magdalena had been seized on the galley of Corrado Doria. Recalled and interrogated a second time on Peire's additional claims, Guilhem Limosin acknowledged the truth of the matter. But although Peire had caught Guilhem in a lie, there was nothing he could do about the remaining witnesses. Most of them, surely, knew perfectly well that Magdalena had once been a slave. Nicolau d'Ays, Peire's brother-in-law, said as much when he acknowledged the existence of a rumor about her slave status in the neighborhood. Yet he, like the others, denied having any legal certainty about the matter.

In doing so, had they perjured themselves? This depends on the answer that a thoughtful witness might give in response to the question "Is it true that Magdalena was a slave?" After all, what does it mean to be a slave? Under what conditions can one declare, under oath, that someone is enslaved to another? The legal condition of enslavement, after all, is not an inherent attribute of persons, in the way that hardness is an inherent attribute of diamonds. Seen this way, the collective refusal to acknowledge Magdalena's slave status amounted to a profound philosophical statement about the impossibility of knowing what slavery is. Ordinary people are capable of uncommon feats of wisdom, and we may confidently attribute such wisdom to them even if there is no evidence to suggest that they knew how to articulate that wisdom in learned words.

There were ways to prove slave status, of course, but those strategies did not rely on proofs grounded in positive law. They depended, instead, on performance. As Nicole Giannella has pointed out, what mattered in cases of disputed status in ancient Rome was how people behaved. In cases where an individual acted in the manner of a free person, that person was considered free.[21] Centuries later, the laws of Genoa explicitly defined slavery in this way. As Hannah Barker has put it, a slave, in Genoa, was defined as "she who is held and owned as a slave by her master or mistress, and she who is considered and held to be a slave by the neighborhood of the said master or mistress."[22] The power to define the condition of enslaved and free, clearly, lay not in formal legal mechanisms. The power resided instead in the community, in what Rebecca Scott has described as "vernacular understandings of what it meant to 'be' free."[23]

There were no laws governing slavery in Marseille, but even so, the custom was identical to what we find in Genoa. This much can be deduced through a close reading of the first article presented to the court in September of 1406 by Peire's lawyer, Johan de Ysia: "First, he intends to prove that the said Magdalena was a slave woman of the said Peire Huguet for many years. He held and possessed her as a slave for many years, and rumor of this has worked all across the city of Marseille among neighbors and people in the know." The distinction between the first and second clauses is subtle but interesting, for it shows an awareness that ownership is knowable only when it is regularly and openly performed.

The fact that slavery could not be known independently of its performance presented an insoluble dilemma for Peire. The problem is that performance does not consist solely of the dance of master and slave, involving a constant stream of humiliations emanating from the former and gestures of submission or resistance from the latter, but also includes a far more complex choreography involving members of the community. All members of the community participate in the making of slavery through their assent and approbation.[24] Without that participation, what is left?

Let us translate these philosophical musings into practical terms. When an enslaved person first arrives in a community—and for these purposes, it is helpful to imagine a frightened and bewildered teenage woman—it is not difficult to imagine scenarios in which a master identifies her to members of his household and neighbors as his slave. In a situation where she had been acquired by sale, those present as witnesses would have participated directly in the legal act that defined her condition. To others, however, her legal condition would have been knowable only by word of mouth, a rumor confirmed in the minds of observers by speech patterns, physiognomy, and other cues emanating from the posture and deportment of enslaver and enslaved alike.

Yet these kinds of cues are prone to fade over time. As the enslaved woman's linguistic skills improve and her accent diminishes, and as her body language absorbs local gestures and comportments, the signs distinguishing her from an ordinary housemaid gradually fade. To counteract this, a master might

A ROLL OF THE DICE   163

perform ever more insistently the many routines of domination that continually made a slave a slave. Outside the household, however, turnover among the
members of the community would have caused the once-clear social memory
of the slave's identity to gradually fade. It took work for the community to
know, and to continue to know, that a slave was a slave. Forgetting was the
default setting in the borderlands of slavery. Slave status in places like Marseille, in short, was inherently unstable and prone to degrade over time. It is
particularly easy to conceive how a female domestic slave could slide, incre-
mentally, into the ubiquitous sociological slot of the housemaid.

If the instability of status helps explain how Peire's friends, neighbors, and
dependents were able to deny knowledge of Magdalena's condition without
perjuring themselves, what explains why they chose to do so? It is not because
they deemed there to be anything wrong with slavery per se. In 1407, abolition-
ism lay far over the horizon. To the extent that unstated norms were in force,
the witnesses may have felt that the duration of slavery should be limited, and
that enslaved people who were willing to be assimilated should be allowed in.
But there was no rule requiring masters to manumit slaves. What we are seeing
instead are inklings of resistance to the idea that Peire possessed the moral
standing needed to be worthy of slave ownership.

All societies have an interest in controlling access to the symbols of power
and prestige. In a world where anyone could purchase a slave from a Genoese
or Catalan merchant, or for that matter sail off and grab one on the high seas,
it was difficult for a community to regulate the prestige associated with slave
ownership. But given a situation where the definition of slave status resided in
a suite of embodied behaviors and community perceptions of those behaviors,
the power to control ongoing access to slave owning gradually shifted, over
time, from the master to the enslaved individual and the community.

In all probability, no one, with the possible exception of his wife, Bertomieua, begrudged Peire the slave he had acquired in 1387 as part of the spoils
of war. Subsequently, the community would have had little interest in regulating his access to this symbol of prestige had success softened his behavior and
turned him into an upstanding citizen. But Peire was a social climber, and he
planted his boot on a lot of upturned faces while clambering up the ladder. His
high-handed behavior set him at odds not only with his current and former
business partners but also with members of his own family. By 1399, when
Magdalena got married, community opinion had begun to solidify around the
opinion that Peire was not worthy of the prestige that came with being a slave
owner. The notaries had already withdrawn the honorific *providus vir*, and a
short time later, he was sued by two women in his family. By the time the trial
opened in 1406, Peire had few supporters left. He did have the law on his side,
or at least the law as he and his lawyer, Johan de Ysia, understood it. That, along

with the witnesses who were willing to testify for him, gave him enough power to make life miserable for Magdalena. But it was not enough to persuade his employees and neighbors and even his relatives to support him in his claims.

A marked reluctance to support a plaintiff is not unusual in court cases from Marseille. Episodes like this indicate how witness groups in Roman-canon law courts could nullify truth-claims in a way that is analogous to a practice known as jury nullification in Anglo-American law. A jury is said to have nullified the law when it arrives at a finding contrary to the letter of the law. The witnesses in this case did not constitute a jury in the literal sense of the word, but by declining to attest to something that was true but legally indefinable, the witnesses made it difficult for the judge to find for Peire. Once the testimony of Nicolau de Sala had been repudiated by the testimony of Alaeta Columbe and her friend, Peire lacked the two witnesses needed for proof. In effect, Peire's neighbors and acquaintances had voted for Magdalena's freedom.

Justice Bends Toward Magdalena

Numerous references to Magdalena are peppered throughout the record of proceedings between 1406 and 1407. Whenever names appear in legal records, they are sometimes accompanied by identity labels or attributes, such as "Magdalena, the slave of Peire Huguet." These labels were generated by the individuals who participated in the hearings: plaintiffs, defendants, procurators, judges, and so on. The notaries who transcribed the proceedings into court registers typically did so in a way that was faithful to the language used by actors. Differences in the labels selected, therefore, can be meaningful. By way of example, we have already seen how Peire Huguet persistently labeled Magdalena as a slave in the present tense, "my slave," whereas his procurator, Johan de Ysia, invariably used the past tense or used expressions such as "formerly a slave." The difference in tense betrays a fundamental difference in their understanding of the legal logic driving their claims.

What did the judges and the notaries of the court think? What kinds of labels did they attach to Magdalena's name?

In early March, when Peire Huguet recused the judge of the second of the two lesser courts, he asked for a complete transcript of the proceedings so that they could be annexed to the case already underway in the first court. The notary of the issuing court, as was customary, wrote a salutation to the receiving judge, and gave the proceedings a title. On the 8th of March, the proceedings were received and entered into the record. This is how the salutation read:

> To the noble and distinguished gentleman, lord Johan Raynaut, a licentiate in laws, judge of one of the lesser courts of the city of Marseille, or to his

lieutenant. All the proceedings transacted before the noble and outstanding man, lord Antoni de Raude, doctor of laws, judge of one of the lesser courts of Marseille, involving Peire Huguet, the plaintiff, on the one hand, and Magdalena, the former slave woman of the said Peire, on the other, closed, corrected, and faithfully sealed.[25]

On the inside, the proceedings were similarly entitled "The case of Peire Huguet against the former slave woman, Magdalena."

As this wording indicates, the personnel of the court, at least in the early stages of the dispute, tacitly accepted the proposition that Magdalena had once been but was no longer a slave. The heading of the appellate case, drafted in August of 1407, became dramatically less favorable to Peire's claims, for it omitted any reference whatsoever to her possible slave status: "The appellate case of Peire Huguet against Mandalena [sic] and others." Throughout the proceedings, moreover, notaries scrupulously avoided making any reference to Magdalena as currently a slave, except when recording Peire's direct speech. The only exception occurs in the lurid scene that unfolded in July of 1407, when the lieutenant judge, Elziar Autrici, incautiously echoed Peire's reference to "the said slave woman." This was a gaffe, committed by a secular officer with no formal legal training who was temporarily occupying the position of judge in the absence of his superior.

The personnel of the court understood that Peire's claim of Magdalena's current slave status was just that: a claim, not a statement of fact. This was a neutral and appropriate stance. Elsewhere, however, fragmentary evidence suggests that at least some of the judges who heard the case were not neutral. Rather, they were actively biased against Peire.

The first clue occurs in proceedings from March of 1407, when Peire launched his second claim before Antoni de Raude, the judge of the second of the lesser courts. Soon after, he declared the judge "suspect" and had the proceedings transferred to Johan Raynaut's court. Peire had good reason to doubt Antoni's neutrality. After all, Antoni had required Peire to deposit Bertomieua's 10 l. legacy in escrow, a peculiar decision to say the least, since it was unrelated to the matter at hand.[26] The appropriate response, when Magdalena appeared in court to lodge the complaint, would have been to tell her to initiate a separate procedure to collect on an unpaid legacy.

A more serious irregularity arose in the wake of Magdalena's exception to the testimony of Nicolau de Sala on the grounds of a prior hatred. Like all such legal moves, this one was governed by procedures that required the party to name witnesses, draw up articles, and give the adversary time to draw up interrogatory questions. This could take days or even weeks to arrange. Johan de Ysia appeared in court and declared, as a matter of form, that he could not consent to the taking of testimony unless the usual procedure was respected. Yet the judge, in a stunning departure from the norms of procedural law, moved with indecent haste to hearing testimony on the exception.

Unsurprisingly, Peire declared *this* judge suspect as well, thereby bringing the case into the Palace court, Marseille's major court of first instance. Accordingly, the judge, Johan Raynaut, ordered that the necessary letter be written for Peire. Truly breathtaking, though, is what the judge then did with the deposit that Peire had left with the notary of the court several months earlier. This involved a departure from procedure so remarkable that the notary of the court felt duty-bound to enter a strong protest in the transcript of the proceedings:

> Following this, the said lord judge, despite the fact that he had been recused for suspicion, desired and ruled that the said deposit be handed over to Magdalena, ordering me, the notary whose name is written below, to hand it over to Magdalena, which I did. At the same time, the lord judge ordered that a certain hand-note concerning the aforesaid deposit, which I myself had written out and which the said Peire Huguet had received in written form, be given back to me. Here again, I feared infringing on the liberties of this city by virtue of imposing some novelty following this recusal for suspicion. I, Arnaut Barran, the notary of the aforesaid court, wrote this.[27]

The notary's expression of deep concern about the judge's procedural shenanigans is without precedent in Marseille's extensive judicial records.

We have, then, three procedural irregularities: placing the deposit in escrow, sidestepping the procedures that governed the hearing of an exception procedure, and releasing the deposit prior to any ruling on the matter. The judges of the two lesser courts were not only ill-disposed to Peire and his claims. They were actively working against him.

What about the lieutenant judge, Elziar Autrici, who presided over the Palace court in the absence of the viguier, Mathieu de Bella Valle? The transfer of the case to the Palace court had taken place after Peire had completed his own arguments, meaning there was little more he could do. Now that Peire's evidence phase was over, Hugonin reappeared, with his wife at his side, to relaunch the plea filed the previous August. The testimony offered by Antoneta Poncie and Catherina Limosine in July, as we saw in the previous chapter, was vague and indecisive.[28] Shortly afterward, the evidence phase had drawn to a close, all the available procedural moves had been considered and stilled, and the lieutenant judge issued a sentence. According to his sentence, both parties had lost.

Although any number of reasons may explain the failure of Peire's case, the most likely is that the successful repudiation of Nicolau de Sala's testimony meant that Peire only had one witness to attest to his claim that Magdalena had been given to him as a slave. The personnel of the court knew that Magdalena had formerly been a slave, since that is how they referred to her. Yet the presiding magistrate was unable to know this in a lawful sense. What is interesting, therefore, is that the lieutenant, Elziar Autrici, either failed to note the procedural irregularity associated with the exception to Nicolau de Sala's testimony or, having noticed it, failed to discount it. Equally interesting is the fact that he confirmed the ruling of the judge of the lesser court that the 10 l. legacy be given to Magdalena, regardless of the manifest irregularity of this move. Despite the gaffe he had committed by referring to Magdalena as "the said slave woman," it seems that Elziar ultimately chose to side with his colleagues in the lesser courts in doubting the merits of Peire's arguments.

In his appeal, Peire referred to the ruling of the magistrate of the Palace court as iniquitous and unjust. The expression is formulaic, appearing in all appeals from the era. Even so, there seems to be little doubt that the early phases of the trial, from start to finish, were tainted by procedural irregularities.

A Servile Bitch

Over the next two months, Peire and his procurator pursued an appeal before Antoni Barreme, the judge of the first appellate court. When Antoni's term in office ended in mid-October, his successor, Guilhem Arnaut, took over. After two months of legal wrangling, the transcripts of all the previous hearings were transmitted from the Palace court and entered into the register of the appellate court. None of it made any difference. Within a few weeks, Guilhem ruled against Peire, and he was back to the drawing board.

Yet the fall was not entirely without drama. One day, Peire and Magdalena appeared in court in the presence of the appellate judge and the notaries of the court. Although we hear Magdalena speaking at frequent intervals over the span of two years, those references, following the style of the courts, are always formatted in the third person, as in "Magdalena Coline appeared in court, having first recalled her procurator, and accused the adversary party of contumacy" and so on. The salty exchange that took place in the fall of 1407 occurred off-stage, providing one of those rare moments where we actually hear a fragment of direct speech.

The record of the exchange survives because in the second trial, launched in January of 1408, Peire sought to show that Magdalena had failed to demonstrate the respect and gratitude that a freedperson was obliged to display toward a patron.[29] To prove this, Peire claimed that she had insulted him in the court of first appeals the previous fall. The witnesses to this claim consisted of none other than the presiding appellate judge, along with one of his notaries. Here is what they said:

In the year above, on Monday, the 19th of March, the noble and distinguished gentleman, the jurist Lord Guilhem Arnaut, testified that he knows nothing about this other than that on one occasion, when he was serving as a tribune in the court of first appeals, he heard Magdalena, who was in court at the time, say that Peire Huguet had called her "a slave woman" and "a servile bitch." To this, Magdalena responded that Peire Huguet was lying through his throat, since Peire, despite all his efforts, had failed to prove that she was a slave. He heard many other insulting words spoken by Magdalena against Peire Huguet, though he doesn't remember them.

On the year and day above, master Guilhem Morenon, notary, a witness summoned and produced on behalf of Peire Huguet, swore on the holy gospels to speak and testify truthfully about the matters under interrogation. This witness, interrogated and diligently examined on the fifth of the articles presented above on behalf of Peire Huguet, these having first been read to him in the vernacular, and the preceding ones omitted with the permission of the plaintiff, said and testified on his oath that he knows nothing about this other than that during the present year, while he was at the court of first appeals of this city, together with Guilhem Arnaut, the judge of the court, and Raymon Elie, notary of the court, he heard from the aforesaid Magdalena—who was engaged in a lawsuit with Peire Huguet, according to people in the know, at the court of the palace judge—that this same Peire had treated her badly, and had called her "a slave woman" and "a servile bitch." To this, Magdalena responded that Peire Huguet was lying through his throat, and brought forth several other insulting words against Peire, which he said he doesn't remember, since Peire had failed to prove that she was a slave despite his best efforts. Asked about the day, month, and hour and the names of those present, he said he did not remember.[30]

To accuse someone of "lying through his throat (*mentre per gulam*)," as Magdalena apparently did, was sufficiently bad to qualify for prosecution. Similar insults, in court records from the early 1400s, earned fines upward of 10 s. To take a pertinent example, one of Peire's associates from the 1380s, Hugo de Relhana, was fined 25 s. for insulting Peire's brother-in-law, Nicolau d'Ays, having "injuriously given the lie to him through the throat."[31]

Peire had reason enough, then, to feel affronted by this verbal assault. Even more piercing, though, is the insight we gain into Magdalena's state of mind: her sense of dignity, her anger and resentment over the years of humiliation, her understanding of what it was all about. Standing before the judge, having forcefully rejected the label "slave," she mocked her former enslaver for his pathetic inability to prove her servitude. Although the notary's language is characteristically imprecise, it is likely that Magdalena directed the remarks not to Peire but instead to the judge. If so, we can imagine her saying words such as this: "Your honor, I beg you to understand that this man has treated me badly for years. He has insulted me by calling me a 'slave woman' and a 'servile bitch.' But he is lying through his throat, because he has never been able to prove that I was once enslaved."

Also revealing is the insult, *cana mastina*, that Peire hurled at her. Insults based on dogs (Lat. *canis*; Occ. *can, cana*) were not common in the arsenal of insult in Marseille. The only examples I have found come from a register of criminal fines paid to the treasurer from the fiscal year 1330–1331.[32] The insult was sometimes hurled by Christians against one another, as when one Christian woman insulted another by saying "Get lost, shitty whore for dogs and pigs."[33] But they were used more commonly against Jews, as when a Christian, Jacme Coysinier, insulted a Jew named Petit by calling him a "smelly renegade dog." The tendency to connect Jews to dogs was cleverly turned around by a Jewish woman named Astruga, wife of Comprat, who said to a Christian woman "you are more of a dog than I am."[34] To call Magdalena a "bitch," therefore, was to highlight her foreign origins and liken her to Jews and strangers.

The adjective *mastina* is even more interesting. Etymologically, the literal meaning is "mastiff," or guard-dog. In Old French, Middle French, and Occitan, *mastin* and its variants, in both adjectival and verbal forms, acquired the transferred meaning of servile or subservient, and sometimes dirty, bad, or stubborn. In later centuries, it also took on the sense of someone who is a mongrel or impure.[35] In the creative imagination of the troubadour Marcabru, the verbal form carries the suggestion of a woman whose lust induces her to couple with a social inferior, just like a bitch in heat, however well bred, will couple with any available mongrel.[36] Who knows whether Peire was listening to troubadour songs in the early fifteenth century, but if he knew this verse, then he was condemning Magdalena for the lustful desire that had induced her to leave his house, foregoing his refined and courtly lovemaking in favor of the crude attentions afforded by the country bumpkin from Savoy with whom she had cast her lot.

By the fall of 1407, Peire had come to understand Magdalena as a servile hound sent by Fate to bite and snap at him and drag him down into hell. Everything started to go wrong for him from the moment he had taken her as a slave. Even more revealing is the sense we get of how Magdalena's own understanding of the lawsuit had evolved. Once upon a time, it may have been a lawsuit over a debt of 6 florins, but it had since turned into a suit about her freedom. The crucial issue did not even concern the question of when or whether she had become free. It was instead about whether she had ever been a slave.

11

A Pyrrhic Victory

IN JANUARY OF 1408, a dispute that Magdalena had every reason to believe was over and done with came roaring back to life. On the 26th, Peire appeared in court with a list of grievances, complaining that his former slave—and the wording merits emphasis: his *former* slave—unmindful of all the nice things he had done for her, had pursued him in court without receiving permission to do so. She failed to show the necessary reverence to any of the judges. Worse, she failed to show him, Peire, any reverence at all, even going to the extent of insulting him in public. Given that the witnesses who might speak to these truths are aged and verging on senility, he declared, and given his fears that any might depart at any moment, he asked for and received permission to move directly to the presentation of his articles of proof.

Four days later, an astonished Bertran Gombert, Magdalena's lawyer, appeared at court, telling the judge that the plea merited no reply whatsoever, since a legal matter that has been adjudicated cannot be heard again. But Peire anticipated this rebuttal. The suit, he argued, was grounded in a new claim. In one of the rare victories granted by members of Marseille's judiciary, the judge of the Palace court, Hugo Vincens, agreed with Peire and allowed the plea to go forward.

The arguments laid out by Peire have elements that are by now familiar to us. In the first three articles, we are told that Magdalena was captured in a just war in the vicinity of Naples. Knowing herself to be a slave, she served him for ten years and more. But the fourth and fifth articles introduced a strikingly different claim:

> Next, he intends to prove that an ungrateful Magdalena, to Peire's injury, caused her patron and master to be summoned in justice for the purpose of litigating with him. She litigated for many months in the royal court of Marseille without having requested or received license from a judge having the power to grant and bestow such license. It is public and notorious that she had Peire distrained, summoned, and convened before various judges belonging to Marseille's royal court, litigating with him.

A PYRRHIC VICTORY 171

Next, he intends to prove that the said Magdalena said every bad thing and did what she could against the said Peire, both in court and elsewhere.[1]

These were serious challenges indeed.

Legal Peril

As scholars have had occasion to remark before now, the twinned concepts of freedom and slavery were deeply embedded in the thought of the ancient Roman world.[2] As a result, regulation of the boundary between freedom and servitude was a matter of concern for the law and suffuses the body of Roman law gathered by the emperor Justinian and published in 536 in a legal text known as the *Corpus iuris civilis*. Two matters were of special interest. First, slaves were human. Since they were human, they could suffer injury, form conjugal unions, provide evidence in court, and similar actions. Second, slaves could become free.[3] Both of these matters required regulation.[4]

When the Corpus iuris civilis resurfaced in western Europe in the eleventh century, it became the subject of much juristic commentary and discussion. The body of Roman legal thought about slavery came along for the ride. As the Bolognese glossators thought more and more about the matter, it occurred to them that there were a great many people in their world who didn't fit neatly into the legal categories of enslaved and free as laid out by the Roman jurist Gaius and his successors. These people were sometimes described as *servi* in contemporary texts, a label that historians today are inclined to translate as "serfs." To the Bolognese glossators, though, the word *servi* was all wrong, because serfs and bondsmen had rights and privileges that would never have been accorded to Roman slaves. This bothered them. They began to think carefully about what had gone wrong, and to consider the possibility that *servi* should be restored to their proper condition.[5]

By a curious coincidence, the recuperation of Roman law took place at a moment when the trade in chattel slaves in Mediterranean Europe was beginning to accelerate, as we saw in chapter 1. The slavery of the age, based as it was on the enslavement of those who were not co-religionists, was very different from the bondage associated with serfs or *adscriptii*, one of the words invented by the glossators to describe this category. As they became aware, chattel slavery fit the Roman legal concept far better than did serfdom. In several areas, however, there was friction, much of it arising from the fact that Christianity itself had changed a good deal since the days of Justinian. Christianity was hardly opposed to slavery. Among other things, canon law deemed the enslavement and forcible conversion of pagans and Muslims to be a pious and laudable action, inasmuch as it brought souls to salvation. In addition, medieval Christendom was just as inclined as ancient Rome to sort people into status categories. The major differences arose from changes in the Christian understanding of marriage, and, to a lesser degree, from ideas about the special legal status of the priesthood.

As it happens, the Romans had anticipated the situation that confronted Peire, that is, one in which a freedman or freedwoman pursued litigation against a patron. The relevant laws or principles, assembled in the Code and the Digest, lie at the headwaters of a stream of legal thought that resurfaced vigorously in the twelfth century.[6] One of the laws published in the Siete Partidas in 1252 mentions the principle in a general title concerned with the honor that a slave should exhibit toward a master: "An emancipated person should not bring his master into court or make any statements against him, or claim anything of him except after permission is asked of the judge of the district; or bring any accusation against him or defame him in any way."[7] Unlike the Siete Partidas, the Occitan law text Lo Codi did not have a separate section on slavery, and instead followed the Roman habit of considering matters pertaining to slavery in the contexts in which they were relevant. The relevant passage in Lo Codi appears in the law *De in ius vocando*, or "Concerning summons to court," an amalgamation of several passages in the Code and the Digest.

> In the same manner, a freedman may not call his patron in justice, that is to say he who had been a slave and was made free may not summon the person who made him free, without approval of a judge. Similarly, in the kinds of cases where a son may not call his father in justice, a freedman in the same way may not call his patron. If a son shall in fact have summoned his father or mother, or if a freedman shall have summoned his patron or his patron's wife or his children, except in the manner described above, he shall suffer a penalty of fifty of gold, that is to say, fifty bezants.[8]

Following his complaint that Magdalena, as a freedwoman, had summoned him without permission, Peire added a second novel argument: "Next, he intends to prove that the said Magdalena said every bad thing and did what she could against the said Peire, both in court and elsewhere." Laws related to this are found in the sixth book of the Code, in the chapter on freedmen and their children.[9] Related laws are amply attested in texts such as the Siete Partidas and Lo Codi. In the latter, the law, which represents a significant elaboration on the corresponding passages in the Code, appears under the heading *Quomodo libertinus uel libertina efficiuntur serui*, or "How a freedman or freedwoman may be turned back into slaves":

> If a freedman or a freedwoman following their manumission shall have offered any ingratitude toward their patron or his wife or son or any of his heirs, and if the patron or his children can prove it, they should be restored

to servitude and be made slaves. The instances of ingratitude for which a freedman or freedwoman may be returned to servitude are these: if the freedman threatened to strike his patron, or if he treated him with contempt of any kind, for instance by striking him, or if he damaged his patron's goods.[10]

The key word here is "ingratitude," for it allowed Peire to define the insults he had received from Magdalena as violations of the law.

Strikingly, a pastiche of the language associated with the Roman laws governing the reverence due to a patron had already appeared in the unformed plea initially presented by Peire at the very outset of the first trial, in August 1406:

> And owing to her ingratitude, she ought to be restored to servitude, *salvo iure*, since she had never been manumitted by Peire nor in his name. And because she had him called in justice, license not having been requested or received, and had him summoned by the said master Hugonin, therefore, she ought to be punished under the legal penalty for summoning a patron in justice, for having lodged a plea against him for six florins for the reasons provided in the so-called "petition" that was presented by the said master Hugonin in Magdalena's name.[11]

Rather strangely, however, when it came time to present the articles in September 1406, both claims had silently been dropped. Nor do they appear in the additional articles presented that month and six months later, in March 1407. Peire's lawyer, Johan de Ysia, clearly knew about the law and its potential relevance. Why did Peire decide to abandon this line?

The answer is quite straightforward. Throughout the first trial, as we saw in the previous chapter, Peire was extremely reluctant to acknowledge that Magdalena had ever been manumitted. The law governing the reverence due to a patron, however, applied only to freedpersons. An acknowledgment of Magdalena's freedom would have clashed with Peire's heartfelt belief that Magdalena was still his slave. But there was another problem, potentially even more significant, for the first trial had been initiated not by Magdalena, but by her husband, Hugonin. Peire claimed that Magdalena was behind it all and he was probably right. Yet there was no way he could prove this suspicion. If Magdalena had been so indiscreet as to have made an appearance at one of the hearings in the fall, then perhaps Peire and Johan could have leapt upon this to invoke *De in ius vocando*. But she did not, and for this reason, the law did not apply. In light of this, one of the striking features about the second trial lies in how Peire's language shifted dramatically to accommodate the new understanding of Magdalena's status. Throughout much of the second trial, he referred to Magdalena as "formerly his slave."[12] The insistent nagging of his procurator, Johan de Ysia, had apparently gotten through to him.

But this is getting ahead of the game, so let us return to the 16th of February 1408, which is when Peire's witnesses began to appear. This time, he managed to dig up not two but five highly disciplined witnesses who were ready and willing to speak to his claims regarding Magdalena's condition as a slave. This time, he took pains to coach them carefully on what they should say, to avoid any surprises. Two of the witnesses had appeared in the first trial: the barber-surgeon, Nicolau de Sala, and the shipwright, Guilhem Limosin. We have already met the third, the ship's scribe, Aycart Vedel, whose careful testimony was so helpful for reconstructing some of the circumstances of Magdalena's early life.[13] All five witnesses confirmed Peire's account of Magdalena's acquisition and subsequent servitude. A comparison of the testimony of the two men who had also testified in the first trial, Nicolau de Sala and Guilhem Limosin, is revealing, for the second depositions of both men were more detailed, either thanks to the careful coaching, or because their memories had improved following months of reflection.

On the crucial 4th and 5th articles, however, the testimony was more tentative. Three witnesses, Jacme Aurelhe, Clari Borays, and Aycart Vedel, disclaimed all knowledge of Magdalena's suits and acts of ingratitude, probably out of a sense of sullenness that is common among witnesses in this era, perhaps because they had been at sea the previous year and genuinely knew nothing about the first trial. Nicolau and Guilhem confirmed the claim that Magdalena had litigated against Peire—they could hardly have done otherwise, having testified in the first trial—but denied any knowledge of the insults attributed to Magdalena. To demonstrate Magdalena's ingratitude, therefore, Peire called two additional witnesses, namely, the judge and the notary of the first appellate court whose depositions were featured at the end of the previous chapter.

The testimony of these two men was devastating for Magdalena's cause. All the elements that had worked so powerfully in her favor during the first trial suddenly began to work against her. In the spring and summer of 1407, performing her freedom in court seemed like a winning strategy. But under the terms of *De in ius vocando*, all the energy she had put into the case merely served to make her, a freedwoman, guilty of having litigated against her patron. So powerful was the resulting argument that it is possible to imagine that Johan de Ysia's strategy, all along, had consisted of goading Magdalena into making a legal response that could then be used to discredit her.

But what about the escape clause? *De in ius vocando* allowed freedpersons to sue their patrons under the condition that they first receive permission from a judge. The point that doing so hadn't occurred to Magdalena's inexperienced

A PYRRHIC VICTORY   175

legal counsel, Antoni Arnaut, in the spring of 1407, may be a symptom of the fact that the laws pertaining to slavery were not very well understood in Provence—or at least, not sufficiently understood by a no-name procurator like Antoni Arnaut. It would have been a simple enough matter, after all, to have acquired the necessary permission from a judge. By July, Magdalena had hired an expert pleader, Bertran Gombert, who probably did know about *De in ius vocando*. By then, however, it was too late.

As a point of law, it is not clear which party had the obligation to prove that the request for permission to litigate had or had not taken place. Peire and Johan, however, left nothing to chance. On the 27th of March, they brought forth a letters patent delivered to them by the judge of the first appellate court, Guilhem Arnaut. On their request, Guilhem had taken time to reread the transcripts of the first trial in search of any evidence indicating that Magdalena had requested an indulgence to summon Peire in justice.[14] He found none.

The final thread in the skein of legal arguments assembled by Peire arrived on the 28th of May, when Peire placed in evidence a long and learned legal brief (*consilium*) issued by a doctor-of-laws named Antonius Virronis, a minor figure in Provençal legal circles based in Aix-en-Provence.[15] Through the briefs they wrote, jurists such as Antonius can be thought of as providing expert testimony concerning the domain of law itself. By the fourteenth or fifteenth centuries, such briefs were commonly sought by litigants in trials that involved complex points of law. Typically, the consulting jurist was paid to conduct research into the relevant legal precedents and to assemble the arguments in the form of a brief.

At the outset of his brief, Antonius declared that proceedings had clearly shown that Magdalena had long been the slave of Peire Huguet, who had held her in servitude continuously up to the time of her manumission.[16] Subsequently, as the most ungrateful of ingrates, she irreverently summoned her patron in justice without having received an indulgence to do so and litigated with him on many occasions. Even worse, she proffered horrible contumelies against him. For all of this, he declared, she was liable to the penalty of fifty pieces of gold. The brief bristles with learned references to the Code, the Digest, and the Institutes. From the older corpus of laws assembled in the Digest, he pulled out several elements of the section 2. 2, *De in ius vocando*, which declared that freedpersons, like sons, were restricted in their ability to summon a patron or a father before a court. The case was also bolstered by references to sections of the Code which insisted on the reverence due to a patron by a freedperson. Antonius was also learned in contemporary law, as shown by his great familiarity with the extensive body of glosses on the Corpus iuris civilis found in the works of the glossators Odofredus, Bartolus, Cynus de Pistoia, and Albericus de Rosate.

In a passage that must have been particularly alarming to Magdalena and Bertran, Antonius pushed the logic beyond the claims made by Peire, declaring that "I believe that it could be said that, by reason of the injuries inflicted by her on her patron, she may be recalled into slavery."[17] The fact that she is married, he continued, offers no obstacle to re-enslavement, since slaves can be married and continue to serve their masters.[18] Summing it up, he declared that "a freedwoman can be restored to slavery on account of her ingratitude, and she can be married and serve her master."[19]

Peire Is Undone, Again

Between February and May of 1408, as the web of Peire's arguments gradually tightened around her, Magdalena's response was uncharacteristically limp and flagging, a symptom of deep and gnawing anxiety. The only legal strategy deployed by her loyal procurator, Bertran Gombert, was to protest, repeatedly, that the case had already been ruled on the previous year, but the judge appears to have accepted Peire's argument to the effect that articles 4 and 5 were new, as indeed they were. When Hugo Vincens, the judge of the Palace Court, recessed on Tuesday, the 29th of May, things looked bleak.

On Saturday the 9th of June, Hugo, like a deus ex machina, returned with a verdict in Magdalena's favor. The judge's ruling, astonishingly, held that Peire's suit had failed because he neglected to check the paperwork that allowed Magdalena's procurator, Bertran Gombert, to represent her at court:

> [W]e declare this trial to be a nothing of nullities . . . since nowhere in the acts do we find any reference to the ruling or authority that authorized Bertran Gombert, Magdalena's procurator, who had joined the plea and carried out many actions in the case. It behooves the plaintiff, through his vigilance, to verify everything that is relevant to his case, lest it be corrupted by the defect of nullity, given how we glean the law from his actions. Therefore, with this, our ruling, we condemn Peire Huguet, the actor in this case . . . to pay all the expenses arising from this plea.[20]

Peire was astounded by Hugo's perplexing ruling and so are we. Among other things, as he pointed out, Bertran Gombert's power of attorney had been entered into the record during the first trial, and since that trial was the foundation upon which the second was built, there was no obligation to refile the paperwork. Peire may have been wrong on the point of law here, since by his own argument, the trial initiated before the Palace court in January of 1408 was grounded in a different claim. But even so, it was unprecedented for a plaintiff to be held responsible for the paperwork of the adversary party.

As we have already seen, the judges who supervised the first trial, from the lesser courts up to the first appellate court, stretched and bent procedure in an

A PYRRHIC VICTORY   177

effort to find for Magdalena. The bizarre decision of Hugo Vincens in the second trial confirms the extent of a deep judicial bias against Peire. The problem lies in explaining why this should have been the case.

We might be tempted to say that the bias arose from the fact that the judges simply disliked Peire, or were moved by a pretty face, or found Magdalena's personal story so compelling. Records of criminal fines collected in the first decade of the fifteenth century include several that arose from insults directed at members of Marseille's judiciary, accusing them of exactly the kind of bias that worked in Magdalena's favor. In 1413, a weaver was fined 40 s. for telling the judge of the Palace court, "Better justice will be found in the land of the Moors than is found here."[21] Equally vivid was an insult hurled by a notary at a judge around the same time: "I have been attending this court for sixteen years, and I have never seen it so badly governed as it is today."[22] These and other insults, which appear in registers of fines paid alongside sentences issued against judges themselves for corrupt behavior, reveal a widespread sense that the courts were being badly run. But if "corruption" occupies one face of the coin of explanation, the reverse bears the logo "equity." Procedure is the enemy of fairness whenever it generates a decision that is legally correct but intuitively wrong. The judges in both trials simply knew that Magdalena had right on her side. Knowing this, they concocted specious arguments that allowed them to issue the rulings they wanted to issue.

Along with this, it is helpful to consider what could have happened to Magdalena if a judge had ruled in Peire's favor. In both trials, such a ruling could have entailed a restoration of servitude. It is highly doubtful that anyone associated with the law had any moral objections to slavery per se. The public notaries, to take a noteworthy instance, routinely participated in slave sales. As this demonstrates, there was no *favor libertatis*, no preference for freedom, among members of the legal community. But it is easy to imagine how the spectacle of arresting Magdalena, dragging her from her house, and returning her to bondage could have made some judges feel queasy. It would have required imposing a condition of sexual dishonor on a respectable married woman. For judges in the borderlands, where the practice of slavery was unfamiliar, this might have been a step too far.

The King Rules

Undaunted by the latest setback, a resilient Peire launched another appeal in June of 1408. The judge of the appellate court was Guilhem Arnaut, the very same judge who had ruled the previous fall in Magdalena's favor. This time, however, the circumstances were different. Guilhem himself had entered evidence on Peire's behalf, for he had not only testified to the insults Magdalena had spoken against Peire in his court the previous fall but had also scoured the

178   CHAPTER 11

trial proceedings of the previous year to confirm that Magdalena had never acquired a license to sue her patron. In a sense, Guilhem was primed to rule in Peire's favor. Yet Peire was not one to leave anything to chance. He had one last trump card to play in an effort to ensure that Guilhem would rule in his favor, and that was to petition the king.

In medieval Europe, justice was inextricably associated with the image of good kingship. Since the days of the Carolingians, it was the duty of the good king to hear the cries of his subjects and correct wrongs. Louis IX of France, the great-great-great-great grandfather of the present King Louis II of Naples, was famed for his solicitous attention to doing what was right. Supplying justice was not merely a case of placing the merits of two cases on a balance and seeing how things tipped but also ensuring that the poor and the humble were not victimized by those who administered the realm and issued justice in the king's name. The deluge of appeals would have swamped any well-meaning king. With the rise of administrative kingship in the thirteenth century, procedures emerged that allowed appellants to file petitions and pleas for mercy of many sorts. These became formalized within royal bureaucracies across Europe.

Scholarship in recent decades has explored aspects of the vast system of petitioning that emerged in the later Middle Ages and accelerated dramatically in the early modern period.[23] Upon payment of the necessary fees, pardon letters were issued by royal courts to mitigate the harsh sentences meted out by local judges. But petitions could also be lodged at any prior stage of a trial or dispute where the objective was to short-circuit local justice through the king's ruling. This was the card that Peire now sought to play. Thanks to a chance note entered in the record on Saturday the 11th of August, we learn that a visit to Marseille from King Louis II of Anjou was imminently expected. A few days later, Peire managed to wangle an audience with the king or with one of his courtiers. We know this because on Tuesday the 21st, a triumphant Johan de Ysia appeared in the court of first appeals bearing a royal response to Peire's petition. Magdalena was summoned to court and the letters patent was registered in the proceedings. The letter, issued from Marseille, was dated the 16th of August.

Following the formula in use at the Angevin court, the letter began with a conventional salutation to the judge of the appellate court and then noted that the king had recently received the following supplication:

> To the sacred royal majesty of Jerusalem and Sicily, with all humility, reverence, and honor that is fitting, Peire Huguet, a loyal servant and subject of your majesty, is submitting a supplication. In years not long past, while in the vicinity of Naples in an armada of galleys belonging to your royal majesty, a certain slave named Magdalena was captured in a galley of the rebels along

with several other slaves, and in a just war. Then, in compensation for the good services provided by Peire to the same armada, the slave was given as a slave to the supplicant by the ship captains of the other galleys, and he held her as a slave, in the same condition of servitude, for ten years and more.[24]

Here, the text of Peire's supplication turned to the matter of his complaints, first noting that the slave woman had summoned him in justice without having received license, and then observing that the Palace judge, strangely, had condemned him for a mistake made by the adversary party. The supplication notes that Peire had appealed to the court of first appeals, where the matter was currently pending. It ended with a plea to the king to be mindful of the services provided by Peire and to intervene in the matter in his favor, by ordering the judge to sentence the slave woman to pay the 50 pieces of gold prescribed by *De in ius vocando*. In the remainder of the letter, the official writing on the king's behalf, Johan de Sado, did not absolutely order the judge to do as Peire had requested, but simply declared that summary justice should be delivered without any of the usual legal wrangling. Nevertheless, it is clear what the king wanted.

On the evening of Monday, the 27th of August, at the hour of the evening prayers, the judge of the appellate court issued his sentence, declaring that Peire had successfully proven his case. The text of his ruling has not survived, so we cannot know whether he ruled on the merits of the case alone, which in any event were airtight for Peire, or whether the king's letter was decisive in determining the outcome. Magdalena declined to be present for the reading of the sentence. Instead, she appeared in court moments later to request a copy in writing.

During this time Magdalena had not been passive. Another chance entry in the record several folios earlier indicates that she had traveled to Aix-en-Provence three weeks before, around the 7th of August.[25] The only conceivable reason for her to be in Aix is because she, too, had hoped for an audience with the king. If so, she may have been dismayed to learn upon her arrival in Aix that the king was on his way to Marseille, and even more dismayed upon her return to discover that Peire had gotten to the king first. Yet not all hope was lost. Immediately after receiving a copy of the sentence, she set out once again for Aix-en-Provence. She was probably accompanied by her procurator, Bertran Gombert, given the legal advice she was going to need.

Aix-en-Provence lies about 30 kilometers to the north of Marseille. Walking at a brisk pace all night, you could get there the following day, following the route that heads north and passes through the ridge known as the Massif de l'Étoile at the village of Septème-les-Vallons. Magdalena did not belong to a class of people who normally would have traveled by horse or donkey. Bertran did, however, and it is possible that he was able to arrange transport for them.

Regardless of the mode of travel, we know that Magdalena reached Aix quickly, for she acquired an audience with the king or a courtier with astonishing celerity, on Tuesday or Wednesday, a day or two after receiving a copy of the sentence.

It is worth pausing for a moment to consider the spectacle of Magdalena begging special grace and favor at the court of the king in Aix-en-Provence. A quarter of a century earlier, the assassination of Queen Johanna in 1382 inaugurated an era of political instability for the realm of Naples. In 1387, a military expedition launched by officials attached to the court of Queen Marie dislodged Magdalena from her first enslaver and placed her in the hands of her second. Two decades later, Magdalena Coline, now a free woman, Provençale in speech and dress, appeared before the royal court to ask Louis II, son of Queen Marie, to confirm her free status. Rarely do we come across so vivid a glimpse into a moment when the lives of the great and powerful intersect with those of the poor and humble.

As the adage goes, she who laughs last, laughs best. On Wednesday, the 29th of August, Louis II, king of Naples, Sicily, and Jerusalem, having heard Magdalena's supplication either directly or via one of his courtiers, issued a letters patent on parchment, sealed with a red-wax pendant seal, to Pons Cays, judge of the court of appeals in the counties of Provence and Forcalquier.[26] The letter included a verbatim copy of the supplication that had been submitted by Magdalena, which opened as follows:

> To the sacred royal majesty of Jerusalem and Sicily, it is not without bonds of bitterness that this is being told to his royal majesty, on behalf of his humble servant, Magdalena, the wife of Hugonin de lo Chorges, a shoemaker and citizen of Marseille. A little while ago, a lawsuit was directed against Magdalena, born of free parents. It was brought before the wise and honorable man, Lord Johan Raynaut, a licentiate in laws, judge of one of the lesser courts of the city of Marseille. The suit was initiated through the unjust importunings of a certain Peire Huguet, citizen of the aforesaid city. Sometime earlier, he had married off Magdalena, not as a slave, but as a pure and free woman, and had in part provided her with a dowry. Now, he is claiming that Magdalena was and is a slave woman. This suit traveled by way of suspicion to the court of the lord viguier and judge of the city, presided over by Lord Hugo Audivin, a judge appointed as a replacement for the deceased Johan Ysoart, formerly the judge of the Palace court of the city. Through his definitive sentence, he declared Magdalena absolved of the charges made by Peire Huguet, her adversary.[27]

The narration, continuing to unfold for another page or so, went on to describe events that are mostly familiar to us, apart from the revelation that late

A PYRRHIC VICTORY   181

in the fall of 1407, Peire had pleaded his case before Marseille's court of second appeals, where it hung in an unresolved state. Magdalena also revealed that Peire, pretending to be aggrieved by the decision of the appellate judge, simultaneously lodged a claim in the court of first appeals of Provence and Forcalquier, before the very same judge, Pons Cays. But not content to wait for a ruling from Pons, Peire launched into yet another suit—and here, the language that pours forth from Magdalena's supplication is so charged and bitter that it is worth returning to her words:

> Nonetheless, despite all this, in no small detriment and injury to these same proceedings and to Magdalena and her rights in this matter, Peire, in order to oppress this poor woman and enmesh her in suits and legal expenses, once again dragged Magdalena before the lord judge of the city over a claim of 50 pieces of gold on the grounds that Magdalena had summoned Peire to court without having requested a license to do so.

This judge, as we know, declared the trial a nullity, inducing Peire to lodge an appeal. Here things get interesting again, because according to Magdalena, the judge of the court of first appeals, possibly motivated by a letters patent "deviously petitioned from his royal majesty," issued a ruling against her, even though this same judge had ruled in her favor the previous fall. The next passage lingers on the irony by which Magdalena had been both absolved and condemned by one and the same judge. Following this, a curious phrase indicates that Magdalena did not bother to take her case to the court of second appeals in Marseille, "because the judges there are not fully learned."[28] This explains why Magdalena preferred to skip Marseille's second appellate court and bring the case directly to the king. The supplication closed with a plea to the king that he resolve the case by ordering Pons Cays to return to the case lodged by Peire the previous December and issue a ruling.

By Friday, Pons drafted an order to the judge of the court of appeals in Marseille, appending Magdalena's supplication and Louis II's response, and delivered the document into Magdalena's hands. She and Bertran traveled back to Marseille and appeared in court the following Monday, the 3rd of September, to have the letter inserted into the proceedings.

As is the case with all such rulings, the king and his appellate judge refrained from making a definitive ruling in the absence of further hearings. Pons did order the judge of Marseille's appellate court to transcribe the relevant proceedings and remit them to him within fifteen days, at Tarascon. Peire Huguet was told to come to Tarascon to witness the unsealing of the acts if he so desired, but if he chose not to, they would be opened regardless and justice pursued. The proceedings end abruptly at this point, and what this means is that we cannot know for certain how Pons ruled. Yet every sign, including the rapidity with which the case was taken up at the royal court, the dismissive tone in which Peire is addressed at the end of the letter, the pattern whereby the king's true wishes could be discerned from his indirect statements, and the very fact that Magdalena and Bertran thought it worth their while to have the ruling registered, indicates that Peire had played his last card and lost.

But although Peire had lost, it is not easy for us to say that Magdalena had won. The roll of the dice in 1406 had inaugurated two years of intense anguish, expense, and humiliation for her and her husband. The case was touch-and-go until the very last minute and could have derailed at any point. In public, she had repeatedly been called a slave woman, an ingrate, a thief, and a servile bitch. In moments of desperation, she had had to call in favors from those who wished her well, and had done so in ways that may have set husbands against wives and neighbors against one another. Although some of her well-wishers stood by her during the first trial, notably Lady Alaeta Columbe and her friend, they may have been troubled by the fact that they had been asked to do so. It had been Magdalena's choice, after all, to launch the suit. Anyone with knowledge of Peire's irascible nature might have told her to let sleeping dogs lie.

The victory may have been barbed in another way. Magdalena was a displaced person. Years ago, she had been dragged violently from her homeland and put through the pain and indignity of enslavement. The escape route that she cobbled together required her to adopt the persona of a free Christian woman. She had learned how to wear Christian dress and behave as Christians do: attending religious services, taking communion, invoking the name of God in ways that were very different from how she had been taught as a child. She had to deny the woman she had become when the elders of her community, long ago, marked her arms with the tattoos of her people. We don't know whether she missed her home and her family, but if she did, she would have had to sequester those feelings away in a deep inner place, since it would have been perilous to acknowledge the ache. On this reading, Magdalena may have achieved a victory, but it was a Pyrrhic victory. It had come at great cost, the cost of assimilation.

Coda: Bertran Gombert

The path that took Magdalena beyond slavery may have been rather different from that pursued by enslaved men and women elsewhere in the Mediterranean, notably those who sought freedom through flight, but it required just as much fortitude and stamina, just as much planning, and just as much good fortune. Her own pursuit of freedom was enabled by the network of supporters who negotiated the terms of her first and second marriages and then by a broader group of neighbors and others in the know, most of whom refused to aid and abet Peire's desire to put her back in servitude or punish her for having wriggled free. In a perverse way, she was assisted by Peire himself, who was unable to pursue his grievances without undermining his own claim that she had never been manumitted. Judges of the courts bent their rulings in her favor.

At the top of the hierarchy, the king himself was sympathetic to her claims. It is striking that he appears to have favored a freedwoman over a man who had served his own father and mother, Louis I of Anjou and Queen Marie. In this instance, it seems very likely that Bertran Gombert, no doubt the author of the Latin text of Magdalena's supplication, had struck the right chord by framing Magdalena as a poor, defenseless woman beset by the tribulations of a powerful man. Louis II would have had no moral objection to slavery per se. But it would have been very hard for him not to see Magdalena as a free woman deserving of his mercy. Delivering mercy to the poor and the weak oppressed by the rich and the powerful was how kings showed that they were kingly.

Magdalena's freedom, in short, was a team effort. And on this team, there is one person who has yet to be given the credit due to him. Bertran Gombert worked as her procurator for over a year, appearing at court, responding to summons, reading transcripts of proceedings, drafting acts, and almost certainly accompanying Magdalena on her dramatic trip to Aix-en-Provence. Bertran was an interesting and complex man. As a jurist who occasionally served as judge in one of Marseille's lesser courts, he himself was prone to bending the law, usually, it seems, for reasons having to do with pecuniary gain. In 1407, he was accused of partiality by one of the petitioners who appeared before him. In 1409, he was fined 100 l. for soliciting bribes.[29] As a lawyer, moreover, he was not above committing fraud on behalf of his clients. In 1409, he was fined 200 l., a substantial amount, for fraudulently representing himself as the procurator of an accused man in the court of first appeals.[30] In 1410, he was fined yet again, this time 100 l., for having committed a fraud that consisted of surreptitiously changing the date on a letters patent.[31] His wife, Margarita, was an equally doubtful character, having been hauled before the criminal court in 1409 and fined 100 l. for committing usury against two of her debtors, a Jewish couple. This is one of the few known usury trials from the time period.[32]

Yet alongside the fraud and corruption, Bertran served on more than one occasion in a more noble role, that of public defender. A few years before the trial of Magdalena, he made a cameo appearance in another sensational case. This case, a criminal trial, involved a Jewish midwife named Floreta d'Ays who had been accused of murdering her client, a Christian woman. After the baby was delivered, the woman's placenta failed to detach itself from the uterus. When the efforts of the Christian midwives in attendance proved to be in vain, Floreta was called in to provide expert care to the stricken woman. This story

184 CHAPTER 11

has been told elsewhere.[33] What matters here is that at a key moment in the trial, Floreta was asked to name a procurator to represent her pro bono in the upcoming criminal trial. The procurator she asked for was Bertran Gombert. In the event, Bertran happened to be away from the city, so Floreta had to turn elsewhere. But her stated preference gives us some idea of the city-wide reputation he appears to have earned as someone who would go to considerable lengths for his clients.

12

Afterlives

ON MONDAY, the 3rd of September 1408, the letters patent that Magdalena received from Louis II was faithfully copied into the register of the court of first appeals. On the evening of the following day, the parties assembled for the last time to draw the proceedings to a close. It fell to Raymon Elie, the notary, to enter the concluding details into the record. Bertran Gombert and Magdalena were present, as well as Johan de Ysia. Peire could not bring himself to acknowledge his defeat and refused to join. His defeat, after two years of persistent litigation, must have been a humiliating blow. The judge informed the parties that he had been superseded in the case and that everything would be done as required by the king. Johan de Ysia asked for a copy of the letter. And with that, the notary drew things to a close. The remainder of the page was left blank. There was nothing more to say.

That summer, nine cases had been aired before the court of first appeals. Since early May, the proceedings had been piling up on the notary's desk, new quires of paper progressively added to the back of each case as the paper record grew over time. By the time Raymon Elie set down his quill on Tuesday, the pile had gotten rather thick, and he deemed it time to bind everything into a register. To make the cover, he or one of his assistants took an old parchment from a stack of recycled legal instruments purchased from the scrap dealer and stitched the quires inside in chronological order, by date of initiation. The case of Peire Huguet against Magdalena Coline was the eighth. A ninth case had opened in early August, and the quires associated with that case were the last ones to be bound into the register. That case, however, petered out after only a few days. The entry that terminated the appeal of Peire Huguet was Raymon's last contribution to the register.

On the cover, Raymon set out a brief description of the contents and drew a little box around the rubric (figure 10). Subsequent damage has made it difficult to make out much of what he had written, although even with natural light we can make out some of the words, including his name and part of the date clause. Further down on the cover, he inserted a table of contents listing

FIGURE 10. The cover of the second Magdalena register. *Source:* ADBR 3 B 861.

all nine cases in the register. Although the ink has faded, we can just make out "Next, the suit of Peire Huguet against Magdalena Coline" toward the bottom. His work done, the notary deposited the register in the archive, alongside hundreds of other court registers that had been accumulating for over a century.

The Corridors of Time

As they sat there, gathering dust, the two registers preserving the details of the drama of Magdalena Coline and Peire Huguet entered a new phase of their existence. Up to this point, both records had served both practical and symbolic ends. As a practical matter, they were essential to the machinery of justice. Judges read them carefully because their contents mattered at law. From time to time, we see traces of their passing, in the form of marginal notations or manicules pointing to crucial passages. The proceedings also mattered in a symbolic sense, as the historian François Otchakovsky-Laurens has argued in a related context.[1] The shuffling of paper, the scratching of the quill on the paper, the ceremonial moments where a party handed over documents to be bound into the register: these constituted a set of visual and auditory cues telling everyone present that they were witnessing the law in action.

Within a few months or a year at the most, however, the phase of legal utility had come to an end, for once the proceedings had been read, they were rarely of any further use to judges and parties alike. The shift from active register to archival document brought about changes in the meaning or function of the registers, as legal utility gave way to a different kind of utility. Archives can and do store documents that preserve their original relevance, but collections of documents, as objects, also contribute to the construction of prestige, power, and authority for those who control them.

Elsewhere in the city, year in and year out, other notaries were generating registers. They had been doing so for decades and centuries, since at least the later twelfth century, which is when we catch an indirect glimpse of some of the first notarial instruments produced in Marseille.[2] These registers were archived by the notaries in their own bureaus, where they slowly accumulated, typically at the rate of one register per year. Though the legal utility of most notarial acts was also ephemeral, some acts, including house sales and dowries, could retain their legal relevance for years or even decades to come. In time, though, even these lost their original function, and were henceforward preserved, if preserved at all, for their political and symbolic utility.

Ordinary people, too, kept their own archives, storing not only household cartularies but also legal instruments generated by the notaries. They put them in sacks or chests or sometimes stacked them in loose piles. By 1408, Magdalena herself had acquired several such instruments. The one we know about for sure is a record of Bertomieua's legacy of 10 l., since Magdalena had brought the instrument to court to show the judge. It is also quite likely that she had instruments recording one or both dowries arising from her two known marriages. The many stages of the dispute with Peire Huguet generated numerous legal instruments which would have come into Magdalena's possession, the royal letters patent from Louis II, presumably, occupying pride-of-place among them.

The documented activities of all the dramatis personae in the case, freeze-dried in a form that preserves only their essential and emotionless details, settled into this vast, multi-form archive like sedimentary particles. At one time, the meanings and memories and emotions that gave the particles life and bound them one to another in a narrative were fresh in the minds of everyone familiar with the drama. Most everyone in the tight circle of acquaintances in the neighborhood of Lansaria would have known many of the details that we can now only surmise. They would have known the "real" reason that motivated Magdalena and Hugonin to sue Peire Huguet for a 6-florin debt in August 1406. They would have understood why the witness Guilhem Limosin provided conflicting testimony on three separate occasions. When news of the story of attempted seduction by the barber-surgeon, Nicolau de Sala, as told by Alaeta Columbe and her friend, Gassenda, began to circulate in the community, listeners would have been able to parse the intimate details. But the context that once provided meaning was systematically stripped out as the particles were reduced to a written form in Latin translation and as the connections that bound the fragments into a coherent whole were broken. As the memories faded, the documented facts grew progressively more isolated from one another. Over time, the drama that Magdalena Coline had helped stage as a bid to cement her freedom, a drama she had followed from its bleakest moments through to its bitter triumph, broke up into its archival pieces, decoagulated, and was lost.

Along with the loss of the ligatures of memory, some of the documented pieces that once slotted into the story themselves winked out of existence. Following the inexorable logic of time, archives typically erode from back to front. Episodes of fire, flood, and pillage periodically wreak havoc on their contents. In 1408, Marseille had been relatively lucky, and the communal archive, several hundred years old at that point, would have been largely intact. But disaster lay on the horizon, for in 1423, Aragonese troops landed to the south of the port, breached the walls, and pillaged the city for three days. Fire broke out and devastated many neighborhoods. As luck would have it, the two Magdalena registers survived the flames, along with a substantial fraction of the judicial records, but much was lost, including a substantial percentage of Marseille's notarial archive to that date. Whole bureaus went up in flames and all the registers produced by those notaries were lost.[3] Had Magdalena ever made the shift from a pawnbroker to a moneylender who relied on notarized instruments? Perhaps. But if she did, and if she had used a notary whose registers are now lost, we will probably never know it.

Archival decay also arises from more simple human actions and desires, such as the inclination to throw away old and worthless stuff. The domestic archives, in particular, were relentlessly pruned. The citizens and residents of Marseille regularly brought old parchments to resellers who would purchase them for pennies and sell them in bulk back to the very same notaries who had created the acts in the first place, to be recycled as the covers of registers. The inside of the cover of the 1408 register, to take the example closest to hand, records the sale of a plot of land by someone named Pellegrin to Johan somebody. Many of the details of the transaction, including the surnames of the actors and the date, have been lost, since the parchment was cut to size and otherwise damaged and its contents partially obscured in the binding. Even so, we can make out some of the elements, including the fact that Pellegrin's wife, Sanxia, needed to give her consent to the sale, foregoing any rights her dowry may have given her over her husband's estate. The orthography is old and the notary, Bonetus Traverii, is unfamiliar. The instrument may have been a century old before entering a new phase of life as the cover of a register.

There Was Slavery on French Soil

For a century or two, the two registers, along with a supporting cast consisting of the notarial registers and other documents that survived the sack of 1423, sat there in their respective archives, quietly performing their role as components of the city's proud heritage. When Marseille's Hôtel de Ville was erected in the sixteenth century, it is likely that the archives were transferred into the new building. There, they began to capture the attention of antiquarians, who were fascinated by all manner of fragments of the past and avidly sought them out in documents, collections, and the physical environment.[4] They picked up the registers housed in the city's archives, including the two Magdalena registers, and leafed through them in search of wonders. Unknown hands scribbled notes on the covers, the first stage in the long and ongoing process whereby archives, over centuries, become indexed, and thereby are made findable.

On the 1408 register, just below the rubric written by Raymon Elie, the hand of an unknown antiquarian or early archivist has drawn a large plus sign, followed by the year in Arabic numerals. Below that appears the name of the notary in its Latinized form, "Raimundus Elie." The cover of the previous register, which extends over the years 1407–1408, is much cleaner. It bears a single line in a contemporary hand indicating that it was a register of the court of first appeals concluding in 1408. Below it, a later hand has added the name of the notary.

As they perused the monuments of the past, one of the many things that antiquarians were surprised to discover was evidence of slavery in the Middle Ages. In France, when the history of slavery started coming together as a narrative thread in the general history of the country, it told the story of an institution that had flourished in antiquity and decayed ever since.[5] The French historians who wrote about slavery differed on the question of how to explain the trend. But all agreed that the ancient system of slavery had withered away, following the so-called Christian amelioration hypothesis which held that slavery was incompatible with Christianity.[6] After Louis X supposedly emancipated the tiny remnant population of slaves in 1315—a particularly resilient historiographical fantasy—there were supposedly no more slaves to be found in France.[7] By the early seventeenth century, as Sue Peabody has discussed, the related "free-soil principle"—the idea that a slave who had crossed the border into France and had received baptism was thereby free—was widely known throughout the country.[8] A national myth, carefully curated over the course of the seventeenth and eighteenth centuries, claimed that freedom had planted deep roots on free French soil.

Hence the astonishment to discover that this was not quite true. One of the first to publish his findings was a French lawyer and antiquarian named Alexandre de Fauris de Saint-Vincens. In 1814, Fauris de Saint-Vincens published a study entitled *Mémoires et notices relatifs à la Provence*, a quirky selection of the quaint facts and stories concerning times past that he had gathered during his perquisitions through the libraries, archives, and attics of Provence.[9] Like others of his age, he was drawn to the days of the good King René of Anjou. He wrote about the art of painting on glass and the characteristic types of furniture and table wares. He ruminated on the cost of oats, honey, and wax, and described the Feast of Fools, celebrated in Aix-en-Provence until 1543. Toward the end of his reminiscences, following several pages dedicated to the songs played at the court of the king, he turned abruptly to a new theme, desiring to make known the status of the persons in that age.

At the outset of this section, Fauris de Saint-Vincens explains to the reader that he will reveal several historical facts that have hitherto remained unknown. In the county of Provence of the fifteenth century, he tells us, there were still slaves to be found. Not serfs bound to the land, but genuine slaves, "ordinary" slaves as he calls them, who could be bought and sold on the market. "I've seen the acts myself," he writes, somewhat breathlessly. He mentions having visited the bureaus of notaries who were the successors of those who wrote the original acts. He tells a story he came across one day, the story of a man named François Grillo who, in 1465, had manumitted his slave, Marguerite, with a dowry of 200 florins, only to marry her himself. But shortly afterward, Fauris de Saint-Vincens lost interest, and flitted on to the next subject to catch his fancy, that of prostitution and sexual decadence.

Despite his claims of novelty, Fauris de Saint-Vincens was probably not the first antiquarian to discover and be shocked by the slave sales and manumissions littered across the notarial acts of Provence, and he certainly wasn't the last. A small book could be written about the continuing expressions of surprise southern French antiquarians and amateur historians felt in the nineteenth century as they came across evidence for slavery every time they rummaged through the enormous pile of notarial registers and other administrative documents that survives from the later Middle Ages. Surprisingly, the surprise exists to this day. It is a defensive mechanism, one that makes it possible to cling to the romance that there were no slaves on French soil.

The instinct that had motivated Fauris de Saint-Vincens sprang from little more than the desire to collect and present the curious facts of yesteryear. But in his day, the topic of slavery was circulating widely in France, as it was across Europe and the world. Slavery in France's overseas colonies had been abolished during the French Revolution, only to be reinstated by Napoleon in 1802, with the second and final emancipation not coming until 1848. In this atmosphere, a new generation of scientifically minded historians realized that they could contribute to the debate about slavery by systematically assembling acts from the medieval archives of southern France.

One of the first to do so was a local historian of Marseille whom we have already met: Jean-Anselme-Bernard Mortreuil (1806–1876). Anselme Mortreuil had been born in Perpignan in 1806 and moved to Marseille with his family when he was five years old. He became a lawyer, judge, and a member of the Académie de Marseille, one of the many local learned societies that proliferated in that century.[10] As a scholar, Mortreuil gained renown as the author of a well-regarded three-volume legal history of the Byzantine Empire.[11] But alongside his legal scholarship, he was one of the first to systematically explore the local notarial archives, which at the time were either housed in Marseille's Hôtel de Ville or kept in the bureaus of local notaries, often in damp and insalubrious conditions, to judge by the water and insect damage that marks some registers.

Like Fauris de Saint-Vincens before him, Mortreuil was stunned to discover the existence of slave sales and manumissions. Such records pointed to the presence of an active trade in chattel slaves that Mortreuil, like virtually all the scholars of his day, thought had withered and died in the centuries after the fall of Rome. Unlike Fauris de Saint-Vincent, Mortreuil worked diligently through a mass of registers from the later medieval centuries, harvesting a selection of acts pertinent to slavery and transcribing them, in his fine, flowing hand, into a notebook. These sources, in turn, became the basis for an article he published in a local journal in 1859, one of the earliest contributions to the history of slavery in the medieval Mediterranean.[12] After his death, some of the registers that he had acquired, along with his extensive notes and transcriptions, were donated by his widow to the Bibliothèque nationale de France.

The enduring belief that there were no slaves in France generated longlasting historiographical blind spots. Nearly a century later, in 1929, the great historian Marc Bloch published a review of a study of slavery in later medieval Sicily.[13] In it, he declared that Mediterranean France, like Sicily, had had slaves, but that the subject passed unnoticed in the scholarship. "I would be delighted," he wrote, "if these words should ever come to the attention of some scholar in search of unfamiliar things and might incite that person to tackle the job." A few years later, in 1933, he met Charles Verlinden, who would do exactly that, finally bringing to light a history that Mortreuil, a century earlier, had labored to make known.

The notarial sources favored by Verlinden, like Mortreuil before him, lend themselves to the quantitative approaches featured in chapter 2 above. From such acts, we learn a great deal about trends and patterns. But what is missing in such an approach are stories of lives and afterlives, insights that are rarely found in single documents but instead lie in their interstices. It is only when the pieces are put together that the story can be told. In Mortreuil's day, this act of re-assembling the fragments of the Magdalena story would have been nearly impossible, in the absence of the finding aids that enable archival research today. Even in Verlinden's day, the indexes and inventories upon which we now rely were only partly developed. So it was that the Magdalena story lay undiscovered, in its limp and decoagulated form. Only by the 1990s and early 2000s, thanks to the patient work of a brilliant archival staff and the finding aids that they so painstakingly assembled, has it become possible to reconstitute that history.

Magdalena Moves On

So much for the afterlives of the documents. What about the afterlives of the persons of the drama? In the preceding chapters, we have already had occasion to hear about some of the lives after 1408. Alaeta Columbe lived out her remaining years with her friend, Gassenda Olivarie. Johan Huguet and Lady Alaseta Huguete lived to a ripe old age and participated in the resettlement of the ravaged city in 1429. Here and there, we catch glimpses of other members of the dramatis personae.

Magdalena and Hugonin, sadly, are not among them. After 1408, both vanish from the record, apart from an ambiguous entry found in a 1412 court register that may refer to Hugonin.[14] In some ways, it is a surprising absence. In 1406, as we have seen, Hugonin de lo Chorges had taken an apprentice under his wing, the type of act that would normally mark the moment when an immigrant, having settled into the social fabric of a new city, would begin appearing with greater regularity in the sources. The silence of the archival record, in light of this, is striking. The ending, in other words, doesn't fit a story that in so many respects seems to follow the usual narrative arc of a romance.

But this is not necessarily a bad thing. It means that we are free to imagine several possible endings.

It is possible that Magdalena died soon after the trial, although this seems unlikely: after all, we should still expect to find Hugonin de lo Chorges.[15] By the same token, if Hugonin had died, then Magdalena might have remarried a third time and dissolved into the persona of one of the many women named Magdalena who appear in Marseille's records around this time. Of the dozen or so who have been documented apart from our Magdalena, the likeliest candidate is the wife of Bertran de Sosquiers, a laborer or urban peasant. Among other things, the size of the dowry, at 20 l., roughly approximates the wealth Magdalena Coline might have held at the time of the marriage, in 1412, and the fact that the bride constituted her own dowry is also suggestive of a woman who was remarrying and was kinless.[16] A third possibility is that, after two years of traumatic litigation, the couple decided to abandon Marseille and move to another city, or perhaps even return to Hugonin's home village of Chorges. Geographical mobility in the decades around 1400 was high and the barriers to migration low. If so, they may yet be found in the archives of Aix, Toulon, Barcelona, Genoa, or anywhere that they or their well-wishers had friends and relations willing to look after them.

Is it possible that Magdalena left her second husband and returned home to North Africa? Though that outcome is exceedingly unlikely, it is not impossible, since the rise of religious orders dedicated to the redemption of slaves and captives meant that ships bearing the unfortunate victims of the trade traveled regularly back and forth across the Mediterranean.[17] The search has not ended. In time, we may learn more about the fate of Magdalena Coline.

A Shattered Man

An abundant documentation records the final days of Peire Huguet in vivid detail. In the years before the trial, Peire was already falling into insolvency, pursued by his daughter-in-law, Hugoneta, and his other creditors. Between 1406 and 1408, his creditors appear to have paused their pursuits. The perverse logic associated with litigation recommended this respite, because he might have won, and indeed probably should have won, and had he done so, he may have been in a better position to pay off his debts. But the letters patent issued by Louis II of Anjou made an already bad situation nigh impossible. Payment of the hundreds of florins he probably owed in court costs would have weakened his already parlous financial condition.

The world of the later Middle Ages was defined by dense and dynamic webs of credit and debt. Court records are filled with references to acts of debt collection, and sergeants were constantly kept busy seizing innumerable pledges from the houses of debtors, pushing the items into circulation as coin substitutes. Debt collection, in short, was omnipresent and unremarkable. Given the shortfall in the money supply, almost everyone was periodically insolvent.

Full-blown bankruptcy, however, was another matter. When creditors in this world found out that a debtor was verging on bankruptcy, they naturally got nervous, even if they often refrained from outright action. There are complicated reasons for this. At first blush, it would seem to make sense for a creditor to lodge a simple debt claim before the court or to bring a lawsuit. But every such action raised at least a specter of doubt among the onlookers about the debtor's finances, and if word got out that insolvency was verging on bankruptcy, then outstanding credits were instantly withdrawn and all the nervous creditors descended upon the court in a throng, all clamoring for repayment. Somewhat paradoxically, creditors tended to pursue debt claims when they knew their debtors' assets were sufficient to cover the debt. Otherwise, their actions risked ruining their debtors' creditworthiness and with it, their own chances of being repaid. Why? When a case moved into the bankruptcy court, at least in Marseille, claims were determined on a first-in, first-out basis. In cases where the bankrupt individual was a man, the debt given top priority was typically his wife's dowry, and by extension the dowries of any daughters-in-law. The remaining creditors were reimbursed in strict chronological order, beginning with the oldest debts first. Unless a creditor knew that he or she was at the front of the line, aggressively pursuing unpaid debts from insolvent debtors could backfire.

In a few rare cases found in late medieval court records, it is possible to witness the undignified spectacle of frantic creditors piling on a suddenly bankrupt individual. The evidence comes to light whenever there was a dispute among creditors about the priority of their claims, meaning that a lawsuit was joined to determine the proper order.

By February 1410, Peire Huguet could stave off bankruptcy no longer, and steps were taken to wind up his estate in the Palace court, before Hugo Vincens, the very same man who had ruled against him in the second trial. One of the creditors who managed to get something from the wreckage of the estate was Peire's old partner and investor, Isnart de Sant Gilles. Isnart had acquired the 100-florin debt originally owed to Bertomieu Simondel in 1395 and was therefore among the first in line to be reimbursed. Another individual, named Isnart Ricau, whose claims preceded even those of Isnart de Sant Gilles, was awarded 30 florins by the judge.[18] But the principal creditor to Peire's estate was his daughter-in-law, Hugoneta, and various entries in the records of the court capture the final stages of her efforts to recover her dowry.[19] One entry suggests that Hugoneta may have even had Peire imprisoned, since the judge told Hugoneta that he might "release" him if she were to fail to appear in court on a designated day. The total cost of the proceedings of the bankruptcy court, which was billed to Hugoneta, came to 3 florins and 3 ½ gros.

A series of entries in a register from 1412 record some of the last known references to Peire Huguet. The register was a daybook in which the notary of the court entered a series of roughly penned notes about the day's events in court. Most of the entries concern stages of debt collection, but occasionally, extracts of witness testimony made their way into the register, alongside fragmentary notes concerning legal actions. At some point in July of 1412, a woman named Sicarda Raynerie had initiated a claim against Peire Huguet.[20] The debt that she was pursuing must have been relatively small, since the item seized was described as a *bassinet*—probably a basnet, or a basin-shaped helmet, but possibly a small ceramic bowl, and in either case almost certainly worth less than a florin.

What is interesting about the act is that the object was not taken from Peire Huguet. It was seized from master Peire Tenchurier, almost certainly a notary, who was holding the item in pledge. The notary could have come into possession of the pledge in several different ways. For instance, Peire Huguet might have left it with the notary as a pledge to cover a fee for notarization. Alternatively, the notary could have had the item seized from Peire's house in order to repay a debt. But either way, what is clear is that Sicarda had proven to the satisfaction of the court that her credit was prior to the notary's, so the item was handed over to her and the notary was stiffed. This exchange is a relatively common event during the very late stages of bankruptcy.

A few days later, a representative of the cellarer of the monastery of Saint-Victor came before the court, asserting that Peire owed back rent amounting to 5 florins for a wheat field under the cellarer's lordship in Saint-Giniez, a district located a few kilometers south of the city.[21] The harvest was underway at the time. A crier was sent to the field with orders to ensure that a portion of the harvested grain equal in value to the back rent be set aside for the cellarer. The crier, upon his return, reported that he issued the warning to Johan Huguet and his nephew, Lazar Huguet, who were apparently undertaking the harvest at the time. The entry provides an interesting insight into relations between father and son. It tells us that, in the dispute between Peire and Hugoneta, Lazar had either sided with his father or had somehow managed to make peace with him afterward. It also suggests how a family whose fortunes had once been associated with the sea and whose lives had intersected with the great and the powerful had been reduced to the status of tenants unable to pay the ground rent on a single wheat field.

Immediately afterward, the register records the first of a series of entries, beginning on 9 August 1412, generated by a new lawsuit setting him once again against his daughter-in-law. It is not entirely clear who had sued whom. The first entry bears the rubric "The Case of Peire Huguet," which would normally indicate that Peire was the plaintiff, but the brief extracts of witness testimony that follow appear to have been called by Hugoneta. Since the procedural envelope is entirely lacking, we have no idea about the exact nature of the dispute. What we can discern, though, is that it concerned ownership of a plot of land from which wheat was being harvested. This is quite possibly the same plot of land targeted by the cellarer of Saint-Victor. Hugoneta claimed that the land was hers by right of dowry, and had come to her via her mother, Lady Alaseta Huguete, who had inherited it from her father, Johan Bertran. Peire, in turn, claimed it was a plot of land listed in the 1374 dowry act of his unnamed wife, presumably Bertomieua.[22]

Amid this suit, someone named Durant Salvayre launched proceedings against Lazar Huguet for a debt of 5 florins. A few days later, Durant's wife appeared in court to give testimony about the source of the debt:

> Loisa Salvayre, the wife of Durant Salvayre, said on her oath that . . . she asked Peire Huguet whether he knew of anyone who might wish to sell her some wheat up to the value of 5 florins. Peire Huguet answered that he would provide her with good and decent wheat up to the value of 5 florins if she would give him an advance of 3 florins so he could undertake the harvest. Loisa immediately handed over the 3 florins, and a short while later paid another 2 florins. Maritona Boquerie, Ayglina, the wife of Raynier Niel, and Lady Catherina Colime saw this. Asked where this took place, she said in the street. Asked where her husband was, she said in the galleys.[23]

Although this incident seems to have been a separate legal action, it nonetheless provides some clues as to what the lawsuit was all about. For years, Peire and his brother Johan had been harvesting wheat from the field. When Peire went bankrupt, all or most of his assets had gone to pay his creditors, Hugoneta above all. But in the meantime, winter wheat that had been sown by Johan Huguet the previous fall was ready for harvest, and Peire, acting with his brother and his son, tried to sneak in and harvest wheat that nominally now belonged to Hugoneta. Lacking the necessary funds to hire agricultural laborers, Peire received an advance from Loisa Salvayre. Judging from the fact that her husband, Durant, worked for a living on galleys, she seems to have been the wife of one of his old shipmates. Clearly, Hugoneta had gotten wind of what was going on, and managed to nip in to seize the harvest from Peire, which presumably occasioned the suit. In the meantime, Durant and Loisa, who had not received the wheat promised them, had launched their proceedings. Despite everything that had happened, in other words, Peire was still in the business of trying to defraud his own family members. Perhaps the most telling aspect of this incident lies in what it reveals about Peire's new status. He had become little better than a peasant, earning a living off the land by the sweat of his brow.

In 1413, Peire Huguet made his last known appearance in the records consulted to date. He was probably in his early sixties. He appeared before the royal treasurer to pay a fine of 60 s. arising from a criminal prosecution. In a physical altercation with Peyret Bertran, the brother of his daughter-in-law, Peire had drawn his knife, which was widely perceived as a threatening gesture, and in return had been struck on the arm with a rock.[24]

After this, he vanishes from the record. More accurately, he no longer appears in the documents that our team has consulted, and it is possible that further revelations will appear. But even so, it is likely that he died a shattered man. We do not know whether Magdalena was present to witness his downfall. If she were, it is hard to imagine that she would have had any pity to spare.

ACKNOWLEDGMENTS

I FIRST CAME ACROSS THE two appellate cases at the heart of this book in 1998, while undertaking archival work for the book that eventually became *The Consumption of Justice* (2003). In 2009, Magdalena played a starring role in a graduate seminar I taught in the Department of History at Harvard University, where the first appellate case served as a paleographical exercise for the students in the class and as an excuse for all of us to engage with the emerging literature on medieval slavery. The seeds of this book were first planted amid the exhilarating conversations I had with Naor Ben-Yehoyada, Rowan Dorin, and Rena Lauer in that seminar. A decade later, I had a chance to revisit the case in another graduate seminar, and I thank all the students as well as my colleague, Orlando Patterson, who kindly joined us for a class meeting. In the summer of 2019, Ryan Low, then a doctoral student at Harvard, joined me in the archives to initiate the search of Magdalena. Ryan has lived with the project ever since and has contributed to it in ways that are far too numerous to list. A second campaign conducted in the summer of 2023 was dedicated to building up the collection of slavery-related contracts from Marseille, and I thank Ryan, Angela Zhang, and Louie Escobar for their many contributions and conversations. Magdalena also featured in a Harvard undergraduate honors thesis written by Kevin Wang in 2022–23. Among other things, Kevin worked tirelessly on the transcription of the consilium of Antonius Virronis featured in chapter 11.

Where studies and methodologies in the history of medieval slavery are concerned, I have benefited enormously over the years from the guidance and suggestions offered by Hannah Barker, Debra Blumenthal, Sally McKee, and Rebecca Winer. On matters concerning the Roman and medieval laws of slavery, I received invaluable advice and suggestions from Mike Humphreys, Attilio Stella, Charlie Donahue, Florent Garnier, and Marie Bassano. Several colleagues, including Cynthia Becker, Suzanne Blier, and Claudia Stella Valeria Geremia, kindly answered the many questions I had about Amazigh tattoos and provided bibliographic suggestions. Omar Abdel-Ghaffar, Luis Girón Negrón, and other colleagues helped with questions related to Arabic and Berber onomastics, in the effort to explain Magdalena's surname "Coline." Elizabeth A. R. (Peggy) Brown and Paul Freedman provided wise counsel about matters pertaining to the literature on slavery and serfdom in medieval Europe; I have learned much from them about the complex historiography, and, with many colleagues, greatly miss dear Peggy, who died before this book was published.

For matters pertaining to the history of Provence and the Angevin realms, I received generous assistance and advice from Michel Hébert and David Abulafia. Charlie Steinman's undergraduate thesis on slavery in Marseille was the source for some important ideas concerning Catherina of Tartary, and files he shared made it easier to navigate the transcriptions of Anselme Mortreuil. Elizabeth Casteen's brilliant insight about the "marks made with fire" on Magdalena Coline's arms, shared with me at a conference some years ago, has been invaluable to this project. François Otchakovsky-Laurens not only advised me about the deliberations of Marseille's city council but also graciously provided images from several important registers and assisted with gaining access to archival materials. I had a chance to discuss women moneylenders in Marseille with Laure-Hélène Gouffran and have been inspired by her work. Patrick Hegarty-Morrish offered guidance on the *gajaria* contract as practiced in Provence. Where the realm of Naples is concerned, I still marvel at the fact that Enrico Basso, from his vast wisdom and mastery of the sources, was able to identify both Corrado Doria and Manfredi Chiaramonte using the thinnest of clues provided in the sources. Rowan Dorin also provided much guidance on these matters as well as on the chronicle evidence concerning the events of 1387, along with sage advice on legal history. Alex Csiszar helped me track down information about Anselme Mortreuil, the historian of slavery in Marseille. Valuable conversations about narrative and microhistory with Mita Choudhury and Ulinka Rublack got me started in important ways, and conversations with Sara McDougall, together with an invitation to share early chapters with her students, have provided constant inspiration on modes of historical writing. Sara also read the complete manuscript and provided much valuable counsel.

Over the last five years, I have had numerous opportunities to present aspects of the work in progress. I began the project in earnest in the fall of 2019, as a Donald Bullough fellow at the University of St Andrews, and I thank many friends and colleagues there, including Frances Andrews, Justine Firnhaber-Baker, John Hudson, Caroline Humfress, Attilio Stella, and Alex Woolf. In 2019 and 2020, I presented an early version of the story in seminars at Trinity College Dublin, the University of Cambridge, and Université de Paris 1 Panthéon-Sorbonne, and I am grateful to my hosts, Ruth Mazo Karras, John Arnold, and Laurent Feller for their invitations. Certain features of the case appeared in a plenary address I delivered to the Society for French Historical Studies in July 2020, and it is a pleasure to thank Christine Adams, Tracy Adams, Kirsty

ACKNOWLEDGMENTS 201

Carpenter, and David K. Smith for the arrangements. Jeff Ravel and the Boston Area French History group gave me an opportunity to discuss a written version of that talk, and I thank Jeff and friends and colleagues in the BAFH for their comments and Malick Ghachem for his response. Exchanges with Sue Peabody during this time enlightened me on many aspects of the historiography of slavery in early modern France.

An invitation from Andrew Jotischky to address the European History 1150–1550 seminar at the Institute for Historical Research at the University of London in January 2022 offered me the first opportunity to think about lives beyond slavery, and I thank all the participants for their valuable feedback. I also had my first opportunity to talk about the search for Magdalena in March of 2022, thanks to an invitation from the organizers of the Vagantes conference: at Harvard, Jonas Hermann, Sama Mammadova, Lydia Shahan, and Nicholas Thyr; and at Case Western Reserve, Reed O'Mara, Sam Truman, and their colleagues. Invitations from Mackenzie Cooley and Jay Rubenstein made it possible to revisit the search for Magdalena at Hamilton College and the University of Southern California, and I want to especially thank Jessica Maya Marglin and Nathan Perl-Rosenthal at USC for their many insights on the case. Anne Lester invited me to present a paper at the History Department seminar at Johns Hopkins University in April 2023, and I thank the members of the seminar for an illuminating discussion and Anne and Scott Bruce for their warm hospitality. I also thank Pablo Sanahuja Ferrer and the Real Colegio Complutense at Harvard for an opportunity to present Magdalena in April of 2023.

In the fall of 2023, an invitation from Tamar Herzig to participate in the conference "Gender and Enslavement in Mediterranean Europe, 1250–1800," at the Israel Institute for Advanced Studies at Hebrew University, allowed me to develop the chapter that became "Magdalena the Moneylender." I thank Naama Rachel Cohen Hanegbi for her comments and Stefan Hanß, Juliane Schiel, and many colleagues for important insights. I delivered the 2023/2024 Lecture in the History of Slavery at the University of Edinburgh and am grateful to Sonia Tycko for the invitation and to colleagues for their inspiring comments. A sabbatical allowed me to spend time in the fall of 2023 as a visitor at King's College Cambridge, where I rebuilt the existing book manuscript. John Arnold was a princely host, and Kathleen and I warmly thank many friends and colleagues there for their hospitality and friendship, including Caroline Goodson, Irene Ferreira, Timothy Griffin, John Robb, and Miri Rubin. I received invaluable advice from Giulia Boitani on the interpretation of the insult "cana mastina," and benefited from discussions about the phrase with Paul Russell. Thanks to an invitation from Emmanuel Huertas, I was able to spend three weeks in February 2024 in Toulouse, where I presented aspects of the case in seminar and had many opportunities to discuss it with colleagues,

202 ACKNOWLEDGMENTS

including Florent Garnier and Marie Bassano. In April of 2024, I had the immense honor of delivering the Lawrence Stone Lectures at the Shelby Cullom Davis Center, Princeton University, over a period of three days, which gave me the unparalleled opportunity to present the entire arc of the project. I owe an enormous debt of gratitude to David Bell and to many colleagues at Princeton for the invitation and for the rich conversations that ensued. It has been a joy to work with Priya Nelson, my editor at Princeton University Press, together with Emma Wagh, Sara Lerner, Karen Verde, and all who so expertly shepherded this book through production. The anonymous reader 2 read the manuscript great care and made a number of exceedingly valuable and erudite suggestions, all of which improved the manuscript significantly. The many failings that no doubt remain are my own responsibility.

I am very grateful to Scott Walker, the Digital Cartography Specialist in the Harvard Map Library, for his assistance in preparing the maps, and to Samantha Kelly, for her help with maps of Naples. The many colleagues with whom I have discussed the case and from whom I have received valuable suggestions and advice include Abigail Balbale, Shane Bobrycki, Didier Boisseuil, Guillaume Calafat, Sidney Chalhoub, Christopher Clark, Beatrice del Bo, Hussein Fancy, Brian Forman, Paul Friedland, Cecilia Gaposchkin, Guy Geltner, Henry Gruber, Tom Kuehn, Eduardo Manzano Moreno, Therese Martin, Tiya Miles, Maureen Miller, Laura Morreale, Michèle Plott, Riccardo Rao, Kay Reyerson, Rebecca Scott, Elena Shadrina, Andrew Shryock, and Catherine Verna.

Shortly before this book was published, Kathleen and I celebrated forty years of marriage. In addition to reading and editing the entire manuscript, Kathleen has been a constant companion with me in the search for Magdalena, always patient, always willing to hear new thoughts and perspectives and to offer her own valuable insights. This book is dedicated to her, with love.

NOTES

Abbreviations

ADBR Archives départementales des Bouches-du-Rhône

AMM Archives municipales de la Ville de Marseille

BNF Bibliothèque nationale de France

NAL Nouvelles acquisitions latines

DALME "The Documentary Archaeology of Late Medieval Europe," edited by Daniel Lord Smail, Gabriel H. Pizzorno, and Laura Morreale, available at https://dalme.org

For Roman legal sources, the numbering follows the *Corpus iuris civilis*, edited by Theodor Mommsen et al., 6th ed., 3 vols. (Berlin: Weidmann, 1954).

COD. *Codex Iustinianus*

DIG. *Digesta Iustiniani*

NOV. *Novellae Constitutiones*

Prologue: The Spoils of War

1. Crane, "Digging Up the Present."

2. This dynasty is also known as the Second House of Anjou and the House of Anjou-Provence. The house was founded in 1382 by Louis I, Duke of Anjou, adopted son and heir of Johanna of Naples.

3. The major study is Salicrú i Lluch, *Esclaus i propietaris d'esclaus*.

4. See Desimoni, Belgrango, and Poggi, *Leges genuenses*, 676; Romano, *Housecraft and State-craft*, 52; Schiel, "Mord von zarter Hand"; Epstein, *Speaking of Slavery*, 97–98.

5. Gross, *What Blood Won't Tell*; Scott, "Social Facts, Legal Fictions"; Scott and Fornias, "María Coleta and the Capuchin Friar."

6. A point made by Sidney Chalhoub for the case of Brazil; see Chalhoub, "Precariousness of Freedom"; Chalhoub, "Politics of Ambiguity."

7. Planas, "Des héritages et des affranchis," 45, referring to *le sas*.

8. Sobers-Khan, "Slavery in the Early Modern Ottoman Empire," 409.

9. At present, opinions vary on the degree to which racial constructs shaped perceptions of slaves in medieval Europe. Contributions generally favoring the idea that medieval slavery had a racialized dimension include Blumenthal, *Enemies and Familiars*, 272–77; Patton, "What Did

Medieval Slavery Look Like?"; Zhang, "Rethinking 'Domestic Enemies'"; Armstrong-Partida, "Race, Skin Colour, Enslavement and Sexuality in the Late Medieval Mediterranean." Hannah Barker (*That Most Precious Merchandise*, 45) notes the important degree to which late medieval Mediterranean slavery was anchored in a hierarchy of power built on religious difference. Provençal sources generally provide little evidence one way or the other, though see Coulet, "Négritude et liberté."

10. Smail, *Consumption of Justice*, 33–34.

11. Low, "Notarial Information and the Production of Knowledge," 116–17.

12. For the term and its application, see Polanyi, *Personal Knowledge*; Polanyi, *The Tacit Dimension*.

13. Farge, *Allure of the Archives*, 17. My thanks to Rebecca Scott for discussing this point.

14. See, inter alia, Davis, *Women on the Margins*; Davis, *Trickster Travels*. A variant lies in Saidiya Hartman's much-discussed idea of "critical fabulation"; see Hartman, "Venus in Two Acts," 11.

15. Miles, *All That She Carried*, 89.

16. Perry et al., eds., *Cambridge World History of Slavery*; Schiel and Pargas, *Palgrave Handbook of Global Slavery*.

17. Smallwood, "Politics of the Archive," 128: "The counter-history, the history that is accountable to the enslaved, cannot fulfill our yearning for romance, our desire to hear the subaltern speak, or our search for the subaltern as heroic actor whose agency triumphs over the forces of oppression."

18. Jordan, *Apple of His Eye*.

19. Rubin, *Cities of Strangers*.

20. Whence the force of Frederick Cooper's argument against the assimilationist tendencies characteristic of African slavery, as described by Suzanne Miers and Igor Kopytoff. See Cooper, "Problem of Slavery in African Studies"; Miers and Kopytoff, *Slavery in Africa*.

21. Wolfe, "Settler Colonialism and the Elimination of the Native."

22. de la Fuente, "From Slaves to Citizens?"

23. Cooper, "Problem of Slavery in African Studies"; Miller, *Problem of Slavery as History*.

24. Vlassopoulos, "Does Slavery Have a History?," esp. p. 12, citing one of Nietzsche's aphorisms: "Nothing that has history can have a definition." See also the cogent remarks in Karras, *Slavery and Society*, 5–11.

25. In the records, the Latin word for slave broker was typically spelled *prozoneta*, the root of the modern French *proxénète*, which means "pimp" or "procurer."

Chapter 1. Practices of Slavery

1. Perry et al., eds., *Cambridge World History of Slavery*.

2. One of the prominent early studies is Bensch, "From Prizes of War." Henri Bresc locates the onset of a "slavery revolution (*révolution esclavagiste*)" in the final conquest of Menorca in 1287, which was accompanied by the reduction of many of the island's population to slavery. See Bresc, "L'esclave dans le monde méditerranéen."

3. Biran, "Forced Migrations and Slavery."

4. Barker, *That Most Precious Merchandise*; Cluse and Amitai, "Introduction."

5. Bensch, "From Prizes of War"; Constable, "Muslim Spain and Mediterranean Slavery"; Martín Casares, "Maghrebian Slaves in Spain."

NOTES TO CHAPTER 1   205

6. Balard, "Remarques sur les esclaves," 635.

7. Both Henri Bresc and David Abulafia suggest that as many as 40,000 of Menorca's indigenous Muslim population may have been enslaved in 1287; see Bresc, "L'esclave dans le monde méditerranéen," 89; Abulafia, "Last Muslims in Italy," 282. Brian Catlos, however, indicates that members of the island's Muslim population were invited to purchase their freedom for a fee of 7 ½ *duplas*, equivalent to 30 sous; see Catlos, *Muslims of Medieval Latin Christendom*, 76. Catlos notes only "hundreds" of warrants of sale in register 70 of the royal archive, rather fewer than suggested by Bresc and Abulafia.

8. The act concerns the manumission of Sibilina, a woman described as a Cuman. See Verlinden, *Esclavage* (1977), 2:447.

9. Balard, "Slavery in the Latin Mediterranean," 238–39.

10. Barker, *That Most Precious Merchandise*, 136–37.

11. Salicrú i Lluch, "Slaves in the Professional and Family Life"; Catlos, *Muslims of Medieval Latin Christendom*, 263.

12. Kopytoff, "Slavery"; Patterson, *Slavery and Social Death*; Meillassoux, *Anthropology of Slavery*.

13. Miller, *Problem of Slavery as History*, 25.

14. Bresc, *Un monde méditerranéen*, 1:446–450. See also Verlinden, *Esclavage* (1955), 1:361. The trade did not pass through points further west such as the port city of Bejaia; see Valérian, *Bougie*, 412–13.

15. ADBR 381 E 81, fol. 138r, 19 Mar. 1359.

16. Boni and Delort, "Des esclaves toscans," 1070.

17. Balard, "Le transport des esclaves," 363. Balard also discusses the volume of the slave trade in "Esclavage en Crimée," 12–13. Annika Stello suggests lower numbers for exports of captives, from 180 to 600 per year in the first half of the fifteenth century; see Stello, "Caffa and the Slave Trade," 384.

18. Marmon, "Domestic Slavery in the Mamluk Empire," 9.

19. Christ, *Trading Conflicts*, 124.

20. Bono, *Schiavi*, 73–74. See also the discussion in Bonazza, "Slavery in the Mediterranean," 227–28.

21. Heers, *Esclaves et domestiques*, 110–12.

22. For Barcelona, see Salicrú i Lluch, "L'esclau com a inversió?," 51n5. The figure is derived from an insurance register indicating the presence of 1,379 male slaves in 1424; for discussion, see Salicrú i Lluch, *Esclaus i propietaris d'esclaus*, 71. To this, Salicrú adds a number of female slaves on the assumption that the population of female slaves was at least half again as large as that of male slaves and as much as three times larger. The population of Barcelona at this time was between 30,000 and 40,000 people. For Palermo, see Bresc, *Un monde méditerranéen*, 1:439. For Mallorca, see Mummey, "Women, Slavery, and Community," 51–55.

23. The image used in Bradley, "Freedom and Slavery," 627, to describe the embeddedness of slavery in ancient Rome.

24. Estimates from Gioffré, *Il mercato degli schiavi*, 69–70, 79; Balard, *La Romanie génoise*, 2:816. Their sources have been checked and reworked by Barker, *That Most Precious Merchandise*, 62–65. Barker writes (p. 65) that "Overall, it seems that slaves made up 1 to 2 percent of the total Genoese population in the thirteenth century and 4 to 5 percent in the fifteenth century."

25. Capet, "Les étrangers au travail." For Perpignan, see also Brutails, *Étude sur l'esclavage*; Romestan, "Femmes esclaves à Perpignan."

26. Figures summarized in Angiolini, "Schiave," 99. For Pisa, see also Luzzati, "Schiavi e figli di schiavi." For Menresa, see Fynn-Paul, "Tartars in Spain."

27. McCormick, *Origins of the European Economy*, 733–77; McCormick, "New Light on the 'Dark Ages.'"

28. The question has been examined recently in Arnoux, "Effacement ou abolition?"

29. Karras, *Slavery and Society*; Hellie, *Slavery in Russia*.

30. Heers, *Esclaves et domestiques*, 116–17. Further to the west, there are slaves to be found in Montpellier, Narbonne, and especially Perpignan but not Toulouse; see pp. 118–19.

31. Romestan, "Femmes esclaves à Perpignan," 197–99; Peabody, "Alternative Genealogy"; Peabody, *'There Are No Slaves in France'*; Débax, "1446, un esclave noir."

32. Patterson, *Slavery and Social Death*, x: "One of the mistakes frequently made in comparative research is the exclusion of all societies in which the object of one's inquiry, even though it may occur, does not attain marked systemic importance."

33. Bensch, "From Prizes of War," 84.

34. Balard, "Remarques sur les esclaves," 649–50.

35. Budak, "Slavery in late medieval Dalmatia," 761.

36. Bresc, *Un monde méditerranéen*, 1:439–44.

37. Boni and Delort, "Des esclaves toscans," 1070.

38. Gioffré, *Il mercato degli schiavi*, 79.

39. In late medieval Dalmatia, Neven Budak describes a shift in slave labor from agriculture and cattle-breeding to urban tasks associated with households, crafts, and shipping. See Budak, "Slavery in Late Medieval Dalmatia," 750.

40. Romano, *Housecraft and Statecraft*. See also Heers, *Esclaves et domestiques*.

41. Verlinden, *Esclavage*, vols. 1–2; McKee, "Inherited Status and Slavery"; McKee, "Domestic Slavery in Renaissance Italy"; McKee, "Slavery"; McKee, "Familiarity of Slaves."

42. Del Bo, "Schiave bianche."

43. Bensch, "From Prizes of War," 79.

44. Blumenthal, *Enemies and Familiars*, 4.

45. Bonnassie, *La organización del trabajo*, 99; Martín Casares, "Maghrebian Slaves in Spain"; Blumenthal, *Enemies and Familiars*; Salicrú i Lluch, "Slaves in the Professional and Family Life."

46. Bernardi, "Esclaves et artisanat," 79.

47. Angiolini, "Schiave," 98.

48. The most important study of the general phenomenon of slave identity is Epstein, *Speaking of Slavery*.

49. See, inter alia, Cluse and Amitai, "Introduction," 17.

50. Barker, *That Most Precious Merchandise*, 40.

51. Bresc, *Un monde méditerranéen*, 1:449–50. For the Africanization of the slave market in Barcelona, see Armenteros Martínez, "Towards the Atlantic Mediterranean."

52. Budak, "Slavery in Renaissance Croatia," 84.

53. Bloch, "Comment et pourquoi finit l'esclavage antique."

54. Bonnassie, "Survie et extinction."

55. Schiel and Hanß, "Semantics, Practices," 11.

NOTES TO CHAPTER 2   207

56. Bonnassie, "Survie et extinction," 310. The translation is from Bonnassie, *From Slavery to Feudalism*, 5.

57. Blackburn, "Old World Background."

58. Armenteros Martínez and Ouerfelli, "Réévaluer l'économie de l'esclavage," paragraph 13.

59. Harper, *Slavery in the Late Roman World*.

60. Bernardi, "Esclaves et artisanat"; Salicrú i Lluch, "L'esclau com a inversió?"

61. See, inter alia, Boserup, *Woman's Role in Economic Development*; Goldin, *Understanding the Gender Gap*. For an evaluation of the impact of Boserup's work, see Benería and Sen, "Accumulation, Reproduction."

62. See p. 39.

63. Watson, *Roman Slave Law*, 9–23. For discussion, see Skoda, "People as Property," 251–54.

64. Blumenthal, "Masters, Slave Women." See also Blumenthal, "'As If She Were His Wife.'"

65. Fuentes, *Dispossessed Lives*; Johnson, *Wicked Flesh*; Morgan, *Reckoning with Slavery*.

66. Sobers-Khan, "Slavery in the Early Modern Ottoman Empire," 409.

Chapter 2. Slavery in Marseille, 1248–1491

1. This relates to an argument developed by Susan Mosher Stuard to the effect that the presence of enslaved servants sent a message to free servants to moderate their wage demands; see Stuard, "Ancillary Evidence," 25.

2. Darwin, *On the Origin of Species*, 310–11.

3. AMM 1 II. Many of the acts in this register are edited in Blancard, *Documents inédits*.

4. ADBR 381 E 15, fol. 58v, 24 July 1287. This act is edited in Verlinden, *Esclavage* (1955), 1:883–84.

5. Jordan, *Louis IX and the Challenge of the Crusade*, 71–72; Richard, *Crusades*.

6. Strayer, "Crusades of Louis IX," 165.

7. AMM 1 II, fol. 79r. For Mortreuil's transcription of the act, see BnF NAL 1325, p. 146.

8. ADBR 3 B 1, fol. 11r, 12 kalendas Aprilis 1264. The appellate judge ruled that Maria, the enslaved woman, did not actually belong to the debtor but instead to a woman also named Maria, wife of Peire Thomas. For Mortreuil's transcription of the act, see BnF NAL 1325, pp. 51–52.

9. Pernoud, *Les statuts municipaux de Marseille*, book 1, statute 39, p. 52. This entry concerns the fees paid to public criers, fees that varied according to the type of proclamation. One of the entries lists a fee of 2 d. "for male and female slaves" (*de servo et de serva*), presumably referring to proclamations about fugitive slaves.

10. Mabilly, *Inventaire sommaire, série BB*. The first reference to a slave in this inventory of the series occurs in BB 28, covering the years 1380–1383 (see p. 159).

11. ADBR 351 E 2, fol. 221r, 19 Oct. 1353: *tartaresa*. For Mortreuil's transcription of the act, see BnF NAL 1325, p. 77.

12. For Greek slaves, see Grant, *Greek Captives and Mediterranean Slavery*.

13. ADBR 351 E 2, fol. 348v, 23 Feb. 1354. For Mortreuil's transcription of the act, see BnF NAL 1325, p. 78.

14. Jackson, *The Mongols and the Islamic World*, 62; Jackson, *The Mongols and the West*, 38; Favereau Doumenjou, *The Horde*.

208 NOTES TO CHAPTER 2

15. Many insights concerning Tatars may be found in Quirini-Poplawska, "Venetian Involvement."

16. For the latter, see Bresc, *Un monde méditerranéen*, 1:444.

17. Kowalesky, *Die ökonomische entwicklung Europas*, 5:341–44.

18. Origo, "Domestic Enemy," 324.

19. One of the most vigorous proponents of the wage thesis in recent years has been Jeffrey Fynn-Paul; see Fynn-Paul, "Tartars in Spain"; Fynn-Paul, "Empire, Monotheism and Slavery"; Fynn-Paul, "Reasons for the Limited Scope." The wage thesis is central to the recent synthesis of Hocquet, *Maîtres et esclaves*.

20. See p. 26.

21. This argument has been made vigorously in Bernardi, "Esclaves et artisanat"; Martín Casares, "Evolution of the Origin of Slaves," 410.

22. Salicrú i Lluch, "L'esclau com a inversió?," 63–65. See also the thoughtful discussion in Armenteros Martínez, *L'esclavitud a la Barcelona*, 35–42.

23. Verlinden, *Esclavage* (1977), 2:437–40.

24. Barker, *That Most Precious Merchandise*, 141–44.

25. A model proposed by Boni and Delort suggests that free labor in post-plague Florence would have been cheaper, in the long run, than enslaved labor, although they acknowledge the schematic nature of the argument; see Boni and Delort, "Des esclaves toscans," 1075–76. Juliane Schiel also casts doubt on the wage thesis, although her arguments are specific to the situation in Venice; see Schiel, "Die Sklaven."

26. Valérian, *Bougie*, 122. Mark Meyerson speaks of the "almost-incessant raiding and piracy so characteristic of Muslim-Christian contact in the western Mediterranean" in the fourteenth and fifteenth centuries; see his "Slavery and Solidarity," 289.

27. All three acts were drafted by the notary Raymon Audebert; see ADBR 351 E 2, fol. 221r, 19 Oct. 1353; fol. 348v, 23 Feb. 1354; fol. 357r, 5 Mar. 1354. For Mortreuil's transcription, see BnF NAL 1325, pp. 77–79.

28. Perry, *Slavery in a Medieval Islamic Society*. See also Hershenzon, *Captive Sea*, 24–27, and Barker, *That Most Precious Merchandise*, 85: "Although a slave's first owner was his or her gateway into slaveholding society, most slaves passed through the hands of several owners over the course of their lives."

29. The use of this clause was not unique to Marseille. For a case that had arisen in Genoa, see Epstein, "Late Medieval Lawyer," 55–56.

30. ADBR 351 E 50, fols. 354v-356r, 5 Mar. 1381; this act is duplicated in an extenso, ADBR 351 E 650, fols. 198r-199r. An edition of the act is available in Verlinden, *Esclavage* (1955), 1:889–890; for a discussion of the case, see p. 821.

31. Peres, "'She Wants to Do It Her Own Way,'" 315.

32. On other methods used by members of the Datini network to get rid of or conceal the "threatening presence" of enslaved mothers, see Peres, "'She Wants to Do It Her Own Way,'" 315–28.

33. Heers, *Esclaves et domestiques*, 128.

34. The figures here and below for the demographic importance of broad occupational sectors derives from a database listing approximately 13,000 unique individuals identified in records from 1337 to 1362 (see Smail, *Imaginary Cartographies*, appendix 1). Of the 7,200 individuals

whose occupations can be identified with reasonable accuracy, 837 (11.6 percent) are members of the clergy. The figure almost certainly overstates the overall demographic importance of the clergy, since members of the clergy were more likely than members of other occupational groups to appear in notarial and administrative records.

35. See Armstrong-Partida, "Priestly Wives," 180; Sommar, *Slaves of the Churches.*

36. For the example of Genoa, see Gioffré, *Il mercato degli schiavi*, 86; Balard, "Remarques sur les esclaves," 664.

37. Killerby, *Sumptuary Law.*

38. ADBR 5 G 775, fol. 97v.

39. For extensive comments on legal practices bearing on manumissions in Provence, see Aubenas, "L'esclavage en pays de droit écrit."

40. ADBR 381 E 81, fols. 124r-125v, 8 Feb. 1359.

41. ADBR 381 E 83, fols. 43r-44r, 28 May 1361.

42. For Mortreuil's transcription of the act, see BnF NAL 1325, p. 166. It is likely to be found in ADBR 351 E 68, fol. 166r, 30 Jan. 1395, although current archival policy has restricted the availability of this register. Note that this is not the same person as Magdalena Coline.

43. The act is described though not transcribed in Mortreuil, "Moeurs et institutions marseillaises," 163. It was subsequently referenced by Verlinden, *Esclavage* (1955), 1:820. It is likely to be found in ADBR 355 E 19, ADBR 355 E 38, or ADBR 391 E 22, although current archival policy has restricted the availability of these registers.

44. Peres, "'She Wants to Do It Her Own Way,'" 248. The practice, according to Peres, was common (p. 251): "Temporary slavery, as attested in the documents of the Datini archive, was not a marginal phenomenon. It was widely practised in the cities of the Iberian and Italian peninsulas."

45. McKinley, "Financing Freedom."

46. Balard, "Slavery in the Latin Mediterranean," 243, 248.

47. See the discussion on pp. 78–79, suggesting that the median age for women at the point of acquisition was probably closer to 14.

48. See the discussion of manumission in Barker, *That Most Precious Merchandise*, 86–88.

49. ADBR 351 E 44, fols. 106r-108r, 21 Jan. 1376. For a complete transcription of the act and discussion, see Verlinden, *Esclavage* (1955), 1:820–821, 897–900; Steinman, "The Bond of Said Child's Blood."

50. BnF NAL 1325, p. 141.

51. Verlinden, *Esclavage* (1955), 1:898: *extraneus et de remotis partibus dicebatur.* It is likely that the potential buyer was in fact from no further than Alghero.

52. Barker, *That Most Precious Merchandise*, 117–19. Hannah Skoda has argued that consent clauses are a distinctive feature of Ragusan sales; see Skoda, "People as Property," 244–49.

53. ADBR 355 E 16, fols. 56v-57r, 18 Sept. 1367. It is conceivable that Catharina was pregnant and that the act was arranged to ensure that the child would be raised as another man's offspring. My thanks to Sara McDougall for this insight. A related possibility is that her master, Obertus Avogarii of Piacenza, had concerns about men other than a lawful husband having sexual access to her.

54. See the illuminating discussion of this phenomenon in Peres, "'She Wants to Do It Her Own Way,'" 252–55. The experiences of Catherina of Tartary are remarkably similar to those of

210 NOTES TO CHAPTER 3

an enslaved woman named Margherita who worked in branch offices of the Datini network in the Crown of Aragon and similarly took flight to claim her freedom; see pp. 255–57.

55. Shoemaker, *Sanctuary and Crime*.

56. The notary noted the involvement of Raymon's circle of friends and kin with this phrase: *Et volens propria tractantibus et consulentibus cunctis suis amicis dictam Catherinam afranchamenti beneficio premiare.*

Chapter 3. Peire the Privateer

1. Retrieved from https://newsroom.churchofjesuschrist.org/article/church-completes-major-microfilm-digitization-initiative on 23 October 2023.

2. An argument especially associated with Baratier, *De 1291 à 1423*.

3. In general, see Pryor, "Ship Types and Fleet Composition"; Dotson, "Everything Is a Compromise."

4. ADBR 351 E 147, fol. 52r, 5 May 1391.

5. ADBR 381 E 72, fols. 56r-57v.

6. AMM BB 21, fol. 6r. The name of the committee was *Ad expellendum meretrices*, "For the purpose of expelling prostitutes."

7. AMM BB 21, fol. 41v.

8. AMM FF 532, fol. 31r (the lawsuit); ADBR 355 E 8, fol. 19r-v, 17 July 1355 (the witness). The handwriting is difficult to make out; it may read "Perronus."

9. *Perrotus* appears three times in records between 1337 and 1362, referring to two or three unique individuals. All three were immigrants, one from Savoy, a second from Dijon, and a third from France. See, respectively, ADBR 355 E 35, fol. 34v, 17 May 1357 (Perrotus Pellipparii, an artisan from Savoy); 355 E 10, fol. 11r-v, 27 Apr. 1359 (Perrotus de Digon, a shoemaker); and 381 E 86, fol. 191v, Nov. 1354 (Perrotus de Insula, a shoemaker from France).

10. AMM BB 22, 13 Sept. 1357, fols. 11r-13v. The passage has been damaged by humidity; the sense of the passage given here is based on the summary provided in the index; see Mabilly, *Inventaire sommaire, série BB*, 68.

11. ADBR 3 HD H 12, pièce 7. The inventory, edited by Christine Barnel and Daniel Lord Smail, is available in DALME, retrieved from https://purl.dalme.org/a0a9e400-2191-4354-9793-660c55c536c7/ on 23 Oct. 2023.

12. AMM FF 557, unfoliated, entry dated 7 Aug. 1384.

13. ADBR 351 E 38, fols. 96v-97r, 2 Sept. 1381.

14. ADBR 351 E 38, fols. 161r-162v, 3 Feb. 1382.

15. See pp. 85–86.

16. For a transcription of the act by Anselme Mortreuil, see BnF NAL 1325, pp. 179–83, 26 Apr. 1387. I have been unable to locate the original register. It is possible that the act is preserved in ADBR 351 E 655, a type of register known as an "extenso" that corresponds to the years in question (1386–1388), but archival restrictions currently in place prevent consultation of this register.

17. ADBR 351 E 68, fol. 12r, 28 Apr. 1395. An extenso version of the same act appears in ADBR 351 E 659, fols. 51v-52v. Although the act concerns a loan of 100 florins for the purchase of a sail—on which more below—a marginal note entered in both the original act and the extenso version explicitly states that this loan was in addition to the existing debt.

NOTES TO CHAPTER 4   211

18. ADBR 351 E 57, fol. 157v, 24 Nov. 1387, in which Peire acknowledges a debt of 50 florins to Johan.

19. ADBR 3 B 100, unfoliated, entry dated 24 Dec. 1384.

20. ADBR 351 E 668, fol. 102r-v, 27 Oct. 1387. For Peire's encounter with Queen Marie, see p. 64.

21. ADBR 3 B 150, fol. 67r, entry dated 16 Aug. 1412. The entry records the appearance in court of Johan de Ysia, Peire's lawyer, bearing a dowry act that supposedly gave Peire rights to harvest wheat from a certain plot of land, the matter of contention in the dispute. Context suggests very strongly that the dowry act was Bertomieua's, since there are no other women in the Huguet family (e.g., a daughter-in-law) through whom he could have acquired rights to the land. The act is incompletely dated, for it literally reads (in translation) "In the year of the Lord one thousand seventy-seven 74, Tuesday, the 1st of the month of April."

22. ADBR 351 E 39, fol. 244r, 3 Mar. 1384.

23. ADBR 355 E 76, fols. 154v-155r, 20 Nov. 1392.

24. Details on Alaseta's marriage to Johan and her dowry are revealed in a legal action setting her against her son, Peyret, a fragment of which appears in a register of the court in September of 1406; see ADBR 3 B 144, fols. 130r-133v, 4 Sept. 1406. Since the early stages of the suit are missing, it is difficult to ascertain the nature of the dispute. To rebut his mother's plea, Peyret noted that he was 10 years old at the time of her marriage to Johan Huguet, and that her father, Bertran Colin, was named guardian of the estate Peyret had inherited from his own father. But Bertran was a poor man, lacking the wherewithal to pay a dowry of 300 florins, so he paid the dowry with funds supposedly embezzled from Peyret's estate. Additional details indicate that Peyret subsequently married at the age of 18, probably around 1399, and was therefore 25 years old in 1406. At the end of the case (fol. 133v), the judge ruled against Peyret and required him to pay 50 l. to Alaseta.

25. ADBR 351 E 66, fols. 39v-40r, 29 May 1393. This act also provides details about Alaseta's first husband and her children. Her father, Bertran, was living in Ceyreste in 1403; see ADBR 355 E 76bis, fol. 79r, 30 Apr. 1403. In this act, Johan Huguet appears as a procurator for his father-in-law.

26. ADBR 355 E 92, fol. 20r-v, 28 May 1429.

Chapter 4. The Expedition to Naples

1. Léonard, *Histoire de Jeanne Ire*; Casteen, *From She-Wolf to Martyr*.

2. For connections between Marseille and Naples, see Rambaud, ed., *Marseille et ses rois de Naples*.

3. Arlot, "Dans la tourmente," 73.

4. The most detailed narrative of the events described in this section may be found in Valois, *La France et le grand schisme*.

5. Baratier, *De 1291 à 1423*, 46–47.

6. Bourrilly, "Duguesclin et le duc d'Anjou."

7. Coulet, "L'Union d'Aix"; Venturini, "La guerre de l'Union d'Aix"; Xhayet, "Partisans et adversaires."

8. Arlot, "Dans la tourmente"; Matz, "Un grand officier"; Matz, "Princesse au pouvoir"; Hébert and Matz, *Journal de Jean Le Fèvre*.

212 NOTES TO CHAPTER 4

9. de Blasiis, ed., *Cronicon siculum*, 70.

10. Hébert and Matz, *Journal de Jean Le Fèvre*, 390.

11. Arlot, "Dans la tourmente," 166, note 56; Hébert and Matz, *Journal de Jean Le Fèvre*, 395.

12. Hébert and Matz, *Journal de Jean Le Fèvre*, 401: *Le quart jour Madame fu devers nostre Saint Pere a Rauquemaure et entre eulz fu accordé que dedens le XXe jour de ce mois, le pape et elle feront finance de XXX^M florins de chambre, quilibet XV^M et conducetur galea, que de Neapoli venit, ad unum mensem, que defferet istos Neapolitanos; et usque ad diem conductionis domina sustentabit eam ut melius poterit; et portabitur peccunia per litteras cambii de Avinione Pisis et de Pisis ad Neapolim.* In the journal entry for 27 Sept. 1387 (p. 432), Jean indicates that Marie agreed to remit the 15,000 florins she had promised to the Italians.

13. Hébert and Matz, *Journal de Jean Le Fèvre*, 431–32.

14. A sense of the tension is indicated in Valois, *La France et le grand schisme*, 2:120–121.

15. Baratier, *De 1291 à 1423*, 50. Arlot, "Dans la tourmente," p. 166, indicates that the pope agreed to provide 22,000 florins to fund the expedition, to be led by the Duke of Bourbon, but I have been unable to confirm this claim.

16. Hébert and Matz, *Journal de Jean Le Fèvre*, 437: *Item pro Petro Hugueti de Massilia, cui rex Ludovicus concessit officium tercenalis civitatis Neapolis, quod officium domina confirmat. Item pro eodem confirmacio donacionis sibi facte per regem Ludovicum de delacione armorum per comitatus Provincie et Forcalquerii et aliarum donacionum eidem Petro factarum. Item pro eodem confirmacio immunitatis et exempcionis solucionis gabellarum et pedagiorum.* It is possible that Peire had also received similar concessions in August of 1387, since an entry that month refers to a letter *pro Perro de Hugot* (p. 390).

17. Baratier, *De 1291 à 1423*, 47, fns. 1–2.

18. BnF Ms Lat. 5913A, fols. 99r-101v.

19. ADBR 351 E 87, fols. 64r-65r, 23 Nov. 1387.

20. These acts were discovered by Édouard Baratier and are discussed in *De 1291 à 1423*, 50–51.

21. ADBR 351 E 57, fols. 156v-157r, 24 Nov. 1387.

22. ADBR 351 E 57, fols. 157v-158r.

23. BnF Ms Lat. 5913A, fols. 50r-51v. The reference to La Stella, which was being assigned to a nobleman named Guillelmus Canet, appears on fol. 50r: *Et primo predictus reverendissimus dominus camerarius vice et nomine quibus supra promisit dicto domino Guillelmo Canet solemniter stipulanti et recipienti traddere et realiter assignare seu traddi et assignari facere quandam galeam dicta domini nostri pape vocatam galea de Stella.*

24. ADBR 351 E 57, fols. 158r-159r. The *Sanctus-Georgius* appears in an act from January of 1384. Like *La Stella*, the galley belonged to the papal curia, and it was being assigned to Peire Enguayte of Majorca, a shipowner who appears elsewhere in association with other Massiliote shipowners around this time. The *Sanctus-Georgius* was a large galley with 29 banks of oars. See BnF Ms Lat. 5913A, fols. 47r-49v, 26 Jan. 1384.

25. BnF Ms Lat. 5913A, fols. 46r-101v. Some acts in this series are duplicates.

26. BnF Ms Lat. 5913A, fol. 50v.

27. E.g., BnF Ms Lat. 5913A, fol. 55v: *exeptis vestibus sive vestimentis et aliis utensilibus sive ordilhiis que dimictuntur marinariis et aliis qui ea ceperunt tam in terra quam in mari.*

28. E.g., BnF Ms Lat. 5913A, fol. 50v: *Hoc exepto quod si capitaneus guerre terre vel maris vel alter official caperetur per dictum dominum Guillelmum quod dictus dominus Guillelmus habeat*

ipsum reddere et reddere tenetur dicto domino nostro pape aut dicto domino regi pro iusto precio et racionabili secundum conditionem persone.

29. For a study of commenda contracts in Marseille, see Pryor, *Business Contracts.* A recent study of marine insurance is Ceccarelli, *Un mercato del rischio.*

30. Details of the scene are found in several passages in ADBR 3 B 117, fols. 58v-69v, case opened 14 Feb. 1391. This case consists of a lawsuit and countersuit pitting the former partners against one another. For a fuller discussion, see pp. 95–97.

31. de Blasiis, ed., *Cronicon siculum,* 72–73.

32. For the identification, see Cappelletti, *Le chiese d'Italia,* 19:659–60. Francesco III had been named to the see in 1380. Within a year or two, perhaps because of his capture in 1387, he abandoned Urban VI and threw his support behind Clement VII.

33. Cutolo, *Re Ladislao d'Angiò Durazzo,* 74.

34. Personal communication, 21 July 2019.

35. ADBR 3 B 117, fol. 62r: *Item dixit et proponit quod dictus Petrus retrocedens de partibus Neapolis ubi dimiserat dictum Anthonium cum sua gualea quem noluit sequi ad discurendum in costa de Malpha iuxta preceptum factum per dominum viceregem.* This was one of the claims made by Antoni de Lueys against his former partner. The name of the vice-regent is not specified.

36. ADBR 3 B 117, fol. 68r.

37. ADBR 3 B 117, fols. 67v-68r.

38. Abulafia, *Western Mediterranean Kingdoms,* 169.

39. ADBR 355 E 76, fols. 205r-206v, 14 Feb. 1393. An extenso version of this act is found in ADBR 355 E 311, fols. 73v-75r. Substantial sections of the act are written in eastern Occitan.

40. ADBR 351 E 658, fols. 201r-204v, 13 Feb. 1393.

41. Ryder, "Angevin Bid for Naples," 56–57.

42. BnF NAL 1349, fols. 18v-20v, 17 May 1398.

43. AMM BB 32, fol. 52r.

Chapter 5. Magdalena Comes to Marseille

1. ADBR 3B 861, fols. 441v-443v.

2. ADBR 3B 861, fols. 437v-439v.

3. Verlinden, "Orthodoxie et esclavage au bas Moyen Âge"; Barker, *That Most Precious Merchandise,* 20–22; Grant, *Greek Captives and Mediterranean Slavery,* 144–52.

4. For Sardinians, see Livi, *Sardi in schiavitù;* Mummey, "Women, Slavery, and Community," 63–78. For the *anime,* see Heers, *Esclaves et domestiques,* esp. 153–54; Romano, *Housecraft and Statecraft,* 47–48; McKee, "Domestic Slavery in Renaissance Italy," 320.

5. Boni and Delort, "Des esclaves toscans," 1065.

6. ADBR 3B 858, fol. 216v.

7. ADBR 3B 858, fol. 244v. The phrase is *ipsa erat sclava domini cuius era[n]t.* The sense of this passage is garbled, hence the suggestion of a scribal error that can be repaired by adding the "n." My thanks to Shane Bobrycki for his assistance with the Latin.

8. ADBR 3B 861, fol. 438r-v.

9. ADBR 3 B 858, fol. 228r-v. The relevant phrase is *Item probare intendit quod dicta Magdalena et cetere sarracene que capiuntur de partibus Barbarie habent magnam differenciam cum Christianis pro eo quia habent certa signa cum igne facta in brachis.*

214 NOTES TO CHAPTER 5

10. Casteen, "'Just War' and 'Conspicuous Sins,'" 533n7.

11. Valentin Groebner (*Who Are You?*, 110) has used entries in the Florentine *Registro degli schiavi* as the basis for his argument that the practice of branding slaves with scars and tattoos was widespread in the later Middle Ages. The register (edited in Livi, *La schiavitù domestica nei tempi di mezzo e nei moderni*), compiled between 1366 and 1397, contains descriptions of 357 enslaved people in Florence. Groebner's phrasing, in both the English translation and the German original, appears to suggest that of the 357 individuals listed in the register, all but one were marked with dots or signs (*puncta* or *signa*). In fact, a reading of the register indicates that the words *puncta* and *signa* were not commonly used, appearing in the descriptions of just seven individuals. It is likely that Groebner intended to say that all but one include descriptions of marks on the skin, the vast majority of which are moles, scars, and other blemishes. Groebner does not seem to have considered the possibility that at least some of the *puncta* and *signa* may have been indigenous in origin. My thanks to Hannah Barker for discussion of this passage.

12. Phillips, *Slavery in Medieval and Early Modern Iberia*, 75–77.

13. The forehead and chin are among the most common sites attested in contemporary populations, and tattoos were also made on the arms, wrists, the back of the hand, and other sites. See Garanger, *Femmes algériennes 1960*; Martín Casares, "Maghrebian Slaves in Spain," 106; Bouabdella et al., "Les tatouages traditionnels au Maroc."

14. Unclothed slaves could be subjected to physical examination at the point of sale; see Ferragud, "Role of Doctors in the Slave Trade," 147. For the Islamicate world, where there are some contradictions in the normative literature, see Barker, "Purchasing a Slave," 12.

15. Barker, *That Most Precious Merchandise*, 68.

16. Barker, *That Most Precious Merchandise*, 135–36.

17. Peres, "'She Wants to Do It Her Own Way,'" 136.

18. Becker, *Amazigh Arts in Morocco*, 56.

19. ADBR 3 B 861, fol. 469r: *de liberis parentibus procreatam.*

20. Bresc, *Un monde méditerranéen*, 1:444.

21. Valérian, "La course maghrébine."

22. ADBR 5 G 775, fols. 44v-46r.

23. Ganchou, "Valentina Doria."

24. de Blasiis, ed., *Cronicon siculum*, 70: *comes Cerreti regni Cicilie amiratus.*

25. Stella, *Georgii et Iohannis Stellae Annales Genuenses*. The phrase reads *Manfredi de Claramonte admirati nuncupati seu armiragii regni Trinaclie.*

26. See Battilana, *Genealogie delle famiglie nobili di Genova*. To my knowledge, no member of Corrado's family after the death of Raffaele Doria (d. ca. 1341) bore the title. This doesn't preclude the possibility that a relative of his was claiming the title in 1387.

27. In addition to the reference cited above, see Pontieri, *Storia di Napoli*, 315.

28. See Fancy, *The Mercenary Mediterranean*.

29. Cutolo, *Re Ladislao d'Angiò Durazzo*, 79. For further details on the raids, see Antoninus, *Divi Antonini Archiepiscopi florentini*, 405–6. My thanks to Rowan Dorin for identifying this source. Note that owing to a printer's error, there are two pages "405" in this edition; the first reference is on the second page 405, dated 1386. The phrases read *Circa id tempus infideles, qui dicuntur Mauri, discurrentes per mare Siculum cum suis lignis ceperunt aliqua navigia Christianorum quae ad partes suas adducentes servos vendiderunt inventos in eis* (p. 405) and *Sequenti anno Mauri cum nonem navigiis venerunt usque ad insulam Gelbae, ibique captis pluribus lignis et Christicolis in*

NOTES TO CHAPTER 6   215

regionem suam duxerunt servituti captos addicentos (p. 406). On p. 406, the chronicle describes another assault by the Moors, this time with a fleet of seven ships, all across the Western Mediterranean. In 1388, according to the chronicle, a fleet led by count Manfredi Chiaramonte in response to this attack took the island of Djerba, killing more than 2,000 Muslims. This episode is also described briefly in Pignatelli, *I Diurnali del Duca di Monteleone*, 50.

30. A faint possibility is the given name *Kahina*, derived from al-Kahina, a legendary figure in the Amazigh resistance to Arab incursions in the seventh century.

31. Origo, "Domestic Enemy."

32. ADBR B 1946, fol. 29r.

33. The story emerges from an appeal that was later filed by Johan Martin; see ADBR 3 B 845, case opened 6 July 1391 on fol. 234r. See also ADBR 3 B 119, fol. 2r and following, 16 Jan. 1392.

34. ADBR 3 B 845, fol. 253v.

35. The insult, which exists in modern French as "ribaud," has a meaning close to "vagabond" or "truant" in English.

36. Smail, *Legal Plunder*, 79–83.

Chapter 6. The Wheel of Fortune

1. AMM BB 32, fol. 42r, 20 May 1391. One of the last references to Peire as a member of the city council appears in a record from 30 Jan. 1409; see ADBR 3 B 147bis, fols. 27r-31v. A list of counselors for the year 1408–1409 appears on fol. 31r-v and includes Peire Huguet on fol. 31r and his brother Johan Huguet on fol. 31v. The final appearance occurs on 16 Feb. 1410, see ADBR 355 E 309, fol. 16v.

2. ADBR 355 E 298, fols. 99r-100r, 15 July 1390.

3. ADBR 355 E 76, fols. 205r-206v, 14 Feb. 1393.

4. This is the series FF in the Archives municipales de la Ville de Marseille.

5. AMM FF 55, unfoliated, entry dated 7 Aug. 1384. This action targeted a moneychanger named Laurens Fulco.

6. ADBR 3 B 100, unfoliated, entry dated 5 May 1385.

7. ADBR 351 E 670, fol. 76v, 8 May 1388.

8. ADBR 3 B 840, fol. 102r, 10 June 1388. A marginal note reads "It is not being pursued (*non prosequitur*)."

9. ADBR 351 E 124, fols. 311v-312r, 27 Oct. 1388.

10. A flotilla of five ships, apparently without *La Stella*, left Marseille for Naples on 18 October 1388; see the brief reference to this expedition in Pontieri, *Storia di Napoli*, 314.

11. ADBR 3 B 115, fol. 4r, 10 Jan. 1391.

12. ADBR 3 B 115, fols. 8v-9r, 27 Jan. 1397.

13. ADBR 3 B 115, fols. 6v-7v.

14. ADBR 3 B 117, fol. 68r: *fuit repertum quod dictus Johannes Hugueti frater dicti Petri de lucrata quantitate in dicta galiota elevavit due centos florenos.*

15. ADBR 351 E 47, fols. 10v-11r, 9 Dec. 1391.

16. ADBR 351 E 659, fol. 137r-v, 28 Apr. 1395 (the pavises); ADBR 351 E 68, fol. 12r, 28 Apr. 1395 (the sail), with a copy in ADBR 351 E 659, fols. 51v-52v.

17. BnF NAL 1348, fols. 284r-286v, 19 Jan. 1398. The reference to a debt of 100 florins owed by Peire Huguet and his wife appears on fol. 285r. The original act, drafted by the notary Antoni Raynaut, is not extant.

216   NOTES TO CHAPTER 7

18. ADBR 351 E 64, fol. 86r, 29 Sept. 1391.

19. ADBR 351 E 47, fols. 19v-20v, 30 Dec. 1391.

20. ADBR 351 E 659, fols. 51v-52v, 28 Apr. 1395.

21. ADBR 355 E 68, fol. 100r-v, 6 Feb. 1410.

22. BnF NAL 1348, fols. 284r-286v, 19 Jan. 1398.

23. ADBR 355 E 51, fol. 126r-v, 27 Nov. 1398.

24. See Claustre, *Faire ses comptes au Moyen Âge.*

25. Van Allen, "Sitting on a Man," 165–81, here 170. For commentary, see Day, "Judith Van Allen and the Impact of Her Article."

26. BnF NAL 1352, fol. 32r.

27. AMM BB 32, fol. 91r, 20 Oct. 1402.

28. ADBR 3 B 137, fol. 72v, 5 Jan. 1403.

29. AMM FF 588, fol. 2r.

30. ADBR 351 E 222, fols. 62v-64r, 21 Dec. 1403.

Chapter 7. Magdalena Gets Married

1. As the French historian Robert Fossier put it, "there was no such thing as Liberty, then as now; liberties did exist but no one possessed all of them." Fossier, *Enfance de l'Europe*, 1:515. See also the discussion in Patterson, "Revisiting Slavery, Property, and Social Death." Patterson argues that the property definition cannot fully define the category of slave, and the reason lies in the fact that in kin-based societies, few if any people can ever be considered entirely free of claims made on them.

2. ADBR 351 E 80, fols. 53v-54r.

3. For a discussion of the fragment of evidence that we have for Bertomieua's dowry, see p. 56.

4. ADBR 351 E 80, fol. 53v: *tractatu tamen precedenti aliquorum amicorum comunum partium earumdem.*

5. ADBR 351 E 80, fols. 91v-92r, 22 Feb. 1400, and fol. 96v, 7 Mar. 1400.

6. ADBR 355 E 290, fols. 61r-62r, 4 Apr. 1355. This register also preserves a peace act or composition involving the two parties, made with the involvement of "many other common friends of the same parties (*pluribus aliis amicis communibus partium earumdem*)"; see fols. 20r-21r.

7. In general, see Wisnoski, "It Is Unjust for the Law of Marriage."

8. For an edition of the Decretum, see Friedberg, *Eine neue kritische Ausgabe des Corpus iuris canonici*, causa 29. The translation is by John T. Noonan, retrieved from http://legalhistorysources .com/Canon%20Law/MARRIAGELAW.htm on 11 July 2024. For discussion, see Anders Winroth, "Neither Slave nor Free."

9. A number of related concerns arose in situations where individuals in bondage had married without their lords' consent; see Landau, "Hadrians IV. Dekretale 'Dignum est.'"

10. *Cod.* 7. 6. 1. 9, from 531 CE. I am indebted to Mike Humphreys for this and other references.

11. *Nov.* 22. 10–11, from 536 CE.

12. Ricardus Pisanus, *Lo Codi*, 7. 2, p. 245: *Quomodo seruus efficitur liber contra uoluntatem domini.*

13. My thanks to Rowan Dorin for this image.

14. Burns, *Las Siete Partidas*, 4. 22. 5, p. 983.

NOTES TO CHAPTER 8   217

15. Desimoni, Belgrango, and Poggi, *Leges genuenses*, 583.

16. The names of pedicequas in Marseille include thoroughly Provençal names such as "Biatris." A loose folio at the end of ADBR 381 E 393 describes the interesting case involving another pedicequa with the conventional Provençal name "Bertrandeta." The suit identifies her as the daughter of Bertomieu Vincens of the castrum of Gemenos; she was serving as an *ancilla* or pedicequa in the house of Berengier Matairin when she was raped by Berengier's nephew.

17. See p. 46. The act is ADBR 355 E 16, fols. 56v-57r, 18 Sept. 1367. The relevant phrase is *dicta Catharina pro pediceca ad tempus cum aliqua persona se conduceret existens tamen sine marito*.

18. See ADBR 3 B 96, fol. 113r-v.

19. ADBR 3 B 861, fol. 469r: *antea perprius dictam Magdalenam non ut sclavam sed ut meram liberam maritaverat et in parte dotaverat*.

20. On this important question, see Lauer, "From Slave to Wife."

21. Epstein, *Speaking of Slavery*, 24–33.

22. As suggested by an acknowledgment of debt arising from negotiations involving these products in an act from 1394; see ADBR 355 E 78, fol. 72v, 1 Sept. 1394.

23. An instance of both is found in AMM FF 563, fol. 8r-v, 7 Nov. 1388. Earlier in the day, Elena appeared at court pursuing some claim against Peire Imbert. Later that same day, an entry in the register indicates that a woman named Dulcieta (her surname is unclear) had been pursuing her for an unrelated claim.

24. ADBR 351 E 179, fol. 17v, 28 May 1395.

25. See ADBR 355 E 2, fol. 44r-v, 30 June 1349. In the act, a woman named Elena Fabressa, from the town of Moustiers in Upper Provence, was getting married to Peire Gregori, a shoemaker and resident of Marseille.

26. I gratefully acknowledge the contributions of Ryan Low and Angela Zhang.

27. ADBR 351 E 39, fol. 145r-v, 26 Sept. 1384.

28. ADBR 351 E 286, fols. 205v-206r, 5 Mar. 1423.

29. Lesnick, "Insults and Threats in Medieval Todi"; Vise, *Unruly Tongue*.

30. ADBR 351 E 92, fols. 35v-36r. Undated, but it appears after a record dated 7 July 1393. The expression is *Vay caytieva que si yeu non fossa tu feras putan.*

31. The text, which is uncertain, appears to read: *Vay caytieva que yest tu aguda en ton tenps trueia escladas foras si non ho aguessas contat al juge merdos*. Jaumona denied this, admitting only to having said *Tu yest lo juge merdos*.

32. For striking insights on the prostitution of slaves in the Crown of Aragon, see Peres, "'She Wants to Do It Her Own Way,'" 159–73.

33. AMM FF 583, unfoliated, case opened 24 July 1402.

Chapter 8. Magdalena the Moneylender

1. ADBR 3 B 858, fol. 203r.

2. ADBR 3 B 858, fols. 209v-211r. The translation of the fifth claim is awkward because an inattentive notary, in the act of making a fair copy from the original trial proceedings, inadvertently dropped a line, leaving the expression "she appropriated to herself" dangling. The text supplied in brackets is a conjecture.

3. Pernoud, *Les statuts municipaux de Marseille*, book 5, chapter 40, 184.

218 NOTES TO CHAPTER 8

4. Kaye, *History of Balance*.

5. BnF NAL 1342.

6. Graeber, *Debt*.

7. ADBR 5 G 775, fols. 90r-100v.

8. A sample of several hundred inventories is available in DALME, https://dalme.org/, retrieved on 30 March 2025.

9. Smail, *Consumption of Justice*, 39–40, 144.

10. ADBR 4 HD B 4. An index appearing at the front of the register, alphabetized by first name, lists close to four hundred property owners owing rents to the hospital. The figure excludes several institutions, including monasteries and convents, that were listed among the owners. Also excluded are several names that cannot easily be made out. Of the 372 readily legible entries, there are 294 male and 78 female property owners.

11. The extent of her business operations is revealed by a lawsuit that stretched from February 1407 to November 1408; see ADBR 3 B 147, fols. 21r-96v, case opened 24 Feb. 1407. The lawsuit originally involved her son, Jacme Niel, but Jacme died in the midst of the proceedings and the suit was taken over by Resens. By 1407, Resens Cambale had stepped back from running the day-to-day operations, but according to the procurator for the plaintiff, the shop was still named after her. The relevant claim (fol. 48r-v) reads: "Commonly, the stations and shops of merchants are named after the oldest and worthiest of the society, and, on the letters and receipts of the shop, the trade goods are signed with the *marca* or sign of the oldest or worthiest. In the shop of the late Jacme Niel, all the things carried out there were done for the greater utility of Jacme rather than Lady Cambale his mother, but nevertheless that shop was called and was continually called and is still called the 'Apotheca of Lady Cambale.'" Resens died around 1410. Her inventory is available in DALME, retrieved from https://purl.dalme.org/d92ab61d-68ee-4ced-8b06-0e3863c7b805/ on 11 July 2024.

12. ADBR 5 G 775, fols. 90r-100v. See also the discussion of Laureta's account book in Smail, *Legal Plunder*, 93–113.

13. Jordan, *Women and Credit*; Petti Balbi and Guglielmotti, eds., *Dare credito alle donne*; Dermineur, ed., *Women and Credit*.

14. Reyerson, "Women in Business," 132.

15. Ifft Decker, *Fruit of Her Hands*.

16. Auruola's activity has been studied at length by Laure-Hélène Gouffran in a study unpublished as of this writing.

17. ADBR 355 E 28, fol. 81r, 11 Mar. 1383. The phrase reads *de propria pecunia dicte domine Auriole*. Pons was identified in this act as his wife's procurator or legal representative.

18. This is typical of most loans in Marseille.

19. The registers recording procedures for debt collection where we might have expected to find Auruola taking action against debtors in default are AMM FF 556 (1380–1381), FF 557 (1383–1384), FF 558 (1385–1385), FF 559 (1385–1386), FF 563 (1388), FF 564 (1389–1390), FF 565 (1389–1390), and FF 566 (1391–1395).

20. ADBR 3 B 858, fol. 237v.

21. ADBR 3 B 858, fols. 238v-242r.

22. AMM FF 581, unfoliated, 8 Nov. 1397. The entry reads *Pro uxore Petri Hugueti*.

23. ADBR 3 B 859, fols. 221r-224v.

NOTES TO CHAPTER 9   219

24. ADBR 381 E 6, 2 Dec. 1318. Owing to archival restrictions currently in place, I have been unable to view this act. For Mortreuil's transcription, see BnF NAL 1325, p. 4. The case is discussed in Verlinden, *Esclavage* (1955), 1:812. See also Bernardi, "Esclaves et artisanat," 87n42; Michaud, *Earning Dignity*, 112.

Chapter 9. Alaeta and Her Friend

1. ADBR 3 B 858, fols. 228v-229r.

2. For private distraint, see Smail, "Enmity and the Distraint of Goods."

3. ADBR 3 B 858, fols. 212v-213v.

4. ADBR 3 B 858, fols. 248r-249r.

5. Bailey, "Handmaids of God," 364. For the Roman world, see Perry, *Gender, Manumission, and the Roman Freedwoman*.

6. ADBR 351 E 146. The table of contents lists a contract by this name on fol. 145. The register has been damaged, however, and the corresponding pages have been lost. The phrase is *Emptio caprarum et bimonorum et inhitio societam pro Alaeta Columbe*.

7. ADBR 351 E 152, fols. 104r-105r, 14 Aug. 1399. In Provence, sharecropping and shareherding were known as *mejaria* or *mègerie*; see Malaussena, *La vie en Provence orientale*, 139–52. I thank Patrick Hegarty-Morrish for drawing my attention to this. Monet d'Esparon resurfaced six years later when Alaeta acknowledged receipt of a debt amounting to 74 florins; see ADBR 351 E 158, fols. 131v-132r, 29 Sept. 1405. The date is unclear.

8. ADBR 351 E 158, fol. 106r, 31 Aug. 1405. The act is duplicated in ADBR 351 E 159, fol. 50r-v.

9. See, respectively, AMM FF 564, fol. 193v, 24 Sept. 1390 (Lois Davin plundered for 10 s.) and AMM FF 570, unfoliated, entry dated 21 Aug. 1392 (Siffren Gassin plundered for 1 florin).

10. ADBR 351 E 148, fol. 113r, 4 Aug. 1393.

11. ADBR 351 E 148, fols. 163v-164r, 13 Oct. 1393. The two men from Auriol are named Bertran Fabre and Jacme Fabre. Notaries occasionally made mistakes when writing names, so it's possible that this is one and the same person. The Marseille moneylender in whose house Alaeta named her procurator was Isnart Ricau, who shows up repeatedly in the same register as a moneylender.

12. ADBR 392 E 4, fol. 92r-v, 26 Mar. 1407.

13. Respectively, ADBR 351 E 672, fols. 27r-28r, 3 June 1408, and ADBR B 1946, fol. 29r.

14. ADBR 351 E 150, fol. 214r, 14 Jan. 1398.

15. ADBR 351 E 268, fols. 251v-252r, 24 Feb. 1398.

16. ADBR 351 E 152, fols. 104r-105r, 14 Aug. 1399.

17. ADBR 351 E 150, fols. 77v-79v, 23 Nov. 1397.

18. In an act from 1398, Antoni Jay acknowledged a debt of 10 florins to Alaeta, who accepted his acknowledgment in both her own name and that of Gassenda Olivarie. See ADBR 351 E 150, fol. 252r-v, 24 Feb. 1398. A further reference to this same debt occurs in ADBR 351 E 268, fols. 252v-253r, 19 Aug. 1399. An act of 1395 provides evidence for Gassenda's separate business interests; in this act, she took steps to pursue a debt of 10 l. from a woman named Borgueta. In the act, she was described as "Gassenda Olivarie alias Ortolane." The nature of the alias is not clear: it could mean that she was a gardener (*ortolana*); it could indicate that she had once been

married to someone with the surname *Ortolan*; or it could be a sobriquet, like Alaeta's sobriquet *La Gavota*. See AMM 573, unfoliated, entry dated 30 July 1395.

19. ADBR 351 E 148, fols. 177v–179r, 30 Oct. 1393. A duplicate may be found in ADBR 351 E 670, fols. 118r–120r.

20. The street was called *carreria Balneorum Tennerii*.

21. It is also possible that they had purchased the house in the Baths of the Tannery as an investment since there is no evidence they ever lived there.

22. ADBR B 1946, fol. 29r. The entry reads "By Alaeta Columbe and Gassenda Olivarie, in place of Honorat de Sant Gilles (*ab Alayeta Columbe et Garsendis Olivarie loco Honorati de Sancto Egidio*)." As suggested by this phrasing, the notary understood that the house belonged to Honorat. This is contradicted by the unambiguous statement in Alaeta's testament that the house belonged to her and Gassenda.

23. Gassenda's testament may be found in ADBR 351 E 166, fols. 43v–44v, 12 July 1413.

24. In a series of acts from 1421, we learn that the recently deceased Honorat de Sant Gilles was survived by his widow, Dalfina, and his three sons, Ludovicetus, Peyretus, and Antonetus, so it is unlikely that he was living with Alaeta and Gassenda. For an example, see ADBR 351 E 286, fols. 55v–56r, 27 Mar. 1421.

Chapter 10. A Roll of the Dice

1. BnF NAL 1351, fol. 171v, 1 June 1406.

2. BnF NAL 1351, fols. 189v–190r, 20 Aug. 1406.

3. ADBR 3 B 861, fol. 464r.

4. Simmons, *Crescent City Girls*, 83.

5. See p. 124.

6. ADBR 3 B 858, fols. 224v–225r. The date is actually given as the 19th but this seems to have been scribal error.

7. It was not in the least unusual for women to argue their own cases in the law courts of medieval Marseille. For perspectives on women and litigation beyond Marseille, see Phipps and Youngs, *Litigating Women*. For Marseille, in addition to my *Consumption of Justice*, see McDonough, "Mothers and Daughters and Sons."

8. See pp. 157–58.

9. Smail, *Consumption of Justice*, 33–34.

10. See p. 137.

11. ADBR 3 B 858, fol. 203v.

12. As discussed in a previous chapter, any lawyer could have easily argued that he had tacitly manumitted her by virtue of providing her with a dowry. Doing so, however, would have required an admission that Magdalena had in fact been his slave, an acknowledgment that could have had serious legal repercussions.

13. As discussed in chapter 7, canon law made it quite clear that individuals in bondage were free to marry without their lord's consent; see Landau, "Hadrians IV. Dekretale 'Dignum est.'"

14. ADBR 3 B 858, fol. 181r: *ob quod debet et est in prima servitute redigenda . . . cum non sit digna libertate.*

15. ADBR 3 B 858, fol. 228v.

NOTES TO CHAPTER 11   221

16. Rio, *Slavery After Rome*, 15.

17. ADBR 3 B 858, fol. 250v.

18. ADBR 3 B 858, fols. 250v-251v.

19. ADBR 3 B 858, fols. 216v and 217r.

20. ADBR 3 B 858, fols. 234r-245r.

21. Giannella, "Free in Fact?," 92. See also Ando, "Race and Citizenship in Roman Law."

22. Barker, *That Most Precious Merchandise*, 26–27.

23. Scott, "Social Facts, Legal Fictions," 11.

24. Patterson, *Slavery and Social Death*, 35. Patterson notes that masters need "the recognition and the support of the nonslave members of his community for his assumption of sovereign power over another person."

25. ADBR 3 B 858, fols. 220v-221r.

26. ADBR 3 B 858, fol. 224r-v.

27. ADBR 3 B 858, fols. 249v-250r.

28. See p. 142.

29. In Roman law, freedmen and freedwomen had a duty to honor their former masters, known as "patrons," in the same manner that children had a duty to honor their father. See Mouritsen, *Freedman in the Roman World*. As Hannah Skoda has put it, what resulted from this was "a very particular, restrained kind of liberty." Skoda, "People as Property," 253.

30. ADBR 3 B 861, fols. 443v-445v.

31. ADBR B 1944, fol. 13v: *iniuriose dismentitus fuit per gulam*.

32. ADBR B 1940. Curiously, canine insults do not appear in the registers from the early 1400s (ADBR B 1943, B 1944, B 1945, and B 1947).

33. ADBR B 1940, fol. 129v: *va estratassa merdosa puta de canis et de porcs*.

34. Respectively, ADBR B 1940, fol. 85r: *can pugnays renegat*; fol. 107r: *vos estis melius canis quam ego*.

35. Godefroy, *Dictionnaire de l'ancienne langue française*, s.v. mastin; Mistral, *Lou trésor dóu Felibrige*, s.v. mastin, mastina. Many thanks to Giulia Boitani for helping me sort out the etymologies, and also to Paul Russell.

36. See Gaunt, Harvey, and Paterson, *Marcabru*, 392. "A lady who loves a menial within the household/ knows nothing about *fin' amor*, since her desire/ cross-couples (*mastina*), like a greyhound bitch/ does with a lap-dog./Alas!"

Chapter 11. A Pyrrhic Victory

1. ADBR 3 B 861, fol. 421r-v.

2. For a recent overview, see Bradley, "Freedom and Slavery."

3. See Mouritsen, *Freedman in the Roman World*.

4. Some of the complexities arising from how these general principles interacted with local conditions in medieval Europe are treated authoritatively in Skoda, "People as Property."

5. This delicate matter is treated in Conte, "Declino e rilancio della servitù"; Carrier, "De l'esclavage au servage."

6. The principal source in Roman law was *Cod.* 2. 2. 2, a title under the heading *De in ius vocando*, which declares that a freedperson may not summon a patron to court without

obtaining permission to do so in advance. Other Roman law passages concerning the honor and respect due to patrons are found in *Cod. 6. 6. 6–7* and *Dig. 2. 4. 25.*

7. Burns, *Las Siete Partidas*, 983–84.

8. Ricardus Pisanus, *Lo Codi*, 9–10.

9. *Cod. 6. 7. 1–4.*

10. Ricardus Pisanus, *Lo Codi*, 193.

11. ADBR 3 B 858, fol. 203v. The relevant phrase is *de conveniendo patronum in judicio.*

12. Later, in June, he returned to the habit of naming Magdalena as his slave, but this shift may have arisen from the bitterness he experienced when his arguments, once again, were rejected by a member of Marseille's judiciary. See ADBR 3 B 861, fol. 410r.

13. See pp. 73–74.

14. ADBR 3 B 861, fols. 445v-447v.

15. ADBR 3 B 861, fols. 454r-459r. Antonius figures in two legal texts printed in the seventeenth century.

16. My thanks to Kevin Wang for the extensive work he put into interpreting this consilium. It is reasonably certain that Antonius understood her marriage of 1399 to be the moment of her manumission, since there is no evidence of an independent act of manumission and ample reason to believe that there never was one.

17. ADBR 3 B 861, fol. 456r: *credo dicendum quod ratione iniuriarum ab ipsa illatarum patrono revocari posset in servitutem.*

18. ADBR 3 B 861, fol. 456v: *cum possit esse matrimonium cum servo vel ancilla.*

19. ADBR 3 B 861, fol. 456v: *propter ingratitudinem liberta redigi possit in servitutem, et poterit esse in coniugio et servire domino.*

20. ADBR 3 B 861, fol. 405r.

21. ADBR B 1947, fol. 38v. The words attributed to the weaver, Peire Donzelet, were *meilhor iusticia si troberia en terra de moros qua non si troba ayssi.*

22. ADBR B 1947, fol. 44r: *lo a xvi ans que jeu acostumi aquesta cort, mays jamays jeu non la vi si mal gouvernada coma es al jorn duey.* The insult cost the notary, Vincens Riquet, a fine of 8 l.

23. Prominent contributions include Gauvard, *De grace especial*; Davis, *Fiction in the Archives*; Smith and Killick, *Petitions and Strategies of Persuasion*; Israeli, "Politics of Records."

24. ADBR 3 B 861, fol. 464v.

25. ADBR 3 B 861, fol. 463r.

26. A brief biography of Pons Cays (d. 1420) is provided in Cortez, *Les grands officiers royaux*, 181–82. My thanks to Michel Hébert for this reference.

27. ADBR 3 B 861, fol. 469r-v. Note that although this petition identifies the judge of the Palace court as Hugo Audivin, the actual sentence was handed down by the lieutenant judge, Elziar Autrici.

28. ADBR 3 B 861, fol. 470r: *non sunt judices multum litterati.* Although the phrase could mean that they weren't sufficiently versed in the facts of the case, the suggestion is that they did not fully understand the laws that had a bearing on the matter.

29. Respectively, ADBR B 1943, fol. 44v, and ADBR B 1944, fol. 36v.

30. ADBR B 1944, fol. 12v.

31. ADBR B 1945, fol. 14r: *eo quia in quibusdam litteris patentibus inhibitoriis mutavit certam datam raendo in eis et rescribendo dolum et falsitatem ac barateriam committendo scienter.*

NOTES TO CHAPTER 12   223

32. ADBR B 1944, fol. 38v. She had loaned 300 l. to Astrug Robert and his wife but demanded 1,000 l. in payment.

33. Green and Smail, "Trial of Floreta d'Ays."

Chapter 12. Afterlives

1. Otchakovsky-Laurens, *La vie politique à Marseille.*

2. Balossino, "Notaire et institutions." See my "Inventory of Petrus Audeberti," in DALME, retrieved from https://purl.dalme.org/6a0fbaff-19a5-410a-b856-2858df74537e/ on 19 Apr. 2024. This act, from the year 1258, contains a reference to a notarial instrument produced by a Marseille public notary on 6 July 1196.

3. Low, "Notarial Information and the Production of Knowledge," 247–84.

4. Miller, *Peiresc's History of Provence.*

5. Bodin, *Les six livres de la Republique*; Biot, *De l'abolition de l'esclavage ancien en occident*; Tourmagne, *Histoire de l'esclavage ancien et moderne.*

6. The major contemporary contribution to the debate was Wallon, *Histoire de l'esclavage dans l'antiquité.* For discussion, see Finley, *Ancient Slavery and Modern Ideology*, 12.

7. The proclamation emancipated unfree peasants (for a fee), not slaves. A stubborn myth arose in the early modern period and was grounded in the ambiguity of the word *servi*, which in the Latin of ancient Rome meant "slaves" but in the medieval context meant "serfs."

8. The jurist Antoine Loisel included a version of it on the first page of his collection of legal maxims, published in 1607; see Loisel, *Institutes coustumieres.* The phrase reads *Toutes personnes sont franches en ce Royaume, et si tost qu'un esclave a attaint les marches d'iceluy, se faisant baptiser, il est affranchy.* See Peabody, *'There Are No Slaves in France.'*

9. Fauris de Saint-Vincens, *Mémoires et notices.*

10. Perrier, *Les bibliophiles et les collectionneurs*, 366–68. An obituary of Mortreuil by M. Dieulafait can be found in the *Mémoires de l'Académie des Sciences, Belles-Lettres et Arts de Marseille*, 3 Feb. 1878, pp. 205–8. My thanks to Alex Csiszar for his assistance in tracking down biographical elements pertaining to Mortreuil.

11. Mortreuil, *Histoire du droit byzantin.*

12. Mortreuil, "Moeurs et institutions marseillaises."

13. Bloch, "L'Esclavage en Sicile."

14. The register ADBR 3 B 150, from the years 1411–1412, was used as a daybook to record a miscellaneous set of procedures initiated in one of Marseille's courts. It may constitute the original set of rough or ephemeral notes that were intended to be copied in longer form in court registers. On fol. 10r, reference is made to "Hugonin Sabaterii," who was being pursued for a debt around 9 gros in value. The first name is a somewhat unusual form of the diminutive version of the name "Hugo," which was more commonly rendered as "Huguetus" in Latin. The suggestion of a connection to Hugonin de lo Chorges is also found in the surname, with its allusion to the shoemaker's profession. The complicating factor is that "Sabaterii" was a perfectly ordinary surname, one that had emerged generations earlier, and by the early fifteenth century, the habit of creating new surnames from trades had largely ceased. If the notary intended to refer to "Hugonin the shoemaker," he would have written "Hugonin sabaterius" or even "Hugonin lo sabatier."

224 NOTES TO CHAPTER 12

15. It is important to be aware that another man bearing a very similar name, Hugo Chaorge or Sahorge, was active around the same time. This Hugo was a butcher who was married for over thirty years to a woman named Batrona, the natural daughter of another butcher, whom he married in 1394. See ADBR 355 E 79, fol. 81v, 18 Nov. 1394. He and Batrona survived an attempt to poison them in 1426; details of that case may be found in ADBR 351 E 731, fols. 106v-135r, 7 Dec. 1426.

16. ADBR 351 E 108, fol. 34v, 30 Nov. 1413.

17. Rodriguez, *Captives and Their Saviors*; Kaiser and Calafat, "Economy of Ransoming"; Fancy, "Captivity, Ransom, and Manumission."

18. ADBR 351 E 68, fol. 100r-v. Both credits are mentioned in this act. As mentioned in an earlier chapter, Peire borrowed 100 florins from Bertomieu Simondel in 1395 to purchase a sail. Following Bertomieu's death, the debt was inherited by his brother, Esteve, who sold it to Isnart de Sant Gilles in 1405. In the court register ADBR 3 B 149, fol. 12v, Isnart de Sant Gilles and Bertran Gombert were summoned to court to formally witness the cancellation of Isnart's debt instrument. It is possible that Bertran Gombert, Magdalena's lawyer, was also being reimbursed, but more likely that he was serving as Isnart's lawyer at the time.

19. The several entries relative to Hugoneta's claim appear in ADBR 3 B 149, fols. 31r-v and 35r.

20. ADBR 3 B 150, fol. 57r.

21. ADBR 3 B 150, fol. 63v.

22. The elements relevant to the case are scattered across ADBR 3 B 150, on fols. 65v-67v, 71v, and 86v.

23. ADBR 3 B 150, fol. 73r.

24. ADBR B 1947, fol. 33r. The entries in this register are not dated.

BIBLIOGRAPHY

Abulafia, David. "The Last Muslims in Italy." In *Dante and Islam*, edited by Jan M. Ziolkowski, 235–50. Fordham University Press, 2014.

———. *The Western Mediterranean Kingdoms, 1200–1500: The Struggle for Dominion*. Longman, 1997.

Ando, Clifford. "Race and Citizenship in Roman Law and Administration." In *Xenofobia y racismo en el mundo antiguo*, edited by Francisco Marco Simón, Francisco Pina Polo, and J. Remesal Rodríguez, 175–88. Edicions de la Universitat de Barcelona, 2019.

Angiolini, Franco. "Schiave." In *Il lavoro delle donne*, edited by Angela Groppi, 92–115. Storia delle donne in Italia. Laterza, 1996.

Antoninus, Saint, Archbishop of Florence. *Divi Antonini archiepiscopi Florentini, et doctoris sanctae theologiae praestantissimi Chronicorum tercia pars*. Ex officina Iuntarum, 1587.

Arlot, Françoise. "Dans la tourmente du XIVe siècle. Marie de Blois, comtesse de Provence et reine de Naples." *Provence historique* 56 (2006): 53–90, 155–94.

Armenteros Martínez, Iván. *L'esclavitud a la Barcelona del Renaixement (1479–1616): un port mediterrani sota la influència del primer tràfic negre*. Fundació Noguera, 2015.

———. "Towards the Atlantic Mediterranean. Catalan Participation in the Early Atlantic Slave Trade (Late Fifteenth—Early Sixteenth Century)." In *Schiavitù e servaggio nell'economia Europea, secc. XI–XVIII / Serfdom and Slavery in the European Economy, 11th–18th Centuries*, edited by Simonetta Cavaciocchi, 2:631–50. Atti delle settimane di studi et altri convegni 2. Firenze University Press, 2014.

Armenteros Martínez, Ivan, and Mohamed Ouerfelli. "Réévaluer l'économie de l'esclavage en Méditerranée au Moyen Âge et au début de l'époque Moderne. Une introduction." *Rives méditerranéennes* 53 (2016): 7–17.

Armstrong-Partida, Michelle. "Priestly Wives: The Role and Acceptance of Clerics' Concubines in the Parishes of Late Medieval Catalunya." *Speculum* 88, no. 1 (2013): 166–214.

———. "Race, Skin Colour, Enslavement and Sexuality in the Late Medieval Mediterranean." *Journal of Medieval History* 50, no. 4 (2024): 477–99.

Arnoux, Mathieu. "Effacement ou abolition? Réflexion sur la disparition de l'esclavage dans l'Europe non méditerranéenne (XIe–XIVe siècles)." In *Mediterranean Slavery Revisited (500–1800) / Neue Perspektiven auf mediterrane Sklaverei (500–1800)*, edited by Stefan Hanß, Juliane Schiel, and Claudia Schmid, 49–74. Chronos, 2014.

Aubenas, Roger. "L'esclavage en pays de droit écrit." In *Cours d'histoire du droit privé*, 2nd ed., 1:67–77. La Pensée Universitaire, 1956.

Bailey, Lisa Kaaren. "Handmaids of God: Images of Service in the Lives of Merovingian Female Saints." *Journal of Religious History* 43, no. 3 (2019): 359–79.

Balard, Michel. "Esclavage en Crimée et sources fiscales génoises au XVe siècle." *Byzantinische Zeitschrift* 22 (1996): 9–17.

———. *La Romanie génoise: XIIe–début du XVe siècle*. 2 vols. Atti della Società ligure di storia patria, 18. École française de Rome, 1978.

———. "Le transport des esclaves dans le monde méditerranéen médiéval." In *Slavery and the Slave Trade in the Eastern Mediterranean (c. 1000–1500 CE)*, edited by Reuven Amitai and Christoph Cluse, 353–74. Brepols, 2018.

———. "Remarques sur les esclaves à Gênes dans la seconde moitié du XIIIe siècle." *Mélanges d'archéologie et d'histoire* 80, no. 2 (1968): 627–80.

———. "Slavery in the Latin Mediterranean (Thirteenth to Fifteenth Centuries): The Case of Genoa." In *Slavery and the Slave Trade in the Eastern Mediterranean (c. 1000–1500 CE)*, edited by Reuven Amitai and Christoph Cluse, 235–54. Brepols, 2018.

Balossino, Simone. "Notaire et institutions communales dans la basse vallée du Rhône (XIIe–moitié du XIIIe siècle)." In *Le notaire: Entre métier et espace public en Europe VIIIe–XVIIIe siècle*, edited by Lucien Faggion, Anne Mailloux, and Laure Verdon, 183–97. Presses universitaires de Provence, 2008.

Baratier, Édouard. *De 1291 à 1423*. Vol. 2 of *Histoire du commerce de Marseille*, edited by Gaston Rambert. Plon, 1949.

Barker, Hannah. "Purchasing a Slave in Fourteenth-Century Cairo: Ibn al-Akfani's Book of Observation and Inspection in the Examination of Slaves." *Mamluk Studies Review* 19 (2016): 1–24.

———. *That Most Precious Merchandise: The Mediterranean Trade in Black Sea Slaves, 1260–1500*. University of Pennsylvania Press, 2019.

Battilana, Natale. *Genealogie delle famiglie nobili di Genova*. 3 vols. Pagano, 1825.

Becker, Cynthia J. *Amazigh Arts in Morocco: Women Shaping Berber Identity*. University of Texas Press, 2006.

Benería, Lourdes, and Gita Sen. "Accumulation, Reproduction, and 'Women's Role in Economic Development': Boserup Revisited." *Signs: Journal of Women in Culture and Society* 7, no. 2 (1981): 279–98.

Bensch, Stephen P. "From Prizes of War to Domestic Merchandise: The Changing Face of Slavery in Catalonia and Aragon, 1000–1300." *Viator* 25 (1994): 63–94.

Bernardi, Philippe. "Esclaves et artisanat: une main d'œuvre étrangère dans la Provence des XIIIe–XVe siècles." *Actes des congrès de la Société des historiens médiévistes de l'enseignement supérieur public* 30, no. 1 (1999): 79–94.

Biot, Edouard. *De l'abolition de l'esclavage ancien en occident*. Renouard, 1840.

Biran, Michal. "Forced Migrations and Slavery in the Mongol Empire (1206–1368)." In *The Cambridge World History of Slavery*, Vol. 2, *AD 500–AD 1420*, edited by Craig Perry, David Eltis, David Richardson, and Stanley L. Engerman, 76–99. Cambridge University Press, 2021.

Blackburn, Robin. "The Old World Background to European Colonial Slavery." *William and Mary Quarterly* 54, no. 1 (1997): 65–102.

Blancard, Louis, ed. *Documents inédits sur le commerce de Marseille au Moyen Âge*. Barlatier-Feissat, 1884.

Bloch, Marc. "Comment et pourquoi finit l'esclavage antique." *Annales: économies, sociétés, civilizations* 2, no. 1 (1947): 30–44.

BIBLIOGRAPHY 227

———. "L'Esclavage en Sicile depuis la fin du Moyen Âge." *Annales d'histoire économique et sociale* 1, no. 1 (1929): 91–94.

Blumenthal, Debra. "'As If She Were His Wife': Slavery and Sexual Ethics in Late Medieval Spain." In *Beyond Slavery: Overcoming Its Religious and Sexual Legacies*, edited by Bernadette J. Brooten, 179–89. Palgrave Macmillan, 2010.

———. *Enemies and Familiars: Slavery and Mastery in Fifteenth-Century Valencia.* Cornell University Press, 2009.

———. "Masters, Slave Women and Their Children: A Child Custody Dispute in 15th-Century Valencia." In *Mediterranean Slavery Revisited (500–1800) / Neue Perspektiven auf mediterrane Sklaverei (500–1800)*, edited by Stefan Hanß, Juliane Schiel, and Claudia Schmid, 228–56. Chronos, 2014.

Bodin, Jean. *Les six livres de la Republique.* Jacques du Puy, 1576.

Bonazza, Giulia. "Slavery in the Mediterranean." In *The Palgrave Handbook of Global Slavery Throughout History*, edited by Damian A. Pargas and Juliane Schiel, 227–42. Springer International Publishing AG, 2023.

Boni, Monica, and Robert Delort. "Des esclaves toscans, du milieu du XIVe au milieu du XVe siècle." *Mélanges de l'École française de Rome. Moyen Âge* 112, no. 2 (2000): 1057–77.

Bonnassie, Pierre. *From Slavery to Feudalism in South-Western Europe.* Translated by Jean Birrell. Cambridge University Press, 1991.

———. *La organización del trabajo en Barcelona a fines de siglo XV.* Anuario de estudios medievales. Anejo 8. Consejo Superior de Investigaciones Científicas, 1975.

———. "Survie et extinction du régime esclavagiste dans l'Occident du haut Moyen Âge (IVe-XIe s.)." *Cahiers de civilisation médiévale* 28, no. 112 (1985): 307–43.

Bonnot, Isabelle, ed. *Marseille et ses rois de Naples: la diagonale angevine, 1265–1382.* Edisud, 1988.

Bono, Salvatore. *Schiavi: una storia mediterranea (XVI–XIX secolo).* Il mulino, 2016.

Boserup, Ester. *Woman's Role in Economic Development.* St. Martin's Press, 1970.

Bouabdella, S., S. Aouali, S. Sefraoui, N. Zizi, and S. Dikhaye. "Les tatouages traditionnels au Maroc." *Annales de dermatologie et de vénéréologie - FMC* 2, no. 8 (2022): A260.

Bourrilly, Victor-Louis. "Duguesclin et le duc d'Anjou en Provence, 1368." *Revue historique* 152 (1926): 161–80.

Bradley, Keith R. "Freedom and Slavery." In *The Oxford Handbook of Roman Studies*, edited by Alessandro Barchiesi and Walter Scheidel, 624–36. Oxford University Press, 2010.

Bresc, Henri. "L'esclave dans le monde méditerranéen des XIVe et XVe siècles: problèmes politiques, religieux et moraux." In *XIII Congrés d'Història de la Corona d'Aragó*, 1:89–102. Palma de Mallorca, 1990.

———. *Un monde méditerranéen: économie et société en Sicile, 1300–1450.* 2 vols. École française de Rome, 1986.

Brutails, Auguste. *Étude sur l'esclavage en Roussillon du XIIIe au XVIIe siècle.* L. Larose et Forcel, 1886.

Budak, Neven. "Slavery in Late Medieval Dalmatia/Croatia: Labour, Legal Status, Integration." *Mélanges de l'École française de Rome. Moyen Âge* 112, no. 2 (2000): 745–60.

———. "Slavery in Renaissance Croatia: Reality and Fiction." In *Mediterranean Slavery Revisited (500–1800) / Neue Perspektiven auf mediterrane Sklaverei (500–1800)*, edited by Stefan Hanß, Juliane Schiel, and Claudia Schmid, 75–96. Chronos, 2014.

228 BIBLIOGRAPHY

Burns, Robert I., ed. *Las Siete Partidas*. Translated by Samuel Parsons Scott. University of Pennsylvania Press, 2001.

Capet, Élodie. "Les étrangers au travail Perpignan, milieu XIVe siècle–fin XVe siècle." PhD Dissertation, Université Paris 8 Vincennes-Saint-Denis, 2020.

Cappelletti, Giuseppe. *Le chiese d'Italia: dalla loro origine sino ai nostri giorni. Volume 19, Chiese delle provincie napoletane*. Giuseppe Antonelli, 1864.

Carrier, Nicolas. "De l'esclavage au servage: pour une étude des dynamiques de la servitude." *Médiévales 81*, no. 81 (2022): 179–96.

Casteen, Elizabeth. *From She-Wolf to Martyr: The Reign and Disputed Reputation of Johanna I of Naples*. Cornell University Press, 2015.

———. "'Just War' and 'Conspicuous Sins.'" *French Historical Studies* 47, no. 4 (2024): 531–48.

Catlos, Brian A. *Muslims of Medieval Latin Christendom, c. 1050–1614*. Cambridge University Press, 2014.

Ceccarelli, Giovanni. *Un mercato del rischio: assicurare e farsi assicurare nella Firenze rinascimentale*. Marsilio, 2013.

Chalhoub, Sidney. "The Politics of Ambiguity: Conditional Manumission, Labor Contracts, and Slave Emancipation in Brazil (1850s–1888)." *International Review of Social History* 60, no. 2 (2015): 161–91.

———. "The Precariousness of Freedom in a Slave Society (Brazil in the Nineteenth Century)." *International Review of Social History* 56, no. 3 (2011): 405–39.

Christ, Georg. *Trading Conflicts: Venetian Merchants and Mamluk Officials in Late Medieval Alexandria*. Brill, 2012.

Claustre, Julie. *Faire ses comptes au Moyen Âge: les mémoires de besogne de Colin de Lormoye*. Les Belles Lettres, 2021.

Cluse, Christoph, and Reuven Amitai. "Introduction." In *Slavery and the Slave Trade in the Eastern Mediterranean (c. 1000–1500 CE)*, edited by Reuven Amitai and Christoph Cluse, 11–27. Brepols, 2018.

Constable, Olivia Remie. "Muslim Spain and Mediterranean Slavery: The Medieval Slave Trade as an Aspect of Muslim-Christian Relations." In *Christendom and Its Discontents: Exclusion, Persecution, and Rebellion, 1000–1500*, edited by Scott L. Waugh and Peter D. Diehl, 264–84. Cambridge University Press, 1996.

Conte, Emanuele. "Declino e rilancio della servitù: tra teoria e pratica giuridica." *Mélanges de l'École française de Rome. Moyen Âge* 112, no. 2 (2000): 663–85.

Cooper, Frederick. "The Problem of Slavery in African Studies." *Journal of African History* 20, no. 1 (1979): 103–25.

Cortez, Fernand. *Les grands officiers royaux de Provence au Moyen Âge*. A. Dragon, 1921.

Coulet, Noël. "L'Union d'Aix dans l'historiographie provençale XVIe–XVIIIe siècle." *Provence historique* 40 (1990): 443–54.

———. "Négritude et liberté. Un contrat de dedicatio personalis. Aix, 1455." *Revue Historique* 282, no. 1 (571) (1989): 59–82.

Crane, Sheila. "Digging Up the Present in Marseille's Old Port: Toward an Archaeology of Reconstruction." *Journal of the Society of Architectural Historians* 63, no. 3 (2004): 296–319.

Cutolo, Alessandro. *Re Ladislao d'Angiò Durazzo*. A. Berisio, 1969.

BIBLIOGRAPHY 229

Darwin, Charles. *On the Origin of Species.* John Murray, 1859. Reprint, Harvard University Press, 1964.

Davis, Natalie Zemon. *Fiction in the Archives: Pardon Tales and Their Tellers in Sixteenth Century France.* Stanford University Press, 1987.

———. *Trickster Travels: A Sixteenth-Century Muslim between Worlds.* Hill and Wang, 2006.

———. *Women on the Margins: Three Seventeenth-Century Lives.* Harvard University Press, 1995.

Day, Lynda R. "Judith Van Allen and the Impact of Her Article "'Sitting on a Man': Colonialism and the Lost Political Institutions of Igbo Women' in the Classroom." *Journal of West African History* 3, no. 2 (2017): 183–89.

Débax, Hélène. "1446, un esclave noir à Pamiers." In *Histoire mondiale de la France*, edited by Patrick Boucheron et al., 233–37. Seuil, 2017.

de Blasiis, Giuseppe, ed. *Cronicon siculum incerti authoris ab anno 340 ad annum 1396 in forma diary ex inedito Codice ottoboniano vaticano cura et studio Joseph de Blasiis.* Ex regio typographeo Francisci Giannini et filii, 1887.

de la Fuente, Alejandro. "From Slaves to Citizens? Tannenbaum and the Debates on Slavery, Emancipation, and Race Relations in Latin America." *International Labor and Working-Class History*, no. 77 (2010): 154–73.

Del Bo, Beatrice. "Schiave bianche nelle città del basso Medioevo: la fortuna di un tema di ricerca nel secondo Ottocento." *Storia in Lombarda* 37 (2017): 142–62.

Dermineur, Elise M., ed. *Women and Credit in Pre-Industrial Europe.* Brepols, 2018.

Desimoni, Cornelius, Aloisius Thomas Belgrango, and Victorius Poggi, eds. *Leges genuenses.* Historiae patriae monumenta, vol. 18. E regio typographeo, 1901.

Dotson, John E. "Everything Is a Compromise: Mediterranean Ship Design, Thirteenth to Sixteenth Centuries." In *The Art, Science, and Technology of Medieval Travel*, edited by Robert Bork and Andrea Kann, 31–40. Ashgate, 2008.

Epstein, Steven A. "A Late Medieval Lawyer Confronts Slavery: The Cases of Bartolomeo de Bosco." *Slavery & Abolition* 20, no. 3 (1999): 49–68.

———. *Speaking of Slavery: Color, Ethnicity, and Human Bondage in Italy.* Cornell University Press, 2018.

Fancy, Hussein. "Captivity, Ransom, and Manumission, 500–1420." In *The Cambridge World History of Slavery*, Vol. 2, *AD 500–AD 1420*, edited by Craig Perry, David Eltis, David Richardson, and Stanley L. Engerman, 53–75. Cambridge University Press, 2021.

———. *The Mercenary Mediterranean: Sovereignty, Religion, and Violence in the Medieval Crown of Aragon.* University of Chicago Press, 2016.

Farge, Arlette. *The Allure of the Archives.* Translated by Thomas Scott-Railton. Yale University Press, 2013.

Fauris de Saint-Vincens, Alexandre Jules Antoine. *Mémoires et notices relatifs à la Provence.* J. B. Sajou, 1814.

Favereau Doumenjou, Marie. *The Horde: How the Mongols Changed the World.* The Belknap Press of Harvard University Press, 2021.

Ferragud, Carmel. "The Role of Doctors in the Slave Trade during the Fourteenth and Fifteenth Centuries within the Kingdom of Valencia (Crown of Aragon)." *Bulletin of the History of Medicine* 87, no. 2 (2013): 143–69.

Finley, M. I. *Ancient Slavery and Modern Ideology.* Chatto & Windus, 1980.

BIBLIOGRAPHY

Fossier, Robert. *Enfance de l'Europe: Xe–XIIe siècle: aspects économiques et sociaux.* 2nd ed. 2 vols. Presses universitaires de France, 1989.

Friedberg, Emil. *Eine neue kritische Ausgabe des Corpus iuris canonici: I. Das decretum Gratiani.* Druck von A. Edelmann, 1876.

Fuentes, Marisa J. *Dispossessed Lives: Enslaved Women, Violence, and the Archive.* University of Pennsylvania Press, 2016.

Fynn-Paul, Jeffrey. "Empire, Monotheism and Slavery in the Greater Mediterranean Region from Antiquity to the Early Modern Era." *Past & Present* 205 (2009): 3–40.

———. "Reasons for the Limited Scope and Duration of 'Renaissance Slavery' in Southern Europe (ca. 1348–ca. 1750): A New Structuralist Analysis." In *Schiavitù e servaggio nell'economia europea, secc. XI–XVIII /Serfdom and slavery in the European economy, 11th–18th centuries,* edited by Simonetta Cavaciocchi, 1:337–350. Firenze University Press, 2014.

———. "Tartars in Spain: Renaissance Slavery in the Catalan City of Manresa, c.1408." *Journal of Medieval History* 34, no. 4 (2008): 347–59.

Ganchou, Thierry. "Valentina Doria, épouse de Francesco II Gattilusio seigneur de l'île de Mytilène (1384–1403), et sa parenté. Le Lesbian puzzle résolu." *Nuova rivista storica* 88 (2004): 619–86.

Garanger, Marc. *Femmes algériennes 1960.* Atlantica, 2002.

Gaunt, Simon, Ruth Harvey, and Linda M. Paterson, eds. *Marcabru: A Critical Edition.* D.S. Brewer, 2000.

Gauvard, Claude. *"De grace especial": crime, état et société en France à la fin du Moyen Âge.* 2nd ed. Publications de la Sorbonne, 2010.

Giannella, Nicole. "Free in Fact? Legal Status and State in the Suits for Freedom." In *The Discovery of the Fact,* edited by Clifford Ando and William P. Sullivan, 98–118. University of Michigan Press, 2020.

Gioffré, Domenico. *Il mercato degli schiavi a Genova nel secolo XV.* Bozzi, 1971.

Godefroy, Frédéric. *Dictionnaire de l'ancienne langue française, et de tous ses dialectes du IXe au XVe siècle.* 10 vols. F. Vieweg, 1881.

Goldin, Claudia Dale. *Understanding the Gender Gap: An Economic History of American Women.* Oxford University Press, 1990.

Graeber, David. *Debt: The First 5,000 Years.* Melville House, 2010.

Grant, Alasdair C. *Greek Captives and Mediterranean Slavery, 1260–1460.* Edinburgh University Press, 2024.

Green, Monica H., and Daniel Lord Smail. "The Trial of Floreta d'Ays (1403): Jews, Christians, and Obstetrics in Later Medieval Marseille." *Journal of Medieval History* 34, no. 2 (2008): 185–211.

Groebner, Valentin. *Who Are You?: Identification, Deception, and Surveillance in Early Modern Europe.* Translated by Mark Kyburz and John Peck. Zone Books, 2007.

Gross, Ariela Julie. *What Blood Won't Tell: A History of Race on Trial in America.* Harvard University Press, 2008.

Harper, Kyle. *Slavery in the Late Roman World, AD 275–425.* Cambridge University Press, 2011.

Hartman, Saidiya V. "Venus in Two Acts." *Small Axe: A Journal of Criticism* 26, no. 26 (2008): 1–14.

Hébert, Michel, and Jean-Michel Matz, eds. *Journal de Jean Le Fèvre: chancelier des ducs d'Anjou et comtes de Provence (1381–1388).* Presses universitaires de Rennes, 2020.

Heers, Jacques. *Esclaves et domestiques au Moyen Âge dans le monde méditerranéen.* Fayard, 1981.

BIBLIOGRAPHY 231

Hellie, Richard. *Slavery in Russia, 1450–1725*. University of Chicago Press, 1982.

Hershenzon, Daniel. *The Captive Sea: Slavery, Communication, and Commerce in Early Modern Spain and the Mediterranean*. University of Pennsylvania Press, 2018.

Hocquet, Jean-Claude. *Maîtres et esclaves en Méditerranée: Xe–XIXe siècle*. CNRS, 2022.

Ifft Decker, Sarah. *The Fruit of Her Hands: Jewish and Christian Women's Work in Medieval Catalan Cities*. Penn State University Press, 2022.

Israeli, Yanay. "The Politics of Records: Petitions and Depositions in the Legal Struggle of a Fifteenth-Century Converso." *Viator: Medieval and Renaissance Studies* 48, no. 2 (2017): 279–303.

Jackson, Peter. *The Mongols and the Islamic World: From Conquest to Conversion*. Yale University Press, 2017.

———. *The Mongols and the West: 1221–1410*. 2nd ed. Routledge, 2018.

Johnson, Jessica Marie. *Wicked Flesh: Black Women, Intimacy, and Freedom in the Atlantic World*. University of Pennsylvania Press, 2020.

Jordan, William C. *Louis IX and the Challenge of the Crusade: A Study in Rulership*. Princeton University Press, 1979.

———. *The Apple of His Eye: Converts from Islam in the Reign of Louis IX*. Princeton University Press, 2019.

———. *Women and Credit in Pre-Industrial and Developing Societies*. University of Pennsylvania Press, 1993.

Kaiser, Wolfgang, and Guillaume Calafat. "The Economy of Ransoming in the Early Modern Mediterranean: A Form of Cross-Cultural Trade Between Southern Europe and the Maghreb (Sixteenth to Eighteenth Centuries)." In *Religion and Trade: Cross-Cultural Exchanges in World History, 1000–1900*, edited by Francesca Trivellato, Leor Halevi, and Catia Antunes. Online edition. Oxford Academic, 2014.

Karras, Ruth Mazo. *Slavery and Society in Medieval Scandinavia*. Yale University Press, 1988.

Kaye, Joel. *A History of Balance, 1250–1375: The Emergence of a New Model of Equilibrium and Its Impact on Medieval Thought*. Cambridge University Press, 2014.

Killerby, Catherine Kovesi. *Sumptuary Law in Italy 1200–1500*. Clarendon Press, 2002.

Kopytoff, Igor. "Slavery." *Annual Review of Anthropology* 11 (1982): 207–30.

Kowalesky, Maxime. *Die hofrechtliche Verfassung des Gewerbes und des Zunftwesens. Der schwarze Tod und seine wirtschaftlichen Folgen*. Vol. 5 of *Die ökonomische entwicklung Europas bis zum beginn der kapitalistischen Wirtschaftsform*. R. L. Prager, 1911.

Landau, Peter. "Hadrians IV. Dekretale 'Dignum est' (X.4.9.1) und die Eheschließung Unfreier in der Diskussion von Kanonisten und Theologen des 12. und 13. Jahrhunderts." *Studia Gratiana* 12 (1967): 511–53.

Lauer, Rena N. "From Slave to Wife: Manumission and Marriage in Venetian Crete." *Medieval People: Social Bonds, Kinship, and Networks* 36, no. 1 (2022): 107–32.

Léonard, Émile G. *Histoire de Jeanne Ire, reine de Naples, comtesse de Provence (1343–1382)*. Imprimerie de Monaco, 1932.

Lesnick, Daniel R. "Insults and Threats in Medieval Todi." *Journal of Medieval History* 17 (1991): 71–91.

Livi, Carlo. *Sardi in schiavitù nei secoli XII–XV*. F. Cesati, 2002.

Livi, Ridolfo. *La schiavitù domestica nei tempi di mezzo e nei moderni: ricerche storiche di un antropologo*. Casa editrice dott. Antonio Milani, 1928.

Loisel, Antoine. *Institutes coustumieres ou manuel de plusieurs et diverses reigles sentences et proverbes tant anciens que modernes du droict coustumier et plus ordinaire de la France*. Chez Abel L'Angelier, 1607.

Low, Ryan K. "Notarial Information and the Production of Knowledge in Rural Society." PhD Dissertation, Harvard University, 2024.

Luzzati, Michele. "Schiavi e figli di schiavi attraverso le registrazioni di battesimo medievali: Pisa, Gemona del Friuli, Lucca." *Quaderni storici* 36, no. 107 (2) (2001): 349–62.

Mabilly, Philippe. *Ville de Marseille. Inventaire sommaire des Archives Communales antèrieures à 1790. Série BB*. Imprimerie Moullot fils ainé, 1909.

Malaussena, Paul-Louis. *La vie en Provence orientale aux XIVe et XVe siècles. Un exemple: Grasse à travers les actes notariés*. Librairie générale de droit et de jurisprudence, 1969.

Marmon, Shaun E. "Domestic Slavery in the Mamluk Empire: A Preliminary Sketch." In *Slavery in the Islamic Middle East*, edited by Shaun E. Marmon, 1–23. Markus Wiener, 1999.

Martín Casares, Aurelia. "Evolution of the Origin of Slaves Sold in Spain from the Late Middle Ages till the 18th Century." In *Schiavitù e servaggio nell'economia europea, secc. XI–XVIII / Serfdom and Slavery in the European Economy, 11th–18th Centuries*, edited by Simonetta Cavaciocchi, 1:409–30. Firenze University Press, 2014.

———. "Maghrebian Slaves in Spain: Human Trafficking and Insecurity in the Early Modern Western Mediterranean." In *Mediterranean Slavery Revisited (500–1800) / Neue Perspektiven auf mediterrane Sklaverei (500–1800)*, edited by Stefan Hanß, Juliane Schiel, and Claudia Schmid, 97–117. Chronos, 2014.

Matz, Jean-Michel. "Princesse au pouvoir, femme de pouvoir? L'action politique de Marie de Blois d'après le Journal du chancelier Jean Le Fèvre (1383–1388)." *Mélanges de l'École française de Rome. Moyen Âge* 129, no. 2 (2017): 379–91.

———. "Un grand officier des princes angevins: le chancelier Jean Le Fèvre d'après son journal (1381–1388)." *Provence historique* 64 (2014): 313–25.

McCormick, Michael. "New Light on the 'Dark Ages': How the Slave Trade Fuelled the Carolingian Economy." *Past & Present* 177 (2002): 17–54.

———. *Origins of the European Economy: Communications and Commerce A.D. 300–900*. Cambridge University Press, 2001.

McDonough, Susan. "Mothers and Daughters and Sons, in the Law: Family Conflict, Legal Stories, and Women's Litigation in Late Medieval Marseille." In *Litigating Women: Gender and Justice in Europe, c.1300–c.1800*, edited by Teresa Phipps and Deborah Youngs, 14–31. Routledge, 2022.

McKee, Sally. "Domestic Slavery in Renaissance Italy." *Slavery & Abolition* 29, no. 3 (2008): 305–26.

———. "Inherited Status and Slavery in Late Medieval Italy and Venetian Crete." *Past & Present* 182 (2004): 31–53.

———. "Slavery." In *The Oxford Handbook of Women and Gender in Medieval Europe*, edited by Judith Bennett and Ruth Karras. Oxford University Press, 2013.

———. "The Familiarity of Slaves in Medieval and Early Modern Households." In *Mediterranean Slavery Revisited (500–1800) / Neue Perspektiven auf mediterrane Sklaverei (500–1800)*, edited by Stefan Hanß, Juliane Schiel, and Claudia Schmid, 501–14. Chronos, 2014.

McKinley, Michelle A. "Financing Freedom: Self-Purchase and Reenslavement in Seventeenth-Century Andalucía." *William and Mary Quarterly* 81, no. 4 (2024): 651–86.

Meillassoux, Claude. *The Anthropology of Slavery: The Womb of Iron and Gold*. University of Chicago Press, 1991.

Meyerson, Mark D. "Slavery and Solidarity: Mudejars and Foreign Muslim Captives in the Kingdom of Valencia." *Medieval Encounters: Jewish, Christian, and Muslim Culture in Confluence and Dialogue* 2, no. 3 (1996): 286–343.

Michaud, Francine. *Earning Dignity: Labour Conditions and Relations during the Century of the Black Death in Marseille*. Brepols, 2016.

Miers, Suzanne, and Igor Kopytoff. *Slavery in Africa: Historical and Anthropological Perspectives*. University of Wisconsin Press, 1977.

Miles, Tiya. *All That She Carried: The Journey of Ashley's Sack, a Black Family Keepsake*. Random House, 2021.

Miller, Joseph Calder. *The Problem of Slavery as History: A Global Approach*. Yale University Press, 2012.

Miller, Peter N. *Peiresc's History of Provence: Antiquarianism and the Discovery of a Medieval Mediterrranean*. American Philosophical Society, 2011.

Mistral, Frédéric. *Lou trésor dóu Felibrige*. 2 vols. Veuve Remondet-Aubin, 1879.

Morgan, Jennifer L. *Reckoning with Slavery: Gender, Kinship, and Capitalism in the Early Black Atlantic*. Duke University Press, 2021.

Mortreuil, Jean-Anselme-Bernard. *Histoire du droit byzantin, ou du droit romain dans l'Empire d'Orient, depuis la mort de Justinien jusqu'à la prise de Constantinople en 1453*. E. Guilbert, 1843.

———. "Moeurs et institutions marseillaises au Moyen Âge. L'esclavage." *Revue de Marseille* 4 (1858): 153–74.

Mouritsen, Henrik. *The Freedman in the Roman World*. Cambridge University Press, 2011.

Mummey, Kevin. "Women, Slavery, and Community on the Island of Mallorca, 1360–1390." PhD Dissertation, University of Minnesota, 2013.

Origo, Iris. "The Domestic Enemy: The Eastern Slaves in Tuscany in the Fourteenth and Fifteenth Centuries." *Speculum* 30 (1955): 321–66.

Otchakovsky-Laurens, François. *La vie politique à Marseille sous la domination angevine (1348–1385)*. École française de Rome, 2017.

Patterson, Orlando. "Revisiting Slavery, Property, and Social Death." In *On Human Bondage: After Slavery and Social Death*, edited by John Bodel and Walter Scheidel, 265–96. Wiley-Blackwell, 2017.

———. *Slavery and Social Death: A Comparative Study*. Harvard University Press, 1982.

Patton, Pamela A. "What Did Medieval Slavery Look Like? Color, Race, and Unfreedom in Later Medieval Iberia." *Speculum* 97, no. 3 (2022): 649–97.

Peabody, Sue. "An Alternative Genealogy of the Origins of French Free Soil: Medieval Toulouse." *Slavery & Abolition* 32, no. 3 (2011): 341–62.

———. *'There Are No Slaves in France': The Political Culture of Race and Slavery in the Ancien Régime*. Oxford University Press, 1997.

Peres, Corinna. "'She Wants to Do It Her Own Way.' Enslaved Women, Their Work, and Their Children in the Datini Merchant Community, 1380s–1410s." PhD Dissertation, Universität Wien, 2024.

Pernoud, Régine, ed. *Les statuts municipaux de Marseille*. Picard, 1949.

Perrier, Émile. *Les bibliophiles et les collectionneurs provençaux anciens et modernes: arrondissement de Marseille*. De Barthelet, 1897.

234 BIBLIOGRAPHY

Perry, Craig. *Slavery and the Jews of Medieval Egypt: A History*. Princeton University Press, 2026.

Perry, Craig, David Eltis, Stanley L. Engerman, and David Richardson, eds. *The Cambridge World History of Slavery*, Vol. 2, *AD 500–AD 1420*. Cambridge University Press, 2021.

Perry, Matthew J. *Gender, Manumission, and the Roman Freedwoman*. Cambridge University Press, 2014.

Petti Balbi, Giovanna, and Paola Guglielmotti, eds. *Dare credito alle donne. Presenze femminili nell'economia tra medioevo ed età moderna*. Centro studi Renato Bordone, 2012.

Phillips, William D. *Slavery in Medieval and Early Modern Iberia*. University of Pennsylvania Press, 2014.

Phipps, Teresa, and Deborah Youngs. *Litigating Women: Gender and Justice in Europe, c.1300–c.1800*. Routledge, 2022.

Pignatelli, Ettore. *I Diurnali del Duca di Monteleone*. Edited by Michele Manfredi. Rerum italicarum scriptores, Nuova edizione 21.5. Nicola Zanichelli, 1958.

Planas, Natividad. "Des héritages et des affranchis (Majorque au XVIe siècle)." In *La cité des choses: une nouvelle histoire de la citoyenneté*, edited by Simona Cerutti, Thomas Glesener, and Isabelle Grangaud. Anacharsis, 2024.

Polanyi, Michael. *Personal Knowledge: Towards a Post-Critical Philosophy*. Enlarged ed. University of Chicago Press, 2015.

———. *The Tacit Dimension*. Rev. ed. University of Chicago Press, 2009.

Pontieri, Ernesto, ed. *Storia di Napoli*. Società editrice Storia di Napoli, 1967.

Pryor, John H. *Business Contracts of Medieval Provence: Selected Notulae from the Cartulary of Giraud Amalric of Marseilles, 1248*. Pontifical Institute of Mediaeval Studies, 1981.

———. "Ship Types and Fleet Composition at Genoa and Venice in the Early Thirteenth Century." In *Logistics of Warfare in the Age of the Crusades*, edited by John H. Pryor, 95–108. Routledge, 2006.

Quirini-Poplawska, Danuta. "The Venetian Involvement in the Black Sea Slave Trade (Fourteenth to Fifteenth Centuries)." In *Slavery and the Slave Trade in the Eastern Mediterranean (c. 1000–1500 CE)*, edited by Reuven Amitai and Christoph Cluse, 255–98. Brepols, 2018.

Reyerson, Kathryn L. "Women in Business in Medieval Montpellier." In *Women and Work in Preindustrial Europe*, edited by Barbara A. Hanawalt. Indiana University Press, 1986.

Ricardus Pisanus. *Lo Codi: eine Summa Codicis in provenzalischer Sprache aus der Mitte des XII. Jahrhunderts*. Edited by Hermann Fitting and Hermann Suchier. Niemeyer, 1906.

Richard, Jean. *The Crusades, c. 1071–c. 1291*. Translated by Jean Birrell. Cambridge University Press, 1999.

Rio, Alice. *Slavery After Rome, 500–1100*. Oxford University Press, 2017.

Rodriguez, Jarbel. *Captives and Their Saviors in the Medieval Crown of Aragon*. The Catholic University of America Press, 2011.

Romano, Dennis. *Housecraft and Statecraft: Domestic Service in Renaissance Venice, 1400–1600*. Johns Hopkins University Press, 1996.

Romestan, Guy. "Femmes esclaves à Perpignan aux XIVe et XVe siècles." In *La Femme dans l'histoire et la société méridionales (IXe–XIXe s.): Actes du 66e congrès de la Fédération historique du Languedoc méditerranéen et du Roussillon*, 187–218. Fédération historique du Languedoc méditerranéen et du Roussillon, 1995.

Rubin, Miri. *Cities of Strangers: Making Lives in Medieval Europe*. Cambridge University Press, 2020.

Ryder, Alan. "The Angevin Bid for Naples, 1380–1480." In *The French Descent into Renaissance Italy, 1494–95: Antecedents and Effects*, edited by David Abulafia, 69–84. Ashgate, 1995.

Salicrú i Lluch, Roser. *Esclaus i propietaris d'esclaus a la Catalunya del segle XV: l'assegurança contra fugues*. Consell Superior d'Investigacions Científiques, Institució Milà i Fontanals, 1998.

———. "L'esclau com a inversió? Aprofitament, assalariament i rendibilitat del treball en l'entorn català tardomedieval." *Recerques: història, economia, cultura*, no. 52–53 (2006).

———. "Slaves in the Professional and Family Life of Craftsmen in the Late Middle Ages." In *La Famiglia nell'economia Europea secc. XIII–XVIII / The Economic Role of the Family in the European Economy from the 13th to the 18th Centuries*, edited by Simonetta Cavaciocchi, 325–42. Firenze University Press, 2009.

Schiel, Juliane. "Die Sklaven und die Pest. Überprüfung Forschungsnarrativs am Beispiel Venedig." In *Schiavitù e servaggio nell'economia europea, secc. XI–XVIII / Serfdom and Slavery in the European Economy, 11th–18th Centuries*, edited by Simonetta Cavaciocchi, 1: 365–375. Firenze University Press, 2014.

———. "Mord von zarter Hand: Der Giftmordvorwurf im Venedig des 15. Jahrhunderts." In *Mediterranean Slavery Revisited (500–1800) / Neue Perspektiven auf mediterrane Sklaverei (500–1800)*, edited by Stefan Hanß, Juliane Schiel, and Claudia Schmid, 201–28. Chronos, 2014.

Schiel, Juliane, and Stefan Hanß. "Semantics, Practices and Transcultural Perspectives on Mediterranean Slavery." In *Mediterranean Slavery Revisited (500–1800) / Neue Perspektiven auf mediterrane Sklaverei (500–1800)*, edited by Stefan Hanß, Juliane Schiel, and Claudia Schmid, 11–23. Chronos, 2014.

Schiel, Juliane, and Damian A. Pargas. *The Palgrave Handbook of Global Slavery throughout History*. Springer Nature, 2023.

Scott, Rebecca J. "Social Facts, Legal Fictions, and the Attribution of Slave Status: The Puzzle of Prescription." *Law and History Review* 35, no. 1 (2017): 9–30.

Scott, Rebecca J., and Carlos Venegas Fornias. "María Coleta and the Capuchin Friar: Slavery, Salvation, and the Adjudication of Status." *William and Mary Quarterly* 76, no. 4 (2019): 727–62.

Shoemaker, Karl. *Sanctuary and Crime in the Middle Ages, 400–1500*. Fordham University Press, 2011.

Simmons, LaKisha Michelle. *Crescent City Girls: The Lives of Young Black Women in Segregated New Orleans*. University of North Carolina Press, 2015.

Skoda, Hannah. "People as Property in Medieval Dubrovnik." In *Legalism: Property and Ownership*, edited by Georgy Kantor, Tom Lambert, and Hannah Skoda, 235–60. Oxford University Press, 2017.

Smail, Daniel Lord. "Enmity and the Distraint of Goods in Late Medieval Marseille." In *Emotions and Material Culture*, edited by Gerhard Jaritz, 17–30. Der Österreichischen Akademie der Wissenschaften, 2003.

236 BIBLIOGRAPHY

Smail, Daniel Lord. *Imaginary Cartographies: Possession and Identity in Late Medieval Marseille*. Cornell University Press, 2000.

———. *Legal Plunder: Households and Debt Collection in Late Medieval Europe*. Harvard University Press, 2016.

———. *The Consumption of Justice: Emotions, Publicity, and Legal Culture in Marseille, 1264–1423*. Cornell University Press, 2003.

Smallwood, Stephanie E. "The Politics of the Archive and History's Accountability to the Enslaved." *History of the Present* 6, no. 2 (2016): 117–32.

Smith, Thomas W., and Helen Killick. *Petitions and Strategies of Persuasion in the Middle Ages: The English Crown and the Church, c. 1200—c. 1550*. York Medieval Press, 2018.

Sobers-Khan, Nur. "Slavery in the Early Modern Ottoman Empire." In *The Cambridge World History of Slavery*, Vol. 2, *AD 500–AD 1420*, edited by Craig Perry, David Eltis, David Richardson, and Stanley L. Engerman, 406–28. Cambridge University Press, 2021.

Sommar, Mary E. *The Slaves of the Churches: A History*. Oxford University Press, 2020.

Steinman, Charlie. "'The Bond of Said Child's Blood through Her, His Slave': The Social Worlds of Slavery in Late Medieval Marseille." Undergraduate thesis, Brown University, 2020.

Stella, Giorgio. *Georgii et Iohannis Stellae Annales Genuenses*. Edited by Giovanna Petti Balbi. Rerum italicarum scriptores, Nuova edizione 17.2. Zanichelli, 1975.

Stello, Annika. "Caffa and the Slave Trade during the First Half of the Fifteenth Century." In *Slavery and the Slave Trade in the Eastern Mediterranean (c. 1000–1500 CE)*, edited by Reuven Amitai and Christoph Cluse, 375–98. Brepols, 2018.

Strayer, Joseph R. "The Crusades of Louis IX." In *Medieval Statecraft and Perspectives of History: Essays by Joseph Strayer*, edited by John F. Benton and Thomas N. Bisson. Princeton University Press, 2015.

Stuard, Susan Mosher. "Ancillary Evidence for the Decline of Medieval Slavery." *Past & Present* 149 (1995): 3–28.

Tourmagne, Amédée. *Histoire de l'esclavage ancien et moderne*. Guillaumin, 1880.

Valérian, Dominique. *Bougie: port maghrébin, 1067–1510*. École française de Rome, 2006.

———. "La course maghrébine à la fin du Moyen Âge: une forme maritime du djihad?" In *La frontière méditerranéenne du XVe au XVIIe siècle: échanges, circulations et affrontements*, edited by Albrecht Fuess and Bernard Heyberger, 115–26. Brepols, 2013.

Valois, Noël. *La France et le grand schisme d'Occident*. 4 vols. Alphonse Picard, 1896.

Van Allen, Judith. "'Sitting on a Man': Colonialism and the Lost Political Institutions of Igbo Women." *Canadian Journal of African Studies* 6, no. 2 (1972): 165–81.

Venturini, Alain. "La guerre de l'Union d'Aix (1383–1388)." In *1388, La Dédition de Nice à la Savoie*, edited by Rosine Cleyet-Michaud et al., 35–141. Éditions de la Sorbonne, 2019.

Verlinden, Charles. *L'esclavage dans l'Europe médiévale*. Vol. 1, *Péninsule Ibérique. France*. De Tempel, 1955.

———. *L'esclavage dans l'Europe médiévale*. Vol. 2, *Italie - Colonies italiennes du Levant - Levant latin - Empire byzantin*. Rijksuniversiteit te Gent, 1977.

———. "Orthodoxie et esclavage au bas Moyen Âge." In *Mélanges Eugène Tisserant*, 5:427–56. Biblioteca Apostolica Vaticana, 1964.

Vise, Melissa. *The Unruly Tongue: Speech and Violence in Medieval Italy*. University of Pennsylvania Press, 2025.

Vlassopoulos, Kostas. "Does Slavery Have a History?" *Journal of Global Slavery* 1, no. 1 (2020): 5–27.

Wallon, Henri. *Histoire de l'esclavage dans l'antiquité*. 3 vols. Hachette, 1847.

Watson, Alan. *Roman Slave Law*. Johns Hopkins University Press, 1987.

Winroth, Anders. "Neither Slave nor Free: Theology and Law in Gratian's Thoughts on the Definition of Marriage and Unfree Persons." In *Medieval Church Law and the Origins of the Western Legal Tradition*, edited by Wolfgang P. Müller and Mary E. Sommar. Catholic University of America Press, 2012.

Wisnoski, Alexander L. "'It Is Unjust for the Law of Marriage to Be Broken by the Law of Slavery': Married Slaves and Their Masters in Early Colonial Lima." *Slavery & Abolition* 35, no. 2 (2014): 234–52.

Wolfe, Patrick. "Settler Colonialism and the Elimination of the Native." *Journal of Genocide Research* 8, no. 4 (2006): 387–409.

Xhayet, Geneviève. "Partisans et adversaires de Louis d'Anjou pendant la guerre de l'Union d'Aix." *Provence historique* 40 (1990): 403–27.

Zhang, Angela. "Rethinking 'Domestic Enemies': Slavery and Race Formation in Late Medieval Florence." *Speculum* 99, no. 2 (2024): 409–31.

INDEX

Note: Page numbers in italic type indicate figures or tables.

al-Andalus, enslaved persons from, 15, 16,
   23–24, 32
Alazacia (manumitted enslaved woman),
   33, 39
Albericus de Rosate, 175
Alfonso the Wise, 110
al-Ghuzuli, 19
Amalric, Giraud, register of 1248, 32–33
Amazigh origins, of Magdalena, 4, 77–79, 82
Angevin dynasty conflict, 60–62. *See also*
   Valois Angevins
Annales (journal), 25
archives: in Marseille, 7, 8, 187–89, 191–92;
   of slavery, 15–16, 29, 32, 34
Armenteros, Ivan, 26–27
Arnaut, Antoni, 144, 155, 175
Arnaut, Guilhem, 7, 8, 167, 175, 177–78
assimilation, 13, 18, 107, 115, 120, 154,
   163, 182
Audebert, Antoni, 56
Audivin, Hugo, 180, 222n27
Aurelhe, Jacme, 174
Auruola de Jerusalem, 93, 133, 147
Ausier, Jaumona, 120
autonomy/freedom, 103–4. *See also*
   manumission
Autrici, Elziar, 7, 158, 165–67, 222n27
Aycart, Laurens, 65, 101, 128
Aymeric, Bertomieu, 65, 74, 76
Aymes, Raymon, 102
Ays, Floreta d', 183–84
Ays, Nicolau d', 136, 160–61, 168
Ays, Rayneria d', 136, 160

Bailey, Lisa, 145
Baiul, Guilhem, 86
Balard, Michel, 19, 43–44, 46
bankruptcy, 194–96
Baratier, Édouard, 64
Barban, Guilhem, 120
Barker, Hannah, 24, 78, 162
Barran, Arnaut, 166
Barreme, Antoni, 167
Bartolus, 175
Basso, Enrico, 68, 80
Baussan, Antoni, 135, 140–41, 160
Baussane, Gabriella, 135, 141–42, 160
Becker, Cynthia, 79
Bella Valle, Mathieu de, 7, 166
Bellissens, Johan, 55, 64–65, 98
Bellomonte, Johan de, 160
Bernardi, Philippe, 24
Berra, Bernat de, 97
Bertran, Johan, 196
Bertran, Peire, 58
Bertran, Peyret, 58, 196, 211n24
Black Africans: enslavement of, 16, 24;
   manumission of, 24
Blackburn, Robin, 26
Black Death. *See* plague/Black Death
Black Sea, as source of enslaved persons, 16
Blanc, Johan, 119
Bloch, Marc, 25, 192
Blumenthal, Debra, 23, 28
Bonaffazy, Laureta, 42, 129–30, 132
Bonaffazy, Peyret, 129–30, 132
Boni, Monica, 19

239

240 INDEX

Boniface IX, Roman pope, 71

Bonnassie, Pierre, 25–27

Bono, Salvatore, 20

Borays, Clari, 174

Boserup, Ester, 27

Bourdon, Duke, 71

Brachio, Bertran de, 83

brands, 77–78, 214n11

Bresc, Henri, 23, 24

Budak, Nevan, 25

Calafat, Antoni, 52, 53

Calafat, Peire, 52

Calvin, Peire, 91, 99–100, 113

Cambale, Resens, 132, 218n11

canon law, 74–75, 108–10, 164, 171, 220n13

Canton of the Masters of the Adze, 2

Capet, Élodie, 20

Casaulx, Julian de, 43, 128, 131

Casteen, Elizabeth, 77

Catherina of Tartary, 44–48

Cays, Pons, 180–81

Cerreto, Niccolò Sanframondi, count of, 63, 67, 74, 76, 80, 91, 94, 96

Charles of Durazzo, 54, 60–62, 71

Charles V, King, 61

Charles VI, King, 61

Chaupin, Laureta, 120–21

Chaupin, Lois, 120–21

Chiaramonte, Costanza, 81

Chiaramonte, Manfredi, 80–81, 82

children: of enslaved women and their masters, 27–28, 39, 45–47; enslavement of the masters' own, 39

Christianity: labeling of others by, 12–13, 172; Magdalena's exposure to, 88–90; Muslim converts to, 13; and slavery, 16, 23–24, 74–75, 109–10, 171, 190, 220n13. See also canon law; papal schism; sanctuary, ecclesiastical

Church of Latter-Day Saints, 49

Clement VII, Avignonese pope, 4, 61–62, 69, 71

clothing: of enslaved persons, 90, 103–4; of Magdalena, 7, 56, 90, 103–4, 136–38, 157; as plunder, 66, 69, 70; sumptuary laws, 41

Cochet, Johan, 160

Code, Justinian's, 109, 172, 175. See also Corpus iuris civilis

Lo Codi, 109–10, 172

Colin, Bertran, 58

Coline, Magdalena: age of, 78; Bertomieua Huguete's dealings with and legacy to, 107, 122, 136–39, 155–56, 165, 167, 187; clothing of, 7, 56, 90, 103–4, 136–38, 157; dignity of, 154–55, 168; documents kept by, 187–88; dowry of, 105–7, 109–13, 122, 143, 187; enslavement of, 4, 48; free status of, 108–13, 154–55, 159, 173–74, 222n16; Gassenda Huguete and, 56, 122, 136–38, 157; life of, after trials, 192–93; marriages of, 5, 43, 79, 104–13, 118–22, 125, 139–40, 143, 152, 159, 163, 222n16; as moneylender, 5, 123–25, 134–38, 142–44; North African heritage of, 48; occupation assigned to, 111; parents of, 79; in Peire's house, 82–90; performance of free status by, 6–7, 174; place of origin of, 77–79, 82, 105; prior slave status of, 75–81; religion of, 88; social support received by, 12, 107, 139–52, 182–83; surname of, 81–82; tacit knowledge of Marseille gained by, 103; transfer to Peire, 73–77. See also trials involving Magdalena and Peire

Columbe, Alaeta, 140, 144–47, 149–52, 154, 156, 164, 182, 188, 192; map showing business world of, 148; rubric for house purchase by, 150

Columbi, Bermon, 150

Comitis, Franciscus, 65

common law, 109, 158

consilium (expert legal opinion), 8, 175, 199

Corpus iuris civilis, 171, 175. See also Code, Justinian's; Digest, Justinian's

Cronicon Siculum, 67–69, 80

crusades, 33, 61

Cynus de Pistoia, 175

INDEX 241

Darwin, Charles, 31–32
Decker, Sarah Ifft, 133
De in ius vocando, 172–75, 179, 221n6
Delort, Robert, 19
Digest, Justinian's, 172, 175. *See also* Code,
  Justinian's; Corpus iuris civilis
domestic labor, 23, 27
Doria, Corrado, 68–70, 73, 74, 76–77, 80–81
Doria, Pietro, 68
dowries, 25, 43, 56, 58, 81, 99, 101, 102, 105–7,
  109–13, 119–20, 122, 131, 149, 187, 196
Durkheim, Émile, 20

Elie, Martin, 55
Elie, Raymon, 168, 185–86, 189
Engles, Johan, 85
Enguayte, Peire, 64
enslaved persons: agency of, 47–48; age
  of, at time of enslavement/sale, 44, 78;
  clothing of, 103–4; community's role
  in determining status of, 111, 161–63;
  duration of servitude of, 43–44;
  ecclesiastical sanctuary sought by, 45–46;
  gender of, 22–25; Greeks as, 11, 16, 18, 23,
  34, 114; labeling of, 12–13, 24; law's role in
  determining status of, 5–6, 162; men as,
  23–24; multiple owners of, 208n28;
  names of, in Marseille, *114*; numbers of,
  19–20; paths out of enslavement available
  to, 5; performance of status by, 161–63;
  places of origin of, in the Mediterranean,
  11; social support received by, 47, 48;
  Tatars as, 11, 16, 18, 23, 34–37, 44–48;
  women as, 22–25, 27–28. *See also* freed
  slaves; slave sales
Epstein, Steven, 114
Ermini, Johan and Guinarda, 33

Fabre, Martin, 47
Farge, Arlette, 10
Fauris de Saint-Vincens, Alexandre, 190
Felip, Raymon, 80
Flote, Guigo, 94
Fossier, Robert, 216n1

France, slavery in, 21–22, 28, 189–92
Francesco III, bishop of Pozzuoli, 67–69,
  213n32
Frayre, Guilhem, 115
freedom/autonomy, 103–4. *See also*
  manumission
freed slaves: performance of status by, 6–7,
  162, 174; permission to sue their patrons,
  170, 172–76; persistence of memory of
  former status of, 118–21, 154–55, 162–63;
  respectful behavior required of, by
  Roman law, 8, 167–68, 172–73, 221n29.
  See also manumission
free-soil principle, 190

Gaius, 171
galleys, furnishing of, 65–66
Garda, Andrea de, 85, 87–89
Garda, Hugueta de, 89
gender: of enslaved persons, 22–25; of
  enslaved Tatars, 35
Giannella, Nicole, 161
Giraut, Guilhem, 98, 99
Gombert, Bertran, 79, 156, 170, 175–76, 179,
  181–85
Gracian, Antoni, 54–55, 56, 85–86
Graeber, David, 128
Gratian, 108–9
Greek slaves, 11, 16, 18, 23, 34, 114
Groebner, Valentin, 214n11
Gross, Ariela, 5
Guesclin, Bertrand du, 62

Hanß, Stefan, 26
Harper, Kyle, 27
historiographical method, 5–6, 8–11. *See also*
  scholarship
houses, descriptions of interior and
  inventories of, 85–90
Hugonin de lo Chorges, 7, 123, 125,
  139, 142–43, 152–57, 166, 173, 180,
  192–93
Huguet, Johan: civic records concerning,
  57; harvesting of wheat field by, 195–96;

242 INDEX

Huguet, Johan (*continued*)
  litigation involving, 95; and litigation
  involving Peire, 99, 101; marriage and
  subsequent life of, 57–59, 192; Peire's
  relationship to, 57, 58; as shipowner and
  privateer, 2, 4, 65, 69–70, 92; unlawful
  plunder retained by, 4, 69–70, 92, 95–97
Huguet, Lazaret, 56, 58, 88, 99, 101, 195–96
Huguet, Peire, the elder: civic service of,
  51–52; as an immigrant, 52–53; marriage
  of, 56; as a merchant, 51–53; murder
  charge against, 52, 53; name of, 50–52;
  relationship of, to his son, 53–54
Huguet, Peire, the younger: and Antoni de
  Lueys conflict, 95–98, 101; bad reputation
  of, 12, 92, 97–100, 163, 177; business
  associates of, 54–56; civic service of, 91;
  debts incurred by, 5, 71, 97–102, 123,
  193–96; harvesting of wheat field by,
  195–97; historical documents on, 49–50;
  Johan's relationship to, 57, 58; life of, after
  trials, 193–97; litigation involving, 93–95,
  101–2, 193–97; location of house of,
  64–65, 83, 84, 85; Magdalena in the house
  of, 82–90; marriages of, 56–57, 134;
  and the Naples expedition, 4, 64–70;
  ownership of shipyards by, 2;
  performance of slave ownership by, 6–7;
  as shipowner and privateer, 4, 53–56,
  69–72, 82, 91–92, 95–96, 98, 99; as a
  shipwright, 50, 53, 100; social ascent of,
  42, 56–57, 91, 92, 163; unlawful plunder
  retained by, 4, 69–70, 92, 95–97. *See also*
  trials involving Magdalena and Peire
Huguete, Alaseta (née Coline), 57–59, 82,
  101, 196, 211n24
Huguete, Bertomieua (née Durante), 56,
  82–90, 107, 122, 136–39, 142, 155, 163, 165,
  187, 196
Huguete, Gassenda, 56, 88, 122, 136–39, 155
Huguete, Guillelmona, 134, 142–43
Huguete, Hugoneta (née Bertrana), 58, 99,
  101–2, 193–96

Igbo women, 100
Institutes, 175
insults, 120, 168–69, 173, 177

Jews, 12, 127, 128, 133, 169, 183
Johanna, Queen of Naples, 54, 60–62,
  180
Jordan, William Chester, 13
jury nullification, 164
Justinian, Emperor, 109, 171. *See also* Code,
  Justinian's; Corpus iuris civilis; Digest,
  Justinian's; Institutes

Kaye, Joel, 126
Kowalesky, Maxime, 36

Lacydon, 1
Ladislas of Naples, 62, 71, 81
Lansaria, street/neighborhood of, 2, 12, 55,
  64–65, 84, 85
Laurens, Lois, 118
law: open-air conduct of, 6–7, 157;
  performance of, 6; slave status as
  determined by, 5–6; suits concerning
  money and business dealings, 92–95, 126;
  women's resort to, against men, 100–102.
  See also canon law; common law; Roman
  law
Le Fèvre, Jean, 62–63
Lenski, Noel, 13
Limosin, Guilhem, 55, 73–77, 79–81, 142,
  144, 161, 174
Limosin, Jacme, 55–56, 65, 83, 86, 94, 95, 97,
  188
Limosine, Catherina, 142–44, 166
Lombart, Antoni, 147, 150
Louis I, Duke of Anjou, 4, 61–62, 64, 183
Louis II, King of Naples, 4, 8, 62–63, 69,
  70–71, 79, 178–83, 188
Louis IX, King of France, 33, 178
Louis X, King of France, 190
Lueys, Antoni de, 55, 65, 67, 69–70, 73–74,
  76, 94–98, 101, 160

INDEX 243

Magdalena, women in Marseille named, 115, 116–17

Magdalena Coline. *See* Coline, Magdalena

manumission: acts of, 42–43, 45–47; age of persons at, 44; of Black slaves, 24; in France, 190–91; incidences of, 24, 43; marriage of enslaved women as means of informal, 43, 108–13; in Marseille, 33, 42–43, 191; in Mediterranean slavery, 27; tacit, 111, 113–18, 222n16; testamentary, 42–43, 46, 118. *See also* freedom/ autonomy; freed slaves

Marcabru, 169

Margaret of Durazzo, 4, 62, 67–69, 80–81

Maria (enslaved woman), 120–21

Marie of Blois, Queen, 4, 56, 62–63, 180, 183

Marmon, Shaun, 19

marriage, manumission/free status and, 108–18. *See also* dowries

Marseille: crusades launching from, 33; founding of, 1; historical documents of, 9–10, 191–92; insults in, 120, 168–69, 173, 177; judicial archives of, 7, 8, 187–89; law and litigation in, 92–95, 100–101; money and credit in, 125–34; names given to enslaved women in, *114*; recent history of, 1–2; shipyards of, 50; slavery in, 13–14, 29–48, 162–63, 191; slave sales in, *30*; Valois Angevins and, 4, 50, 60–61. *See also* Provence

Marta (formerly enslaved woman), 119–20

Martin, Antoni, 83, 86

Martin, Jacme, 65, 74, 76, 160

Martin, Johan, 85–89, 93

Martín Casares, Aurelia, 77

Marvan, Ferrar, 86

Massilia. *See* Marseille

masters. *See* slave owners

McCormick, Michael, 21

McKee, Sally, 23

Mediterranean: map of western basin, *17*; slavery in, 11, 21, 26–27, 171

men: as enslaved persons, 23–24; names of, 50–51

Miles, Tiya, 11

Miller, Joseph, 16

money and credit, 125–34

Mongols, 11, 15, 34

Montels, Guilhem de, 101

Morenon, Guilhem, 168

Mortreuil, Jean-Anselme-Bernard, 29, 43, 138, 190, 192

Muslims: as converts to Christianity, 13; enslavement of, 16, 79–80; labeling of, 12; slave-raiding by, 79–80; tattoos on female, 77–79

names. *See* patronymics

Naples, 4, 54, 56, 60–71; Bay of Naples, *68*

Napoleon, 190

Nicolai, Reynier, 105–7

Nigri, Jacme, 119

Odofredus, 175

Old Port, Marseille, map of neighborhood around, *3*

Olivarie, Bertran, 150

Olivarie, Gassenda, 140, 144–45, 149–51, 154, 156, 164, 182, 188, 192; rubric for house purchase by, *150*

Olivier, Peire, 65

Origo, Iris, 36, 82

Otchakovsky-Laurens, François, 187

Otto of Brunswick, 61–63

Ouerfelli, Mohamed, 26–27

owners. *See* slave owners

Palermo, slavery in, 18

papal schism, 9, 60–61

patronymics, 50–51

Patterson, Orlando, 22, 216n1

pawnbroking, 129–31, 134, 136–38, 142

Peabody, Sue, 190

pedicequa (housemaid), 111–12

Peres, Corinna, 39, 43, 79

INDEX

Perry, Craig, 38
petitions to the king, 5, 8, 79, 178–79, 181
Petre, Johan, 105–6, 109, 121–25, 139, 159
Peytamin, Jacme, 101
Phillips, William, 77
Phocaeans, 1
Piloti, Emmanuele, 19
plague/Black Death, 10, 34–37, 43, 53, 58, 87, 121–22, 149
Planas, Natividad, 6
Plaza of the Shipyards, 2, 3, 83, 84
pledges, for loans, 130–31, 143, 195
Polanyi, Michael, 10
Poncie, Antoneta, 142–43, 166
Poncilionis, Esteve de, 119–20
Poncilionis, Franses de, 119–20
Pons, Jorgi, 142
Pouillon, Fernand, 2
profiteering and plunder, 66, 68–69
Provence: naming conventions in, 50; and the Naples expedition, 63–67; revolt of, 62–63; slavery in, 11, 13, 21–22, 38, 190. *See also* Marseille

Raude, Antoni de, 7, 155–56, 165
Raynaut, Guilhem, 177–78
Raynaut, Johan, 7, 137, 164–66, 180
Raynerie, Sicarda, 195
Relhana, Hugo de, 160, 168
René of Anjou, King, 190
Reyerson, Kathryn, 133
Ricau, Isnart, 194
Rio, Alice, 157
Robert, Antoni, 94
Romanete, Guillelmeta, 134, 160
Roman law: enabling jury nullification, 164; on marriage of enslaved persons, 109–10; on side work done by enslaved persons, 136; on slavery and the duties of the enslaved, 8, 11, 113, 161–62, 167–68, 171–73, 221n29; on the two-witness rule for proof of claims, 77. See also *De in ius vocando*
Romano, Dennis, 23

Rubin, Miri, 13
Ruffe, Magdalena, 115

Sado, Johan de, 179
Saint-Jean church, 85, 89
Saint-Laurent church, 2, 67, 89, 95
Sala, Nicolau de, 86, 93, 121–22, 140, 144–45, 151, 154, 160–61, 164–67, 174, 188
Salicrú i Lluch, Roser, 36–37
Salvayre, Durant, 196
Salvayre, Loisa, 196
Salves, Mosse, 86
Sancta-Catherina (ship), 55, 65, 69
sanctuary, ecclesiastical, 45–46, 86
Sanctus-Georgius (ship), 65, 212n24
Sanctus-Johannes-Evangeliste (ship), 71, 102
Sanctus-Urbanus (ship), 54–55
Sant Gilles, Alayeta de, 140, 143–44, 151
Sant Gilles, Guilhem de, 97
Sant Gilles, Honorat de, 147, 150–51
Sant Gilles, Isnart de, 54, 55, 98–101, 143, 147, 151, 194
Scalis, Pons de, 101
Schiel, Juliane, 26
scholarship: economic perspectives in, 24–25, 36–37; historiographical method, 5–6, 8–11; individuals vs. structure as frameworks in, 106, 107; and marginalization of Mediterranean slavery, 25–27; metaphors and analogies used in, 31–32; particularity and variety as subject of, 16, 18–19; phenomenological approach in, 5–6; shortcomings arising from text-based character of, 8–9; silences in, 28, 30–31, 44, 104, 188, 192; on slavery in Eurasia, 15–28; on slavery in France, 189–92; social perspectives in, 24–25, 40–42; tacit knowledge employed in, 10; topographical metaphor used in, 22; and typological classification, 13–14
Scott, Rebecca, 5, 162
serfs, 21, 25, 103, 171, 190
Serviers, Blacassia de, 102, 140, 143–44, 151
Serviers, Peire de, 102, 144
shipwrights, 2, 50

Siete Partidas, 110, 172
Simmons, LaKisha Michelle, 154
Simondel, Bertomieu, 55, 71, 98, 194
Simondel, Esteve, 98
slave brokers, 14
slave owners: characteristics of, 40–42; enslaved persons' multiplicity of, 208n28; norms applicable to, 41; performance of role of, 162–63
slavery: archives concerning, 15–16, 29, 32, 34; brief account of, across Eurasia, 15–22; Christianity and, 16, 23–24, 74–75, 109–10, 171, 190, 220n13; data and scholarship on, 15–28; demographic data on, 19–20; economic perspectives on, 24–25, 36–37; in France, 21–22, 28, 189–92; and gender, 22–25; in Giraud Amalric's 1248 register, 32–33; legal framing of, 5–6, 162; in Marseille, 13–14, 29–48, 162–63; in medieval period, 25–26; Mediterranean, 11, 21, 26–27, 171; norms of, 18–19, 31, 41; performances of, 161–63; phenomenology of, 5–6, 8–10, 28, 31; in Provence, 11, 13, 21–22, 190; Roman law and, 8, 11, 113, 161–62, 171–73, 221n29; as a social fact, 20, 28; social perspectives on, 24–25, 40–42; topography of, 19–22; typological classification of, 13–14; unanswered questions about, 30–31; varieties and diversity of, 16, 18–19, 21. *See also* enslaved persons; slave owners
slaves. *See* enslaved persons; freed slaves
slave sales: age of persons at, 44; domestic and foreign buyers and sellers in, 37–39; enslaved persons' consent to, 45; in France, 190–91; increase of, in later fourteenth century, 10; manumissions in relation to, 43; in Marseille, 30, 191
social status: Peire Huguet and, 42, 56–57, 91, 92, 163; slave ownership and, 24–25, 40–42; sumptuary laws and, 40–41
Sosquiers, Bertomieu de, 115
Sosquiers, Bertran de, 193
Steinman, Charlie, 47

Stela, Peyroneta de, 120–21
La Stella (ship), 4, 61, 65, 82, 94
sumptuary laws, 41
Surda, Antoni de, 94
surnames. *See* patronymics
Syon, Monet de, 45–47
Syon, Raymon de, 44–48

tacit knowledge, 10
Tannenbaum, Frank, 13
Tatar slaves, 11, 16, 18, 23, 34–37, 44–48
tattoos, 77–78, 214n11
Tenchurier, Peire, 195
Theodora (formerly enslaved woman), 119–20, *119*
trials involving Magdalena and Peire, 153–83; characterizations of Magdalena in, 157–59, 164–65; conclusion of, 185; consequences for Magdalena, 182; *consilium* submitted in, 8, 175, 199; documentation of, 8, 10, 185–87, *186*; duration of, 4, 7; Hugonin's role in, 153–57, 166, 173, 180; king's final decision, 5, 8, 178–83; Magdalena's apparent victory, 7, 156, 170; Magdalena's appearances in court, 6–7, 155–57, 167, 179; Magdalena's moneylending as component of, 123–25, 134–36; Magdalena's social and judicial support in, 12, 140, 144, 159–67, 176–77, 182–83; original suit filed by Magdalena, 5, 153–55; Peire's accusation of theft, 7, 135–38, 140–42, 155; Peire's apparent victory, 5, 8, 178–79; Peire's claims about Magdalena's disrespectful behavior, 8, 167–70, 172–75; Peire's claims of ownership of Magdalena, 157–64, 166–69, 174; Peire's countersuits and appeals, 5, 7–8, 155–57, 165, 167, 170–71, 176–78, 181; Peire's transfer of suits to different courts, 7, 156, 157, 165–66; procedural irregularities committed by judges, 165–67, 176–77; procedural ruling against Peire, 8, 12, 176; Roman law brought to

246 INDEX

trials involving Magdalena and Peire (*continued*)

bear in, 11, 77 (see also *De in ius vocando*; freed slaves: respectful behavior required of, by Roman law); testimony about Magdalena's initial transfer to Peire and current slave status, 73–77, 144, 159–64, 174; testimony against the witness Nicolau de Sala, 144–45, 151, 156, 164, 165–66

Urban VI, Roman pope, 61, 62, 67–68, 71

Valencia, Guilhem, 86
Valérian, Dominique, 37
Valois Angevins, 4, 50, 60, 62–63, 68–69, 71. *See also* Angevin dynasty conflict
Van Allen, Judith, 100
Vedel, Aycart, 73–75, 174
Verlinden, Charles, 23, 26, 29, 36, 39, 192
Vincens, Hugo, 8, 12, 13, 170, 176–77
Virronis, Antonius, 8, 175–76, 199, 222n16

wage thesis, 36–37
Watson, Alan, 27
Wolfe, Patrick, 13
women: and domestic labor, 23, 27; as enslaved persons, 22–25, 27–28; and litigation, 100–102, 220n7; masters' children borne by enslaved, 27–28, 39, 45–47; mistress-slave relations among, 82; as moneylenders, 93, 131–34, 146–47, 149, 150–51; names of, 51, 81; networks of social support among, 140–44; rape and sexual exploitation of, 27–28, 47, 90, 145, 154; roles and status of, 9; tattoos on Muslim, 77–79; wealth owned by, 132
writing, 104

Yscla, Nicolau, 115
Ysia, Johan de, 124, 155, 158–59, 162–65, 173–75, 178, 185
Ysoart, Johan, 180

THE LAWRENCE STONE LECTURES

Sponsored by

*The Shelby Cullom Davis Center for Historical Studies
and Princeton University Press*

Daniel Lord Smail, *Magdalena Coline: A Life Beyond Slavery
in Mediterranean Europe*

Lorraine Daston, *Rules: A Short History of What We Live By*

Lyndal Roper, *Living I Was Your Plague: Martin Luther's World and Legacy*

Christopher Clark, *Time and Power: Visions of History in German Politics,
from the Thirty Years' War to the Third Reich*

Frederick Cooper, *Citizenship, Inequality, and Difference: Historical Perspectives*

Chris Wickham, *Sleepwalking into a New World: The Emergence of Italian City
Communes in the Twelfth Century*

Stuart B. Schwartz, *Sea of Storms: A History of Hurricanes in the Greater
Caribbean from Columbus to Katrina*

Ayesha Jalal, *The Pity of Partition: Manto's Life, Times, and Work across
the India-Pakistan Divide*

Thomas J. Sugrue, *Not Even Past: Barack Obama and the Burden of Race*

Mark Mazower, *No Enchanted Palace: The End of Empire and the Ideological
Origins of the United Nations*

A NOTE ON THE TYPE

This book has been composed in Arno, an Old-style serif typeface in the classic Venetian tradition, designed by Robert Slimbach at Adobe.